D1546368

As Long as the River Shall Run

An Ethnohistory of
Pyramid Lake Indian Reservation

Martha C. Knack *and* Omer C. Stewart

UNIVERSITY OF CALIFORNIA PRESS
Berkeley / Los Angeles / London

University of California Press
Berkeley and Los Angeles, California

University of California Press, Ltd.
London, England

©1984 by Martha C. Knack

Library of Congress Cataloging in Publication Data

Knack, Martha C.
    As long as the river shall run.

    Includes bibliographical references and index.
    1. Pyramid Lake Indian Reservation (Nev.) —History.
2. Paiute Indians —History. 3. Paiute Indians —
Government relations. 4. Indians of North America —
Government relations. I. Stewart, Omer Call,
1908 –   . II. Title.
E99.P2K587   1984   979.3'55   83-5005
ISBN 0-520-04868-7

Your father has provided a country large enough for all of you, and he advises you to remove to it. There your white brothers will not trouble you; they will have no claim to the land, and you can live upon it, you and all your children, as long as the grass grows and the water runs, in peace and plenty. It will be yours forever.

President Andrew Jackson to the Creek Nation, 1829

Contents

Plates

Figures

Foreword

Martha Knack, building on notes and research compiled over four decades by her co-author, Omer Stewart, here provides us with the most complete and lucid analysis to date of a native society of the Great Basin—the Northern Paiutes of Pyramid Lake, Nevada. Heretofore the major analyses of native societies in the Great Basin have focused on pre-European Contact adjustments to the cold desert environments that so dominate that massive inland sink, and the first chapter of *As Long as the River Shall Run* takes account of that research tradition, presenting a rich and integrated story of aboriginal Northern Paiute culture, the Pyramid Lake setting in which it was sustained prior to extensive European contact, and the fit between native culture and its native environment.

But this book is much more than a cultural ecological investigation of a pre-Contact Great Basin society, although the pre-Contact environment of Pyramid Lake and the post-Contact changes that were made to that environment are crucial to the investigation. The uniqueness of *As Long as the River Shall Run* lies in the full, deep, and careful ethnohistorical analysis of the Northern Paiutes of the Pyramid Lake Indian Reservation, over a 120-year period, during which time their resources were expropriated, and their waters cut off, while they were crowded into a smaller and smaller niche. The Indians became dominated by local Anglos, the regional economy, and the federal government, and gradually they became dependent upon dole. This ethnohistory is not only the first such study of a Great Basin society, but it is unlikely to be superseded in the near future because it covers so much so well. Here is a complex story with many actors, many institutions, and many levels of power, which is presented with a fair appraisal of both sides of the issues.

The history of agriculture, mining, and lumbering as they influenced Indian and regional history is unveiled, as is the history of white-Indian relations as they were affected by market forces and as, in turn, Anglos and Indians each sought to influence people in the seats of political power to help them. There were no great wars, but there were continual struggles. The Northern Paiutes almost invariably lost on all levels, even in their attempts to get the Bureau of Indian Affairs—the federal bureau charged with administering the federal trust relationship to Indians—to defend their interests and to protect their land and water rights.

But in the 1980s the Northern Paiutes are alive and well. Not only have they endured over a century of expropriations and deprivations but in the past fifteen years they have fought back with vigor in the courts against water expropriations and against Bureau of Indian Affairs mismanagement. They have taken steps to restore Pyramid Lake into a self-sustaining fishery, a fishery that once produced the fabled Lahontan Cutthroat Trout (up to 50 lbs.) and Cui-ui suckers (2- to 5-lb. fish) in huge quantities. The opposition to their efforts has been strong and publicly powerful, but not completely successful.

The monumental research of Julian H. Steward, especially his *Basin-Plateau Aboriginal Sociopolitical Groups* (Bulletin of the Bureau of American Ethnology 120, Washington, D.C., 1938), has influenced two generations of scholars to explain in what ways the Northern Paiutes, Southern Paiutes, Western Shoshones and Washos of the Great Basin organized to extract and consume naturally occurring resources. James Mooney in his classic *The Ghost Dance Religion and the Sioux Outbreak of 1890* (Annual Report of the Bureau of American Ethnology, Part 2, 1896) traced the origins of the 1869 and 1889 Ghost Dances to their respective visionaries—Wodziwob and Wovoka—among the Northern Paiutes of Nevada, and he explained these movements as responses of many American Indians to the deep poverty and ubiquitous oppression they had suffered during prolonged contact with whites. The Great Basin has had these two splendid analyses already, each with great breadth and each stimulating related research. Now Martha Knack manages to join, though not intentionally so, the interests of Steward in cultural adaptations to a demanding environment with the interests of Mooney in explaining social movements among deprived native peoples. *As Long as the River Shall Run* should pave the way for a third and current research focus in the inquiry into Great Basin societies—the inter-ethnic social, political, and economic history of the transformations of Indian and rural Anglo society. This new research focus, replacing breadth with depth, will have applied legal implications for Great Basin scholarship. It is likely that students of other Great Basin societies will learn not only that Paiutes, Shoshones, and Washos have endured, but that they respect their native spaces and places as something much more than a commodity. Martha Knack shows that the Pyramid Lake region is not only home for the Northern Paiutes, but it is the place from which they cull sustenance and to which they attach their own significant meanings. Future researchers of other Basin locales will similarly find that these are not commodities to be bought or sold on the market place, or to be expropriated by force—political, economic or physical.

The following pages will provide general readers, seasoned anthropologists or ethnohistorians, and interested attorneys with a grand map to previously uncharted seas. The clarity, the compelling story, and the wealth of details will surely make all readers question why so many injustices, large and small, have not been dealt with promptly by the courts.

Joseph G. Jorgensen
University of California at Irvine

Preface

Indian history, as it is usually written, is too often merely a series of generalizations broadly outlining wars, cavalry campaigns, and legislation. However, the reality of the intricate and complex human conflict, the historical truth which Indians actually lived, is only visible in detail. This book is the story of one small reservation at Pyramid Lake, home of some of the Northern Paiute Indians of Nevada.

This book is not a tribal history in the usual sense. It is not the life story of the brave men and women of Pyramid Lake. Rather, it is the history of a conflict which has continued now for over 120 years. This is not a conflict made of battlefields and blood; it is an economic struggle for the possession of land, water, and other resources of every kind. This fight was not caused by Indian people, Indian actions, Indian beliefs, or Indian culture. The conflict was born of American culture and American desire to possess, to profit, and to progress. Therefore this history will not deal exclusively with Indian actions, but also with Anglo-American actions. It is the story of the trials Anglos have brought to the Paiutes, of the relentless Anglo legal and illegal pressure, trespass, and progressive removal of valuable property from the Pyramid Lake Indian Reservation.

Unlike most histories dealing with Indians, this book will not end at 1860 or 1885 when the shooting ceased. Rather, its focus is the twentieth century, for this conflict rooted in the historical past continues no less actively today. The unconscionable exploitation to which Indians have been subjected cannot be set aside with a satisfying feeling of guilt and the comfortable assurance that this is now a thing of the past. Anglo society today profits not only from the actions of its forefathers, but also from present actions in the halls of state and federal legislatures which continue to victimize Indian peoples.

There can be no narration of facts without selection and, through that selection, the intrusion of opinion. We have clearly stated our interpretation of the historical facts because that opinion is the very reason for our writing this book. We believe that it is far better to declare our biases openly for your consideration than to hide or insinuate them. Then you may judge and decide for yourself, on the basis of the facts we have marshaled, whether we are right or wrong. We do not ask that you agree with those opinions so much as that you consider the facts presented in order to reach your own conclusions.

The idea for this book was born of a lawsuit. In 1975, the Department of Justice asked Omer Stewart to serve as an expert witness in a case that the Paiutes were preparing, in an attempt to recover water for Pyramid Lake. With Martha Knack aiding as a research assistant, Dr. Stewart gathered documentation and organized his testimony. On the basis of evidence accumulated for that testimony as well as additional researches, the present volume was written by Dr. Knack and verified by Dr. Stewart. We jointly accept responsibility for any inaccuracies of fact or errors of research.

We would like to acknowledge the help of many people in the preparation of this book. First, we express our appreciation for the insight and energy of the late Douglas King, head of the team of lawyers at the Department of Justice who worked on the Pyramid Lake water case. He provided Dr. Stewart with an array of public documents collected for that testimony by the Bureau of Ethnic Research of the University of Arizona (Bureau of Indian Affairs contract H50C-14209178) under the direction of Thomas Weaver, Theodore Downing, and David Ruppert. The staff of the Special Projects Office of the Bureau of Indian Affairs at Reno was most helpful at the time of testimony preparation. We thank also the Inter-Tribal Council of Nevada, and in particular their staff historian Winona Holmes, for opening their archival collection to us. The librarians of the Special Collection at the University of Nevada, Reno, and of the Special Collections Room at the University of Nevada, Las Vegas, have given freely of their assistance, and we are grateful. We also thank Dr. James Deacon of the Department of Biological Sciences at the University of Nevada, Las Vegas, for his advice on ichthyological details.

Dr. Dianne S. Peters of Montana State University has read the entire manuscript with a tireless and critical eye. Her generous cooperation has been invaluable in improving the prose style. Robert Pelcyger of Fredericks and Pelcyger, Boulder, Colorado, and Robbie Ferron of the University of Kansas, Lawrence, have read portions of preliminary drafts and offered most beneficial advice on legal technicalities; their help is gratefully acknowledged. We also thank the Department of Anthropology and the Graduate College of the University of Nevada, Las Vegas, for making available the professional services of Joyce Peters, Joyce Lee, Mary Funcannon, and Mary Lou Carter, who prepared the final typescript with great interest and care.

Above all, we thank the Paiutes of Pyramid Lake, who have lived this history and who have refused to quit.

M.C.K.

Las Vegas, Nevada

O.C.S.

Boulder, Colorado

March 12, 1981

ONE

The Land and Its People

Pyramid Lake, lying amid the deserts of northwestern Nevada, is large by regional standards. Fish abound in its waters, small pockets of agricultural land clutch its shores, and all around, as far as the eye can see, stretch the sage-dotted plains. This is the story of Pyramid Lake and its land, and of those people who have fought and continue to fight for its riches. This is also the story of conflict between ideas of how the land should be used today and tomorrow.

Pyramid Lake itself nestles in the northwestern portion of the Great Basin region, so-called because streams there have no outlet to the sea, but wander until they either sink into the ground or empty into alkaline lakes. The Great Basin encloses over 200,000 square miles, from the Wasatch Range of central Utah and the Snake River tributaries of Idaho and Oregon to the Sierra Nevada on the California border. More than a hundred short mountain ranges stretch north to south through its interior, dissecting the flat valley floors with almost monotonous regularity every ten to twenty miles. The elevation of those valleys varies from below sea level in the south to 4 – 5,000 feet in the north, and the mountains reach above them to altitudes of 7 –10,000 feet. These massive uplifted blocks of bare rock rise abruptly, without foothills.

The Sierra Nevada, on the western border of the Great Basin, generates one of its most striking characteristics—its dryness. Although less than 250 miles from the sea, the western edge of the Basin encompasses such terrain as Death Valley in the south and Black Rock Desert in the north. The prevailing westerly winds, originally carrying much Pacific moisture, are cooled as they lift across the high peaks of the Sierra. Since cool air cannot hold much moisture, it drops this precipitation on the western slopes. But as the air slides down the eastern side of the range, it compresses and grows hotter. Again it can carry more humidity, and so retains all that is left. As a result, the eastern slopes lying in the "rain shadow" are considerably drier than the western ones, and deserts lie under the mountain lea. Similarly, the minor interior ranges receive more rainfall than the lowlands between them. Many valleys get only 5 –8 inches of rain in a year, while the neighboring highlands may receive three times this amount.[1]

Rainfall in the Great Basin comes mostly in winter, although there are a few violent summer thunderstorms. Usually the water immediately runs off the steep, bare mountainsides, rushing down through the rocks to the alluvial fans below. Here the slope changes dramatically and, if not absorbed by the porous fan gravels, the water flows slowly toward the center of the valley. There the rivulets may gather to form a temporary stream which moves on until it is absorbed by the soil or puddles as a playa at the valley bottom. Without outward drainage, these shallow lakes are often miles in extent but only a few inches deep. They exist until evaporation reduces them to a flat pan of hard-baked silt and salt. Such ephemeral streams and playas appear and disappear swiftly after rains in winter and spring.

Where mountains are high enough to trap rainfall as snow, primarily in the high border ranges, the slow melting provides a more uniform water supply and gives rise to the few perennial streams of the Great Basin. These flow into sink lakes or shallow marshes which, although fluctuating in response to long-term weather trends, are far more stable than playas. Such a river is the Humboldt, crossing nearly 300 miles of the Basin before it empties into the alkaline Humboldt Sink. The Carson River rises in the Sierra, and flows north and then east out of the mountains and across a stretch of flatlands to

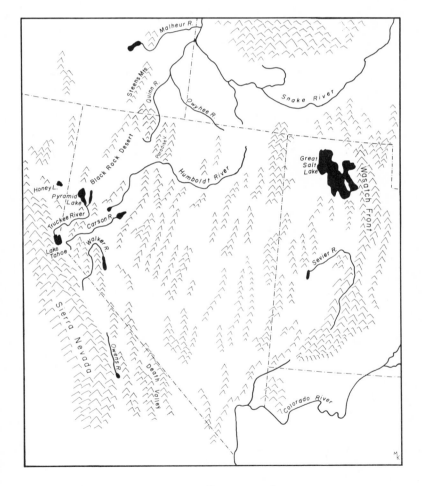

Figure 1. The Great Basin

its terminus just south of Humboldt Sink. Similarly, the Walker River parallels the Carson on its route to nearby Walker Lake. But the most important drainage for our history is the Truckee. It begins far up in the Sierra Nevada, where many short streams and underground springs feed Lake Tahoe. That lake overflows to become the Truckee River, sweeping down mountainsides, through Reno, and out across miles of desert, then cutting through a lower canyon to die a double death in the shallow Winnemucca Lake and the deep, crystalline Pyramid Lake.

Rivers are not the only sources of water in the Great Basin: more widely distributed are numerous small springs and seeps. Nearly every valley has a string of springs along one of its mountain walls. Some may only moisten deep-rooting plants; others actually bubble to the surface, large enough for animals, and man, to drink from. Some are sour with minerals dissolved from the mother rock; others rise under such high pressure that the water is heated and so forms hot springs. But wherever water seeps to the surface, desert vegetation grows and creates a green marker which can be spied from miles away by the sharp eyes of the desert dwellers.

While often called a desert, the climate of the Great Basin is not uniformly hot. Summer temperatures often reach 100°F on the valley floors, but high altitude and low humidity bring evening cooling. Winters in the northern Basin are cold, and snow occurs in most valleys every winter.

These characteristics of altitude, rainfall, and temperature influence plant growth.[2] The actual amount of growth depends on strictly local conditions. Direction of exposure to sun and wind, proximity to a spring or seep, bedrock type, depth of soil, passage of a single summer thunderstorm, and a multitude of other factors permit luxuriant growth of plants in one particular pocket, a single well-sheltered hillside, a turn of the canyon, or a dry wash. These same plants may not appear again for many miles around; but here, because of precisely the right mosaic of factors, they grow abundantly.

Not only are plants very uneven in their regional distribution, but in any given spot they are unpredictable from one year to the next. Rainfall is the most critical factor. Many desert-adapted species are able to lie in the ground as seeds for many years. When the right conditions occur, the accumulated seeds suddenly germinate and grow rapidly to maturity. If plants do not receive the necessary amount of moisture at the proper time during their growth cycle, they will not produce or, perhaps, even appear at all. Because so much of the rainfall here occurs in winter when plants are inactive, it is not directly useful for the summer-growing flora. Summer thunderstorms, on the other hand, are notoriously unpredictable and local in their effects. A particular area may not have a cloudburst for several years in a row—but when one comes, the storm may be of such violence that it washes away rapidly as a flood. Only around springs do plants have reliable access to water, and there they grow as vivid green patches in the gray-brown landscape.

Animals move to where their plant food is growing. Large mammals are usually widely scattered as a result of the thin vegetation, while small game is far more plentiful. Most flat desert valleys have large numbers of rabbits and various small rodents. There are also many birds. Ground-dwelling game birds scurry in the thickets; carrion-eaters wheel overhead. Some species of waterfowl live year-round on the lakes and sinks, while others migrate up and down the Great Western Flyway. Pelicans nest at Pyramid Lake in the summer. Reptiles are very well adapted to the Great Basin area, and lizards and snakes of many kinds are abundant. Many fish live in the lakes and streams—15 native species in the Truckee drainage alone. One of these is the large Lahontan or cutthroat trout (*Salmo henshawi*), which often grows over 2 feet long and weighs 5 pounds or more. The cuiui (*Chasmistes cujus*), a lacustrine sucker unique in the world, lives only in Pyramid Lake and the lower reaches of the Truckee River, where it spawns in the spring.

Together these plants, mammals, birds, reptiles, and fish comprised the potential food sources of the Indians who lived in the Great Basin. Except for a few groups practicing limited agriculture far to the south of Pyramid Lake, all food was provided by nature. Since game was either very small or widely scattered, red meat never provided a dependable subsistence base. Fish, where they occurred, were reliable and fairly plentiful, but strictly seasonal. It was the numerous plants which constituted the basic diet. The great number of plant species assured always that somewhere, something was available to eat throughout the growing season. However, plants grew sparsely in this harsh environment and rarely provided a surplus. People had to travel to many different locations one after another during the course of the year in order to guarantee a constant food supply. They depended on no single species, but utilized many plant and animal species for food. As a result, human mobility was pronounced, frequent, and necessary.

Thus out of the very nature of the land, the climate, and the flora and fauna, a characteristic lifestyle evolved in the Great Basin and persisted for centuries. Adapted to the scarcity, localization, and unreliability of plant and animal foods, this typical Great Basin culture was simple enough to require only the most basic extractive technologies and flexible enough to survive the inevitable periodic failures. Sometimes called the Desert Archaic or simply the Desert Culture, its outstanding characteristic was this sequential utilization of a great variety of plants and animals as they occurred in widely scattered localities.[3] The human groups were small and widely distributed to avoid overexploitation of any one of these resources or harvesting areas. Their technology was simple and portable; each lightweight tool was suitable for a variety of tasks. These tools were fashioned from a variety of materials. Basketry, for example, was useful for harvesting and winnowing seeds, for sandals and other clothing. As bowls and trays, tightly woven baskets were superior to pottery for this mobile people, because they were lighter and did not break easily. Gruel and soups were cooked in these baskets by carefully dropping in heated rocks and stirring vigorously. Other baskets were made watertight with coatings of pine pitch inside and out. Blankets, woven of rabbit-fur strips, were worn over the shoulders on cold days and doubled as bedding at night. These people hunted with stone-pointed spears and later, bows and arrows. Their heaviest tools were the flat milling stones, called metates, and the hand-held manos used on them to grind seeds to flour. With such few and simple tools, these people made an adequate living; the chewed bones of many animals and piles of vegetable waste attest to the effectiveness of their methods.

The people lived in this way for thousands of years. Which particular plants and animals they ate, which tools they used to gather them, and exactly how they wove their baskets varied through time and from one area of the Great Basin to another, according to the species available, personal tastes, and local custom.

Where large bodies of water offered unique resources, these were enthusiastically employed. Around the large lakes of the northwestern Great Basin a way of life emerged, a culture which shared many features with the general Desert Archaic, but which exploited eagerly the comparatively richer resources of the lakeside environment. As early as 2000 B.C. people had discovered the value of this niche and had come to utilize its potential systematically.

Once part of the enormous glacial Lake Lahontan, Pyramid Lake itself is located in a deep crack in the lowest part of that original drainage. With a surface area of 115,000 acres, it measures 360 feet at its deepest. This depth protects it from periodic evaporation and keeps its waters cool, comparable among all Great Basin lakes with only nearby Walker Lake and Tahoe perched high in the Sierra. The Truckee River flows into Pyramid Lake from the south, a few transient mountain streams dribble in on its west side, and springs gurgle up from its floor, but the lake has no outlet. Only evaporation, driven by the thirsty desert sun and the persistent westerly winds, draws off moisture. Precipitation in this region follows a long-term cycle, several years of drought often followed by a number of unusually rainy seasons. This cycle caused fluctuation of the surface level of Pyramid Lake, rising or falling from year to year, but hovering around a fairly predictable average.

The lake edge itself is barren, without beach except in the north and where the Truckee River now enters across a delta. Along most of the shore, desert vegetation stretches right down to the waterline. Much of the surrounding area is sagebrush flats, without trees except near springs or streams. Bunchgrass grows among the sage without forming a ground cover, and smaller or larger patches of open sand are scattered around. In the small canyons of the Truckee River, where both shelter and water are available, large cottonwood trees grow, and there are berry bushes along the banks. On the higher hills, thin stands of piñon used to grow. Reaching up out of the eastern waters of the lake are craggy shapes of raw volcanic tuff, eroded into free-standing columns and irregularities which lure the imagination.

One of these, shaped like a rough-hewn Egyptian pyramid, gave the lake its present name. This is a gray-green landscape dominated by the muted tones of buff-colored sand, dusty green sage, and purple shadows of hills and canyons, broken only by the brilliant presence of Pyramid Lake itself, barren of outlining greenery but more than compensated by its own constantly changing surface, glinting from turquoise to emerald to slate gray to foaming white.

Pyramid once had a sister lake called Winnemucca. When Pyramid was full, the Truckee would overflow through a slough to the east and there flood a flat valley floor. Extensive and shallow, Winnemucca Lake was ephemeral. If water was low in the Truckee, it received no inflow and dried up. In good years, it supported lush playa vegetation—tules and reeds of all kinds which could not cling to the deep, steep shores of Pyramid. Since the Great Western Flyway, the north–south route of migratory waterfowl, passes overhead, these marsh grasses provided a welcome hiding place for weary birds.

Fish preferred Pyramid Lake. Safe in its cool depths, they waited out the hot summer days. The large cutthroat trout were invisible much of the year, but in December they suddenly appeared at the mouth of the Truckee. Rushing up through the cold winter waters, they climbed to Lake Tahoe and even beyond to spawn in their natal waters. For over three months, great schools flashed through the upper rapids and rested in deep pools. They performed a minor secondary migration in April or May. By then the eggs were laid and fertilized; the fry soon returned to Pyramid Lake, where they grew to 9 or 12, sometimes even 20 pounds. Cuiui only emerged from the lake in mid-April to spawn. They ran up the Truckee River nearly as far as Reno and laid their eggs on sandbars with just barely enough water to cover them. Their blunt, stocky bodies, commonly 20–25 inches long, weighed 3–5 pounds. Pyramid Lake teemed with great numbers of smaller suckers, shiners, chub, and minnows as well.[4]

It was this diverse and populous fishery which formed the heart of the economic plan of early peoples who lived near Pyramid Lake; some 750 archaeological sites are known to exist in the immediate vicinity. Along the eastern shore of the lake, on the bluffs above the Truckee River floodplain, and along the channel for several miles upstream, are the extensive remains of campsites, some as large as 250 by 700 feet. These are believed to have been fishing camps, since fish remains are abundant here. At two sites near the river mouth, excavations recovered a great deal of bone, over 80 percent of which was fish bone. More than half of this was Lahontan cutthroat trout, another quarter cuiui, and the rest Lahontan sucker, tui chub, and minor species.[5] From the particular fish species killed and the timing of their spawning runs through this part of the river, it is deduced that the people used these camps in winter and early spring. The fact that the bones are unburned suggests that the fish were being sun-dried for future use, since caches of dry fish are found in many caves in the region, and historically several groups were known to come to Pyramid Lake for just this purpose.

Despite this heavy preponderance of fish remains, a great variety of other materials is found in Pyramid Lake sites as well. In speaking of the broader regional pattern called Lovelock, of which Pyramid Lake archaeology is definitely a part, two researchers summarized the part played by lake resources in the overall economy of prehistoric peoples:

> The aboriginal residents of that area must necessarily have depended primarily on the lake and its products. Since the several successive archaeological cultures notwithstanding specific trait differences were all specialized in the same directions, we may generalize in calling them desert–lake–shore or tule cultures. Throughout the archaeological continuum we find abundant evidence that fish, waterfowl, seeds and water plants were the primary subsistence items. Some desert animals—mice, squirrels, antelope, deer, and mountain sheep—were obtained, but hunting seems to have been only an occasional pursuit. Rabbit hunting is a possible exception. Tule, rushes, willow, and greasewood were the main materials utilized for string, rope, baskets, clothing, and household objects. Aside from stone metates, mortars, sinkers, chipped implements (points, knives, scrapers), a few ceremonial objects, and limited use of bone, the material culture is predominantly based on perishable substances.[6]

Indeed, a vast quantity of the objects found in sites at Pyramid Lake and in similar ecological zones were manufactured from the resources of the nearby marsh. The early residents used fluff from the ripening cattails to line caches and pad their own sandals. Cattail fiber formed the warp and woof of matting, flexible twined basketry, and rope. Marsh rushes became sandals, bags, and yards of rope and twine, while matting of rush was the most common artifact in the dry caves. Most of the arrows were made of swamp cane, tipped with a hard greasewood foreshaft. People also used the cane to make mats and fire drills. They made tule into matting as well as sandals, baskets, rope, fishline, and decoys to lure the migratory waterfowl. Willow was the raw material for literally thousands of basket fragments in many designs and weaves. Digging sticks, cradles, matting, and snares for small game were also made out of willow. Coils of prepared willow wands, split, cleaned, and shorn of bark, were stored in caves for future use.

The prehistoric people of the area not only used the plants of the sinks, but also harvested the seasonal and permanent waterfowl. Bird-bone beads, pipe-stems, and whistles, loose feathers, and robes woven of skin strips attest to their extensive use of marsh birds. They killed Canada geese, herons, swans, and ducks of all kinds. They feathered their arrows with pelican quills, and made flutes and fishhooks from their bones. Entire skins of these and other large birds formed containers. They made mats out of quills and decorated baskets with bright bird feathers.[7]

Other artifacts were made from raw materials laboriously gathered from great distances. The people made wooden tubes out of elder, and cut poles of distant-growing chokecherry and serviceberry to bring home. They collected pine pitch for glue and to seal water jugs. They used greasewood to make digging sticks for prying up the tough roots of desert plants and to make hearths for their fire drills, as well as bows. Spears, and later arrows, were pointed with heads made of obsidian, chert, or jasper, as were scrapers, drills, and a variety of other useful stone cutting-tools. Metates of volcanic basalt, manos of river cobbles, and heavy mortars and pestles, for grinding and pounding seed-grains, were painstakingly manufactured.

With simple bows and arrows these people successfully hunted deer, for there are deer-hoof pendants, deer-hide moccasins, deer-bone awls and tube beads, deer-antler flaking tools, and deer-sinew bowstrings. The hunters sought mountain sheep also, using their horns to make spoons, arrow-shaft straighteners, and sickles for gathering grass seeds; their hooves for rattles; and their bones for awls. In many sites, rabbit bones littered the soil. The people killed many other animals as well, and made blankets from strips of their fur—rabbits most of all, but also woodchucks, muskrats, moles, meadow mice, and perhaps even packrats and dogs. From the bones of coyotes, wildcats, and wolves they made beads and awls, and porcupine quills decorated baskets. The people also caught birds, leaving as evidence stray feathers from eagles, woodpeckers, owls, and bluebirds.

Analysis of human coprolites from two cave sites at Pyramid Lake and another on nearby Humboldt Sink shows that people not only used plants and animals for tools but ate significant amounts of them as well. Such studies show that for over three millennia food habits were remarkably uniform. Nearly all the coprolites contain pollen, seeds, or fiber of tule, with many also having evidence of cattail, panic grass, wild rye, cane, and seepweed. There are also large amounts of unidentifiable vegetable fiber and minute pieces of fish-bone, fish-scales, feather, and hair. The fish parts are from tui chub, Tahoe sucker, cuiui, and Lahontan speckled dace.[8] The researchers summarize the dietary evidence this way:

> Analysis of the food remains found in 300 human coprolites from Lovelock Cave [on the Humboldt Sink] reveals that about 90 percent of the foods known to have been consumed by the occupants of the cave were obtained from the lacustrine resources of Humboldt Sink. Seeds of aquatic or mesophytic flora, such as bulrush, cattail, waterweeds, and wetland grasses (*Panicum, Elymus*) formed the bulk of the diet of the Lovelock population. Wildfowl, especially ducks and mudhens, were important dietary elements. Fish (*Gila bicolor*) were another important food item.... Wildfowl would have been one of the winter mainstays, and seeds, especially *Scirpus,* which were collected during the autumn months, helped to provide a reasonably well-balanced diet during the lean winter months.[9]

To gather all these plants and animals, each growing in a particular niche scattered across the landscape, people known ethnographically from the Pyramid Lake area were highly mobile over a variety of special-purpose sites. Cave sites provided spots to cache perishable goods or materials needed only seasonally. But while cave sites provide us with a sampling of the rich variety of these perishables, few seem to have been habitation sites for more than very brief periods, and certain types of artifacts are characteristically missing from them. Caves do not tell us what the people did in their day-to-day routine, or where they spent other parts of the year. Fortunately, there are also open-air sites, camps on the unsheltered surface of the ground. Perishable goods do not usually endure here, since they were left exposed to the elements for years before actually being buried by silt or wind-blown dust. Stone tools do remain, as well as traces of house structures, remains of meals, and other subtle evidence of family life. Regional surveys, such as those to the west of Pyramid Lake in Warner and Surprise valleys, show a variety of settlement types, each with a characteristic toolkit.[10] Some sites are large winter camps, deep with food remains and evidence of years of campfires. Others are shallow scatters resulting from a single night's stay in a special seed-gathering area, or from a group of men waiting through the night in a hunting blind.

Luckily, there are examples near Pyramid Lake of each of these kinds of sites, giving a fairly complete picture of life there.[11] Along the tuff shores of both lakes are dry storage caves with the typical assortment of perishables manufactured out of raw materials from the marshes: willow basketry, tule matting, cordage of *Apocynum,* blanket fragments woven of coyote and pelican skins, fishnets, and caches of fishbone. One knife, dated roughly from A.D. 600–1100, was found with scales of the Lahontan cutthroat trout still clinging to it. A burial found at the mouth of the Truckee, dating from about A.D. 100, has been interpreted as that of a shaman. Among the other unique artifacts found in it was a stone effigy clearly identifiable as a cutthroat trout. Open-air sites, some winter villages and others less permanently occupied, have yielded manos and metates, arrow and dart points, bone knives, awls, and weights for an atlatl or spear-thrower, which together indicate the utilization of land plants and animals. Bipointed bone fish gorges, fiber fishline, composite fish-hooks including a unique multiple-pointed carved bone harpoon, all prove that the resources of the lake were not neglected.

From the accumulation of such evidence, we see a picture of a stable lifestyle on the shores of Pyramid Lake beginning at least 4,000 years ago. The people who lived there fished extensively along the shore and lower river with lines, nets, harpoons, and spears. They dried and stored fish for later use in caves. Their large, bustling villages were near the river mouth where the late winter spawning runs brought fish out of the deep lake and into their grasp. They gathered

Figure 2. Tribal Distributions in the Great Basin

marsh plants for food and to create many needed household goods. Despite this primary focus on lacustrine resources, they also utilized materials from the dry land. Grass seeds, large and small game, hardwood and pine pitch, they sought out in small expeditions which seasonally spread out across the hinterland. Technologically simple and well adapted to the environment, this pattern of living was practiced at Pyramid Lake continuously right up until the arrival of Anglo-Europeans in the 1840s.[12]

Who were these people on the shores of Pyramid Lake? While the archaeological remains cannot answer that question for antiquity, historical records of the nineteenth century named the later practitioners as the Northern Paiutes. The Great Basin, unlike California and many other regions of North America at the time of Anglo-European entry, had only a small number of ethnic groups, each using a large territory. These Great Basin ethnic groups were culturally very similar to each other, and none had political organizations of any kind which would have united all members of one group and demarcated them from others. They spoke different, but generally related, languages, and these formed the primary ethnic markers within the region. There were four basic languages, three of them related: Southern Numic, spoken by the people called the Southern Paiutes who lived in western Utah, extreme southern Nevada, and Arizona north of the Grand Canyon; Central Numic, spoken by Shoshones in a north–south wedge stretching through central Nevada, up into Idaho and southwestern Wyoming; and Western Numic, spoken by the Northern Paiutes centering in the northwestern part of Nevada and a bit of southern Oregon. The fourth language, Washo, was unrelated to the others in the Basin; Washos lived in the Lake Tahoe area and upper Carson Valley on the very flanks of the Sierra Nevada range.[13]

Of these, the people who form the focus of our history were Western Numic speakers. They called themselves simply "Numa," the people; whites called them Paviotsos, or Diggers, but most properly Northern Paiutes. While they shared the common Great Basin culture pattern with other groups, they introduced emphases of their own, reflecting their unique location on the great lakes of the northwestern Basin, Walker and Pyramid, which have perennial but short rivers feeding in but none flowing out again.

Northern Paiute territory, at the time Anglo-Europeans first arrived, was roughly wedge-shaped, the widest part in the north, stretching 275 miles across the Blue Mountains of Oregon. From there, the boundary ran down 600 miles of the east side of the Sierra Nevada, south to Owens Lake in California. The eastern limit passed west of the future sites of Austin and Battle Mountain, Nevada, and then included the confluence of the Snake and Breau rivers, as well as the Boise area in the northeast, before joining the Blue Mountains again. The Humboldt, Carson, Walker, and Truckee rivers were in the central portion of this region. The important lakes of Pyramid and Walker, the intermittent Humboldt and Carson sinks, and such smaller lakes as Harney and Malheur were included; but Lake Tahoe, along with the present sites of Reno, Carson City, and Markleeville, was in Washo territory. The total area used by Northern Paiutes extended over approximately 78,000 square miles. Within this territory, the Indians spoke similar dialects of a common language, shared a similar culture and traditions, and considered themselves a distinct ethnic group in contrast to Washos or Shoshones.[14]

However, there was no single tribal political organization which involved all the people of this huge area, nor was there any time during the year when the entire population came together for any purpose. Rather, the population was divided into bands, most numbering about 100–200 people. Each band gathered food within a traditional use area recognized by surrounding bands as rightfully theirs. Every usufruct territory contained some relatively productive areas, and also had within it resources for as many seasons as possible. One group or another customarily used specific piñon groves, lakes, streams, and stretches of game trails. Between these rich but small and localized resource areas were often far larger regions not particularly productive or useful, which were rarely visited by anyone.

Not only did the localization of the resources affect band territories, but so did resource unpredictability. If rain did not come during a critical portion of a plant's growth cycle, that species might either fail to grow or grow only in such small quantities that it would not feed the gatherers while they harvested it. In another area, perhaps not even very far away, the same plant may have been watered by a passing thunderstorm and be growing in profusion. Such unpredictability of food resources made it unwise to claim exclusive territories, and the Northern Paiutes did not do so. Their band areas were flexible, groups of people moving across them in response to transitorily rich resources. If one band's terrain failed to produce a critical crop, they moved to an area where the plants were abundant. They sought out the customary users to ask their permission to harvest food, a request that could never ethically be refused. Not only was hospitality customary, but it was also sound policy, for the usufruct holders knew that their territory was just as vulnerable to periodic scarcity as that of their visitors. The day would come when they themselves would have to request food-sharing in turn. Thus, population density readjusted itself to scarcity and plenty. The poor production of one plant species did not necessarily imply that plants later in the seasonal cycle would not have ideal growing conditions. The visiting group soon returned to its own area, sometimes after several weeks foraging in neighboring territories.

There were approximately 21 bands of Northern Paiutes in the mid-nineteenth century. One of these groups, known as the Kuyuidö-kadö, centered its activities around Pyramid Lake. Like other bands, its name referred to its characteristic food source, the cuiui or Pyramid Lake sucker-fish. Kuyuidökadö territory incorporated about 2,000 square miles, including both Pyramid and Winnemucca lakes. It enclosed an area from the Virginia Mountains on the west side of the lakes, then south across the Truckee River to the Great Bend, with a tongue reaching as far west as the Spanish Spring Valley. It went south from there about 10 miles, then east to the Nightingale Mountains and beyond for 15 more miles of desert before turning north past Pyramid Lake to the edge of the barren and forbidding Black Rock Desert. Paiutes from Burns, Oregon, to Owens Lake, California, knew of these boundaries and of the group who lived there.[15]

Within this stark terrain, food resources were localized in small areas. Production of everything except fish was limited and undependable. Paiute technology offered few means of preserving those foods which happened to produce a surplus beyond what the harvesters themselves needed during their days of gathering. Nevertheless, whenever they could, Paiutes sun-dried or parched foods for winter storage. Between the limitations of environment and those of technology, Kuyuidökadö constantly had to renew their food supply, moving in response to natural fluctuations, utilizing a wide variety of foods as they ripened over the year, walking to the places where these could be found, carrying their few possessions with them.

By far the worst part of the year for the Kuyuidökadö was the middle of winter, in January and February, when the snow was on the mountains and ice on the lakes.[16] Seeds had been blown away or eaten by wildlife long since, and many of the small animals were in hibernation. Just a few thin jackrabbits and limited caches of food they had brought down to the lowlands last autumn were available. If the previous summer had not been ideal, this stored food would not last through until spring. This was the hungry time, between the last of the stored food and the appearance of the earliest plant shoots. In the Truckee and Walker rivers there was a winter-spawning trout which appeared in small numbers during this time, and the Paiutes waited patiently on weirs of woven willow to net this winter meat. In February, if the snows were gone from the valley floors, the ground squirrels came out of hibernation; men and boys hunted them avidly with bows and arrows, or traps and deadfalls. The kill was quickly cleaned and roasted.

About a month later, as it began to warm, the migratory birds arrived. In the midst of the dry lands around them, the lakes, shallow sinks, and playas were welcome resting-places for thousands of waterfowl. It is said that in the early days the sky darkened with the numberless birds: snow geese, Canada geese, mallards, pintails, canvasbacks, goldeneyes, teal, stilts, avocets, curlews, killdeer, pelicans, and more. The Indians made lifelike decoys out of tule or rush, covered them with feathers or even whole bird-skins, and carefully attached grass-filled duck heads. Floating in the water, these decoys lured fowl down into nets strung across the marshes, and swimmers herded the birds toward the snare. Waiting until the last minute, the hunters shouted, startling the birds into the entrapping nets where, with heads and necks entangled, they were easy prey for the men's clubs. Along the shores, the cattail and tule were showing new shoots. The vegetable-hungry Indian women waded out into the still-icy water of the marsh shallows and pulled up these first greens for their families. On the flats the first plants soon arrived, led by the much-sought-after carved seed. Women began digging edible roots such as sego lilies and camas as soon as they appeared, and boiled the bitter squaw-cabbage leaves. When the birds had nested and were laying eggs, Paiute men made small one-man boats of bundled tules and poled out among the marsh plants to raid the nests. Mudhens and swans were valued for their feathers as well as their meat.

In April and May, the water was warming and the spring floods roared off the mountainsides and down the rivers. Small shiners, long invisible on the muddy lake bottoms, came to the surface as the great spawning runs began. The Lahontan cutthroat trout and the large, black Pyramid Lake cuiui appeared. During the weeks of the spawning season, these fish filled the river at the mouth and for miles upstream, making the water seem alive with their thrashing. These early fish runs brought bands of Paiutes from miles around, and the Kuyuidökadö hosted friends and relatives whom they had not seen during the entire long winter. This was a time of plenty, of sociality, gossip, conversation, singing and dancing. Amongst the festivities, they built weirs across the river, repaired nets and set lines, and replaced fish-hooks in eager preparation. Soon the fish arrived in short, rushing spurts; alerted by the shouts of fishermen, all the men ran to the shore, spears in hand, and threw fish ashore to the waiting women. Working in groups under a cloud of cheerful conversation, they quickly split the fish, gutted and filleted them, and laid the flesh to dry on pole racks. Now people ate luxuriously of the fresh roasted fish meat. The abundance of the spawning runs assured a surplus for storage. The Kuyuidökadö and their visitors worked busily; they knew the run would not last more than a few weeks.

By the first of June the desert seeds were beginning to ripen, and women took their finely-woven baskets out onto the flatlands. The women beat the tiny seeds of the mustard plant and the mentzelia into flat, tray-like baskets with basketry fans. When the tray was full, they emptied it over their shoulders into a large, funnel-shaped burden basket slung on their backs. Thus equipped, they could work all day, as long as there were plants and light. They brought back even the very smallest seeds, clinging tightly to stalks. These they dampened, placed in a slow fire to burn off the chaff, and then winnowed the now-roasted seeds from the ash. The women sought out the berries of the desert thorn, which ripens at about this time. Meanwhile the men, following the women who were following the plants, set deadfalls for ground squirrels or rats, checked into holes for the tender, young jackrabbits and cottontails, and shot whatever birds or game they saw. "When one crop was harvested they knew where the next one was ripening, and so over the hills they trudged again, with the baskets, blankets, water jugs, and their babies on their backs, sleeping wherever night found them."[17]

In late June and July, the rice grass ripened. This tiny, black seed was the staple food for much of the remaining summer. Women gathered it in huge heaps and singed off the stems. They gathered cattail pollen by the basketful in the marshes, made it into cakes with water, and baked these in hot coals. Men paddled on tule rafts after the molting waterfowl which, without their full feathers, were unable to escape through flight. If there was a surplus, women split and sundried them for later use. Groups of women and girls picked chokecherries, and those they did not eat on the spot they sun-dried for flavoring later soups and stews. In August, the buckberry patches along the river bottoms began to ripen. Women gathered this important fruit, sieved out the seeds, and dried cakes of the pulp for later use. Birds, too, fed on the berries; like the rabbits and squirrels competing with the Indians for greens and seeds, these birds fell prey to Paiute arrows.

In the fall the major crop was piñon nuts, the most important winter food. Northern Paiute dependence on piñon was reflected in the care with which they approached its harvest. In August, men scouted for the most productive groves. Piñon trees, like most pines, are irregular in their output, being very productive one year, but not necessarily the next; any single grove reaches peak production in only one out of every seven or eight years. The scouts looked for the most promising grove, and the entire group made plans for a ceremony there. The people came up to the hills from the valley floors where they had been gathering other foods, and each family picked a few of the immature cones. They encouraged them to open by cooking them slowly in a pit of hot coals. Then there was dancing under the trees, a slow all-night circle dance, to ensure ample rain and a good harvest. The dancers were sprinkled with water from the branches of sagebrush, ever green and a symbol of life itself. The people returned a few of the pine nuts to the earth in thanks and prayer for regrowth. Each person then ate some of the early, green nuts. The next day, the group enjoyed the rare pleasure of a social gathering, competing in sports, gambling, and talking about the fine harvest that they hoped would come.[18] Soon they returned to the valleys to continue their food quest until the sequential ripening of the other plants indicated that the pine nuts were ready. Then the people returned to the hills.

Piñon-gathering time was a time of plenty. A productive grove could feed more than one group, and many families previously separated came together to exploit the rich plant production. Starting at the foothills, they moved gradually up to the later-ripening trees of the higher elevations. All along the way, people talked and gossiped and laughed as they worked. The men climbed the trees to shake down the cones which the women picked up, or else both sexes worked with crooks snapping off the ripe cones. As basket after basket filled, the people carried their crop into camp. There they easily knocked out the nuts from the fully ripe cones. The less ripe ones they laid in the hot sun or roasted slightly in a pit oven to force the leaves open enough for the nuts to fall out. Sometimes women stored them in this form, but often prepared them further so they would be ready to use. If so, after carefully removing the needles and lumps of pitch from the piles of nuts, women prepared hot coals. They tossed the freed nuts and coals together in a winnowing tray, carefully roasting the nuts, but keeping the whole mixture in constant motion to prevent the basket from burning. Then, deftly, they separated and threw the coals off the tray. They took the lightly toasted nuts to a metate or mortar and gently cracked the shells of the nuts, without crushing the meats. Then they used the basketry tray again to separate the broken shells from the whole, unbroken nuts. Adding fresh coals, they roasted the nuts sufficiently dry to keep in cache pits for the entire winter without spoiling. In a good year, a family might cache up to 1,200 pounds.[19] The entire winter subsistence of the group depended on the productivity of the trees and the rapid labor of the people at this time—for as soon as the cones ripened, the animals and the wind would begin competing for the nuts. This was a busy time.

By November the people had gathered, processed, and cached the piñon nuts for winter. Now the rabbits were fat after eating the summer vegetation and had put on their thick winter fur. It was time for the communal rabbit hunt. A rabbit shaman sent runners out with an announcement of the time and place. Many small groups gathered on the valley floors, and each man contributed his rabbit net to the arch of 3-foot-high mesh which grew out across the flatlands. That night they held a round dance. The next day, under the direction of the rabbit shaman, a closing circle of men stampeded the animals out of the brush and drove them into the nets. There rabbits became entangled in the mesh and fell easy prey to clubs and arrows. The men quickly skinned them, and the women sun-dried whatever meat was not eaten immediately. They cut the pelts into long, thin spirals and later twisted them around a string core, making a long rope. These they wove without a loom into thick square blankets to be worn over the shoulders of both men and women. These robes were the major form both of clothing for the cold winter days to come and of covering for the long bitter nights.

As the early snows dusted the hills, most people left the hills and went down to warmer valleys. There the women gathered whatever late seeds had ripened since they had gone for pine nuts. Along the marsh edges the cattails gave yet another harvest, seeds as fine as dust. Women carried the heavy-headed seed-spikes into camp, where they burned the fuzz away. They then winnowed the ash to recover the tiny cooked seeds. They also harvested nutgrass and seablight seeds. Families sought protected campsites for their winter houses, more carefully built than the casual windbreaks and shades of brush which had been all the shelter they had needed from summer sun and the sand. The far more substantial winter house began with a circular ring of poles driven upright in the ground. Pulled together, their tops formed a domed frame for the covering of tules or thatch of grass. Men and women carried in dried seeds, roots, berries, fish, rabbits, and as many of the other prepared foods as possible from the caches left at harvest sites. Women arranged these to be handy and as safe as possible from spoilage and rodents.

After the first frost, the men gathered wild hemp in large heaps, stripping off the tough fibers. These they twisted and rolled during the long winter days into cordage for netting, fishing line, bowstrings, and other useful things. They gathered sage-bark for thick, twined matting. Women went to the willow patches to get the long straight wands which, if taken now, would be most flexible and could be worked without breaking. Throughout the winter, women split and scraped bundles of these willows, peeling off the bark, smoothing and sorting for size, and finally weaving them into the many specialized baskets of differing shapes and weaves so necessary for their summer's work of gathering. When weather permitted, the men went out hunting, using all their skill to catch any unwary mountain sheep, deer, quail, or other game, no matter how small. Despite all hunting efforts, families relied primarily on the stored seeds and nuts that the women had gathered during the summer. Each day the women removed some grain from storage, ground it to flour, mixed it with water, and cooked it as gruel in baskets.

Throughout this economic year, the basic group which lived, moved, produced, and consumed food together was the family. This was most often a nuclear family, with perhaps a few added people related to one or the other adult. Because of the division of labor by sex and age, this family was an indispensable and ultimately indivisible unit. No single individual would have had the time and strength to perform all the necessary tasks by himself, but each such family was economically independent and capable of living alone. Nevertheless, there were some people acknowledged to be better hunters or basketmakers. The population was so thin and surplus goods for exchange so limited that no one was able to support himself by full-time specialization in either crafts or services. Unusually able individuals spent the majority of their time in exactly the same tasks as everyone else, receiving neither leisure nor wealth by their special skills.

Basically, women worked with plants, clothing, and children. Vegetables were far more reliable food sources than game, and more consistently available than fish; hence plants contributed a substantial proportion of the annual diet. If the women saw a small animal among the bushes, they attacked with their digging sticks. A woman working alone, or with a daughter or mother-in-law, gathered efficiently. This activity would not have benefited from large-scale, cooperative work groups. Women did virtually all the seed-gathering and root-digging, although men helped with the piñon harvest, particularly by climbing the trees to shake down cones. In addition to actually gathering the plants, older girls and women cooked and stored the food, did what little housekeeping was necessary, and made the baskets needed for their other work. Further, they made and repaired clothing for the entire family and tended the small children.

Men, on the other hand, did all the large-game hunting. They manufactured tools for their own tasks; chipped stone for points and knives; worked wood to make bows, arrows, and spears; twined fiber for rabbit nets, fish nets, and various kinds of traps. Men helped to transport large quantities of prepared grains to the winter camp. They carried firewood and water into camp in the evenings and built the brush houses. Despite this standardized division of labor, cooperation between men and women was common. This was especially true in times of harvest when large quantities of foods had to be processed quickly, or where more than one pair of hands was necessary to do the job.

At certain times of the year, such as the dry middle of summer, this very basic family unit separated off from the larger winter groups, spreading the population as thinly across the land as the food itself was spread. At other times, as when the great fish runs of the Truckee were at their maximum, nearly all the families of the Kuyuidökadö, as well as visitors from other bands, gathered at the mouth of the river to harvest the trout. Even though large numbers of people could be supported in one location at such times, their essential separation remained unchanged, for each family speared, netted, or trapped fish and cleaned, dried, and stored them alone, each for its own use.

There were a few exceptions to this economic isolation. Sometimes a few men, most often relatives, pooled their labor to build a fishing weir and fish trap. They then took turns standing on the dam to spear the passing fish, or using its built-in chute for their basketry traps.

A more dramatic form of cooperation was the periodic antelope and rabbit drives. Unlike the building of a fish dam, which one lone man could have laboriously built himself if necessary, such a game drive absolutely required the participation of larger numbers of people and amounts of equipment than a single family group could muster. To be efficient, a drive also required an unusually dense game population juxtaposed with enough other foods to support the congregated band of hunters for a week or more. Game drives produced a large quantity of meat which was then dried and stored for winter.

If the quarry was antelope, the people first built a corral, usually hidden out of sight around a sharp corner of a canyon or at the base of a cliff. When in an open area, they used piles of brush or simply uprooted sage-bushes to build V-shaped wings reaching out for a mile or more in front of the corral.

These mechanical preparations were simple, but, as in so many other cases, Paiutes did not consider such material technology effective in and of itself. Ritual, otherwise unelaborated in the Great Basin, was well developed in the cooperative rabbit and antelope hunts. Spiritual preparation was not only to insure the success of the hunt, but also to make certain that the Spirit of the game was not offended by the slaughter, to assure that Spirit that the people did need this food to live, and thus to persuade It to allow Its physical manifestation to be entrapped. For this purpose, special shamans, who had dreamed of the Antelope for instance, chanted and performed certain ritual procedures as directed during their dream experience. Through the Antelope Spirit's cooperation, assured by the ritual, the physical animals would come submissively and not escape. After all the physical and ceremonial preparations were completed, the fastest runners circled behind the herd of antelope, driving them forward by yelling and waving blankets. Once into the wings of the trap, where women and children shouted and sometimes lit fires, the animals were funneled into the corral. There, in a milling, frightened crowd, they were shot with bows and arrows.[20]

In the autumn, groups of Kuyuidökadö men hunted rabbits. Each man contributed his rabbit net, a strong web about 3 feet high and sometimes 30–40 feet long, made of vegetable-fiber twine knotted into 2–3-inch squares. They strung these nets together and propped them on supporting poles or sagebrush in a long arch across an area known to have many rabbits. Of course, the longer this arch, the better, and so the more men participating, the more successful the hunt for everyone. As in the antelope drive, they made spiritual preparations, offered prayers, and sang chants under direction of a ritual specialist. Then the net owners lined up behind the barrier with clubs. Especially fast youths ran in a loop out across the valley, encircling the area where, hopefully, many rabbits hid. Making as much noise as possible, they closed in, driving the rabbits forward into the nets where they became entangled and waiting linemen clubbed them to death.

After both rabbit and antelope drives, the hunters divided the meat among the participating families. There was always a large feast and dance before the groups split up again and spread over the land to harvest the scarce and fickle desert resources.

The entire Northern Paiute lifestyle was one of mobility and flexibility, both of the groups themselves and the resources they utilized. The uneven and unpredictable rainfall pattern of the Great Basin resulted in an undependable, localized plant growth which required people to rely on a great variety of floral resources. This unspecialized pattern assured people that at least one food would be available at any given time somewhere within walking distance. If drought was prolonged over a wide area, women knew of several alternate edible plants which, while not tasty, would support life until the situation improved. When drought reduced the plant food available for people, it also withheld the forage for browsing and grazing animals, and the herds moved rapidly to other areas, leaving neither plants nor animals. Even in the best of times, hunting was unpredictable and difficult; meat from large game, while considered important and much desired, was not a steady part of the diet, and small game was far more common.

Sometimes it happened that two or more food sources became available at the same time in different areas. Then each family had to decide which it wanted to harvest. In reaching this decision, they considered sociability, important in this thinly populated area, and groups tried to stay together as long as possible. The same families tended to regroup at the end of the summer's dispersion, but this was not a hard and fast rule; a family might join another group where they had relatives. Such fragmentation also took place on a smaller scale; if a band were camped for a time near both a seed-gathering area and a region good for hunting, the family often split for the day. Men and women would each go out to do their job alone, rejoining in the evening to share their catch.

This flexibility bespoke a fundamental independence. Each family selected from among their many kinship ties those which they would mobilize to claim connection with a particular band. Other ties could be utilized later for acceptance into another group. Both men and women individually decided where they would concentrate their food-collecting efforts each day. With such freedom of action remaining with the individual, group leadership was rudimentary, adequate for the tasks of the society, but not highly elaborated. Any man could theoretically become the headman of a band or camp group, if he had the personal qualities necessary to inspire attention from the others. A leader was supposed to be a calm man, tactful in dealings with others, and able to speak persuasively in public. A great deal of his task was the organization of the group's food quest. Members of the group chose a man wise in the ways of plants and animals, so that his advice on when and where to move was worth following. He made suggestions on personal matters, such as marital problems, as well. Nevertheless, in this as in all other cases, his authority was not judicial, and he could not pass judgment or give orders. His advice was heeded because of the respect people had for his wisdom and general character, and because his advice was most often based on the traditional values and customs to which they all subscribed. However, every person retained the right to disregard his suggestions, and the headman had no power to enforce his opinion. In other words, his authority sprang from the voluntary adherence of his followers, and it lasted no longer than their individual respect for his character and agreement with his thoughts.[21] Their respect was his only reward, for he received no salary or special services. In all ways he supported his family in just the same way as every other man of the band.

The headman was not the only important person in the community. There were shamans who had special powers because of contact with supernatural beings. In dreams, the Spirit of an animal or other element of nature voluntarily offered him power to cure the sick, foretell the future, control the weather, or perform other acts of benefit to society. In this vision, the guardian Spirit dictated the ritual means by which the shaman was to call It or invoke Its power. Often these rituals consisted of chants, dances, and use of sage incense, tobacco, feather fans, rattles, or other paraphernalia. The resulting ceremony often lasted several days. While it was going on, the shaman was the undisputed leader of the group, since any disobedience to the

Spirit's wishes would result in Its anger and withdrawal, the failure of the ceremony, and often the death of the patient.

Within this class of ritual specialists were those who had been offered power by the Spirits of antelope or rabbits. These were the men who organized and directed the communal hunting drives. Like the other shamans, their authority was restricted only to the event itself, and at other times they were treated like any other men.

The same pattern of limited, situation-specific authority was also characteristic of the miliary head. There is no record of fights, raids, or feuds between the bands of the Northern Paiute tribe itself, and the vast majority of the references to Paiutes fighting with other tribes and peoples were defensive or retaliatory measures. Nevertheless, there apparently was a recognized temporary role of military leader. Such an individual was a younger man, probably respected for his physical strength, boldness, courage, and craft, and perhaps feared for his aggressiveness. In time of a crisis, such a man gathered around himself a group of other young men willing to risk battle to revenge the ambush of a comrade or the theft of a woman. Battles were not fought for land or conquest, as there was easy access to the resources of other groups, anyway, and larger territories meant only that food had to be carried farther into winter camp. There were no particularly valuable goods that were worth risking injury to steal, and accumulation of goods only meant more to carry from camp to camp. Therefore, fighting seemed to be motivated primarily by social offenses rather than hopes of economic gain. Once the immediate goal of the warriors was accomplished, they disbanded and returned to their hunting and the necessary provisioning of their families. With this, the role of war leader ceased to be, as he too returned to being a husband and brother.[22]

Group leadership was thus loose and did not infringe on the individuality and freedom of choice of each family. If some members disagreed with the headman, they could leave, utilize their kinship ties to validate union with another band, and there follow another headman. If enough of the band lost faith in the abilities of an old headman, a new one emerged simply by the group's heeding his opinions and ignoring those of the elder. There were no strong political loyalties to chiefs. Paiutes did, however, recognize band territories where a group of people led by a headman usually spent part of each year together, moving in a customary route in search of food. Each one of these loose territories contained zones of each major food crop, so that in most years the band successfully foraged within its limits. However, there was always the threat of failure of the wild crops forcing people to look elsewhere for food. Thus, while there was nominal territoriality, the right to use a home region was always extended to another band in time of need. Further, if a band's territory contained a particularly rare resource, like salt, or an especially rich resource, like a fish-spawning grounds, they commonly let visitors share the annual harvest.

To while away the long, cold winter months, the people told and retold the stories of how their world had been created and how the Paiute way of life had been set down immutable by the superhuman ancestors and animal spirits while the earth was yet young. Theirs was a way of life rooted in the nature of the plants and animals of the land and in the small social groups which spent their entire lives together within the same circle of relatives and friends, a thinly populated world full of uncertainty, unpredictable food, and potential starvation. In response to this, the people had spread out over the land and developed a strong ethic of hospitality to visitors and kinsmen, no matter how distantly related nor how long unseen. The myths explained that this was the way the world had been created to be. That all Paiutes were kinsmen and should share with each other and be friendly. That this was how it was, has always been, and would always be.

But after 4,000 years, another philosophy was abroad in the land. Carried by another people, it said that the answer to uncertainty was not group sharing, but private possession.

TWO

Arrival of the Anglos and Their Frontier Culture

Northern Paiutes had always had contact with other Indian groups—with Shoshones to the east, and with Washos, Miwoks, Achomawis, and others to the west. They knew well that there were other tribes with different languages and different customs. However, in the late 1820s they met a new type of people, a people whom they had not previously known even existed, Anglo-Europeans. From all directions came restless waves of white men. While they looked much like each other, these encircling strangers were of different varieties, actively hostile to each other in their competing colonial interests.

White men had lived for a half-century in Spanish southern California, where isolated missions formed the nuclei of extensive settlements. Large haciendas absorbed the fertile, arable land along a strip of coastline. Spanish colonization there was residential, displacing the native tribes and absorbing their remnants as laborers. While tribes east of the Sierra learned of the whites from refugees, they were themselves not directly affected.

From the Far North, Russian colonization extended through Alaska to Fort Ross on the north coast of California. Russian interest lay primarily in trade, and seizure of land was restricted to the sites of trading posts themselves. The few Russians actually in the area were traders, and so the native populations were not displaced. Indians were too valuable to the Russians, because they caught fur-bearing animals in the hinterlands and brought the pelts to exchange for European goods. As the successful Russian trade system expanded, rival nations in Europe and the New World grew suspicious and sought to block Russia's imperial expansion down the Pacific coast.

In the northwest, the large and extremely powerful trading franchise of the Hudson's Bay Company constituted British presence. As in the Russian pattern, British occupation was on a small scale, with trading posts scattered among the tribes. The Company wanted the native economies altered only to the degree that they met European desires for furs, but otherwise to remain self-sustaining. British hegemony was extended aggressively west to the Pacific, blocking Russian movement in many places. Having reached that ocean overland in the vicinity of Vancouver Island, the British turned southward looking for new fur sources. The Columbia River drainage offered an extremely rich area for the Hudson's Bay Company, and it actively encouraged British political and economic imperialism into this northern gateway of the Great Basin.

There were also American fur companies which sent white hunters into Indian territories to bring furs to mobile rendezvous points, rather than rely on Indian tribesmen to provide pelts to stationary trading posts, as did the British and Russians. In the mid to late 1820s, American fur companies previously operating in the upper Missouri drainage met with stout native resistance on the part of Blackfeet, Arikara, Crow, and other tribes. These conflicts exposed the free trappers to great danger, so they sought new territories elsewhere. Some moved through the high passes into the upper drainage of the Columbia River, thus encroaching on the British sphere of influence. Others looked south and west. In the next few years the rendezvous were in Bear Lake Valley, in the Great Salt Lake Valley, and on the upper Green River. From these mobile bases of resupply, exploratory groups stretched out into the Great Basin and eventually found their way to Kuyuidökadö country.

Jedidiah Smith, a fur trapper working for the Rocky Mountain Fur Company, was the first white man of record to cross the Great Basin. In 1826, he sought beaver south and west of the Great Salt Lake, moved down the Wasatch Front, followed the Virgin River to the Colorado, and the Mohave to southern California. There Spanish authorities extracted from Smith a promise to return by the route over which he had come; but knowing that there were few if any beaver along that trail, Smith left Los Angeles and traveled up the central valleys of California until nearly opposite San Francisco. Here he turned east again and found a route over the Sierra Nevada now known as Ebbetts Pass. Then he struck out across central Nevada. He traveled just south of Walker River and its lake, out across the dry flats. He saw few if any Indians, and before reaching Great Salt Lake his most continuous concern was the availability of water and food.

It was not long after Smith's journey that British interests also reached into the Great Basin. On his fifth Snake River Expedition in 1828 and 1829, Peter Skene Ogden, a prominent figure in the Canadian Hudson's Bay Company, traveled down the Snake's southern tributaries to the Malheur. Seeking to reach the Owyhee River, a known tributary of the Snake, and thus return, he crossed over the flatlands of southeastern Oregon, meeting instead a creek which joined the King's River. Finding beaver, he followed it south, trapping along the way, until it joined the Quinn. This he followed downstream farther, still thinking it would eventually return to the Snake. Rather, it joined a far larger stream which, contrary to all expectations, flowed from east to west. This thoroughly confused Ogden, and he designated it "Unknown." Later to be called the Mary, the Ogden, the Barren, this river eventually became known as the Humboldt. It was full of sloughs, swamps, and beaver. Trapping was satisfactory, and the Ogden expedition worked downstream slowly, probably to a point near where Winnemucca now stands.

As winter approached, Ogden sought refuge in the Salt Lake area, but returned as soon as the spring thaw permitted. Following various Indian trails, he explored the northern tributaries and the main stream as far as Humboldt Sink. Here his men were approached by approximately twenty Indians on horseback shouting war cries. There were many more Indians on foot, well equipped with sharp arrows and bows, surrounding his small party. Ogden approached them, gave gifts of tobacco, and held conversation with these men. Although he was the first white man through this area, he observed that they already carried rifles and had fresh ammunition.[1] The Indians informed him that although the river to the west had abundant salmon trout, it had no beaver. He decided to move south instead. He passed by Walker Lake and followed the Carson River upstream until he crossed the Sierra Nevada into southern California. Ogden's widely read journals indicated only fair trapping in this distant country, which he described generally as bleak and difficult of access. Politically, British claim to the central Paiute lands was increasingly untenable, and so they did not pursue possession of this unprofitable tract.

All of these early explorers changed the lives of Great Basin Indians, despite the brevity of their visits and a lifestyle made compatible by their years of association with Indians in the Rockies. Trappers were selectively interested in only one animal, beaver, which was not plentiful. Thus, each company tried to trap out the territory and leave none of the furs for their competitors. In exterminating fur-bearing species along the Humboldt River, they unsettled the native economy. The Indians in the Great Basin were not brought directly into the mercantile market as suppliers, because the small numbers of beaver could be adequately harvested by the transient whites themselves. However, the tribes had previously utilized beaver as they had used nearly every other resource in this scant environment, and were forced to find a substitute, which was necessarily less satisfactory. In addition to killing off beaver systematically, the trappers also sought food for themselves and their horses, which further consumed native resources. Otherwise, trappers had very little interest in the region, seeking neither conquest nor settlement.

These early trappers saw few Indians in the Great Basin area, and when they did the contacts were mostly cautious, marked with conversation through interpreters and exchange of gifts. However, to the Indians of the area trappers were an object of marked curiosity. Sarah Winnemucca, a Paiute woman writing in the 1880s, remembered how her grandfather had told her of first sighting whites near Humboldt Lake:

> He immediately gathered some of his leading men, and went to the place where the party had gone into camp. Arriving near them, he was commanded to halt in a manner that was readily understood without an interpreter. Grandpa at once made signs of friendship by throwing down his robe and throwing up his arms to show them he had no weapons; but in vain,—they kept him at a distance. He knew not what to do. . . . But he would not give up so easily. He took some of his most trustworthy men and followed them day after day, camping near them at night, and travelling in sight of them by day.[2]

Relations between the white trappers and the Indian populations were destined not to remain neutral, however. The first recorded fight occurred during an expedition which Joseph Rediford Walker led into the area in 1833. As the trappers followed the Humboldt River to its sink, more and more Indians appeared. The recorder of the expedition wrote, "The Indians issued from their hiding places in the grass, to the number, as near as I could guess, of 8 or 900, and marched straight towards us, dancing and singing in the greatest glee. When within about 150 yards of us, they all sat down on the ground, and dispatched five of their chiefs to our camp to inquire whether their people might come in and smoke with us."[3] Undoubtedly fearing that this large number of Indians posed a personal threat to them, Walker and his group of men rejected this obviously open and peaceful advance. Instead, the trappers arranged a shooting demonstration in hopes of discouraging further approach by the tribesmen. With their rifles they blasted holes in a beaver pelt before the onlooking Indians. The natives were impressed with the unexpected "thunder and lightening" of these weapons, and fled.

Despite their artillery display, the Walker party was somewhat surprised the next day to find Indians again in their vicinity, walking through the tall grass on the sides of the swamps. "We had not travelled far," the chronicler said,

> until the Indians began to move after us—first in small numbers, but presently in large companies.—They did not approach near until we

had travelled in this way for several hours, when they began to send small parties in advance, who would solicit us most earnestly to stop and smoke with them. After they had repeated this several times, we began to understand their motive—which was to detain us in order to let their whole force come up and surround us, or to get into close quarters with us, when their bows and arrows would be fatal and more effective then [*sic*] our firearms. We now began to be a little stern with them, and gave them to understand, that if they continued to trouble us, they would do it at their own risk. In this manner we were teased until a party of 80 or 100 came forward who appeared more saucy and bold than any others. This greatly excited Capt. Walker . . . and he gave orders for the charge, saying that there was nothing equal to a good start in such a case. This was sufficient. A number of our men had never been engaged in any fighting with the Indians, and were anxious to try their skill. When our commander gave his consent to chastise these Indians, and give them an idea of our strength, 32 of us dismounted and prepared ourselves to give a severe blow. We tied our extra horses to some shrubs and left them with the main body of our company, and then selected each a choice steed, mounted and surrounded this party of Indians. We closed in on them and fired, leaving thirty-nine dead on the field—which was nearly the half—the remainder were over-whelmed with dismay—running into the high grass in every direction, howling in the most lamentable manner.[4]

Said to be chastisement where in fact no wrong had been committed other than curiosity, this pointless killing of Indians seemed to have no other function than to provide green boys a chance to kill a native after having traveled 300 miles without an opportunity to do so. Even the apologist narrator offered no explanation other than nervous trail-weariness and groundless suspicion for the trappers' violent response to the Indians' peaceful approaches. This pattern of violence and overreaction was to become a hallmark of American contact with Northern Paiutes in the vicinity of Pyramid Lake.

Walker's attack at the Humboldt in 1833 has remained in the memory of Northern Paiutes up until the present time. Lalla Scott, recording Paiute oral tradition a century later, reported the beaver-pelt shooting incident. She emphasized that nearby Paiutes had previously perceived the whites as objects of extreme curiosity. Having seen a few pass in the distance along the road, several of the leading men felt that, as custom dictated, these strangers should be approached in a spirit of friendship and accorded the welcome of traditional hospitality. They gathered at Humboldt Sink to greet the next passing expedition, which happened to be the Walker party. "From this vantage point they could keep hidden and yet observe the movements of the white caravan. . . . It was a thrilling adventure, as many of the young men had never been away overnight from their relatives. They passed the time playing games and telling stories. They laughed and pretended that they would not be afraid of the strange creatures they were expecting to meet. . . . Waves of excitement ran through the crowd of two hundred young Paiutes as they boldly marched toward the white man's camp."[5]

But their curiosity and eager anticipation were not to be returned. Scott continued:

> Thinking these were the Shoshones come to drive them away, the long-suffering Walker gave orders to his men to prepare for battle. The trappers hastily made a barricade of their tents and baggage two hundred feet from the camp. The men were divided, those with guns were sent out to stop the savages before they reached the camp. Instead of halting when they saw the men pointing their guns, the Paiutes, with smiles on their painted faces, lifted their prancing feet higher and came forward. At the sound of the guns, the reception party scattered and fell to the ground. They had never heard gunshot, and they thought it was a clap of thunder. After a few volleys, the Paiutes knew the white men were fighting with deadly weapons and did not want to be friends.[6]

Here then were two different perceptions of the same incident, one from the official recorder of the Anglo expedition and the other from Indian memory preserved through generations of oral transmission. Native curiosity and excitement at the arrival of strange new people was met with fear, hostility, and a lethal new technology. The whites were continuing a pattern of Indian fighting carried over from their previous contacts with eastern tribes. On the other hand, the Paiutes had to learn a new pattern, and their confusion was evident in their tribal account. Their attempts to meet these strangers as other travelers and traders had always been met were rebuffed. Instead of joining in conversation and telling entertaining tales of distant places, the whites attacked. Eventually, the Paiutes learned that the behavior of these new people was unpredictable, that they responded not as friends but as enemies.

The Walker expedition passed out of Paiute territory into California only to return early the next spring, again following the Humboldt River as the easiest route. As again they neared the Humboldt Sink, Indians appeared in large numbers. The trappers feared retaliation for their previous actions, and the narrator of the expedition recorded:

> All along our route from the mountains we had seen a great number of Indians, but now when we reached the vicinity of the place where we had had the skirmish with the savages when going to the coast, they appeared to rise in double the numbers that they did at that time, and as we were then compelled to fight them, we saw by their movements now that this would be the only course to pursue. We had used every endeavour that we could think of to reconcile and make them friendly but to no purpose. We had given them one present after another, made them all the strongest manifestations of a desire for peace on our part, by promising to do battle against their enemies, if required, and we found that our own safety and comfort demanded that they should be severely chastised for provoking us to such a measure. Now that we were a good deal aggravated some of our men said hard things about what they would do if we should come in contact with these provoking Indians; and our captain was afraid that, if once engaged, the passions of his men would become so wild that he could not call them off while there was an Indian left to be slaughtered. Being thus compelled to fight, as we thought, in a good cause and in self-defense, we drew up in battle array and fell on the Indians in the wildest and most ferocious manner as we could, which struck dismay through the whole crowd, killing fourteen besides wounding a great many more as we rode right over them. ... This decisive stroke seemed to give the Indians every satisfaction they desired as we were afterwards permitted to pass through their country without molestation.[7]

This unprovoked attack by the white trappers consolidated the new pattern of white–Indian relations. It confirmed the fears of the previous year and convinced Indians of this region that violent hostility was to be expected from whites whenever encountered. The record of Indian relations changed dramatically at this point. Indians no longer approached white strangers with curiosity, with interest, and with peaceful intent. Instead they became extremely timorous and fearful, an attitude which was reflected in nearly all of the subsequent records. Lalla Scott gave a graphic description of this fear in telling of her own group's memory of their first frantic contact with whites:

> A group of them heard a woman scream and saw the familiar signal to move, they knew at once that they must get across the water to safety as fast as they could. They were camping at this time on the east side of what was later known as Humboldt Lake. They thought if they could get to the opposite side they would be safe, so sometimes they waded and sometimes they swam. They were fleeing for their lives.[8]

The profound fear recorded in Paiute history, a fear of death, a fear of personal violence, cannot be overestimated. It was even expressed in the subconscious thought of dreams. Sarah Winnemucca described how her father had told her:

> I dreamt this same thing for three nights,—the very same. I saw the greatest emigration that has yet been through our country. I looked North and South and East and West, and saw nothing but dust, and I heard a great weeping. I saw women crying, and I also saw my men shot down by the white people. They were killing my people with something that made a great noise like thunder and lightening, and I saw the blood streaming from the mouths of my men that lay all around me. I saw it as if it was real. . . . You may all think it is only a dream,—nevertheless, I feel that it will come to pass. And to avoid bloodshed, we must all go to the mountains during the summer. . . . Let us keep away from the emigrant roads and stay in the mountains all summer. There are to be a great many pine-nuts this summer, and we can lay up great supplies for the coming winter, and if the emigrants don't come too early, we can take a run down and fish for a month, and lay up dried fish. I know we can dry a great many in a month, and young men can go into the valleys on hunting excursions, and kill as many rabbits as they can. In that way we can live in the mountains all summer and all winter too.[9]

But summer was not the time to be in the mountains. Summer was when the rice grass and other important seeds had to be gathered on the valley floors. Because they feared for their lives, Northern Paiutes retreated into the mountains, into the distant lands far from the trails, far from the Humboldt River. They moved far also from this most rich of resource areas, thus disrupting the delicate annual balance by which they had traditionally eked out a scanty existence in this harsh country. Lalla Scott reported, "As the white men came in ever increasing numbers, the Indians continued to be afraid and to run and hide when they received the signal that a caravan was coming. During the spring and summer they fled over Ragged Top to the beautiful Pyramid Lake where trout were so plentiful."[10] Although Pyramid Lake at this time was still undiscovered by white men and therefore was a safe place of refuge for this fearful people, it was not long before the influx of population severely pressed the resources of this and other remote areas.

The Walker expedition proved to the world that a fairly level route existed through the numerous craggy mountain ranges of the central Great Basin. This roadway became heavily traveled by California immigrants, as soon as its practicality for wagon travel was proven by the Bidwell–Bartleson party in 1841. This group traveled around the north shore of the Great Salt Lake and on to the head of the Humboldt River, and then westward along its drainage. They reached Humboldt Sink and then crossed south to Carson Sink. A scouting party traveled farther down to Walker Lake, where the Indians gave them pine nuts and fresh fish. More than food, however, they pointed out a pass through the Sierra which enabled the immigrants to climb out of the Great Basin before the winter snows crushed hope of progress. These travelers proved that wagon transit was feasible from St. Louis to San Francisco, allowing not only the hardy mountainmen but also settlers to cross the central Great Basin. That route became a funnel for later travelers, concentrating them along the single roadway which passed through the heart of Northern Paiute territory.

Bartleson and Bidwell were soon followed by many other groups of immigrants, such as the Chiles party in 1843. Stevens in 1844 introduced one of many variations in the trail, crossing west over the Forty Mile Desert from the Humboldt Sink to the Truckee River and tracing its course upward and over what later became known as Donner Pass, leading emigration nearer and nearer to Pyramid Lake.

The lake itself was yet to be discovered by Anglo-Europeans. Although many trappers and travelers had passed near that body of water, no recorded account of it appeared until Fremont's survey for the government in 1844. This party traveled south from the Columbia River past Klamath Lake, and on January 10, 1844, they spied Pyramid Lake from a mountain peak. Fremont described the discovery this way:

> Leaving a signal for the party to encamp, we continued our way up the hollow, intending to see what lay beyond the mountain. The hollow was several miles long, forming a good pass; the snow deepened to about a foot as we neared the summit. Beyond, a defile between the mountains descended rapidly about two thousand feet; and, filling up all the lower space, was a sheet of green water, some twenty miles broad. It broke upon our eyes like the ocean. The neighboring peaks rose high above us, and we ascended one of them to obtain a better view. The waves were curling in the breeze, and their dark-green color showed it to be a body of deep water. For a long time we sat enjoying the view, for we had become fatigued with mountains, and the free expanse of moving waves was very grateful. It was set like a gem in the mountains, which, from our position, seemed to enclose it almost entirely.[11]

Fremont and his men soon moved down onto the eastern shore of the lake, where they found an Indian trail leading southward. They passed many strange tufa formations, including the one which Fremont thought resembled an Egyptian pyramid, and so gave the lake its English name. Along the way they saw a group of shy Indians, one of whom they enticed toward them. Wearing a Great Basin rabbitskin robe, he pointed out the trail south and told them of a great river which entered the lake there. He guided them past several caves, where people had stored baskets and caches of seeds but from which all had fled in fear of the oncoming whites. But the Indians noted the whites' direction, for three or four Paiutes with bows blocked their trail a few miles farther down. The whites conversed with these guards, who eventually led them to a large village just east of the river mouth. There a chief was standing in the middle of the encampment, orating in a loud voice, and groups of curious Indians armed with bows and arrows quickly surrounded the white party. This village was quite large, and Fremont soon explained why:

> An Indian brought in a large fish to trade, which we had the inexpressible satisfaction to find was a salmon trout; we gathered round him eagerly. The Indians were amused with our delight, and immediately brought in numbers; so that the camp was soon stocked. Their flavor was excellent—superior, in fact, to that of any fish I have ever known. They were of extraordinary size. ... They doubtless formed the subsistence of these people, who hold the fishery in exclusive possession. I remarked that one of them gave a fish to the Indian we had first seen, which he carried off to his family. ... These Indians were very fat, and appeared to live an easy and happy life. ... such a salmon trout feast as is seldom seen was going on in our camp; and every variety of manner in which fish could be prepared—boiled, fried, and roasted in the ashes—was put into requisition; and every few minutes an Indian would be seen running off to spear a fresh one.[12]

Although white men had apparently not known of Pyramid Lake before Fremont's expedition, the Indians there certainly knew of white men. Fremont saw among them brass buttons and several articles of "civilized manufacture." The Indians' caution at the approach of the white men, the abandonment of camps, and the personal retreat, were all evidence that they had heard of the behavior of white men on the Humboldt. These Paiutes permitted the carefully controlled entrance of Fremont into their main camp only after several days of observation along the lake shore had assured them that his party was relatively harmless. Even then, all the while Americans were in their camp, the men kept arms in hand.

Fremont sought information from them about the land ahead, the flowing of streams and the presence of mountain passes. He related in his journal that he was unable to secure a guide and that he left Pyramid Lake going south to Walker Lake and over the passes into California. However, Sarah Winnemucca recorded that her grandfather, Captain Truckee, befriended Fremont at Pyramid Lake and accompanied him as guide to California. There he remained for several seasons, taking part in the Mexican War and returning with extensive experience with white culture, a discharge paper from Fremont, and a medal for good service.[13]

Meanwhile, the number of wagon trains using the Humboldt River route increased steadily. For the several years following Fremont's expedition, Paiute bands avoided the valley. Sarah Winnemucca recounted that while her grandfather was in California, purportedly with Fremont, the people completely abandoned the Humboldt in the summertime. When Captain Truckee returned, emboldened by his familiarity with whites, he led the people down to the Humboldt River to fish. Sarah wrote:

> They brought back a great many fish, which we were very glad to get; for none of our people had been down to fish for the whole summer. When they came back, they brought us more news. They said that there were some white people living at the Humboldt sink. . . . We remained there all winter; the next spring the emigrants came as usual, and my father and grandfather and uncles, and many more went down on the Humboldt River on fishing excursions. While they were thus fishing, their white brothers came upon them and fired on them, and killed one of my uncles, and wounded another. Nine more were wounded, and five died afterwards. . . . Our people had council after council, to get my grandfather to give his consent that they should go and kill those white men who were at the sink of the Humboldt. No; they could do nothing of the kind while he lived.[14]

While Sarah may have inserted this last statement in response to later events and political realities during her time, there was nevertheless a real reluctance on the part of early Paiutes to engage in open fighting with whites. Forbearance and avoidance were the general rule.

Group after group of whites moved down the Humboldt and through Paiute terrain, driving Indians from their summer resources during the travel season, competing with them for those grasses which immigrants desired for their livestock and Indians desired for their own food. Not only were Paiute lands expropriated and their lives put into jeopardy, but so also was their property threatened. What little they had was often destroyed. In one such incident, Sarah Winnemucca reported, "While we were in the mountains hiding, the people that my grandfather called our white brothers came along to where our winter supplies were. They set everything we had left on fire. It was a fearful sight. It was all we had for the winter, and it was all burnt during that night. My father took some of his men during the night to try and save some of it, but they could not; it had burnt down before they got there."[15]

Sarah commented further that this party, which did such pointless harm to her people, themselves met a terrible fate. They tried to cross the mountains of the upper Truckee River too late in the season. Caught in the snow, and dying, they were forced by starvation to eat even each other. This was an Indian recount of the famous Donner expedition, in which 40 of the 86 members died. Even into the twentieth century, Paiute and Washo oral history related native shock at this cannibalism, and they said this was the reason they so feared the whites.[16] Once Sarah's mother, when she could not flee fast enough, had buried her children under sagebrush to protect them from being thus eaten. Nearly all Indian oral histories in western Nevada portrayed white men as cannibals both of land and of body.

Other white immigrants, hearing of the Donner tragedy in 1846 and the dangers of the Humboldt route, shifted south to the Old Spanish Trail or north to the Oregon Trail. The reprieve the Northern Paiutes thus enjoyed was short-lived, however. Between 1846 and 1848, the United States waged successful war against Mexico and gained cession of California and Nevada. In 1848, placer gold was found in California, and in 1849 the famous Sutter's Mill discovery brought thousands to the West in search of quick profit.

The new wave of immigrants sought the quickest route to the gold fields, and the most direct route lay along the grassy banks of the Humboldt River. The main Humboldt trail, its Truckee River variant, and the Lassen–Applegate Cutoff across the Black Rock Desert to Honey Lake, each passed through Northern Paiute territory, although none went directly through the Pyramid Lake basin. Thus Kuyuidökadö remained relatively isolated from the mass migration, but were not unaffected by it. Those Paiute groups which were unfortunate enough to have their territories expropriated by large, highly organized wagon trains passing through each summer simply withdrew. Yielding that area to the intruders, they crowded in on their more isolated neighbors. As a result, few of the diaries of white travelers during the early immigrant period ever mention seeing Indians in Nevada at all, for most travelers restricted themselves to a very thin strip along the main trails and did not linger. The very harshness of their land protected the natives, because "few of the human [white] family of the many who in passing through had seen portions of western Utah [as Nevada was then called] had observed anything in it that if appropriated would have been of advantage to the possessor."[17]

Despite the brief presence of any single wagon train, the cumulative effect of the immigration was substantial. Large numbers of livestock ate precisely those grasses on which Paiutes had previously depended for their summer mainstay and for winter supplies. The frequent arrival of the whites disrupted fishing and fowling, making it difficult and dangerous to gather winter preserves. This basic competition for food resources led inevitably to friction and eventually to hostility between the Paiutes and the immigrants.

Because the Humboldt Paiutes were squeezed out of the valley during portions of their annual cycle, they sought, with their customary flexibility, alternate regions during those periods. They spent more and more time away from the Humboldt in the remote areas untraveled by Anglos, thereby overcrowding the safe areas of their Paiute neighbors. In this way, the resource bases of even the distant bands, those without direct contact with whites, were affected by the transient presence of wagon trains along the Humboldt.

Trail-weary immigrants, after crossing hundreds of miles of desert and barren terrain, now faced the prospect of crossing the rugged High Sierra. Horses, mules, and oxen were weary after months of travel with scant grass and often insufficient water. Personal goods, laboriously carried across the continent, were abandoned at this point in order to lighten the load for those last few miles. The travelers' need for resupply and the availability of furniture, jaded animals, and other valuable property created a ready market which was not overlooked by California entrepreneurs. By 1849, California traders were regularly taking pack trains to the eastern side of the Sierra. They preferred to trade for overused draft animals, which they then fattened at leisure on the natural pastures around the sinks and lakes before selling them to other immigrants later in the season. The traders brought in cattle from California, grazed them on the eastern slopes, and sold their meat. By 1850, these traders had built log cabins to house themselves and their goods for the summer and fall trading seasons, but still they left for the winter as soon as the last wagon train had come through. Thus began a new stage in Great Basin history, as traders became the first long-term white residents. Like the trappers and the travelers, they focused their enterprises along narrow roadways near streams.

At most there were 200 permanent white residents in the territory of what is now Nevada in 1854. The majority of these were traders, cattlemen, and a few prospectors overflowing from the gold fields on the California side of the Sierra. In 1855, however, the pattern began to change, when the Church of Jesus Christ of Latter-day Saints sent a group of Mormons into the Carson and Washoe valleys.[18] Immediately they established small farms, organized townships, and turned the trading post of Genoa into a permanent white community. When federal military authorities threatened the Mormon heartland at Salt Lake City two years later, in order to discourage plural marriage, Church authorities withdrew this and other colonies, but permanent occupation by whites continued. Non-Mormons either purchased or simply appropriated the improvements which Mormon families had made.

The next major events in the white history of Nevada involved not ranching, commerce, or travel, but mining. The American West had a large floating population of single males whose primary goal was to be the first to discover a gold strike, make a quick fortune, retire from the western lands to an urban area, and there spend the rest of their lives as leisured millionaires. These men, with their hopes and dreams, migrated from one mining camp to another, prospecting, searching, and rushing after rumors of rich ores. A few at a time, disappointed gold-seekers persistently crossed from California into Nevada, reasoning that if the western slopes of the Sierra were so rich in mineral deposits, then their eastern flanks should be too. In 1850, one such prospector found small quantities of gold about 40 miles east of the California line, in what is now called Gold Canyon. Between 1850 and 1859, the Gold Canyon area supported between 100 and 200 miners, and over that period produced approximately a half million dollars' worth of gold.[19] Encouraged, these men continued prospecting, ever seeking richer deposits. They spread out in all directions through western Nevada, not only in the hills around the original strike but also as far afield as Black Rock Desert. In January of 1859, gold was discovered at Gold Hill near Virginia City, and a few months later silver was found nearby. In June the rich deposits of Six Mile Canyon were found. Before fall some California miners were already arriving at the new diggings, and the following year this immigration became a flood, as word spread of the Comstock Lode. By the end of the summer of 1860, there were 6,000 miners in the vicinity of Virginia City.

In a matter of a few months the white population in Nevada had jumped from a tiny minority of 200 among far more numerous Indians, to an overwhelming majority. Despite the initial trickle of transients, this onslaught of white dominance was sudden, complete, and irreversible. The opportunity for natives to respond and resist was nearly gone before they could even comprehend the threat. The rapidity of this development produced a contact history virtually unique in North America.

In order to understand the effects of the Comstock discovery on the subsequent history of Northern Paiute–white relations, it is necessary to know something of the mining enterprises at the time, of which there were basically two kinds. Initially the work was by individual prospectors. With a gold pan, a shovel, and a mule, these men wandered the hills singly, or in groups of two or three, making exploratory trenches and panning the washes, looking for "color." Once they made a discovery and filed claims, the nature of the enterprise changed dramatically.

Unlike the placer deposits of California, most of the mining areas in Nevada consisted of bedrock ledges having very rich mineral infusions. It required a great amount of equipment to follow these ledges deep into the earth, shore up the rock sides of the shafts with massive timbers, and remove large quantities of rock for smelting. Such enterprise was far beyond the means of the single prospector, who usually sold out to banks, financiers from California and New York, and the rapidly formed mining corporations. These large-scale investments led to quite stable population centers such as Virginia City, with newspapers, banks, wooden buildings, and gambling halls, in marked contrast with the prospector's tent cities.

Despite the development of established mining centers, individual prospecting continued in the surrounding countryside throughout the nineteenth century. Prospectors scattered widely across the landscape, unguarded either by the presence of other white men or by the military. Despite their vulnerability, whites insisted upon the safety of these prospectors, for they carried the potential future of all miners with them. The mining community developed no means of protecting its own members, and yet irrationally insisted on the ability of individual operators to wander at random through territory another people still believed to be its own. There was massive outrage in the mining towns whenever a prospector was killed either by whites with competing interests or, as was more often charged, by Indians. Then the white community lashed out violently against the nearest Indian encampment.

Another source of trouble between Indians and whites was resource competition. Unlike the early trappers, miners were not self-supporting. They did not depend on wild foods, but preferred imported products like bacon and flour. Thus it might appear that there would be minimal competition between native and mining populations for the resources of the area, but this was not so. Piñon trees, virtually the only large trees growing near the Comstock, were selectively cut in order to provide timbers for mine shoring, as well as for building and cook fires. The areas around mining towns were soon stripped bare of all piñon trees, thus effectively removing for non-food purposes one of the major Indian food resources.

In addition to destructive harvesting of piñon, the mining economy also confiscated other resources. As soon as gold-seekers flocked to the Comstock, cattlemen drove their herds from California to feed miners too busy seeking their fortunes to feed themselves. Stockmen rapidly commandeered any available grasslands within easy marketing distance of the Virginia City mines, especially in the Tahoe, Truckee, and Carson valleys. Livestock ate the same grasses that had previously provided a major part of the local Indians' subsistence.

Water, too, was expropriated, as stockmen claimed springs for their cattle. Miners diverted nearby streams for flumes and stamp-mills. Prospectors camped on springs throughout native gathering territories and chased Indians away for fear of theft of their personal possessions. Eventually fences to control cattle and Anglo concepts of private ownership of land further restricted both Indian access to water sources and the mobility on which their indigenous economy had depended.

Thus the enterprises which accompanied Comstock mining increased the ecological competition with Indian groups of the area. Since miners sought out the largest stands of timber and cattlemen wanted the best pastures, whites absorbed the richest productive areas of this region, and they backed up their claims with guns. As a result, nearby native populations were immediately put into a position of dependency during at least part of their annual cycle. Although they much resented this seizure of their land, Indians could respond in only two ways. Some withdrew, as they had from wagon trains; those in the mining areas simply retreated to remote sections. However, because of the nature of prospecting and because of the very rapid development of white industries supporting mining, there were fewer and fewer areas to which they could flee. Regions which had once been isolated, such as Pyramid Lake, were rapidly brought under Anglo-American control. While a few native groups survived by this tactic into the twentieth century in areas devoid of mineral-bearing bedrock, it soon became an impractical alternative for most groups.

The other choice for Indians was to accept the presence of whites and to treat the white developments themselves as productive resources. From even the earliest records of mining towns in Nevada, there was constant reference to Indians in the streets. Very soon, Indians began working for white men in exchange for cast-off clothing, food, and other material benefits. Such work was rarely, if ever, in the mines, the major profitable economic activity in these towns. Rather, Indians found work in menial support services, such as timbering, cattle-tending, loading and unloading wagons. When they failed to find work, they begged. Indian women found work even more easily than their men in these woman-short frontier towns, where they washed clothes, cleaned houses, and served as prostitutes. Despite living in towns, these Indians continued to utilize whatever native resources were unwanted by whites, and they replaced those expropriated portions of their annual cycle with periods spent in the mining towns. The importance of wage labor and town residence varied from group to group, some depending on it more completely than others.

In addition to their patterns of resource use, the white population had other characteristics bound to generate conflict with Indians. Although differing from the East Coast culture of the time in its technological and social simplicity, the frontier culture encompassed most beliefs and values of its original Anglo-European heritage. Some of these basic cultural assumptions, forming the unconscious motivation of white actors in Nevada history, were very much a part of the setting for the events soon to begin at Pyramid Lake.

In the second half of the nineteenth century, American society was very self-conscious. It was convinced of its cultural superiority, and this ethnocentrism often took on racial overtones. Americans viewed Chinese in California, European ethnics in New York, but preeminently, native Indians, as underdeveloped and needing to progress and assimilate into the welcoming melting pot of civilization. The Eastern American way of life saw itself as intrinsically desirable. All people, it thought, should aspire to its heights, and if a "savage" should spurn the gift of participating in this culture, he would be acting in a most "ungrateful" manner. Indians were criticized as being nomadic, individually indistinguishable, and unable to speak the English language. However, these were superficial criticisms camouflaging a more basic set of evaluations.

Some of these underlying assumptions cropped up through belief in Manifest Destiny, that United States hegemony would inevitably spread from the Atlantic to the Pacific. On both the level of political rhetoric and of popular culture, Americans maintained that they had a right to control this territory and that their settlement should fill up the "vacant" land of the Western Wilderness.

That this land could still be defined as vacant, despite numerous wars with native residents throughout the white-occupied sections of the country, was the result of another cultural definition. This assumption stated that if the land were not "used," it was vacant. "Use" was defined to be "best use," which consisted only of intensive, sedentary agriculture, specifically the production of cash crops. During the frontier period, white settlers, government agents, and military men universally expressed this opinion. In the minds of Anglo-Europeans, who saw themselves as fleeing the overcrowding first of Europe and then of the East Coast, there could be no allowance for the native pattern of extensive and transient use of natural resources. Because they perceived their flight as just and their culture as superior, Americans assumed that they must and should dominate the West. An early Indian agent in Nevada, Major Henry Douglas, recorded that during the negotiation with Paiutes on the Walker River Reservation, he warned them, "For when white men come in—fill up the country, you will have no country of your own. Whites will get it all."[20] Such beliefs, stated as unquestionable truths, reveal the strong American faith that white domination of the area was inevitable. For Douglas and others the question was not *if* whites would fill up the land, but *when*.

Whites were selectively interested in a narrow range of productive resources, ones which they could exploit by methods familiar to their own culture. Unfortunately, in Nevada, where productive areas were not broadly distributed, those spots most usable to whites were generally also most productive for the native economy. Conflict was the unavoidable result. For instance, in Paradise Valley, east of Pyramid Lake in Shoshone country, an early settler wrote: "This is One of the Best Valleys for farming in the State + if properly Husbanded will prove of much value to the State. This has been a desireable [sic] home for the Indians as their Old and New Campgrounds denote as well as remarkable good Hunting ground for Nearly all Kinds of game—for which they will not give it up without a long Struggle."[21] Since whites defined farming as inherently superior to gathering and thus considered that farmers had more right to the land than collectors, settlers argued that it was the moral duty of the government to provide them with military protection against the Indians.

Another aspect of this cultural definition of proper use was the concept of monetary value. For example, a newspaper editor stated in reference to Walker Lake, "There is no good reason why a few Piutes should hold this magnificent tract of land to the exclusion of white men who would be glad to settle upon it and make homes which would add greatly to the prosperity of the State."[22] The idea of marketable products from the land, products with familiar values which could be measured in dollars and cents, was very much involved in the white perception of proper use. This was also a very effective argument in securing aid from the government, since such productive lands would be taxable and would validate the expense of military protection.

Driven by their quest for land, local settlers believed that any areas reserved for Indians to the exclusion of whites were a direct blocking of their individual freedom. Therefore, they perceived the federal Bureau of Indian Affairs (BIA), in its role of administrator of Indian reservations, as aimed at denial of their just rights to the totality of western lands. Local whites became adamant adversaries of the Indian Bureau and its agents. A local newspaper editor expressed a common opinion when he wrote, "It is a burning shame and the Interior department should either do justice to the White frontier settlers by throwing open the Reserve for settlement or not act the 'dog in the manger' about the matter. There are no Indian stock no where near to eat the grass and yet the U.S. authorities will not let our people use it."[23] This land hunger found itself blocked by Bureau policy and action; settler frustration was vented against both Indians and their assigned agents. In a clear statement of the assumed moral superiority of Anglo use patterns and the inevitability of their dominance, the editor of the *Reno Evening Gazette* said, "It is very unfair that Indians should control these two great lakes [Pyramid and Walker] and enjoy priveleges [*sic*] that are denied to white men; but it is safe to say that when the hills adjacent to Walker Lake are peopled with miners and prospectors—as they will be in a few years—its waters will be levied upon to supply the wants of the neighborhood, in spite of hoggish Indians and jealous agents."[24]

An early Nevada Indian agent, Franklin Campbell, may have seen most clearly the core of the problem. He reported: "The great cause of complaint by the whites is not that the Reserves are set off for the Indians, but that they are allowed to lay idle furnishing nothing to the Indians but a camping ground, and that in quest of food the latter are compelled to occupy the same amount of territory they did before the country was settled, that the Indians during their migratory trips to and from the pine nut country are continually subjecting them to great annoyance and loss."[25] Since the basic economic system of the Indians had at this time not yet changed fundamentally, it was only reasonable to expect that they would require the same amount of territory they had previously needed to support themselves. The issue really was that the Indians had not modified their way of life, had stubbornly remained hunters and gatherers, and had continued to practice a way of life Americans deeply scorned. Not only did Indians recalcitrantly refuse the proferred Anglo civilization, but whites found it inconvenient to coexist with hunting and gathering societies. They found that native groups crossed and recrossed the sedentary white settlements in pursuit of their subsistence. Indians believed that land was a common value whose products should be used by those in need. Whites, on the other hand, believed in private land "holdings"; a piece of land belonged to the man who held legal title and made "improvements" on it, and then he had exclusive right to its possession and products. Anyone else found on that land was trespassing. Whether or not theft and danger were actually involved, frontier whites feared that some of their private property might be purloined by passing Indians, and found their presence a constant and irritating "annoyance."

Anglo-Americans believed that change in these Indian economic patterns was inevitable, as inevitable and morally right as their own occupation of this country guaranteed them by Manifest Destiny. Frontiersmen did not consider such a change terribly difficult. Hadn't they themselves altered their lifestyles to move West? Hadn't they accepted a ruder and more simplified version of their European-derived culture? Why shouldn't the economy of hunters and gatherers be equally easy to change? Through a curious mixture of condescension, ignorance, and prejudice, Anglos depicted Indians as lacking the traits which they valued and therefore having no culture at all. "They have no government," said an Idaho newspaper, "but their passions, no head, no chiefs except leaders of little bands, who follow them for blood and plunder, no local habitations, no houses, no property except what they steal, never cultivate the soil for anything, and for these reasons can never be put under any restraint to keep the peace, except by putting them away from their wild and extensive wastes, and in some place where they can be easily and at all times repressed."[26] Perceived thus negatively, Indian culture was denied to exist. Therefore white policy to impose Anglo culture on Indians was not seen as replacing anything. There was no competition; it would simply fill a void. Indians would be given something they did not have, a culture, and they should be grateful for this bounteous gift. Governor James Nye of Nevada wrote, "I proposed that these local employees [of the BIA] shall teach the young of the tribe how to read and write and farm; to teach them how to rear sheep and cattle, how to spin, and weave; how to preserve meats, grains, +c. This result is made probable from the natural industrious habits of the tribe. . . . I have no doubt that with the addition of some ox teams, and farm implements, that in the space of five years they will cease to need any further aid from government."[27] Such a simplistic view of culture change was to be controverted by subsequent historical events.

However, at the time, whites perceived such changes as not only easy but also ultimately beneficial to the Indians involved. With comfortable hypocrisy, Anglos believed, "The Piutes and Shoshones have lost nothing by the coming among them of the whites; indeed, they appear to fare better now than in the days when they were in undisturbed possession of the whole land."[28] Such an attitude took the view that domination by the whites was inevitable, and combined it with the idea that they brought with them the benefits of "civilization." Progress, in an absolute sense, was considered to exist, and it was considered intrinsically good. The agricultural and industrial way of life brought by Anglo-Americans was Progress. Therefore, it was inherently superior to the hunting and gathering existence of the Indians. Such superiority gave it the right to displace the native lifeway. Americans were "civilized" in contrast to the nomadic Indians, and Civilization, like Progress, was an absolute "good."

The American cultural concepts which were to generate conflict with Indians not only concerned the evaluation of land use and of lifestyles, but also involved assumptions about the very nature of human society. White Americans believed that all societies were arranged hierarchically like their own, and so lay ultimately under the control of a leader in one form or another. Settlers in Nevada tended to see the band headman as such a commander, and in their writings consistently referred to this figure as a chief. Settlers very much wanted a single man to be liaison between themselves and the Indian population. This man should be a conduit of information, be responsible for the behavior of his purported followers, and be accessible to whites as a reliable contact within this otherwise fluid population.

Thus, the early Honey Lake settlers formed a "treaty" with the band of Indians in their vicinity by gaining the consent of a few of the prominent men. "In the year 1855 the settlers of the valley made a treaty with the Chief Winnemucca, the terms of which were that if any Indian committed any depredation or stole any thing from the whites, the settlers should go to the chief and make complaint to him and not take their revenge indiscriminantly upon the Indians."[29] Whites demanded that these designated chiefs control or deliver to them any Indian found offending white property and personal rights. Thus the new chiefs were made personally responsible for the behavior of the collective Indian population, over whom they had had no real power in aboriginal times. Chiefs were thus cast into a role as representatives, a role totally alien to the system of individualistic democracy which had previously been sufficient to meet native needs for intrasocial peace and limited extratribal contact.

Whites used chiefs freely in solving the problems of their frontier existence, as Sarah Winnemucca related in an incident from about 1859. Two white traders were killed and robbed in the mountains near Reno, slain by Washo arrows. The Washo "chief" was brought into Carson City. When confronted, he insisted that although the arrows were Washo, the slayer was not, because at the time of the killing all his people had been gathering pine nuts in the mountains. At the insistence of the whites and with the complicity of the Northern Paiute leaders, he was forced to bring in three men as the nominal murderers. Whites seized these scapegoats, some saying, "Hang the red devils right off." Within a day the prisoners were given the opportunity to bolt and run, which they did. They were shot trying to escape. Later it was discovered that white men had committed the two original murders and had tried to pass the blame by using Washo arrows. White authorities offered no compensation to the tribe for the deaths of their three men.[30]

The existence of a chief was convenient for the whites, but it was a new role conflicting with traditional values of the small scattered native groups. Whites *created* chiefs in the Great Basin by insisting that they *did* exist. Whites behaved as if headmen were chiefs, chastising and punishing them for the actions of others. And there were Indians willing to assume this role thrust upon them for the benefits in pres-

tige, power, and gifts forthcoming from the whites. Indians themselves often viewed such pretensions to chiefly power as either ridicu-
lous presumption or as traitorous cooperation with the conquerors.
Clinging to their traditional values, the rest of the Indian community
often acknowledged these designated chiefs with little authority and
less respect. Throughout the nineteenth century, the morally based
leadership of the elders and shamans continued to parallel the titular
power of the newly created chiefs so necessary in the new social conditions thrust upon the Paiutes.

One of the outstanding characteristics of the American western
frontier period was its propensity for and admiration of individual violence. The self-image of rugged individuals competitively seeking their
private fortunes and standing up against any opposition which sought
to block those desires was the ideal of western American manhood.
Gunslingers and outlaws were lauded in ballad and story. This pattern
of individual violence was clearly vented in white–Indian relations.

When white settlers had first entered the Great Basin and had been
a tiny minority, they had depended on Indian friendship. During this
very early period, their records described Paiutes as "friendly," "fine
Indians," and "very much inclined to labor."[31] A government report
from 1858 said, "The Pi Utahs are the only peacable [sic] Indians
about there [Honey Lake Valley], and they are altogether a superior
race, compared with the other California Indians. They are fine-look-
ing, intelligent Indians, and are all well mounted and well armed. . . .
they are the most warlike tribe there, and their friendship to the
whites should be cultivated."[32] It was not insignificant that one of the
arguments presented for respect of this tribe was their very military
strength, a characteristic frontier whites could understand.

However, all this was to change dramatically after the influx of
miners to the Comstock Lode, made safe by the military defeat of the
Paiutes in 1860. Indians then no longer formed the majority of population in western Nevada. They need no longer be feared militarily,
since they had been proven vulnerable to Western technology. The
characterization of Indians in white writings changed: "The only
tribe of importance being the Pi-Utes—a lazy, ignorant, predatory
band of irresponsible savages, subsisting chiefly upon herbs and such
wild animals as they could kill with their primitive weapons."[33] Indi-

ans were portrayed as stupid, unreliable, treacherous, bloodthirsty, thieving, and barbaric. They were attributed with an instinctive hate of white men, thus justifying white hostility. Once it was proven that Paiutes could be dominated, they were scorned: "The dull Piute has a large reservation on the south and east side of the lake [Pyramid]. Here, his barbarous ancestors have clubbed the jackrabbit and coyote, and grown browner in their naked filthiness under a sweltering desert sun of countless years, the Great Father has given him a like priviledge [*sic*], secure from the encroachments of the white hunter, of newspapers, or of soap."[34] Such scorn became so entrenched that it lasted well into the twentieth century. In 1910, the *Reno Evening Gazette* editorialized, "The rank and file of the Nevada Indian, particularly those that lie about the cities, are absolutely worthless so far as being employable is concerned. They acquire and disseminate disease. They are drunkards and drug fiends. ... An Indian develops murderous instincts when drunk."[35]

The Anglo propensity for personal violence was a characteristic of the western frontier which was well documented and commented upon by frontiersmen themselves. In an article concerning a shootout over a ranch (incidentally involving one of the Paiute's better Indian agents of the future), the *Deseret News* commented, "The shooting season has commenced in good earnest, and as there is no lack of the necessary means to keep it up, in the absence of all law, excepting that of 'force and arms', there is a fair prospect that personal encounters will be frequent in that region during the mining season."[36] Because of the rapid flood of nearly 6,000 miners into the Comstock area within a few months, it is understandable that there was little established law. All men were interested in getting rich quick and none wanted to work for the low wages of a sheriff. The first law in Nevada was miner's law, which involved simply the enforcement of contracts, claims, and legal titles. Criminal law grew slowly. For many years a man's only defense against personal or property assault by other whites was his own ability to threaten retaliation. This led to a very high homicide rate. The historian Myron Angel recorded 402 homicides between 1846 and 1881. He commented, "Those for which trivial causes, or none at all, is [*sic*] assigned, are more than one half. The majority of these can be safely set down as having begun in frivolous bravado, and never would have occurred had men not gone unnecessarily armed and congregated in places where their cooler thoughts were usurped by those begotten by the insidious wiles of strong drink."[37] Among his listings there were 15 slayings involving possession of land, 13 in resisting arrest, and 15 in quarrels over women. Only 5 noted an Indian as being the slayer. This very small number would seem to belie the prevalent frontier belief that all Indians were lurking behind sage-bushes awaiting the first opportunity to slay any passing white for little or no reason.

There was an attitude of Indian-hating pervading all Nevada which turned the American propensity for violence directly against Paiutes. As early as the trapper days, white men took an aggressive stance against the Indians. The killing of 33 Indians by the Walker expedition for no overt crime was a case in point, but not an isolated one. In Shoshone country, a fur trapper named Meek shot and killed an Indian in 1832. The recorder of the expedition "asked the trapper why he had done this, and was told that it was only a hint 'to keep the Indians from stealing their traps.' 'Had he stolen any?' queried his questioner. 'No,' replied Meek, 'but he *looked as if he was going to.*'"[38] Indian-hating not only arrived early but was a common attitude throughout the Far West. In the Snake River country of Idaho, an editorial suggested in all seriousness, "Let all the hostile bands of Idaho Territory be called in (they will not be caught in any other manner) to attend a grand treaty; lots of blankets and nice little trinkets distributed among them; plenty of grub on hand; have a really jolly time with them; then just before the big feast put stricnine [*sic*] in their meat and poison every last mother's son of them."[39]

A similar Machiavellian attitude was held by many Nevadans, if more temperately expressed. With laudable understatement, one historian, in attempting to sum up the history of violence in the 1860s on the part of a paramilitary group of volunteers, said, "Of course, one must realize that the average Nevadan was violently anti-Indian, and many openly advocated their complete annihilation."[40] The early history of Nevada was littered with unprovoked attacks on Indians. One such narrative was the highly colored and inflated memoir of an "Indian scout" recalling an event in the Truckee Meadows in approximately 1854. He approached three Indians standing with their backs toward him. "I had discovered my game," he wrote, "but how to capture it was what puzzled me. ... Could I only have had Jim [Beckworth] with me, how easy it would have been to follow them to their camp that night, kill and scalp them and capture their horses. ... should I be successful in laying a plan by which I could do away with the Indians, and take their scalps to headquarters as evidence of my work, it would give me a reputation as a scout."[41] This he proceeded to do, sneaking up on their camp in the middle of the night and, without any overt act on the part of these particular Indians, he killed three and scalped them. Some time later he recorded, "I told them [his white friends] I was going out hunting [Indians] and if I struck fresh signs of game I proposed tracking it wherever it went."[42] He went out along one tributary of the Humboldt until he struck a fresh Indian trail. This he followed toward the immigrant route, where the Indians turned away. He interpreted this as evidence of impending attack, although it would seem that they had swerved specifically to avoid trouble. However, calling up cavalry reinforcement, the scout led an attack on the Indians' camp as they breakfasted at sunrise and, without any warning or any reason, killed 67 persons.

Despite the transparent self-aggrandizement of this volume, and even questioning the actuality of some events, it did reveal some features of the popular attitudes of the day. Throughout his narration, the writer used terminology of hunting wild animals in reference to Indians, a trait quite common in the frontier documents. They spoke of The Indian in the singular, or as The Enemy. In this way, Anglos linguistically dehumanized Indian people because they continued to see them as inferior forms of being.

Another clear illustration was purportedly from William Stewart, later an important U.S. Senator from Nevada, recounting his early pioneer days in or about 1860. This story told of how he "cleaned up a party of marauding indians." Stewart was attacked by Indians when prospecting alone one day, but he managed to get away on a mule. He sought the help of a local white man from whom he borrowed a rifle, having been prospecting in this dangerous, savage-ridden hinterland alone with only a Derringer for snakes. As he rode along, he found a white man dead in another camp and "thought we had better clean the red-skins out." Riding into Nevada City, he collected 20 young men who agreed to accompany him back.

> In the morning we rode up the ridge and looked over the ground again [where the first attack had taken place]. It was a little past the full of the moon, so the after part of the night was almost as light as day. The following night we rode up the mountain opposite the camp of the indians, hitched our animals and crawled around the camp, remaining quiet until daylight, when I gave the signal for operations by firing a gun. The indians sprang to their feet at the alarm, but we won the battle before they knew where the enemy was located.

Tracking at night was a notoriously inexact science, and so Stewart and his party had no real evidence to warrant their actions. Nevertheless they felt justified. After two days on a cold trail, they contended violently that the Indian camp harbored those who had harassed Stewart earlier. Big Jim, the leader of the group, denied that any of these Indians had taken part in the original attack. "He was well known to all our party, spoke English perfectly well, and was supposed to be a good, friendly indian. . . . We made a treaty with him that the indians should leave that part of the country and never return. After the treaty was concluded and we supposed the difficulty was all over, we observed Big Jim with a party of his followers fortifying themselves behind rocks and brush." Having just been attacked at breakfast by a group of bloodthirsty white men, this would appear to have been a very reasonable reaction. However, it instantly drew renewed attack from the whites. "We moved on their works, but they fired several shots and slightly wounded one of our men. We hanged Big Jim for his treachery. The indians then left and did not return."[43]

Another, similar event took place in Paradise Valley in 1865. Five or six members of the California Volunteers were guarding government stock in the valley when 50 Indians appeared. The Indians, having long since learned of the whites' propensity for unwarranted attack, immediately raised a white flag. They wanted to come in and talk. The militiamen insisted that they lay down their arms before doing so, which they did. Nevertheless, one of the panicky whites ran for help, and as the Indians and remaining soldiers sat smoking and talking in camp, reinforcements were led to the scene. Without warning they attacked the unarmed Indians under their white flag. The editor of the *Humboldt Register* in describing this event spoke about the "red devils," "treacherous savages," "miscreant dogs," while the attacking white men were termed "good citizens" and "noble." He said:

> No prisoners were taken, in this fight. It was conducted on the system proved by the history of all our border troubles to be the only correct method of quieting Indians—killing them fast as you can lay hands on them. The Indian nature, as developed on the frontiers, is devoid of gratitude, and of all susceptibility to humanizing influences. Be kind to them and they think you fear them; and they grow insolent in proportion as you treat them well. Shoot them down, scourge them with saber and brand, till they cringe and beg for their lives,—and you . . . may get along with him.[44]

In extreme cases this undifferentiating hatred extended even to town-dwelling Indians who had shown no hostility at all. It was enough for some white frontiersmen that a man be an Indian in order for him to be an enemy. For instance, the same *Humboldt Register* editorialized:

> Murdering stragglers keep up a communication with nonparticipating but sympathizing Indians here [in town]. It is even now in discussion among our people, whether it were not good policy and the only security against the Indians, to deliberately put out the light of the "friendly" band managed here by Captain Sou—on the ground that he and his people manifestly have continual intercourse with the murdering bands, affording them information, giving them aid and comfort, nursing their wounded, and furnishing them occasionally with a man. It is in them to hate the white man. Those of them who thirst for adventure seek it in these marauding expeditions; and we would all feel safer from unfriendly Indians if there were fewer of the friendlies about.[45]

Not all Nevadans were paranoid bigots. Some refused to believe that the so-called Indian difficulties on the frontier were solely the biologically determined product of innate Indian hostility. In fact, some believed that the American culture's acceptance of individual violence was itself partly to blame. Thus, in 1852, one touring government agent wrote:

It is my painful duty to report to you, that from all of the information I can get, from Whites and Indians, the great, almost the sole cause of all the difficulties—the destruction of life and property on this route [the Humboldt], is owing to the bad conduct of the whites, who were the first to commence it—and in many instances the whites are the sole depredators of it, they manage to have it charged to the Indians. I am informed by respectable and reliable authority, that many of the whites who travel this road, have been in the habit of persuading the Indians into their camps, under the most solemn assurances of friendship— and then, without any cause on the part of the Indians, they would shoot them down—others are in the habit of shooting the Indians whenever and wherever they can find them, whether the Indians are molesting them or not. These white men, frequently take excursions through the country, in search of the Indians, robbing and plundering them of everything they possess. The Indians retaliate upon the whites whenever they have it in their power, and thus the excitement is kept up. In many instances, innocent persons are made to suffer for the bad conduct of others—the Indian knows no difference between the white men—if injured by one, he takes revenge upon another. Scarcely a day passes, but we hear of some depredations, either of the whites or the Indians. This state of case exists throughout the whole region of country, from within 75 miles of Salt Lake City, to within 100 of Sacramento—some 700 miles. It is very difficult to get any conversations with the Indians on this route—they have been treated so badly by the Whites, that with very few exceptions they have no confidence in any professions of friendship made by a white man.[46]

Regardless of the cause of the interracial hostilities, the fact of continuous violence remained, and frontier authorities believed that the only way to stop it was to physically separate the two groups. It had long been policy in the East to isolate Indians on limited portions of land reserved for their use, and this same policy was introduced in Nevada. The earliest Indian agent to travel in Nevada stated:

Whatever policy may finally be adopted, in relation to these unfortunate people [the Northern Paiutes], I can assure you that none can be worse or productive of more evil to both them and the whites than the present joint and promiscuous occupation of the country. . . . I believe the policy of the Government has been, to withdraw the Indians from such parts of the country as would necessarily expose them to contact with the white settlers, as the only means of averting frequent difficulties. Indians and Whites cannot as a general rule live together. It is not in the nature of things, and it is far from being solely the fault of the Indians.[47]

This view, of course, suited the desires of the Nevada settlers ideally, for it would free the land for their use, a use which they considered a natural result of the rightful westward migration of white Americans according to Manifest Destiny. Settlers often petitioned the Bureau of Indian Affairs to establish reservations as a means of avoiding difficulties, and they favored separation of the races as a peaceful and profitable solution.

The policy of reservationization was instituted in Nevada, but it did not completely accomplish the desired segregation. Indians continued to live both on and off reservations and in towns with whites; the pattern of interracial violence, distrust, and hatred continued for decades. And yet through it all, occasional white men recorded statements which did not fit the dominant pattern of racist epithets. For instance, in 1859 an Indian agent wrote: "The Py-Utes are undoubtedly the most interesting and docile Indians on the continent. By proper management these Indians may be made to compete with the whites in agricultural pursuits. They are extremely anxious to cultivate their lands, and will make excellent men to work. Some of them now take hold of a scythe and mow, drive oxen or a four horse team, equal to a white man."[48]

The agents were not alone in their opinion of Paiute aptitude and flexibility in those changing times. The civilian who had established the first trading post in Genoa, Nevada, recounted:

I established a store there and opened an extensive trade with the Indians. I sold my stock + finding the Indians friendly and disposed to

work I opened a farm and have since followed farming and stock raising Indians being my principal laborers of whom I have often had as
many as twenty five to work for me at one time. They are fine Indians
and are very much inclined to labor. They will work at my kind of
employment faithfully. I have an intimate knowledge of their notions
and are well acquainted with them throughout the Carson Valley. They
have been long expecting and hoping to be permitted to go to work
their lands to support themselves and families and are very anxious to
do so.[49]

Other writers told of the very early peaceful relationships established by some Nevada Indians. As early as 1856, a passing agent
wrote: "The most of those Indians have evidently once lived in California, which accounts for their knowledge of the English language.
Many of them have become domesticated, and are employed by the
settlers of the valley as herdsmen and laborers on their farms."[50]

These descriptions obviously contradicted the earlier-quoted stereotypes of bloodthirsty savages. In the same towns and at the same
time that Paiutes were being reviled, they were occasionally characterized as "friendly," "peace-loving," "cooperative," "trusting," and
"trustworthy." It was a curious paradox that this dual image should
have existed. Even in Paradise Valley, which was the site for so much
racial hatred, there were reflections of this second image of Indians.
Thus, in a letter written by the justice of the peace in 1879, there was
the statement, "The Indians here without exception, are good and
true to the whites. All are willing to work and do work for their living
and it would certainly be unjust to remove them to any reservation to
starve. . . ."[51] Even the U.S. Secretary of the Interior, traveling briefly
through the Reno—Virginia City area, was impressed by the positive
attitude of whites toward Indians, and wrote, "I find that a great
many of the Pi-Utes are off the reservations, residing among the white
people doing work and making a living in a decent way. White people
like them and do not want to part with them."[52]

Why did whites need simultaneously these contradictory images of
Indians? The answer to the paradox is not long to be sought. Indians
were praised in direct relation to their willingness to do menial labor
for whites, to work on farms plowing and harvesting, to do timber-

cutting and road construction, to herd livestock. For this they were paid wages in food, cast-off clothing, or even a little cash. In a mining area where all white men were avidly seeking their own fortunes and were unwilling to work for wages, Indians provided a labor pool in a labor-short, expansionist economy. As such, they were useful to their white neighbors. When their seasonal labor was not needed, they did not have to be kept on wages, for, unlike Anglo hired help, they could be turned loose to support themselves by traditional hunting and gathering. In this way, a symbiotic relationship was established between some Paiutes and particular ranchers and other landholders throughout the valleys of Nevada. In contrast, there were free-ranging Indians not associated directly with farms. These were considered treacherous and dangerous. Their elimination, indeed their annihilation, was actively sought by white frontiersmen. As free-ranging individuals, Paiutes were threatening and much hated. However, as landless laborers offering no competition for the land-base which white settlers coveted for themselves, Paiutes were welcomed.

The events which were soon to begin at Pyramid Lake, and which form the substance of this history, were a small but in no way exceptional manifestation of the great tradition of European imperialism. Modified by local circumstances, these events took on a unique flavor which did not change their essential nature. Rushing to the Great Basin, trappers, immigrants, and miners brought with them a freight of colonialist ideas which found their American expression in the concept of Manifest Destiny. Assured of the moral correctness of their occupation of the land because of the "progressiveness" of their civilization, they freely applied their own ideas of proper and exclusive land use. The American movement west featured settlement and intensive mining capitalism, and had no interest in permitting a self-sustaining native population. In view of the pattern of direct American occupation long established in eastern lands, it was not surprising to find displacement to be a keystone in Great Basin policy as well. Violence and Indian hating were the inevitable accompaniments. The intent of this policy was made obvious by a series of open conflicts with Indians in the 1860s, but its more subtle and all-pervasive machinations were only to appear decades later.

THREE

Open Conflict

During the very earliest white settlement in Nevada, when the small minority of whites needed the cooperation of the majority Paiutes, relations between the two groups were relatively peaceful. For instance, the Anglos at Honey Lake, not far to the northwest of Pyramid Lake, made an unofficial and informal treaty with Winnemucca and other Paiute headmen, pledging to negotiate any crimes committed by members of either race.

This friendly state of affairs persisted until the discovery of silver brought floods of miners into western Nevada Territory in late 1859 and 1860, at which time relations deteriorated rapidly. The miners worked not only in Virginia City but also prospected in the hills, and so came into contact with Paiutes. "Knowing nothing of the treaty which the Honey Lake people had made with Winnemucca or caring nothing to observe it, [the miners] frequently treated the Indians with injustice and cruelty," wrote a contemporary. "The Pah-utes bitterly complained to us [Honey Lakers] of their wrongs and evidently expected that the terms of our treaty should extend to the whites who were flocking into the Southern portion of the Territory. Of course the people of Honey Lake could offer them no redress nor interpose in their behalf."[1] This protest by the Honey Lakers had the convenience of a double standard. In the conflicts to come, many whites considered all Indians to be equally culpable for the behavior of one and, therefore, to be equally subject to attack. Whites would not and did not assume social responsibility for the actions of others of their kind, although they demanded communal responsibility from Indians. This failure to distinguish among individual Paiutes exacerbated the tensions already in evidence both in the mining districts and along the then well-traveled immigrant routes.

One of the primary sources of contention between Indians and whites was economic resources. White immigrants and settlers soon denied Indians those resources on which they relied for food. F. Dodge, an early Indian agent in the Nevada Territory, wrote:

> It is a well-known fact that the loss of life on the Humboldt River for years past, both to the whites and the Indians, has been most lamentable. The Humboldt Indians see by the experience of other tribes, that roads are the harbingers of civilization, and the certain sign of their own subjugation, and final extermination. All they ask is something to eat, and here lies the true secret of most of the Indian depredations upon this great line of travel. The encroachments of the Emigrant have driven away the game upon which they depend for subsistence. They cannot hunt upon the territories of other tribes, except at the risk of their lives. They must therefore steal or starve.[2]

Raids on small wagon trains or isolated groups of travelers were frequent in the late 1850s in the Humboldt country.[3]

Of course, economic competition was not restricted to the Humboldt. By 1860, there were 3,000 white-owned cattle grazing at Pyramid Lake, herded by a few white men and protected by an agreement with local Indians. Headmen committed themselves and their groups not to steal the cattle. In return, a few head of stock were to be given them, a transfer variously interpreted as payment for services or as ground rent. In February of 1860, Winnemucca traveled to Virginia

City and there tried to gain a hearing for complaints against the white herders, who he said had come in the fall and requested and won permission to leave cattle on the grazing grounds around the lake. In return, they agreed to pay him for watching the cattle and making sure that no one stole any. This he did. By late winter, however, the owners refused to give him payment as agreed, and even accused the Indians of pilfering the herd. Smarting from the insult, Winnemucca ordered them to remove the cattle, saying that he wanted the grass for his own horses, which needed it by this time of the season. The cattlemen refused to remove their stock. Not choosing simply to take the cattle due and drive the rest from the range, Winnemucca sought justice from the wider society. However, his appeal was ignored and no retribution was forthcoming.[4]

The rapid rise in the white population with its concomitant pressure on productive resources, coupled with the whites' refusal to consider Indians' legitimate protests, left natives with only military solutions to their grievances. Interethnic tensions heightened. Indian attacks on stragglers from wagon trains and killings of isolated white men became increasingly frequent, and accusations even more so.

The white reaction to these incidents was retaliation. One such occurrence involved the death of Peter Lassen, a popular Honey Lake pioneer and experienced trail guide. He spoke the Paiute language and often served as liaison between Indian bands and the settlers. In the spring of 1859, Lassen went into Black Rock Desert with a few companions to do some prospecting, and there he was slain.[5] He had had good personal relations with the local Indian bands, who promptly condemned the murder and reasserted their own friendship with the whites. However, white reaction was immediate and intense. Despite their long-standing peaceful relations and successful treaty with local Paiutes, Honey Lake settlers immediately suspected them of the slaying and prepared to march against them in bloody revenge. A few of the whites pointed out that supplies carried by the slain men had not been removed, as would have been inevitable if the murderers were Indians. Major Dodge, the Indian agent, rushed to the area to support this rational white minority. For the time being, open hostility was averted, but not for long.

Less than a year later, a young Honey Lake man named Demming was killed in his cabin. Once again the Honey Lake settlement took up arms against the Paiutes. They petitioned Territorial Governor Roop for a military force "to follow and chastise the Indians upon our borders," and he dispatched a small troop of soldiers.[6] Joined by local settlers, they set out across the Black Rock Desert to seek the murderers who, in all probability, were from the Smokey Creek band of Paiutes. They contacted Winnemucca at Pyramid Lake, but he refused to help them. After three days on a cold trail they approached and attacked a fortified Indian camp. For several hours the two parties shot at each other ineffectually before a violent snowstorm forced them to break off. After the storm abated, the whites reentered the now-deserted camp, where they found supplies, several books, and the violin of the murdered man, goods considered to be conclusive proof of the Indians' guilt.

The escalating frequency of such incidents led Governor Roop to petition Army headquarters in February for a troop of dragoons, or at least ammunition and supplies, to mount war against the Paiutes. He asserted, "We are about to be plunged into a bloody and protracted war with the Pah-Ute Indians. Within the last nine months there have been seven of our citizens murdered by the Indians."[7] Thus, the white population from Reno north was expecting a war and arming themselves in preparation for it early in 1860.

Throughout Northern Paiute country, wherever whites and Indians came into contact, the tension was evident. Indians did kill whites, but some whites exploited the situation by blaming natives for their own crimes. In all cases, the settlements immediately struck out in armed groups against the nearest Indian camp. Rational men attempted to curb this violent reaction, but men with guns prevailed. Such men called for war, and their call was soon to lead to the attack on Paiutes at Pyramid Lake.

The winter of 1859–60 was apparently a severe one. The snow lay deep, and movement was difficult. Coupled with the very rapid influx of white population, this winter was one of crisis for the Indians. The newspaper *Territorial Enterprise* reported:

> The Indians in Truckee Meadows are freezing and starving to death by scores. In one cabin the Governor found three children dead and

dying. The whites are doing all they can to alleviate the miseries of the poor Washoes. They have sent out and built fires for them, and offered them bread and other provisions. But in many instances the starving Indians refuse to eat, fearing that the food is poisoned. They attribute the severity of the winter to the whites. . . . The Truckee River is frozen over hard enough to bear up loaded teams.[8]

Equally difficult seasons were undoubtedly common in Paiute life, but this one came at a strategically bad time, complicating already tense interracial relations. The Indians blamed white magic for causing the hardship, a suspicion perhaps generated by whites' comparatively rich food stores and apparent immunity from starvation. It was clear that whites were malevolent toward Indians, and hatred was a traditional sign of witchcraft in Paiute culture. This belief probably explained why the proffered foods were rejected—they were physically or magically poisoned. These fears were merely another indication of the deteriorating interethnic relations.

As usual with the coming spring, many bands gathered at Pyramid Lake to harvest the much-needed spring-running fish and recover from the winter of scarcity. Groups came from all around, including northern groups of mounted Paiutes, then increasingly known by the local whites as Bannocks, as well as families from Truckee Meadows, Honey Lake, Smokey Creek, Carson Sink, Antelope Valley, Black Rock Desert, and Humboldt Sink. They all clustered around the mouth of the Truckee and the lower Pyramid Lake shores to feast.

Ignorant of native ways and looking back from later events, some whites put a military purpose on this gathering. One writer, reflecting the fears typical of the frontier community, declared this congregation to have been not for purposes of food-gathering, but for a council of war. He related that the council was "determined to surround and capture Virginia City, massacre the inhabitants, and take possession of the town."[9] Whites recognized their numerical disadvantage in western Nevada and were very much afraid of Indian attack, but much of this fear came from an unrealistic and false projection of their own military organization onto the Indians. Thus this same narrator continued, "The means of defense, however, were

found too inadequate to cope with the thousands of Indians of the large territory, should they swoop down upon the town en masse."[10]
Even at this time it was patently impossible for Paiutes to have surrounded and laid siege to a town the size of Virginia City. Their bands lacked hierarchical chains of command with which to mobilize the needed number of warriors. Each of their men was allied to a headman only through kinship, friendship, and respect. Otherwise, he retained independence of action. Such ties, while intense, were necessarily on a small scale and did not lend themselves to mobilization of large forces or to unified command. Furthermore, attack on a village the size of Carson or Virginia City needed not only manpower but supplies. Paiute culture provided minimal means for food accumulation and it had been a particularly hard winter. Had an attack force been raised, it simply could not have been fed in the field, and white superiority of weaponry would have prevented any quick success by a small group.

Frontiersmen not only projected American-style military organization onto the Paiutes, but also attributed to them a very highly sophisticated intelligence network: "To accomplish this [military objective], many of their spies, regarded as harmless by the whites, loitered idly up and down the rudely-constructed alkali streets, begging from door to door, and displaying supreme indifference to everything else but the possession of the scraps of food that were given them and the faro games that were in full blast at all hours among the low gamblers of the town; but all the time they were 'sizing up' the defenses of the place, and, transmitting the information to the 'seat of government' further East in the territory."[11]

Anglo fears of a massive Indian military organization lusting to pounce on their settlements, and of hidden networks of disguised spies, generated vigilante groups. Describing Virginia City's response, one writer said, "Every now and then small bands of Indians would menace the town, only to disappear when they met with the least opposition from the whites. Gradually these bands began to increase, and loitered about the outskirts of the town, and it was deemed necessary that drastic measures should be employed against them. To this end some fifty men were chosen, well armed and equipped, to pursue the small bands, and either frighten them into a more remote part of the territory (for the individual Pi-Ute is an arrant coward), or if they remained, to persuade or coerce them into behaving themselves."[12] The "menace" involved with small groups "loitering in towns" hardly seemed worthy of such a drastic reaction. Such a defensive posture anticipating any overt hostility on the part of the Indians was undoubtedly responsible for a great deal of the frontier violence of which the Pyramid Lake War was a prime example.

The lucidity of hindsight led settlers to regard the spring gathering at Pyramid Lake as dangerous and insidious, perhaps even a "war council."[13] But at the time an observer wrote that "the Indians which had been in and around Virginia City suddenly left; not one of the Pah-Utes could be seen; a few of the Washo tribe remained at Carson City and they were among the first to report to us that the Pah-Utes were going to fight the whites. *Up to this time no act had been committed which would lead to the belief that such was really the case.* It was well known to all who were acquainted with the habits of the Pah-Ute tribe that they usually resorted to Pyramid Lake at that season of the year for the purpose of fishing, and this fact kept down all cause of alarm. . . ."[14] Since the Washos were the traditional enemies of the Paiutes, it was natural that they should have fomented such a rumor. Further, the general tenor of interracial relations should have told Washos and whites alike that hostility was imminent. In light of the escalating tensions, it was only natural that the many groups gathered on the shores of the lake should hold conference and discuss the mutual difficulties they were having with their new white neighbors. These difficulties centered on issues of subsistence accentuated by the hard winter—the encroachment of whites on Indian lands, the killing of game, and the cutting of piñon trees.[15] Indians faced the real probability of war with the whites.

Among those gathered at Pyramid Lake were Indians with experience fighting whites on the Humboldt and Snake rivers. When whites massacred noncombatant Indians on a reservation in California, news of the atrocity spread rapidly and was known to those at Pyramid Lake that spring. This contributed to the Paiutes' fear of reservations as potentially lethal traps.[16] Thus at Pyramid Lake there gathered a large group of Indians, smarting from a winter of hunger, pressured by increasing encroachment of whites, and containing among themselves a number of warriors with successful military experience. If no further incident had taken place that spring, this group might well have scattered uneventfully. But this was not to happen.

The particular incident which sparked the flame has remained unclear. One account said that the white settlers at Williams Station, located on a ridge above the bend of the Carson River about 60 miles northeast of Virginia City, stole an Indian's horse left to graze while its owner went duck-hunting.[17] Others maintained that the horse was to have been bartered in an abortive trade agreement, and when the would-be white purchasers broke the agreement, the Indian reclaimed the horse.[18] In still another version, these same white men were detaining two young Indian girls, presumably for immoral purposes. Kinsmen attempted to free the kidnapped girls and fighting broke out.[19] Others, particularly later historians, gave no explanation at all. Rather, they implied that it was an unmotivated outbreak of Paiute racial aggression, a continuation of the frontier stereotype of Indians as naturally and intrinsically Anglo-hating and hostile.[20] In any event, in early May five white men were slain and their cabin burned.[21] The owner of Williams Station, not present at the time, found the bodies the next day and immediately reported the incident to Virginia City.

Cries of "Vengeance!" rang throughout the Comstock Lode. Indian fighters gathered at Genoa, Carson City, and Virginia City. Without having any organized command, these 105 white men hastily rode off toward Pyramid Lake, passing Williams Station, where they buried the dead. A few miles south of the lake, they were ambushed by Pyramid Lake Paiutes and suffered a resounding defeat: 62 were killed; the survivors escaped on foot, in the river, or by sheer chance. When news of this defeat reached the Comstock settlements, panic set in. Whites attempted to fortify the towns and brought women and children into sanctuary locations. Attack on the towns themselves was considered imminent. Urgent cries for help were telegraphed across the Sierra. California's Governor responded with supplies, including guns and ammunition. The town of Downieville sent 165 men, armed and mounted; local volunteers joined the 200 federal troops stationed near Honey Lake. In all, over 750 whites advanced toward Pyramid Lake a month later, well organized under experienced officers. A small detail scouted the main Paiute village at the mouth of the Truckee and then withdrew, but not before the Indians spotted them. Paiutes on horseback and on foot followed. Five hours later, the Indians went down to defeat.[22] While Paiutes claimed that only 4 of their number were killed, understandably minimizing their losses, contemporary white reports correspondingly inflated these, saying that 46 Indians died. By the twentieth century, this figure had grown to 160 Indian deaths.[23] Regardless of the number actually slain, the historical significance of these two engagements was indisputable. Armed Paiute resistance to white settlement ended.

After the second clash at Pyramid Lake, Indians apparently scattered. It was June and fishing season was over. Several reports of the time related that the Indians moved north. Dodge specifically said that old Winnemucca went to Oregon for safety, "disgusted" with the situation around Pyramid Lake and its unhappy memories of defeat.[24]

Anglo troops built a temporary fort near Pyramid Lake, although they were later reassigned to Fort Churchill, a permanent outpost guarding the wagon trail into the Comstock region from the east. There were but a few minor incidents in the following months. A white scouting expedition encircling Pyramid had one man slain.[25] Another minor skirmish occurred in the Black Rock Desert between the northward-retreating Bannocks and Paiutes and a command under F. W. Lander, an engineer constructing an Army wagon road.

It was actually Engineer Lander, annoyed at interruption of his work, who accomplished the peace negotiations. By walking unarmed into an Indian camp after the second skirmish, Lander gained an audience with Numaga, the Paiute war leader from Pyramid Lake. Lander asked the headman why they were fighting, and learned that they were outraged by the whites' seizure of land without remuneration and subsequent claims of exclusive ownership. Nevertheless, Numaga declared, if they were compensated for loss of their homelands, and were given aid to adjust to a new way of life on farms and in building permanent homes, they for their part would be willing to live at peace. Numaga insisted, however, that the shooting of Paiutes without reason, the ravaging of women, and the general hostility of whites toward Indians were further causes of the conflict and must stop. He quickly disclaimed any Paiute involvement in the Williams Station killings, blaming rather a group of Bannocks from the north over whom he, as only the local headman, had no control. In order to establish peace, Numaga offered to try to keep the Paiutes in check for one year, until the following summer. If no further action of hostility took place by that time, a permanent peace would *de facto* be in effect. Knowing he was operating without any authorization, Lander could only promise to forward the Indian grievances to Washington and attempt to get payment for lands taken by whites. Numaga proclaimed himself pleased with this arrangement of peace; for not only had men been killed in the fighting, but also women and children were suffering by being driven away from their usual food-gathering sites.[26] He implied that hostilities would not have taken place if the whites had come to him openly after the Williams Station incident, according to the terms of the Honey Lake treaty.

News of Lander's armistice was spread through all of the communities in the area. Several bands of Indians traveling around the country were threatened by local whites, and armed escorts had to be provided for their safety. Residents of Honey Lake Valley were reported to be still "very indignant against the hostiles, . . . had stated that they would 'kill the Pah-Utes on sight.'"[27] When two Paiutes entered Honey Lake Valley after the peace announcement, they were seized by federal troops and one was shot at several times while trying to escape. After Lander effected their release, the Paiutes complained bitterly about their treatment. Such incidents continued on a small scale for several weeks as news of the armistice spread and tempers cooled.

Both Indians and whites remained tense and watchful. During the fishing season of the following year, as groups of Paiutes congregated at Walker River, whites feared a repetition of the warfare. Not waiting for a sparking incident, Warren Wasson, the local Indian agent, ventured alone into the Indian camp. Direct talk lessened hostilities, and as a result there was no open conflict that year.

Individual members of the Anglo population found Paiute reactions to be less violent and dangerous than their own and so continued to press Indians to the limits of their forbearance. Despite the supposedly dangerous war in progress, whites made mineral discoveries between Honey Lake and Pyramid and filed on them. In late June, even before

Lander's peace negotiations were begun, squatters who were not frightened away by the recent open warfare were establishing farms in Truckee Meadows, on the lower river, and around Pyramid Lake itself.[28] Indian belligerence did not deter white encroachment. Nonetheless, public opinion, citing the hostilities, hardened against the formation of the proposed reservation at Pyramid Lake. Lander reported, "All the citizens of the eastern slope with whom I have conversed deprecate the idea of the Indians being placed on a reserve so near the white settlements as Truckee River and Pyramid Lake. Mineral discoveries have recently been made in those vicinities, and the use of so much good land for the Indians where the fertile sections are so limited in extent and the mining population so rapidly increasing, is regarded as injudicious."[29]

Paiutes for their part, having learned at Pyramid Lake that open resistance was futile, avoided direct confrontation, but their resentment was no less real for all its restraint. In Nevada, the balance of power had changed; the Indians knew this and the whites knew this. A year after the Pyramid Lake clash, Agent Wasson wrote, "It affords me great pleasure to inform you that the Pah-Utes since the unfortunate difficulties with them more than a year ago, have behaved themselves with the utmost propriety till about the middle of April last, submitting to the grossest outrages upon them, committed by villanous [sic] whites, having their men shot and their horses stolen on several occasions without offering to resent the outrages themselves."[30] Nevertheless, isolated stage-drivers and mail-riders on the Humboldt River road were attacked in both Shoshone and Paiute territory, and tension remained high.[31]

That this should have been so was not surprising, since the basic cause of conflict along the Truckee remained unabated. Pyramid Lake was to be only the most famous in a flurry of brush-fire skirmishes in Nevada during this time period. All of these disputes had similar roots—the alienation of a subsistence land-base from the native inhabitants. Two populations simply could not occupy the same territory which one alone had previously filled. The Anglo-American society, shown to be militarily dominant, tried to force a drastic change in the cultural life-way of the Indians, who resisted stoutly and continuously throughout the Great Basin. There resulted cycles of open conflict and simmering antagonism, repeatedly flaring into death.

After the incident at Pyramid Lake, Winnemucca with some of his followers moved north into the Steens Mountains in Oregon and eventually to the Malheur Reservation. There hostile Bannock bands approached the headman in 1878 seeking support for their new war, but he and his family remained neutral.[32] Civil War-trained Army troops, languishing on the frontier, brought a rapid end to those hostilities. The surviving Indians were incarcerated under military guard on the Yakima Reservation. Some of Winnemucca's family, although innocent of any hostilities, were also brought in. There, the more warlike Indians, angered by their neutrality, mistreated them.[33] It was only after years of letter-writing and the intervention of eastern Indian-affairs societies that Paiutes from Oregon and Nevada were permitted to return to their homelands.

Meanwhile, the successful Nevada Anglos were not content with their booty of lives and land, but wanted these benefits at no economic cost to themselves. In December of 1862, the then-Nevada Territorial Legislature petitioned Congress for reimbursement of the private expenses incurred during the fighting. They argued that it was a federal duty to protect the lives and property of citizens. Since rapidly developing circumstances had forced private parties to protect themselves without waiting for aid from Washington, they said, the federal government was liable for the expenses. In presenting the history of the case, their memorial stated only that the Indians "became hostile towards the white settlers, and that in consequence of massacres being committed, it became necessary, in order to save the settlements from annihilation,"[34] that troops be sent. In attempting to place the whites in a powerless, defensive, and pitiable light, no reasons for these Indian "hostilities" were given. Rather, Paiutes were portrayed in classic frontier style as attacking irrationally and without provocation.

The memorial continued that the expenses citizens had thus voluntarily incurred had been a "crushing weight on many worthy individuals, who were deprived of almost their entire subsistence." This overlooked, of course, the massive effects on the Indians, who had lost the bulk of their subsistence base for all time. Congress was willing to reimburse the white Nevadans, but could find no current law which permitted payment for this frontier fray. After admission to statehood, Nevada Congressmen and Senators repeatedly submitted the bill. Every Senate from 1888 to the turn of the century approved this special-interest legislation, and the federal government eventually paid claims of nearly $30,000 to Nevada citizens for their "services, supplies, and expenses incurred" during the so-called Paiute War of 1860.[35]

Conflicts similar to those near Pyramid Lake in 1860 were repeated many times as white population overflowed into areas more remote from the Comstock Lode. In Owens Valley, California, to the southwest, government agents had repeatedly assured the Paiute residents that the lands would be theirs permanently. However, by 1861, whites were bringing in large herds of cattle and expropriating the valley grasslands. The local Indians naturally resented this intrusion, and tensions mounted and eventually broke into open hostilities. The Paiutes at Walker River were aware of these difficulties and sympathetic to the plight of their neighbors. Agent Wasson urged the Walker River people not to become involved, and traveled to Owens Valley himself to attempt a reconciliation. When he arrived he found the local white citizenry organizing militia groups. He reported, "We made known to them our business and instructions but found little or no encouragement to make peace with the Indians, their desire being only to exterminate them."[36] After several small skirmishes in which a few whites were killed, Wasson managed to negotiate a truce involving the establishment of a reservation at Fort Independence. Most of the water-rich valley fell to white cattlemen.

In 1863, there was another "Indian scare," this time at Como near Virginia City. Numaga, a Paiute headman from Pyramid Lake, came into the town in October, and "through his interpreter, uttered a formal protest against any further destruction of the pine nut groves. He said that his people depended upon the nuts from these trees for food; that the *'pine nut groves were the Indians' orchards,'* and they must not be destroyed by the whites. That they were welcome to the fallen or dead timber, but he should not permit a destruction of that portion which yielded food for his followers. This warning was not heeded."[37] It happened that a few unfamiliar Indians showed up in town, and whites declared that the hostiles were bringing in reinforcements. The town hovered in a state of panic through the long autumn day. When two tense citizens met at dusk, "both forgot the password, and 'turned loose' in the most approved style with their revolvers, each supposing he was having a struggle for life with, possibly, Numaga himself. The alarm was general and fearful to contemplate. . . . The next morning the Indians came into town to see what all the row was about."[38]

Such panics based on misinformation, assumption of mutual hostility, and fear, were dangerous potential beginnings of armed combat and were fairly common. Another such incident took place in Unionville the following year.

> From one or two slight acts and movements on the part of the Indians, such as . . . the changing of camping-grounds, the kindling of large fires at night, around which they sit and sleep, and which, in a country like this, with such cool nights, is highly necessary to a nomadic and almost a denuded race of people, these croakers and alarmists [local white settlers] thought they saw specks and signs of disaffection and embryo war on the part of the Indians, and forthwith applied to your excellency [the Governor] to dispatch a military force to the Humboldt for the purpose of overawing and frightening them. Your excellency complying with this request, a troop of fifty mounted men from Fort Churchill visited the Humboldt region. When the troops reached here all was quiet.[39]

While some such encounters, spawned by the anxieties of both Anglos and Indians, passed without bloodshed, other incidents were more lethal. In October 1863, a prominent Indian from Walker River was going to Virginia City to complain about his treatment by a white man. The Anglo ambushed him along the trail and killed both him and his horse. When other Indians found his body floating in the Carson River, they were outraged. Much to the annoyance of the white community, which did not want to set a precedent, reparations were paid. No formal charges were made against the white man. Murdering an Indian in cold blood was not considered a crime.

In the following year, four whites traveling in small groups along the Humboldt were killed in separate incidents. Later the next year, two white prospectors traveling alone were slain in the mountains near Walker Lake.[40]

Small-scale attacks such as these were the typical Indian pattern of conflict in the Great Basin. Camp groups of a few families could mobilize only a limited number of fighting men and but small quantities of supplies. In the prevailing atmosphere of interracial tension, when Indians met isolated white travelers they often raided them for their goods and livestock. Nevertheless, whites continued to travel in small parties. Miners commonly prospected in groups of one or two. Farmers insisted on living on ranches, isolated far from towns. Wagon trains habitually left behind members whose stock tired, anticipating that they would catch up later.[41] Weary livestock were commonly scattered loose along the roadway, it being assumed that they would trail their fellows into camp by evening. When stock had to be kept together in a herd, whites resented it as an imposition and a violation of customary trail methods.[42] Anglo customs of travel and settlement therefore denied and contradicted the real state of affairs. They refused to adjust to the fact that this was a frontier area where the native inhabitants persistently resented white incursions. The attacks on these small groups of whites were therefore predictable and inevitable.

While whites retaliated freely and violently for any of these attacks, they made little effort to assure that punishment fell on those who had actually committed the offense. For instance, in Unionville in the summer of 1863, a few head of cattle disappeared. Whites called the native headmen together, accused the Indians of theft, and threatened severe punishment if the cattle were not brought back. The Indians laboriously gathered all the stock on the range for the farmers. After local whites had profited from this free round-up, undoubtedly netting many mavericks, they threatened that the "whole band will hereafter be held accountable for any misdemeanor of any one of their people, and they have promised that no depredation or other offensive act on their part shall again occur."[43] Clearly, whites had no intention of bothering to differentiate between the actual perpetrators of a crime and any other Indian. The tribes were treated as indistinguishable wholes, and Anglo wrath was vented against the nearest available member of that group.

As local whites pursued this logic, the accumulated number of Indian deaths rose. By 1864, an agent wrote, "I regret to say that within the past year three inoffensive Indians have been unprovokedly killed by the settlers. The Indians have not yet in a single case attempted to retaliate. We have always taught them if any one of their people is injured by the whites to come and inform us at once and in no case to resent the injury themselves. In this way we have prevented serious trouble from time to time. I fear however if the bad white men do not cease their barbarous treatment upon innocent Indians that they will not always bear their injuries so tamely."[44]

The ultimate test of Indian forbearance came in March of 1865, when some cattle were reported stolen near Pyramid Lake. A troop of Nevada volunteer cavalrymen, who had offered to pay their own way to New York just to get in on the Civil War, but had been assigned to protect local roads instead, were now dispatched from Fort Churchill under Captain Wells.[45] They discovered that a few Indians were camped at Winnemucca Lake. Eager for action, but without any direct evidence that this was the band of Indians responsible for the cattle theft, Wells and his men surrounded the camp and attacked without warning. Approximately 30 Indians were killed. Winnemucca, then camped at Pyramid Lake, was afraid to object to the massacre. Powerless, defeated, and afraid, Paiutes stood by and watched their camps attacked and their numbers dwindle. However, memories of the incident rankled in their minds for years. Sarah Winnemucca wrote, "I do not think my Father, will ever come in [to Pyramid Lake Reservation] with his own consent on account of the Brutal Murder by Capt. Wells, then of the Nevada Cavalry ... of all my sisters, and my Father's three wives, but I do not think he will ever again be hostile. They were killed upon the Truckee Reservation and it has had a bad effect on all the Indians ever since."[46] Although white reports said that dried beef was found there, indicating the probable guilt of the group, Indians believed that the people were only fishing and totally innocent of the charge.[47]

Once again in 1865, tension broke into open hostility in the Humboldt River Valley. The fears and counterfears, typical of frontier relations, were vividly enacted there. In April two white men were surrounded and killed by Indians, their friends fleeing for help. When the troops arrived, they attacked the nearest Indian camp, killing 12. Not content with this retribution, a contemporary historian recorded, four more parties of citizen militia within the next few days "succeeded in surprising a camp of Indians near Kane Springs. They charged in among the redskins, dealing death right and left, and brought away with them eighteen scalps as trophies of their work."[48] A bit later, in May, troops under the same Captain Wells who had been responsible for the Winnemucca Lake massacre attacked an Indian encampment, killing an unknown number. The military remained in the area, and killings continued out of all proportion to the original slayings.

After the killing of an isolated military officer along the Quinn River, a squadron of men took retaliatory action against a nearby Indian camp and killed 32. Ten more Indians were surrounded and killed near Table Mountain in September of that same year. Later that month, 31 more Indians, an entire camp, were slaughtered along the Quinn River. All three attacks were supposedly in response to the single original murder.[49]

Because of the disproportionate and indiscriminate pattern of Anglo reaction, Indians justifiably feared any hostile act on the part of their fellows. They actively urged each other to peace, as had Numaga before the Pyramid Lake conflict. If an incident did occur, Indians often steered whites toward other Indian camps in order to protect themselves. Captain Sou was coopted in such a manner in the hunt for Black Rock Tom in the Humboldt country late in 1865. He led whites to Tom's camp and took part in the attack, in which 55 Indians were killed. Forty more Indians were surrounded and killed on Fish Creek still later that year. Both of these last two camps were eliminated in retaliation for the killing of a single ox-cart driver and the plundering of his wagon.

Later that same year, Paiute "chiefs" Soo and John made an informal agreement with officers of the Nevada Volunteers that the Indians would move from the more heavily settled Humboldt to the Carson Valley within one week. Any stragglers would be considered hostiles and killed on sight. "We will never know," wrote a local historian, "how many harmless Indians perished because, in remote regions, they had not heard of this contract."[50] Here again was a clear

Another said:

> Receiving as they [Indians] do little or no assistance from the Government another thing that works against these Indians is the cutting of the timber[.] where in former times they obtained Pine Nutts [*sic*] the discovery of the mines has brought the wood into demand and where the forests of that kind of wood grew five years ago nothing but stumps are left.[64]

And again:

> Their country is rapidly passing from them. Every garden spot and tillable acre of land is now being sought out and occupied by white men. Their groves of piñon are disappearing before the strokes of his axe, their grass-seed is consumed by his herds, the antelope and mountain sheep are killed or driven away, and, although their [*sic*] is some compensation in the employment given in the harvest field and elsewhere, still the Indian must look for a reliable and permanent supply of his wants to the products of these lands sacredly set apart for him.[65]

These refuge lands were the reservations established at Pyramid and Walker lakes. However, history was to prove that these havens were not "sacredly set apart" and inviolable from white incursions, but rather that the acquisitive desires of whites which had brought about their initial necessity were not satisfied by possession of the vastness of Nevada. Rather, these interests persisted in coveting even these limited reservation lands.

FOUR

Reservation Life

Indian reservations are lands held in trust by the United States government for Indian tribes. These are private lands owned by the tribe as a whole, and they are not part of the public domain. This trust relationship between the tribes and the central government grew out of the federal treaty-making power granted in the United States Constitution.[1] Only the federal government, not individual states, could enter into treaties with foreign powers, including Indian tribes. Originally statements of mutual friendship and alliance, these treaties changed over the years into major land cessions which might reserve for the tribe a certain limited portion of its aboriginal territory. These reduced tracts became the first Indian reservations. The U.S. Constitution also specified that the federal government shall regulate commerce with foreign nations and with Indian tribes.[2] Fair trade was necessary for peaceful relations with the large and powerful tribes on the frontiers of the various states. In the early weak days of the United

States, peace with these tribes was critical to the national interest. From these constitutional powers of treaty-making and commerce have issued Supreme Court decisions firmly asserting that relations with Indian tribes are exclusively a federal matter and not subject to state interference.[3]

Federally administered Indian reservations have been created in three different ways. The first way, through treaties, was common before 1871. After that date the United States, grown far more powerful than any of the tribes, refused to recognize them as independent nations with whom bilateral negotiations were appropriate. Unilateral acts of Congress then became the common means for setting up a reservation or changing boundaries of an established one. The third technique, through executive order, required neither negotiations with the tribes nor the approval of Congress. The Pyramid Lake Reservation was founded in this last way.

While executive order reservations had been established since at least 1855, the practice "rested on an uncertain legislative foundation" prior to 1887.[4] Only then did major legislation treat executive order reservations as the same type of legal entity as reserves founded in other ways. Only after 1924 did the Attorney General's Office declare that executive order reservations were not totally arbitrary and were not subject to routine administrative alteration. Only then was it admitted that Indian rights to executive order lands held the same status as rights in treaty-founded reservations. Thus, not until 25 years after the Pyramid Lake Reservation had been set aside was it known by federal attorneys whether such a reserve was even legal, and not for its first 75 years was its legal status defined. This ambiguity strongly affected its early history.

Regardless of the origins of any one reserve, the general policy of reservationization found wide and enthusiastic acceptance in the American West. For the most part, white frontiersmen feared Indians as warriors and hated them as enemies. They also saw them as potential competitors; Indians possessed land which Anglos wanted. By restricting Indians to delimited areas, the physical danger of frontier settlement was removed; at the same time, it opened up lands for Anglo-American pioneers. Frontiersmen perceived reservations not as portions of native territory rightly *retained* but as gifts from whites *to* Indians, areas where their continued existence would be tolerated.

In many areas, whites saw reservations as open-air prisons where tribes defeated in battle would be restricted, penal colonies where they should stay and not "break out." The military should enforce that containment. Good land, it was said, should not be wasted on them, but rather lands not useful for other purposes, Anglo purposes, should be "given back to the Indians."

In contrast to Western pragmatism, which wanted Indians detained if not eliminated, Washington policy during this period was slightly more benign. If Indians were to remain self-supporting and not become a welfare drain on the white society, and yet if they were to be restricted to lands far smaller than those which they had previously needed to earn their living, tribes had to change their economic base. It was assumed that Indians would eventually become small independent farmers, the ideal goal for whites in the nineteenth century. While they were being taught the arts of agriculture, Indians would receive rations to substitute for the game and wild produce on which they had previously subsisted, if these were now in insufficient supply.

This forced economic change was heralded as Progress. The Bureau of Indian Affairs (BIA) perceived itself as bringing Civilization to the Indians, for along with farming would come selected additional changes. Indians would learn to read and write the English language, live in rectangular houses, wear tailored pants and torso-covering blouses, marry only one spouse, embrace Christianity, and sell farm produce to Anglo merchants.

Washington's long-term policy goals, aimed as they were at assimilating Indians into the general population, were completely at odds with the self-perceived interests of frontiersmen. There Indians were not viewed as people to be invited to join American prosperity, but as enemies to be strictly controlled until they should conveniently vanish from the frontier scene. Anglo-American settlers had no wish for independent Indian entrepreneurs who would compete with them for profits and resources. Pioneers saw Washington's Indian policy as an intrusion upon their free rights, an intrusion imposed by eastern do-gooders who, they said, had never been in an Indian fight and therefore did not know the "true character" of Indians.

However, with the desired reservations came the undesired policy and Indian agents to execute it. But in the days before Civil Service, Indian agents were political appointees, and the conflict between federal policy and local interests assured that the job would be difficult at best. The difficulty, the extreme isolation of most western reservations, the low pay, and the still-lower social status of the Indian charges, meant that these jobs attracted few highly capable men. There were compensating factors, however. The isolation permitted ample opportunity for an energetic agent to augment his scant income through a variety of shady deals. Investigations and trials of ex-Indian agents proved that some were in collusion with contractors to defraud Indians of treaty rations. Some defrauded the government of funds allocated for development projects or salaries, and still others engaged in a variety of other imaginative embezzlements. By the mid-nineteenth century, the Indian Bureau had gained an unsavory reputation for scandal. As a result of agent incompetence, outright criminality, inefficiency, and malicious neglect, Indians were not receiving those services which federal policy dictated for them. Late in the 1860s, President Grant attempted to reform the Bureau by delegating the authority to appoint Indian agents to Christian missionary groups. It was hoped that churchmen would be morally exempt from the corruption which had plagued the Bureau.

In such an atmosphere of policy and practice, the Pyramid Lake Indian Reservation was born. On October 6, 1858, the Superintendent of Indian Affairs for Utah Territory, which at that time included what is now called Nevada, wrote to his first agent appointed for the western district, Frederick Dodge: "It is desirable as soon as you have ascertained the where-abouts of the tribes, to make some geographical explorations with a view of selecting suitable reservations for agricultural + herding purposes for the Indians in your Agency. The number and extent of such reservations must be left to your judgment. It would in my opinion be most compatible to the public interest + welfare of the Indians to concentrate them as much as possible."[5]

Accordingly, Dodge reconnoitered the northern Nevada area seeking a suitable territory for the Paiutes of the western river drainages. He found that there were only a few areas that would be appropriate for agricultural colonies as dictated by the BIA policy. Therefore, in November of 1859, he wrote to the Commissioner of Indian Affairs:

> I respectfully suggest that the North West part of the Valley of the Truckee River including Pyramid Lake, and the north east part of the Valley of Walkers River including the lake of the same, be reserved for them, the localities and boundaries of which are indicated on the accompanying map. These are isolated spots, embracing large fisheries, surrounded by Mountains and Deserts, and will have the advantage of being their home from choice.[6]

The Commissioner approved his suggestion and a few days later wrote to the President requesting an executive order to set aside these loosely described lands as Indian reservations. At the same time, the Commissioner asked the General Land Office to withdraw the indicated lands from the public domain. The Surveyor General of Utah Territory was notified, and he closed the proposed reservations to settlement. This withdrawal was duly transferred to the Nevada office on statehood, two years later.

The recorded description of the Pyramid Lake Reservation was vague; it stated simply that a triangular tract varying in width from 25 to 53 miles and including the northwestern portion of the valley of the Truckee River, and Pyramid Lake, was to be withheld from public sale for Indian purposes. When surveys were extended to that vicinity, the lands would be further specified. Although Congress appropriated salaries and the BIA assigned agents to Pyramid Lake, no executive order was issued at this time. Nevertheless, from 1859 on, government documents, agents, local settlers, and even newspapers constantly referred to the Piute, the Truckee River, or the Pyramid Lake Indian Reservation at that location.

Not until 1865 was the reservation surveyed. By then it appeared that the Central Pacific Railroad would cut across the southern tip of the reserve. Therefore, Eugene Monroe was hired to survey the boundaries. Local white interests constantly challenged the lines he set. In order to alleviate the confusion, the BIA once again requested that the President issue an executive order recognizing the existence of the Pyramid Lake Indian Reservation as federal trust territory. He did so in March 1874, with these few brief words:

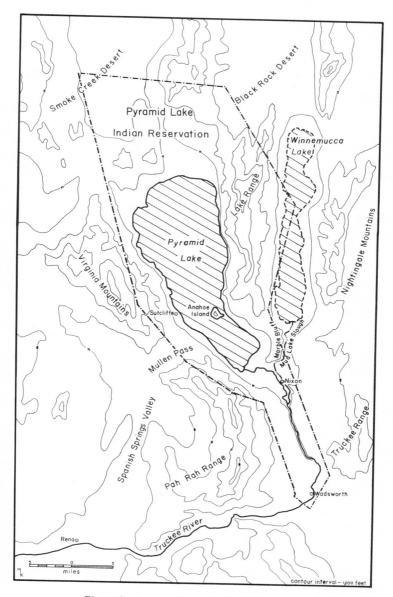

Figure 3. Pyramid Lake Indian Reservation

It is hereby ordered that the tract of country known and occupied as the Pyramid Lake Indian Reservation in Nevada, as surveyed by Eugene Monroe, in January 1865, and indicated by red lines according to the courses and distances given in tabular form on the accompanying diagrams be withdrawn from sale or other disposition, and set apart for the Pah-Ute and other Indians residing thereon.[7]

There were two problems with the founding of this reservation which were to cause much difficulty in coming years. First was its executive order status, then relatively unknown and untested in court. There were many who believed that reservations could be formed only with the consent of Congress—either through Senate ratification of a treaty or through a law approved by both Houses. Northern Paiutes had no treaty following military defeat, nor had Congress legislated a reserve for them. They had only a unilateral declaration of the executive branch that this land was reserved for them.

The second problem was the date of founding. While the executive order was dated 1874, the land had actually been withdrawn from the public domain for Indian purposes 15 years earlier. During the intervening years, Anglo settlers had located on the best farmland, withdrawn water from upstream, and made other claims against the resources of the Pyramid Lake reserve. The ambiguity of the legal status of the reserve during these crucial years was not settled until much later. Felix Cohen, a noted authority on Indian law, explained the legal situation:

It has been held that a reservation in the nature of an Executive order reservation may be established without a formal Executive order if a course of administrative action is shown which had for its purpose the inducing of an Indian tribe to settle in a given area and if the area has thereafter been referred to and dealt with as an Indian reservation by the Executive branch of the Government (Old Winnebago and Crow Creek Reservation, 18 Op. A.G. 141, 1885).[8]

The legal argument made in that 1885 Attorney General's opinion which Cohen cited was based on the fact that the President of the United States delegated authority to his department heads to act in his name. His power to create reservations devolved upon them.

When the Commissioner of Indian Affairs requested the withdrawal of land for Indian purposes, and the Commissioner of the General Land Office concurred, they acted with authority from the President and in his name. Therefore, the Pyramid Lake Indian Reservation was in fact created by this administrative act in 1859. The U.S. Supreme Court and the Indian Claims Commission have both ruled in favor of this date of establishment, but these are recent decisions based on subsequent, complex legal interpretations. In the nineteenth century, many Nevadans simply challenged both the 1859 date and the very existence of the reservation at all.

There was agreement on at least one fact—Pyramid Lake was a small and insignificant BIA post. For a while, it did not even have an agent assigned to it, but was only part of the responsibility of the Nevada Indian Agent or Special Agent in Charge. Headquartered in Reno or Carson City, he was responsible for Pyramid Lake, Walker River, and others. He was to visit these reserves periodically and there conduct the Indian Bureau's programs. As the budget allocation for Pyramid Lake grew, an additional man was hired, entitled the Farmer-in-Charge. He actually lived at the lake. Expected to support himself from his own labors, he was to serve as a model of American farming methods to the Indians and to train them in those technologies and skills.

As the reservation became more important, an agent was assigned solely to Pyramid Lake, and the staff grew. The agent was then to live at the Reservation House and was to direct his full-time effort to the benefit of the Indians. Under his supervision, there might be a farmer, blacksmith, teacher (often the agent's wife, who also provided nursing services), or carpenter. These people lived in a cluster of government housing, apart from the Indian community.

The agent's jurisdiction was limited. A federal officer in charge of federal trust land, he had no authority under state or local law. He had little direct power over local non-Indian citizenry. The 1834 Trade and Intercourse Act gave him the power to arrest non-Indians for civil or criminal acts committed on his reservation. He could remove them from the federal territory, hand them over to a federal marshal, and file formal complaint. However, few frontier whites admitted his authority over them. They argued that he was in charge of the agency for Indians, and therefore his power was limited to them. The small agency staff was ineffective against any white citizens who chose to resist. Many of the agents were unfamiliar with the extent of their authority and were not expert in law enforcement. The agent could call on the U.S. Marshal, often a single man with immense terrain to cover. Agents could also request the aid of the U.S. military, which would be marched in from the nearest command post many miles distant. Since criminal actions on the Indian reservation were performed in federal territory, any suit had to be filed in federal court. The U.S. Attorney was therefore the proper officer to provide the agent legal counsel and to prosecute. However, this federal appointee was a locally prominent lawyer sponsored by the senior senator. His vested interests and clientele were the local whites, who usually supported the defendants. He was often unwilling to offend those interests by actively aiding the unpopular Indian agent. All things considered, despite the agent's legally defined powers and claims to assistance, he was most often on his own. He had very little control over the behavior of whites on reservation lands and absolutely none over whites who abused Indians off-reservation.

In contrast to the Indian agents' weakness against non-Indians, their power over Indians was extensive. They had at their command a variety of means for imposing their wishes on Indian people. These included bribery, control of rations, regulation of work assignments, and brute force. The giving of gifts to Indians was a well-established policy in the United States as early as the American Revolution. Later, both settlers and government agents in the Northern Paiute territory found it expedient to give gifts periodically and to promise more if cooperative behavior were forthcoming from the natives. Initially, presents were distributed whenever and wherever travelers met groups of Paiutes. However, after 1870 Indians complained repeatedly that gifts were no longer given, that they "weren't getting anything." Agents intentionally restricted the distribution of food and clothing to reservation sites. They told Indians they could expect nothing if they did not come in to get it and if they did not live permanently on the reservation. This was one of the primary means agents used to encourage wandering families to concentrate on their reservations.

A special case of this gift-giving was the issuance of rations and supplies. This included food subsidies, wagons, clothing, tools, and seed. Since the Paiutes did not receive these supplies as a result of treaty agreement, distribution was at the discretion of the local agent. Goods were used consciously to force Paiutes to accept cultural changes. Agents throughout the nineteenth century used their control over these goods to reward desirable and to punish unacceptable behaviors. For instance, in 1875 one agent at Pyramid Lake proudly reported that he "issues only to those who work upon the land, and to the sick and the disabled. The Indians who take land and work it are supplied with necessary implements, seed, +c. Those who ramble about in idleness away from the reservation get nothing."[9] A few years later a newspaper reported a little more bluntly that the agent was using "the policy of helping those who help themselves; if an Indian is building a fence, he can have some flour and bacon to live on; if he wants to plow up land, he can get seed, or have his tools fixed at the shop; if he is at work he gets every encouragement, if not, he goes hungry."[10] It was not accidental that all work listed was that associated with Anglo-European subsistence patterns; all else was defined as idleness, including the very labor-intensive traditional Paiute food-getting activities. With the reduction of resources brought about by Anglo-American occupation of the land, the stated alternative of hunger was probably a realistic estimate.

As noted in the above example, agents also controlled access to employment. While Indians were working on agency development projects such as irrigation ditches or farm fencing, they received supplies from the agency stores. The agent controlled who was hired on these crews and when they were fired. Positions as translators, wagoners, carriers for agency supplies from the railhead, and other labor paid in cash or kind, also depended upon the largesse of the agent. In 1879, Sarah Winnemucca declared that she had lost her agency interpreting job in retaliation for her complaint to military authorities about conditions on the reservation at Malheur.[11] Others found that a good reference from the agent was often necessary even for off-reservation employment.

The agent could also throw Indians off the reservation. As late as 1920, Pyramid Lake agents were using the right to live on the reservation as a political weapon to ensure Indian conformity. At that time an official wrote: "Your inspector believes that the action of the Indians in seeking to prefer charges against Superintendent Oliver was precipitated by his (the superintendent's) threat . . . to compel Henry Sampson . . . to leave the Reservation. The grievance of the superintendent had no better foundation than that this Sampson, at the request of older Indians, most of whom, as their thumb prints on the documents attest, were unable to write, had written a letter to the Honorable Commissioner [of Indian Affairs], asking that an inspector be sent to Pyramid Lake."[12] Since the function of the federal inspector was to check up on the efficiency and propriety of agents, the superintendent's motives were transparent.

In addition to such essentially administrative power, agents also used many kinds of brute force, including incarceration after summary judgment in courts where the agent was both judge and jury. The record of sheer physical force was ample, but Sarah Winnemucca provided a series of most graphic examples from her experience at the Malheur Reservation. She told of one incident in which she saw "our agent throw a little boy down on the ground by his ear and kick him. . . . he said, 'Sarah, that little devil laughed at me, because I asked him to go and tell Jarry that I wanted him to come to my house. I will beat the very life out of him. I won't have any of the Indians laughing at me.' . . . I said, 'Mr. Reinhard, that little boy never meant to laugh at you. He thought you were saying something nice to him, and another thing, he cannot understand the English language.'" Not long after, the agent told the same little boy, "'Johnny, go and get some beef; here is the key.' Johnny started off; he got only a little way when the agent called him back, but Johnny kept on. He called him again and again, and at last was so angry he ran after him. . . . he ran up to him and took him by his hair, but the boy was too quick for him and got away, the agent after him saying, 'Stop or I will shoot you.' . . . The same night he took Johnny and put handcuffs on him, saying, 'I will send you to Camp Harney and have the soldiers hang you, for you are a very bad boy.' The boy did not cry or say anything, but his mother ran in crying, and threw her arms around him. She cried." Sarah Winnemucca reported of the same agent, who was apparently very unstable: "He beat an Indian man almost to death for no cause whatever. He asked him to help him carry a sick woman. The Indian was a little too long getting on his moccasins. The agent knocked him down with a great stick, and beat him so shamefully I ran to him and caught hold of him, saying, 'Do not beat him so.' The man rose up, and as he did so, the agent raised his stick again to him. At this point the Indian took hold of it; then the agent took out a pistol to shoot him; but white men came to him and said, 'Do not shoot him.'"[13] Such free use of force, while it did not characterize all agents, was used by some to attain their wishes. There was no one to check such unbridled behavior. Agents had nearly total dictatorial authority within their reservation domains, and Indians dared resist only under most extreme duress.

Since government policy commanded a change in basic Indian life-style, agents could and often did intrude into all aspects of personal life. As more and more Paiutes came to dwell at Pyramid Lake on more than a seasonal basis, the influence of the agents increased. Most intrusive were those with missionary backgrounds, who inter-preted their assignment as the complete alteration of Indian lifestyle. A series of examples chosen from various periods of Pyramid Lake history will show how the agents' all-pervading power over Indian lives was used.

Agents focused their efforts on selected aspects of Indian behavior. Initially, of course, they tried hard to encourage sedentary residence upon the reservation, in order to justify their own continued employ-ment. Gifts and rations were the weapons used, as the 1872 agent reported: "The issue of rations to Indians has, with only a single ex-ception, been to those upon the reservations, discarding all pleas for rations to roving bands or scattering individuals. ... The meager amount of funds at our disposal required that the utmost economy be maintained in the issue of supplies even upon the reservations; thus a strict injunction was laid to issue supplies only to working Indians and their families; to the sick, infirm, and aged, and to prevent actual suffering."[14]

Once resident at Pyramid Lake, agents believed Paiutes should adopt permanent houses and European-style clothing. Early agents considered rectangular houses so important that one of their first proposals was to build a mill, although it was never completed and apparently never produced the desired lumber. Agents also encour-aged Indians to wear European-style clothing, particularly pants for men and blouses for women. The agents' reports systematically praised those Paiutes who adopted such forms of dress. For instance, an inspector once wrote, "Indians at this [Pyramid Lake] Agency are far in advance of all Southern Indians. They are first class Men to work, and I think with few exceptions Sober. They have no long haired ruckets here. These Indians all have short hair and are well dressed."[15] Nevertheless, as the same inspector pointed out, Indian adoption of the European trait of drinking alcoholic beverages was strongly condemned. Many attempts were made to catch whites selling liquor to Indians, but prosecution was noticeably unsuccessful and convictions almost nonexistent.

Another major concern of the agents was for Indian children to attend schools. They believed that while adult behavior could be changed only by force, children were more malleable in their character. If trained in "civilized fashion" at a young age, Paiute ways could be changed in one generation. Parents resisted such forced enculturation, but agents remained adamant. At least one Indian agent thought adult objections should be overcome by force if necessary, and he proclaimed:

> I believe in compulsory education. We have such a law in force in this State; and as the citizens are constantly complaining of Indian children being a great nuisance around their towns and places of business, I have no doubt but that the State law could be readily so amended as to require peace officers to arrest all Indian children of school age and deliver them to Indian agents and superintendents at their terminal points for receiving along the lines of railroads, from where they could be conveyed to schools on reservations at a very slight expense to the Government. This would necessitate the erection of more boarding-schools, but I believe the beneficial results that would accrue by adopting such a course would warrant the expenditure.[16]

In response to such threats, at least one off-reservation Paiute leader begged the Commissioner of Indian Affairs in 1886 that children not be sent 600–700 miles to the boarding school in Grand Junction, Colorado. His petition was not heeded, and the children were taken. Two years later, the parents, who had not seen them since and feared for their safety, asked that their children be allowed to return. Their petition, written for them by a literate local rancher, begged:

> They [the parents] also say that their children are becoming dissatisfied with Grand Junction and they fear when warm weather sets in, they will run away, and that would displease you; and subject them to many hardships. I have written several letters for them to their children, and they have invariably advised them to remain at School until they receive instructions from you to return home.[17]

Powerless before agency seizure of their children and disregard of their wishes, Paiute parents could only cooperate.

Schooling was an issue not only for nineteenth-century agents and parents, but a major concern of those in the twentieth as well. Most Pyramid Lake children went to the day school, available on the reservation after 1878, but a few traditional parents refused to allow their children to attend. One such was Rawhide Henry. The agent described him as "one of the few non-progressive Indians on this reservation." In justification of this judgment, the agent related that Henry had attacked his son-in-law, whom he believed was bewitching a grandchild. By clinging to ancient beliefs in supernatural power and family duty, Henry confronted the agency directly. What finally goaded the agent into hostility was that "he has persistently refused to place his children in school." In 1909, the agent issued the ultimatum of boarding school or day school, both of which Henry rejected. Then the agent brought into play one of his basic weapons, control over the right to reside on the reservation: "I then told him that I would not discuss the matter further with him but would take up the matter with the Commissioner [of Indian Affairs]. He became angry at once, and said he would sell what he had and leave the reservation. . . . I sent him word that as this was his own voluntary act, after he had had time for consideration, that I had no objections to his leaving and would strike the names [of him and his family] from the roll, and also informed him, through the [Indian] police, that after he had left the reservation I did not wish him to return even for a visit, and in case that he should return to the reservation at any time, I should place him at once under arrest."[18]

In addition to imposing such European cultural practices as clothing, formal schooling, and agriculture, the Indian agents also attempted to suppress traditional Paiute behavior as unworthy, uncivilized, and, in many cases, immoral. For instance, gambling had been a traditional pastime with all Great Basin Indians and continued to be so into the twentieth century. Paiutes enthusiastically augmented their old hand and stick games with the new technology of playing cards for poker and faro. As early as 1877, one agent objected that the cash Indians earned was often invested in this form of recreation: "But, beyond their use for food, I doubt if the fish caught, are of any benefit to the Indians. The money obtained from their sale, is almost invariably squandered, and it affords the means for gambling and leads to idleness, and disipation [sic]."[19]

Over time, Paiutes continued to ignore agency moralizing against their favorite games. By 1923, gambling was "still prevalent among all these Indians. It is their chief pastime, and while to a degree it is less harmful than some other pastimes, it nevertheless seriously interferes with the Indian's progress. It is a sad waste of time, to say the least, and cannot help but result in mental and moral deterioration. Efforts to stop gambling have proved futile in this State, as the legislature and public sentiment favor open gambling, and the practice is indulged in by a large majority of the white residents."[20] Another inspector recorded in 1920, "Gambling by the Paiutes of Pyramid Lake is so common as to be nearly universal among adults. Sunday is the most favored day and then the children are taken with their parents to witness the games. . . . They are being reared in an atmosphere wholly deleterious to moral advancement. Gambling consumes whatever money, from the sale of live stock and crops and the proceeds of labor, that these Indians are able to acquire. . . . Jail sentences, the offense being so general, are not practicable. . . . rations [should] be withheld from the gamblers who waste the funds wherewith they could maintain themselves. This recommendation nearly involves suspension of issue of rations. The older women are among the chief offenders."[21] Because they gambled, he suggested that the agent exercise his power of withholding employment until they should "give assurance of abstention from gambling." Indians alone were to be punished for behavior which they saw the surrounding white residents practicing without censure.

Agency interference extended far beyond hobbies and pastimes into the heart of marital relations. Traditionally, Paiutes had permitted polygyny, although in fact it had been rare, because few men could afford to support more than one wife and corresponding sets of children. The agents now insisted on single spouses and waged early, enthusiastic campaigns against multiple marriages. This accomplished, they then demanded from Paiutes their own unattained ideals of marital behavior. Wife-desertion and extramarital liaisons were punished by withholding rations, canceling employment, or ejecting the accused from the reservation.[22]

Another traditional institution the agents tried to suppress was the shaman or "medicine man." Paiutes saw these men as extremely important repositories of supernatural power and continued to respect them. However, toward the turn of the century Washington began providing physicians and nurses, and Indian agents tried actively to discredit the competing native practitioners. In 1914 an agent wrote from Walker River Reservation, "I have, almost completely broken up the practice of the Indian 'Doctors' on this Reservation, and am satisfied that if it is possible to make an example of one or two cases by sending them to the penitentiary, that a great good will be accomplished for those who remain."[23] The true root of agency hostility was made very clear by a report about ten years later which complained about the diffuse power of the medicine men:

> The practice of "medicine men" continues here, and particularly in remote districts. For this reason additional physicians and nurses should be employed, if only for the purpose of combating the evil influences of these Indian "doctors" whose practice means loss of many lives as well as continuation of old pernicious Indian customs and superstitions.
>
> In fact, if the Indian "doctor" can be done away with the civilization and rehabilitation of the whole Indian race would be simplified. The Indian "doctor" is not only "medicine man"—who claims power to heal all physical ills—but is also spiritual adviser, judge in civil and political matters of the tribe as well as in family disturbances, and wields a tremendous influence over practically all old-time Indians and often over a majority of the so-called progressives, returned students. These "doctors," too, are the political agitators who keep the Indians stirred up, wasting time that might be employed advantageously in

honest work and care of families; and, naturally desiring to strengthen and prolong their power, they oppose all efforts of the Government to educate the children or wean the older members of the tribe away from old superstitions and customs that are keeping them down. . . . they form a group of mal-contents, demagogues, dreamers and idlers who are muleting a rather precarious living from the always gullible public—and making trouble for the Government, expenses for the taxpayers and retarding the progress of the real worthwhile Indians. . . .[24]

Shamans were more than physical curers and had always fulfilled a multifaceted role. As men extraordinarily well in tune with supernatural power, their opinions were considered more sound than those of ordinary men; they were often community leaders. They apparently continued this complex role and became the rallying point for Paiutes who clung to more traditional beliefs. This focusing often put shamans in direct opposition to those chiefs who were appointed and supported by the agency. Thus shamans led the resistance to agency policy which, of course, angered the BIA and led to its attempted suppression of traditional medicine.

Other traditional beliefs were also attacked. For instance, Northern Paiutes firmly believed that witches were very real and very dangerous. The community had always defended itself by ostracizing or even killing witches. Such behavior was strongly condemned by the agents as uncivilized. Other native belief systems surrounding the concept of power and the acquisition of grace through peyote were similarly attacked.

In the days before the reservation, Northern Paiutes had gathered after the harvest of a rich crop for sheer social enjoyment and for discussion of political affairs. Agents viewed such seasonal gatherings as a continuation of traditional customs and therefore necessarily heathen. These meetings were also beyond their control and could possibly, they feared, form the foundation for resistance to agency programs. A twentieth-century agent once wrote, "These so-called 'dances', 'big times', 'council gatherings', etc., are the principal factor in the prevention of the Indian's thrift and advancement."[25] He recommended that they be stopped for the benefit of the "ultimate civilization of the Indian." These "fandangos" annoyed agents; they wrote against them and denied their existence, but they could not suppress them.

One of the most spectacular technological innovations Anglos brought to Nevada was the railroad. Paiutes, in their extremely practical and imaginative way, rapidly adapted this tool to their own purposes. The Central Pacific Railroad had granted Indians the privilege of riding ticketless on the roofs and flatbeds of the rail cars. Several of the spur lines, such as the Carson and Colorado which passed through Walker River, had been forced to grant similar privileges to various bands in order to gain right-of-way across their reservations. The custom became institutionalized. Paiutes used the railroad to visit traditional hunting and gathering sites in season. Introduced European weeds sprang up in the disturbed soils along the tracks. Paiutes would pack up their gathering baskets and hop on the rails, take off for a day or two to gather these seeds, and bring their harvest back home again on the car roofs. Men and women used free passes to travel into town or to ranches farther in the hinterlands for jobs. Paiutes adapted the proffered new technology to their mobile lifestyle, which required the utilization of many widely spread resources each in season, much as they had in the old days. Agents did not favor this practice, since they wanted Indians to reside permanently on reservations under their jurisdiction and to participate in their sponsored development programs. They began to write letters urging the discontinuation of free railroad travel. One inspector arriving in Nevada in 1877, wrote in outrage at this local custom:

> The C. P. [Central Pacific] Railroad Company allows Indians to ride free on the platforms of any train of cars, or, in many cases, in the second class cars, and at every station through the State, I found a horde of worthless, shiftless, beggerly Indians. The women especially, gather around passenger trains on their arrival, and beg for cold victuals, and I am told, in this way, support their families, in many cases, including lazy, gambling husbands, and fathers. Men, women, and children get on to any train, and go where they please, without restriction, from either the Govt. Agent, or the Railroad Company. It costs nothing, and naturally, some of the Indians spend a great portion of their time riding on the cars. The injurious effects of this freedom from restraint, and continual change of place, on the Indian, can not be over estimated. On my arival [*sic*] in this city I called on the President, and Officers of the Railroad Company, and talked the whole subject over. They promised to issue orders to their Agents and employees in the

State of Nevada, to allow no Indian to ride free on any train, after the first of July next, without a permit from his Agent, stating where the Indian could go, and how long he could be gone.[26]

Agents found that Indians had adapted to white culture all too well. Paiutes had found a use for Anglo-European technology that had not been anticipated and which conflicted with agency plans.

As much as Indian agents wanted to encourage Paiutes to imitate white lifestyle in clothing, schooling, housing, and religion, still the primary assumption of reservation life had been that they would adopt a new form of subsistence. By the end of the period of open hostilities, it became clear that Indians would no longer be able to hold all of the land in Nevada. They were to be restricted to a limited portion of their previous domain. Because of Anglo mining and ranching, there was very rapid deterioration of the wild food resources that Indians had previously depended on. Therefore, even their previous domain could no longer have fed them. The lands set apart for them could support their entire population only if they made basic economic changes. The BIA assumed that these changes would be toward agriculture. Indians would become farmers, owners and operators of self-sufficient family farms.

This uniform national policy was imported wholesale into Nevada, but warnings arose immediately that it could not be implemented in the Desert West. As early as 1861, the Nevada Indian Agent pointed out that this country was really grazing land, and he recommended that cattle and horses be provided the Indians for a ranching enterprise; he never even considered agriculture a viable alternative. The Nevada superintendent at that time was Governor Nye, who also pointed out that grazing could be very profitable there. He reminded Washington that the Indians were familiar with the characteristics and curing of wild grasses after hundreds of years of their own food-gathering, and that they would work well with hay and pasturage. In recommending the provision of breeding stock, he said, "I have not the fullest confidence in the success of the effort [at agriculture] for the reason the season is so short that the best kind of [agri]culture can produce but few products, and those of an inferior quality."[27] The headmen were nevertheless anxious to attempt agriculture, and Nye suggested satisfying Indian desires with a few hand implements and some seed.

However, nearly ten years later, agents still maintained that Nevada was not reliable farming terrain. One reported: "My opinion regarding the agricultural interests of this reservation is that it will never avail anything of permanence unless at an expense unjustifiable. The land is very difficult to irrigate, lying high above the low-water mark, full of sink-holes, and at a distance from the fall of the water as to require a very long ditch to reach it."[28] He explained that a dam could artificially raise the water to a point that a reasonably short canal would serve; but, he said, the river bank was so sandy and the channel so flat and broad that there would be no footing for such a dam—it would wash out with the first spring flood. This particular scenario proved accurate, not once but many times. None of the officers experienced with local conditions recommended farming for Paiutes. Nevertheless, the BIA struck forth upon a program of agricultural development which they insisted would be the new and permanent subsistence base at Pyramid Lake.

Their program got off to a slow start. A resident farmer was stationed at Walker River quite early, but none was assigned to Pyramid. Ten years after the Pyramid Lake Reservation had been established, Special Agent Lee could report:

> I found no Government improvements on the reserve of any nature whatever; no farming implements, nor evidence that any farming had ever been done or attempted; in short, a remarkable absence of everything which might indicate the existence of an Indian reservation, save about 250 Pah-Ute Indians, (men, women, and children,) who had come in from the mountains and surrounding country to catch what fish they could, and to escape the rigors of winter. Three or four Indians had, with their own limited means, endeavored to cultivate a few acres of ground, had opened an irrigating ditch, but, never having received any assistance from the Government, their success was most trifling.[29]

Not long after Lee had thus brought attention to the situation, a resident agent was posted at Pyramid Lake who immediately perceived the problems of irrigating there. As mentioned above, the slope of the land was so shallow that the ditch needed to be several miles long in order to have enough elevation to get the water out of the river's canyon and onto the farmland. While this was inconvenient, it was not insurmountable. Indians provided the hands to shovel the canal. Only then, however, was the more serious problem confronted—periodic spring flooding. The river rose unexpectedly and roared downstream carrying a great burden of logs, branches, silt, and rock. Water filled the canal to capacity, sometimes crushing the sandy banks. As it receded, this floodwater left thick deposits of sand, especially around the canal mouth, often sealing it shut. After every spring thaw and virtually every upstream thunderstorm, the canals had to be reexcavated. This constant maintenance was extremely time-consuming, especially in the summer thunderstorm season when crops also needed attention. The reservation irrigation system was simply not reliable until the twentieth century, when several dams were inserted upriver to check back the rushing floods. However, by that time there was a serious shortage of water to fill the ditches at the downstream reservation—and this was a very reliable shortage.

Another complication was the flume. Because of the positioning of cliff walls and arable land, the canal had to cross the river in its route downstream. This was done with a flume constructed on the principles of the suspension bridge, a technique much used in mountain mining. This v-shaped plank carrier hung on cables from uprights on each bank. It carried the water above the river quite adequately, except in times of flood. Then the sandy banks washed away from under the posts and the whole arrangement came down. One spring, the floodwater raised high enough actually to grab the bottom of the flume. It wrenched it off the cables and smashed it to smithereens. Nevertheless, agents stubbornly rebuilt the flume year after year.

To overcome the labor expense of maintaining long ditch systems, the agents ordered a brush dam built in 1871. Known locally as The Indian Dam, this was a minor modification of the Paiute wickerwork fishing weir, which had been constructed on the river for generations. The Indians were very expert at this technology and soon had a very adequate brush dam holding back water to the level of the river banks, ready to be drawn off into ditches and carried to their fields.

Upstream Anglos immediately complained that this dam was blocking fish in their spawning run. Whites protested violently that the Indian improvement project was denying them their civil rights to catch fish. The agent was handed a threatening letter that read in part, "Will come down with force enough to take out the dam and clear out the Indians, there is about 150 men armed and ready to turn out at any moment."[30] Only three to four feet high, the dam did apparently function much like a weir. Indians were calmly fishing there until the dam was threatened with dynamiting and they themselves threatened with bodily harm. Eventually the spring runoff raised the water levels above the lip of the dam so that fish swam freely over it and the crisis passed.

Despite technological problems, agents persisted in stressing agriculture at Pyramid Lake. Four years after Lee's despairing condemnation of the lack of farms on the reservation, the agent volubly told Washington in the best bureaucratic style exactly what it wanted to hear: "almost every acre of land that can be made available for farming purposes of any kind has been fenced in, and cross-fenced into fields, and claimed by individuals or families for permanent homes. Much more land has been put under cultivation than at any previous year, and it is not extravagant language when I say that some of the finest ranches in Nevada are upon this reservation, claimed and cultivated by Indians."[31] Subsequent annual reports repeated, in glowing terms, that Paiutes were avidly pursuing the most recent technology on their neat, productive farms.

However, inspectors and other visitors who came to the reserve with great expectations contradicted this hopeful picture. In disappointment, they saw small, poorly kept plots scattered across the sandy bottom lands. Some of the contradiction between the accounts evaporated with examination of the carefully chosen words in the agents' reports. For instance, just after World War I, reports appeared that almost 2500 acres were "under ditch" at Pyramid Lake, which was true.[32] But there was only water enough for Paiutes to farm about 400 acres of this, as other observers stated in superficial contradiction.[33] Of these, only 10 acres were intensively cultivated with row crops and gardens in 1920, while the rest was hay and fodder.[34]

The vast majority of the acreage on the reserve was consistently thus in pasture, haylands, or grains. These extensive and low-value products certainly were not the lucrative row crops the BIA had envisioned to justify the expensive irrigation systems needed to permit any agriculture there at all. Nevertheless, Paiutes continued to grow grains in order to winter cattle and to keep horses. Faced with unreliable weather and water, they chose not to commit themselves to cash crops, and the amount of intensively cultivated acreage remained small throughout the history of Pyramid Lake. In fact, the high point was reached only in World War II when food prices were high. Then gardens attained their maximum of 25 acres, valued at $1600, but this was still only 10 percent of the total value of agricultural crops. The major cash crop at the reserve was potatoes, which reached a maximal aggregate value of $3,000 in 1955. By 1956 there were only 5 acres of garden land, valued at less than $200, and by 1963 there was only 1 acre, a totally insignificant portion of the land base.[35] It would appear that the glowing reports of progressive, intensive, and enthusiastic subsistence and market agriculture at Pyramid Lake were little but agents' carefully phrased attempts to comply with general Washington policy in the face of dry Nevada reality.

Fish always provided a far more lucrative cash crop than agricultural products and a far more reliable subsistence base than farming. Indians continued to fish until well into the twentieth century, and agents, frustrated by Indian loyalty to the lacustrine resources, continued to ignore the value of the fishery. In despair, one irrigation report read, "Some of the Indians still make a good living at fishing and renting boats, while others find that working for the white farmers is more profitable; consequently, it is very doubtful if much progress can be made at this place,"[36] again equating absolute progress with the governmental plan of farming.

Important as physical and environmental limitations were in determining the subsistence program at Pyramid Lake, the Indian agents discovered that a broad variety of auxiliary behaviors also affected it. Paiutes were disinterested in the cash value of crops and refused to specialize in cash-crop production. Most of the agents wanted Indians involved in the cash-market system, and several encouraged that their labor be paid for in cash rather than rations. In this way, it was argued, Paiutes would become accustomed to the dollar value of objects and be more willing to patronize shops. To acquire the goods they desired there, they in turn would have to grow products of value to the Anglo market. In short, they would become valuable consumers for the local non-Indian merchants. Believing that a ration system was paternalistic and that it undervalued Indian labor, one agent decried: "No rations should be issued here for work, but Indians should be paid in money instead. These people are too well advanced to be pauperized by such a system."[37] However, such an opinion was not uniform among agency administrators, for in 1877 a report deprecated fishing, the major cash-producing activity, since the funds were used for gambling and, as he put it, "leads to idleness, and disipation."[38] Games of chance had a central place in Paiutes' culture throughout historic and apparently prehistoric times. Team gambling provided a major recreation. In the midst of the mining frontier, where the flow of gold dust and silver ore through the male Anglo population was to a large degree facilitated by prosperous gambling halls, agents tried to impose Eastern moral standards in this regard. One wrote, "Their propensity for gambling, which is carried on during week days as well as Sundays, probably reflects more adversely on their farming than any other one thing."[39] Paiutes ignored the visible hypocrisy of the agents' demands. Rather, they adapted this introduced cultural phenomenon, cash, as they had the new railroad train, and adjusted it to their own goals, purposes, and desires. They refused to accept wholesale the values which Anglos sought to impose upon them.

Paiutes applied their traditional ethical beliefs and modes of organization to the new farming enterprise itself, as well as to its profits. Groups, probably of kinsmen, did land-clearing, ditch-digging, and other farm-labor activities together, just as native work groups had formed up for harvest in earlier years. They worked on each man's land in turn. The work went faster with the larger group and was more pleasant. Such communalism was incompatible with the American ideal of rugged individualism, however. That alien ethic held that each individual had to maximize his own labor and resources for his own exclusive personal profit. Paiutes found such concepts antisocial and unacceptable. They retained their traditional beliefs of the seniority due age, the cooperation due kinsmen, and the respect due community leaders and shamans, until well into the twentieth century. Agents tried to break down these beliefs immediately. As early as 1873, one reported to the Commissioner, "I regard as second to none the importance of bringing the Indians individually to care for themselves. Co-operative systems, as a rule, are failures. .... It has been my rule to encourage single Indians with their families, or, at most, only small companies, to concert their efforts upon parcels of land cultivated, thus inspiring them to make their work permanent, to have and to hold the same, undisturbed by others."[40] Such ego-centered self-interest and disregard for the needs and desires of one's fellows Paiutes found repugnant; they resisted efforts on the part of agents to individualize their economic activities.

Despite technical difficulties and the Paiutes' overt disinterest, surreptitious evasion, and clandestine modification, agents persisted in their agricultural program. Their annual reports were full of acreage and crop detail, dates of planting, and values of harvest. Year after year agriculture dominated their pages, and yet the financial summaries clearly showed that more Paiutes earned far more money fishing than farming. In fact, fishing contributed virtually the only cash flow into the community. Only when state laws, beyond the control of the Paiutes' community, gutted their fishing enterprise, did they turn to farming, as the agent rightly observed in 1928: "Heretofore, the Indians of this Reservation have made the bulk of their living by fishing, and did not take kindly to farming. Of late years fishing has not been so profitable, for various reasons, and they are giving more attention to farming."[41]

The persistent lack of growth of the farming endeavor at Pyramid Lake was a constant embarrassment to agents. They justified this failure on grounds of the technological difficulties of irrigation there, the lack of funding for development projects, and so on. Finally they simply had to admit that there was little progress being made, and they passed the blame onto the Indians themselves. After 70 years of effort, a BIA irrigation report summarized the attitude rather nicely, saying, "It is very doubtful if many of these Indians will ever be successful farmers. The size of the tentative allotments are such as to discourage farming on a very extensive scale. It is also much easier and far more profitable to work for the neighboring White farmers as laborers. Fishing also offers more pleasant work and is at least as profitable as farming. Raising stock cattle holds promise of interesting some of the Indians and this would probably be quite profitable."[42] The BIA refused to admit that they were trying to introduce the wrong kind of program; Paiutes, they said, were just the wrong kind of Indians.

Viewed in the perspective of Nevada's economy as a whole, the BIA insistence on agriculture as the sole economic activity was clearly unrealistic. Other than in areas of large-scale, twentieth-century reclamation projects, farming is simply not the foundation of any regional economy in the state. It never has been, and chances are it never will be. During the late nineteenth and early twentieth centuries, whites in northern Nevada did not farm, except to grow hay and grain, for the very simple reason that it was neither a profitable nor a secure means of earning a livelihood. Rather, a small subsistence garden was combined into a mixed economy with a cash crop, hay, some cattle, a few fruit trees, and perhaps a little casual prospecting on the side. The BIA itself clearly documented that there was not enough farmland on the Pyramid Lake Reservation for more than a fraction of the Paiutes to farm profitably. Nevertheless, the BIA emphasized agriculture to the exclusion of all else throughout the nineteenth century.

Despite their ultimate failure at farming, Paiutes did adopt a great number of Anglo traits associated with agriculture. For instance, one agent warmly recorded, "These Indians seem endeavoring to conform to the existing order of things, and are making efforts to learn the use of tools in every line; especially they take to blacksmithing; quite a number of them shoe their ponies, and can mend some of the iron work on their wagons. They are encouraged to keep on."[43] Paiutes did keep on. They wove fences of willow basketry and dug irrigation ditches with pointed digging sticks. They hauled agency freight in their wagons. They built houses out of milled lumber at their own expense. Through it all, they continued to fish, to hunt, and to gather wild plants and seeds, contrary to agency hopes.

The agency maintained a written and verbal barrage of dogma, declaring its prejudices over and over again. The agents worked very hard to get Indians to accept their edicts and to rely on their opinions, not only with regard to agriculture, but on a broad variety of issues.

From Governor Nye's very first negotiation with the Paiutes in 1861, they were told that "there would be an agent located among them and they must inform him of any depredations committed upon their rights, and he would inform me [Nye], and that I would see it righted."[44] Agents wanted Paiutes to respond unquestioningly to their word. "We have always taught them," an agent said a few years later, "if anyone of their people is injured by the whites to come and inform us at once and in no case to resent the injury themselves."[45] Throughout the early historic period they stressed constantly that Indians should not act on their own. They should bring their complaints to the agent, who would then act in their name. The agent would protect them in all matters, and they should abandon their independent right to defend their own interests. For instance, at the point when it was very much in doubt whether the coming of the railroad would entirely break up the reservation, a large number of Paiutes gathered at the agency to "receive instructions relative to their duties." They were told "to remain quiet and wait and hear what Mr. Bateman [the agent] said when he came from Wadsworth. . . ."[46]

As late as 1913, Indians were being patronized in the same way. Captain Dave, an Indian leader at Pyramid Lake, feared that a proposed irrigation installation would lead to further loss of land to whites. He approached the agent and declared that he was going to go to Washington at his own expense to find out what the situation really was. He was told to be quiet, go home, and await word from the agency.[47] A few years later, when the Indians were having serious trouble with the state over fish laws, the Pyramid Lake community elected a delegation to go to Carson City and appeal their case directly to the legislature. Their agent intercepted them and forced them to return. He asserted, in a note to the Resident Farmer: "None should go there or undertake anything of this kind without first consulting with me, as I have the fish business in charge and will succeed in getting the law changed if my plans are not upset. In this connection, you must discourage 'meetings' of Indians that take them away from their work and do nothing but unduly excite them. . . . The 'talk habit' must be stopped wherever possible."[48] Consistently throughout reservation history, Paiutes were told not to think for themselves or to reach their own conclusions. This is what a friend of Sarah Winnemucca's meant when she wrote that an Indian agency "prevents civilization by insulting and repressing that creative self-respect and conscious freedom to act, from which alone any vital human improvement can spring."[49]

To assure this ability to dictate to the Indian community, BIA structure systematically removed from Indians the ability to control their own lives. A good example of this came in 1930, when agency power was already well developed. The government was lending the tribe money to buy a cattle herd, but, as the agent reassured a local concerned citizen, "The money will not be loaned outright to the Indians for them to use it as they wish, because you can see how such a plan would not meet with success. We will use our discretion in making purchases [*sic*] for them. . . ."[50] Paiutes were treated as immature children without a sense of responsibility or a capacity to act for themselves. They were not to be trusted with money or with decisions. One classic example of the agency's blatantly overriding a community decision is worth quoting at length:

> Upon investigation, soon after taking charge, I found many of the old Indian residents occupying large enough ranches, fenced in, for two or three Indian farms, and they were not tilling any of the land, nor had they done so for years. They claimed that they owned the land and seemed to want to keep it "just to look at." When I proposed a division, to allow some other families who had no ranches to occupy a portion of the land and thereby afford them an opportunity for support, they hotly made strong objection. I referred the matter to their court of Indian offenses, and the judges' verdict was that "no division could be made". I reversed their decision and made the divisions with full explanation as to who owned the land, etc. Then I informed the original ranchers that unless they cultivated the portion left them (it was ample) I would take that away from them also and give it to someone who would till it.[51]

The community had applied to the question of land holdings their own values of honor for elders and respect for long-standing occupation, while the agent demanded consideration for maximizing profitability. Naturally he met with resistance when he tried to override their wishes and to force a decision which they could see only as arbitrary.

Thus, over and over again, Northern Paiutes were told what to think, what to say, how to act. Their own decisions were ignored. When they voiced justified protests, they were ignored. The cultural values on which their consensus rested were denounced. The agency interfered in free personal movement by demanding railroad passes; it blocked Paiute access to legislative decisions in Nevada and Washington which affected their lives; it intervened in financial arrangements, as for cattle; and it overrode clearly expressed judicial decisions of the group. By the turn of the century, the agency had intentionally removed nearly all power of the Paiute community to govern itself. The agents could offer no higher praise than that awarded Pyramid Lakers in 1914: "Almost all the Indians have been contented and shown a disposition to obey orders and abide by the regulations."[52] This was the agency ideal of the good Indian.

Northern Paiutes did not accept all this interference calmly. They protested constantly. However, they were caught in a structural impasse. As long as they lived on the reservation, they were under the direct authority of the agent who, at this time, was hierarchically responsible to the Commissioner. He had no available superior to whom Indians could appeal. They complained bitterly to military commanders, BIA inspectors, and any other traveling official who happened through their area. They stated repeatedly that whites trespassed on their lands, that goods and annuities promised by one agent were not forthcoming from the next who so rapidly succeeded him, that they did not receive justice at the hands of the local white government, and that their voice was not heard. However, these officials had no authority on the reservation and could do nothing but pass the Paiutes' protests on to the BIA, where the petitions died. As in the case of Rawhide Henry, who refused to send his children to school, petitions were forwarded to the Commissioner of Indian Affairs. The agent was asked to justify his action, and he asserted Henry was a trouble-maker. The agent was believed and the Indian petition was turned back without satisfaction.

Paiutes tried unofficial channels and enlisted the aid of sympathetic local ranchers to write letters and petitions for them. These white men were often declared to be cranks or their motives otherwise called into question. Then they too were ignored. Sometimes, however, their advocacy was effective, as in 1874, when Natchez Winnemucca was arrested and incarcerated on Alcatraz. One account said his crime was refusal to lead his prominent family onto the reserve, coupled with public accusations of agency graft and corruption. Some said he argued with the agent over rations or farming equipment. All sources agreed that his publicly stated disagreement with the agent brought on the retaliation of his arrest. Release came not through regular channels, but after local whites attested to his character and petitioned for his release.[53]

Occasionally Paiutes managed to gain the advocacy of persons who were high in authority but independent of the BIA. For instance, at the beginning of the Depression in 1929 there was a problem regarding rations for the aged and blind. Early that spring, Paiutes heard that once the snow was gone their rations would be discontinued, even for those unable to perform wage work. Indians complained to the agent but received no satisfaction. Then they went to the public press. The *Nevada State Journal* of May 9, 1929, quoted one Paiute declaring that the welfare support was "just like horse. Feed 'em winter time—summer turn 'em in pasture."[54] Such appeals to public opinion received no response. Finally a local mining engineer, John Reid, who was sympathetic to Indian causes, began writing to persons in power. He started locally and received no reply. In October, he wrote the senior Nevada senator, Tasker Oddie. Oddie was moved by the case of Gilbert Natches in particular and wrote the Commissioner of Indian Affairs, who could not ignore a letter from such a source. He ordered the Pyramid Lake superintendent to allow this single Indian $10 a month worth of supplies, but no cash. Reid complained again to Oddie that $10 monthly was inadequate to supply an aged man, his blind mother, and an invalid nephew, all of whom were being supported upon this one annuity. The Bureau replied that a new agent had been assigned to Pyramid Lake and that "the funds so far allotted to us for helping old and indigent Indians are very limited, and we have tried to do the best we could under the circumstances."[55] The end result of this letter campaign was the increase of Natches's rations to $20 per month, to be paid in government subsidized farm produce such as potatoes. Other Paiutes' annuities were not changed at all. When it took the mobilization of senatorial influence to win reversal of such an insignificant and routine administrative decision, it was not surprising that Paiutes lost heart.

Not only did Indians feel helpless against agents, but they also despaired of the administrators' honesty and character. They believed some to be good men and others bad, but saw all as liars and makers of "promises which, like the wind, were heard no more."[56] Paiutes hoped merely to survive on the reservations with as little interference in their daily lives as possible. In 1875, an Indian expressed this view, which reappeared throughout the history of Pyramid Lake, when he said, "Anything the Government says, we will do—if we can keep our homes."[57] Paiutes cooperated with agency demands because of the absence of any practical alternative.

If Paiutes wanted to escape the manipulation of agency life, they could live off-reservation. Having never been militarily defeated or restricted to reservation by treaty, many Northern Paiutes have continuously exercised this option. Sarah Winnemucca wrote eloquently that she and her influential family would rather die than live under the arbitrary authority of the agents from whom they had suffered so much at both Pyramid Lake and Malheur.[58] Other Paiutes were forced off the reservations by the limited subsistence opportunities within them. Often resident Paiutes had to leave the reserve seasonally in order to find food, as when the faulty irrigation system allowed crops to dry up, or pastures burned without rain. In nearby towns or on surrounding ranches, Indians could find wage work, or they might travel into remote sections of the territory to hunt and gather in the traditional ways. Once off the reserve, agents held no power over them, but also accepted no responsibility for them. As a result, situations occurred such as that an agent reported in 1867: he "received a communication signed by the most influential citizens of the place [Mammoth mining district, Nye county] stating that a desperado named Grayson had knocked down with his pistol several peaceable and inoffensive Pi-Utes, and compelled them to pay him $30 for an ox which he accused them of killing, and that they (the citizens) were cognizant of the fact that the ox died from some natural causes. They desired that I should see that justice was done. I regret to say, that not having a single dollar to defray traveling expenses, I was obliged to let the matter pass unnoticed."[59]

Despite such personal abuse, exploitation, and helplessness to defend themselves in a legal system structured against them, many Paiutes chose to live away from the reservations. Many dwelt all or part of the year near white towns, particularly mining towns where they could find day labor. While whites dominated the lucrative mining jobs, Paiutes provided a great deal of the manual service operations that these towns required, such as road-building, teamstering, and gathering firewood. Paiutes built their huts out of native willow and cast-off Anglo canvas and tin in isolated Indian villages at the outskirts of town.[60] Early reports frequently mentioned them gleaning garbage dumps for useable items which they, in their more imaginative poverty, could utilize. Just as the residential zones were strictly segregated, so apparently were social ties. Local whites knew little of what went on in the Indian neighborhoods.

Some off-reservation Indians attempted to imitate the agricultural lifestyle of their white neighbors, while maintaining at least some hunting and gathering of wild crops. However, this was a difficult compromise at best; for just as their native culture was scorned by Anglos, their attempts at conformity were ridiculed. For instance, Natches Winnemucca acquired some land near Lovelock through the intercession of a state senator and, despite the very high cost of lumber, he fenced it in. Water was a problem, so he joined an Anglo ditch-digging cooperative. He mobilized traditional kinship ties to provide the labor of 14 Indian men for a month to dig a section of ditch in return for a share in the resulting water flow. Sarah Winnemucca explained:

> As the wheat grows and tempts the cattle, the water-power people tell him he must leave the gate open so they can get to their ditches, some of which they put on his land without permission. The white men on each side of him have gates, and keep them shut, although their land is used only for grazing. I go to town, find they have no right to say anything about it, and the gate is put up, and the old uncle who has camped by it to keep out the cows and save the wheat can do something else. . . . The next time I go to town, I am told that the water company has decided not to let Natches have any more water, because "Indians are so lazy, they don't want them around," and, for illustration, point to that old man who sat all day by the hole in Natches' fence. I tried to explain; but it is not permitted to explain things here.[61]

Paiutes were caught between sets of contradictions. Whites demanded they conform to American cultural ways, but in doing so they were deterred by preconceived and bigoted stereotypes about what Indians, in general, were like.

Sarah Winnemucca ran into similar problems in her attempt to establish a school at Lovelock for Indian children in the 1880s. She felt the need to have available classrooms independent of the Indian Bureau and its enculturative program. Like a previous short-lived attempt in Virginia City, she too incurred the immediate wrath of the Pyramid Lake agent, who feared the competition and began to spread slander and gossip about both her personal life and the operation of the facility. The local Anglo community opposed her efforts, and her only support came from philanthropic groups in the East. After struggling to overcome many difficulties, she was forced to shut the school down for want of funding.

In addition to prejudice and unpleasant interracial relations, off-reservation Indians were also hampered by legal inequities under Nevada state law. Non-whites, including Indians, were forbidden to marry whites until 1919, and "fornication" between Indians and whites was similarly illegal. The very first legislature in 1861 forbade non-whites from becoming attorneys, serving in the militia, receiving the standard tuition waiver to the state universities, or being sheltered in the state orphanage. The state law outlawing the sale of liquor to Indians was retained from the founding of Nevada until 1949, well after Prohibition had been repealed for the Anglo population. Indians were explicitly forbidden to vote, and hence excluded from holding public office, until 1880. Even after that date, the continued requirement of a poll tax and the specific exemption of Indians from paying that tax effectively prevented them from voting until at least 1910. In many areas of the state, the first records of Indians voting was in 1924 and 1925 after a federal law had specifically declared all American Indians to be citizens of the United States and hence state citizens. Indians could not offer testimony for or against white men in civil court cases until 1869, and in criminal cases until after 1881, nor could they serve on juries. State law denied them public schooling until 1872, when the Nevada Supreme Court declared this unconstitutional. Nevertheless, as late as 1919, the public schools at Wadsworth refused to admit children of the nearly 100 Paiutes living in the township.[62] The 1923 agency report could still bemoan that public prejudice against Indian education was "especially intolerant" in Nevada, and that the rationale used was that there must be "improved methods of sanitation, more general medical supervision and efforts toward personal cleanliness."[63] Thus, local regulations carried on discrimination long after state laws had been adjudicated and repealed.

Perhaps of importance equal to overt legal inequity was the refusal of state law to recognize Indian cultural differences. For instance, Indian marriages performed without authorization by the state of Nevada, or by any church that Anglos recognized, were not legally accepted until 1943. This law affected the property inheritance of many Indian children, who were automatically considered illegitimate under state law. Again, Northern Paiutes firmly believed in the real danger of witchcraft. In 1891, Lovelock Paiutes stoned a self-declared witch in order, according to their beliefs, to protect the lives of everyone in the community. The state arrested three of these defenders, found them guilty of premeditated murder, and sent them to the penitentiary for more than a year. Nevada state law made no allowances for justifiable homicide on grounds of witchcraft. In these and many other ways, Northern Paiutes were held to legal standards incommensurate with their own cultural beliefs and values.[64]

State laws were applied inconsistently to Indians. Many western states, Nevada among them, believed that all Indians were an exclusive federal responsibility. Nevada, however, was unusual in its large percentage of Indians not living on reservations. Coupled with the legal liabilities of Indians under Nevada law, this made Indian persons and property rights very insecure. An early and blatant example dated from 1869. A white man named John Troy, living south of the reserve along the Truckee River, killed a horse belonging to Indian Dave. The horse had been loose and eating the grass on Troy's unfenced ranch. Troy walked several miles to a neighbor's house, borrowed a gun, walked home, and shot the horse. Indian Dave took his case to a military inspector six months later, relating how he "went to Troy—asked him to pay a fair amount for the horse $40—which Troy refused to do. Indian told Troy that if he had caught the horse and tied him up, he (Indian) would have paid him all damages and for his trouble besides. Troy has repeatedly threatened the Indian with personal violence for troubling him about the horse." Indian Dave then requested either that the army force Troy to pay the money or, if that were not possible, that the government reimburse him for the lost horse. The inspector agreed, arguing, "I recommend this from the fact that the majority of Indians feel that there is no protection for them, nor redress of their grievances."[65]

Not only were Indians off the reservation not protected in their property rights, but they suffered similarly on it. The lack of federal authority over non-Indians on reservation land, and the state's refusal to accept jurisdiction over Indians off those lands, opened a wide area for white criminal action. Local Anglos were well aware of this legal hiatus, such as the man who took a horse out of a pasture on the Pyramid Lake Reservation in 1882. The agent called him to trial in the reservation court and found him guilty of horse-stealing. He simply mounted the horse and rode it off the reservation, refusing to acknowledge the jurisdiction of the agent and the court over him. The agent could only complain to Washington but, as he wrote, "The Department has not seen fit to sustain the agent."[66] Incidents such as these, along with actual attacks upon Indians, as illustrated in Chapter Three, led Paiutes to conclude, along with Agent Douglas, that "Indians in this state may be said to be without legal protection."[67]

After the Pyramid Lake War, and as white occupancy progressively caused more and more environmental deterioration, Northern Paiutes found themselves pressured onto the reservations. There they existed under the autocratic rule of an Indian agent bent on redesigning their entire lives. Agents suppressed traditional Indian ways and demanded conformity to Anglo-American practices. Indians were given no opportunity to make their own decisions either as individuals or as a community. While Paiutes cooperated as much as their tolerance allowed, still they were angered and confused by these changes in their lives. Residence away from the reservation, while freeing them from agency control, also opened them to the attacks and scorn of the white citizenry.

Northern Paiutes were not driven far from their homeland as were some tribes, but they did experience a wrenching separation from their cultural past. Their economic livelihood was undercut, their po-

litical rights removed, their cultural ways despised, their remaining
leaders slandered and defamed. In such a situation, all earthly reme-
dies having proven futile, it was not surprising that Northern Paiutes
turned to religious salvation in a last grasp at hope.[68] In 1870 and
again in 1890, Northern Paiute prophets had visions. Like traditional
shamans before them, supernatural beings taught these men a dance,
a song, and a ceremony to bring about a change from an unhealthy
state to a healthy one. Only this time, the patient was not one sick
individual, but an entire society. Thus was the Ghost Dance born. It
was a dance of renewal. It foretold the end of white rule in Nevada. A
disciple of the Prophet Wovoka related the teachings:

> All Indians must dance, everywhere, keep on dancing. Pretty soon
> in next spring Big Man [Great Spirit] come. He bring back all game of
> every kind. The game be thick everywhere. All dead Indians come back
> and live again. They all be strong just like young men, be young again.
> Old blind Indian see again and get young and have fine time. When Old
> Man comes this way, then all the Indians go to the mountains, high up
> away from whites. Whites can't hurt Indians then. Then while Indians
> way up high, big flood comes like water and all white people die, get
> drowned. After that water go way and then nobody but Indians every-
> where and game all kinds thick. Then medicine-man tell Indians
> to send word to all Indians to keep up dancing and the good time
> will come.[69]

Pray and the Good Time would come. Pray and the dead, slain in the
wars with the whites, would return carried on the ephemeral whirl-
winds which dance across Nevada's summer-scorched valleys. Pray
and a flood would come to cover the earth. Or perhaps a frozen wall
of ice. Gone would be white men's cattle, their fences, and their
mines. Gone when Paiutes keep faith in divine intercession.

White men denigrated these Ghost Dances as they had other traditional religious manifestations. The Pyramid Lake agent called
Wovoka a crank, a lunatic, an imposter. He refused to issue passes to
participate in the dances. Blindly sure of his authority, the agent declared, "There are neither ghost songs, dances, nor ceremonials
among them about my agencies. Would not be allowed."[70] Yet in that
same year an inspector at his Walker River jurisdiction saw that Pai-

utes "were almost to a man and woman intensely engaged in dancing."[71] Indians from all over the West flocked to the Paiute prophet. Shoulder to shoulder in great circles around a central fire, forming the symbol of life and hope with their own bodies, Paiutes danced through the dark desert night. Their hope was their song, chanted until the long-awaited dawn:

> The wind stirs the willows, the wind stirs the
>   willows,
> The wind stirs the grasses, the wind stirs the
>   grasses.
> The whirlwind! The whirlwind!
> The snowy earth comes gliding, the snowy earth
>   comes gliding.[72]

PLATE 1.

When he first visited Pyramid Lake in 1844, Fremont camped near a tufa formation which reminded him of an Egyptian pyramid. His naming of the lake, recorded in his official report, became the common English name and has been retained to present times. The next morning, Fremont broke camp and traveled to the mouth of the Truckee. There he found a large and prosperous village and was introduced to the delicacy of Lahontan cutthroat trout. (Courtesy of the Nevada Historical Society.)

PLATE 2.

Numaga, sometimes called Young Winnemucca, was one of the leaders at Pyramid
Lake in 1860 when the natives were attacked by whites. Historian Myron Angel
recorded that Numaga counseled his people to avoid violent confrontation.
Numaga later negotiated with Lander to reestablish peace. (Courtesy of Special
Collections, University of Nevada, Reno, Library.)

PLATE 3.

The running fights which characterized the so-called Pyramid Lake War of 1860 were fought here along the lower reaches of the Truckee River Valley. The steep walls and narrow valley offer little agricultural potential, a factor of importance once this area became established as part of the reservation. (Photo by Martha C. Knack.)

PLATE 4.

Sarah Winnemucca, a member of the important Winnemucca family, figures prominently in Pyramid Lake history. She, with her father, fled north after the violence in 1860 and was incarcerated at Yakima. She learned to read and write the English language, served as an Army interpreter, and wrote endless letters and a book protesting the treatment of her people. With the aid of groups in Boston, she appeared on the East and West Coast lecture circuits, dressed, as shown, as an Indian Princess. She later returned to Nevada and attempted to run a school for Indian children in Lovelock, independent of BIA funding and oversight. (Courtesy of the Nevada Historical Society.)

PLATE 5.

The power and control of the Bureau of Indian Affairs grew at Pyramid Lake. This photo, along with the next five, was made by Lorenzo Creel during his period as Indian Agent there. By 1909, when this photo was taken, the BIA headquarters at Pyramid Lake was a substantial establishment, including housing for the Anglo staff, a school, and a working ranch. (Courtesy of Special Collections, University of Nevada, Reno, Library.)

PLATE 6.

This undated photograph, probably from the 1910s, shows girl students at the Pyramid Lake school. Uniformed regimentation was common in schools of the period. Agent Creel stands at the right. (Courtesy of Special Collections, University of Nevada, Reno, Library.)

PLATE 7.

Joe Mandel had the agency job of carrying mail from Pyramid Lake headquarters to the station at Wadsworth, winter and summer from at least 1908 until 1912. Such jobs for the federal agency were among the few forms of wage employment available to Indians at the time, except for seasonal fish-selling. (Courtesy of Special Collections, University of Nevada, Reno, Library.)

PLATE 8.

Indian police forces were formed on many reservations after 1877. Their primary
task was to see that agency orders were obeyed concerning such minor offenses as
drinking, avoiding school attendance, and domestic issues. During the prolonged
dispute over fishing in the 1920s, agents attempted to use the Pyramid Lake police
force to patrol the reservation and to enforce the prohibition on commercial fish
sales by fellow tribesmen. This photo from Creel's personal collection probably
dates from about 1910, and later-penciled notations on the original identify the
men, from left to right, as Captain Dave Numana, William Paddy, unidentified, Joe
Mandel, and Bob Dodd. (Courtesy of Special Collections, University of Nevada,
Reno, Library.)

PLATE 9.

Until well after the turn of the century, the old mingled with the new at Pyramid
Lake, retained by preference in some cases, enforced by poverty in others. This
remarkable photograph by Creel, probably taken in the 1910s, juxtaposes an
agency-provided milled-lumber house with a modified native *kahnee*. The tule-
matted *kahnee* has a canvas door covering. Five-gallon cans for water are stacked
against the side, next to a hooped barrel with a tin dipper on its top, while an old
woman walks by wearing a traditional rabbitskin blanket. Such selective acceptance of Anglo cultural artifacts has typified Pyramid Lake history. (Courtesy of
Special Collections, University of Nevada, Reno, Library.)

PLATE 10.
One tradition which Paiutes relinquished most reluctantly was the harvesting and drying of fish for subsistence use. Only with the blockage of the Truckee River mouth and falling lake levels in the 1920s and 1930s did this activity decline. (Courtesy of Special Collections, University of Nevada, Reno, Library.)

PLATE 11.

As water was diverted from the Truckee River and the lake level fell, over 34,000 acres of lake bed were exposed, primarily at the south end of the lake near the river mouth. Much of this is now choked with tamarisk, but more lies as long expanses of damp barren sand. The present lakeshore is in the right middle distance. (Photo by Martha C. Knack.)

PLATE 12.

The Marble Bluff Fishway snakes down through the hard rock outcrop on the east side of the river valley. It uses far less water than the natural river would and was designed to facilitate fish-spawning in the face of declining water levels. It seems to be accomplishing its goal, as in 1982 over 13,000 cuiui were counted here as they ascended to spawn. Pyramid Lake is in the right middle distance, extending to the base of the far mountains. The natural channel of the Truckee River is a shiny streak at the extreme left. (Photo by Martha C. Knack.)

PLATE 13.

The Captain Dave Numana fish hatchery, opened in April 1981, is the second tribally operated fish facility at Pyramid Lake. Located in the lower Truckee Valley, it is designed to produce 1.2 million cutthroat trout annually and is an important component in tribal plans for the future. (Photo by Martha C. Knack.)

FIVE

Litany for Reduction and Abandonment

Like many other western areas during the same time period, Pyramid Lake was set aside as an Indian reservation in 1859. There were several explanations for reserves' being established. Official government policy saw them as training grounds, outdoor schools to familiarize natives with Anglo culture and thus permit them to enter the Great Melting Pot of American society. Some men, such as Agent Dodge, saw the reservations as territories set aside for Indians "to enable them to sustain life,"[1] a limited land area where they could pursue their own, albeit necessarily modified, lifestyle. Most white settlers were more crass, openly asserting that the native inhabitants needed to limit the land they used in order to open up portions of the territory for Anglo-American occupancy. Regardless of the degree of benevolence involved, reservation policy remained one of segregation, for it was consistently assumed that the two cultural groups had to be separated from one another.

Closely connected to the Anglos' wish to have Indians removed from their immediate area was their belief that the number of whites in the territory would inevitably increase and that their settlements would expand. When that happened, priority would of course again be given to the whites and the Indians would have to yield. Thus to avoid repeated relocations, it was said, Indians should be established in the most distant sections initially; they "ought to be collected and placed on some reservation more remote from the whites [than Pyramid Lake] and where they can have a permanent home."[2]

The white population in western Nevada did in fact enlarge, rapidly expanding into previously remote areas. With this expansion came demands for security in isolated camps and mines and for subjugation or removal of the Indians. Beginning almost immediately after the first reservation proposal, many individuals attempted to force its abandonment. Not only did local residents constantly yammer about the reserve, but their complaints were supported by governors, superintendents, Indian agents, state legislators as a body, federal inspectors, railroad financiers, and, eventually, the Secretary of the Interior. Considering that even the federal administrators of Indian trust property recommended abandonment, it is astonishing that the Pyramid Lake Reservation survived its first 25 years.

The attack on the reservation began less than a year after it came into existence. As soon as the open hostilities were over, Lander recorded the citizenry's belief that "the use of so much good land for the Indians where the fertile sections are so limited in extent, and the mining population so rapidly increasing, is regarded as injudicious."[3] Within three years the Governor of Nevada, who was also the *ex officio* Superintendent of Indian Affairs, responded to the pressures of his voting constituency and wrote that "the rapid influx of population will soon demand a surrender of one of them [Pyramid Lake or Walker River reservations] as an absolute necessity."[4] He recommended that all the Paiutes be gathered at one of these locations and the other be abandoned to white settlement.

The state legislature also exerted powerful pressures against the land-base of Pyramid Lake Reservation. In 1863, they granted a right-of-way to a toll-road company which would cross the Truckee River just south of Pyramid Lake. The Indian agent immediately objected that the proposed road would cut across reservation lands. This tract would take valuable agricultural land not only for the road-bed itself; but also, since there was a lack of timber for fencing, any nearby crops would be endangered by passing livestock. Further, the road would ford the river at a prime fishing location, where the Indi-ans still gained a substantial portion of their food. He objected to the inevitable grog shops that would spring up along the route to serve the teamsters. He pointed out that there were other established road-ways in the immediate area, and he declared that this new one would serve no necessary purpose. In short, he believed that this toll road was both inimical to Indian interests and superfluous. He said, "I am satisfied that an attempt will be made to get the Reservation abol-ished and I would regard this as an opening wedge to that end."[5] While his protests were endorsed by higher authorities, it was proba-bly economic factors, such as the availability of competitive free road-ways, which defeated construction of this toll road.

The legislature next nibbled at another piece of reserved land. When it was first established, the Pyramid Lake Reservation had as-sociated with it a noncontiguous section of 20,000 timbered acres located high in the Sierra of the upper Truckee drainage. As part of its program for "progress," the BIA desired to house Indians in milled lumber homes, and also the agency itself needed building lumber and firewood. In order to meet this goal in treeless Nevada, the timber reserve was set aside along with the lakeside property; but in 1866, the Indian agent recommended the sale of the upland tract. He pointed out that the timber reserve was in the aboriginal territory of the Washos and that, therefore, no Paiutes did or would occupy it. Again arguing from general policy, he said, "It is not adapted to the purposes of agriculture, and the Indians seldom even pass over it."[6] However, the purpose of the timber reserve was not one of agricul-tural occupancy in the first place, but rather was to serve as a resource base; even the agent could not deny that it served this function admi-rably. In fact, when he really got to the heart of the matter, he said that it contained "nearly one-fifth of the best timbered land in the State. . . . It is found, also, that it is exceedingly difficult to protect this timber. [White] Men gradually encroach upon it, either wilfully or ignorantly, despite all the vigilance which can be used to prevent them. As the timber in other parts of the State is consumed, and as the railroad progresses, this difficulty will increase."[7] In an attempt to prove that the timber reserve was obsolete and therefore not worth the trouble to protect, he claimed that new trees which would serve the agency needs had grown along the river on the main reservation since its founding. Of course, he did not mention that this timber was cottonwood, almost wholly worthless for lumber purposes, while that in the Sierra was pine, the most sought-after timber in the state. So, having argued that the Indians were not using the land advantageously anyway, that they did not need it, and that it could not be protected, he recommended its sale. The Commissioner of Indian Affairs approved the recommendation.[8]

Seeing the opportunity possibly to gain control of this resource before it became available on the open market, the state legislature sent a petition to the Secretary of the Interior requesting that the land be donated for a worthy and charitable purpose, the public school system, which at that time specifically excluded Indians by state law.

Soon, in fact, the agent reported the difficulty he had foretold:

> They [white men] cut down large and valuable trees for the purpose of merely getting the limbs for firewood leaving the trunks to rot on the ground. It is almost impossible to prevent this class of people from committing such depredations. During the winter much valuable timber has been destroyed by them and in order to protect it I have taken the responsibility of appointing an agent to reside there whose duty will be to endeavor to protect it from further destruction. I am satisfied that the duty will be very difficult and that the timber thereon cannot be made of the least value to this Superintendency under the most favorable circumstances.[9]

He then proceeded to discuss in great detail the means by which the most income could be derived from the sale.

Despite this concern, two years later the newly arriving agent reported to Washington, "I can find no record of it [the timber reserve], and no mention of it was made to me by my predecessor. It may have been abandoned before his accession to office."[10] This civil servant was not the only one confused by the sudden disappearance of the timber reserve. At the turn of the century, a very thorough scholar preparing a volume on Indian land cessions for the government could find no record at all of its sale. He concluded that "It was thus tacitly abandoned without any formal relinquishment."[11]

The history of the timber reserve exemplified the roles played by the three main actors concerned with Indian lands in western Nevada—the local white settlers, the state legislature, and the Indian agent. The Anglos had moved west to the Land of Opportunity, and they adamantly wanted the right to exploit that opportunity. It was thus understandable that the state legislature should make every effort to further the acquisitive interests of the white constituency by removing Indian land. However, in addition, some federal agents, sent out from Washington to protect and forward the interests of the Indians, actively agitated to have the Pyramid Lake Reservation reduced in size or abandoned. Sometimes these agents pleaded that they had the Indians' best interests at heart, and at other times their motivations were painfully bald. Their arguments ranged from benevolent removal to a safe distance from the deteriorating effects of the railroad and whiskey of the mining camps to removal for the agents' raw personal gain. However, stripped of rhetoric, the goal of all these groups was control of reservation resources nominally still in the hands of the Indians and purportedly administered by a paternalistic government in their best interests. The Indians themselves were politically powerless; their constant protests remained unheeded by those in the active roles. The drama performed on a small scale over the timber reserve and the toll road would be reenacted over and over, each role recreated until it reached the rituality of litany. But the stake would soon be larger; it would be the lands of the Pyramid Lake Reservation itself.

Early in 1867, the Nevada Superintendent wrote the Commissioner of Indian Affairs to "strongly urge" that the Paiutes be removed totally from the Pyramid Lake Reservation and that those lands be opened for white settlement. He pointed out that the Central Pacific Railroad would soon lay track directly through both the Pyramid Lake and Walker River reservations. He considered that this would "necessarily consume the greater portion of the timber as well as scatter the Indians from their present location." Although the railroad would traverse both reserves, he argued that, being more remote, Indians would be safer at Walker River from the damaging effects of contact with the whites. However, then he made a very telling comment: "Another reason for the removal of these bands besides domesticating them, is, that the lands now occupied by them (and which are producing nothing) are the best farming lands in this portion of the State, and which would at once be settled by whites and cultivated if an opportunity offered, and the product would find a ready market here, saving the people the necessity of importing many of the necessaries of life from California."[12] He was applying the common argument that land ought, by moral right, to belong to those who would use it most intensively for the single purpose of agriculture. Fortunately, the Bureau in Washington remained unconvinced.

With a far more colorful flare, Agent Parker attempted to benefit not the general public but himself by chipping loose the small, "useless" rocky crag of Anahoe Island, then locally known as Goat Island. After leaving the agency in 1869, he requested that the island which lay in the lake a few miles north of the agency headquarters be withdrawn from the reservation lands. Because predators could not reach them there, he explained, Anahoe was an ideal location for the raising of Cashmere goats. He pointed out that some of the local whites had already proven (in a small "pilot project" of most dubious authorization) that goats would thrive there. The agent who replaced him, Major Henry Douglas, rejected the proposal in outrage, and offered cogent arguments against it. He wrote:

> *1st* The topographical situation of the island . . . stands in the way of its withdrawal. It is situated in the *heart* of the Reservation, and its proprietorship by white men would create a *wheel within a wheel* which could not but be detrimental to the interests of the Indians either in the present or future time.
>
> *2nd* If the Island is withdrawn from the Reservation—and it comes into possession of white men, with titles to ownership complete, the purpose for which it would be withdrawn, viz., to encourage the raising of Cashmere goats, would not, and *could not* prevent its being used for any other purpose such as a fishing station, a harbor for the storage and sale of spiritous liquors, or a rendevous [*sic*] for desperadoes. Being outside of the Reservation and at the same time in the middle of it, it could be used for any unlawful purpose with comparative impunity. . . .

4th The Island is just as available for the raising of goats (cashmere or otherwise) for the benefit of *Indians*, as it is for the aggrandisement of any one white man. . . .

5th I am opposed to such an action as the withdrawal of the Island from the Reservation, on general principle. The covetous eyes of white men are constantly cast on the land of the two Indian Reservations in this State, and the withdrawal of Goat Island from the Truckee River Reservation would establish a precedent that would be sure to be followed by numbers of men desiring to locate. I do not think it would be proper or expedient to withdraw a foot of either Reservation, no matter how worthless it may apparently be, or how little available for the immediate use of Indians. . . .

6th There is no real necessity proven, for giving up the Indian title to the Island. . . . could not Mr. Parker receive permission to put as many goats there as he pleases and let the title to the Island remain as it is? He would certainly be as well protected in his interests as far as the *mere raising of goats* is concerned, as if he owned the Island.[13]

Douglas's arguments here were equally applicable to many other attempts upon reservation resources. His point on the strategic importance of such an inroad into the center of the reserve was obvious. Once a foothold had been gained, it would serve as a base for further land seizures.

Douglas stated his opinion bluntly: "I venture to say Mr. Parker's recommendation has for its object the interests of white men rather than the interests of Indians. There is a constant hankering after the lands on these Reservations, and white men are determined to have them if they can by any means obtain them; they will not scruple to hire and make use of the power wielded by 'wickedness in high places' to secure the desired object, and such a conspiracy is now actually in progress."[14] When he suggested that the same type of economic endeavors which could benefit white men could also benefit Indians, he was proposing a rather radical idea for that time and place, one not heard previously in the Pyramid Lake history and rarely heard thereafter.

Further, in answer to the common criticism that Indians did not farm the land, and therefore wasted it, he insisted that, before condemning them as agricultural failures, a concerted effort should be made to encourage them. He reported:

that, until I initiated my own scheme one month ago, no attempt of any kind has been made on either Reservation, to induce Indians to culti- vate the ground—they have not been furnished with the means of do- ing so, no attempt has been made to instruct them in the art of agricul- ture, and there has not been an acre of ground plowed under the direction of a Govt. employe[e], by Indians or white men. The Indians were promised assistance but no assistance was ever given and it was impossible for them to work without this assistance. . . . Mr. Parker further states that though the Indians will not farm for themselves, *"they are good hands for white men"*, without commenting upon this assertion as a plea for the aggrandisement of white men, I think it but reasonable to conclude that if "they are good hands for white men," they would, with proper assistance and good management, *be good hands for themselves.*[15]

Neither of these Reservations have been developed in their resources, no attempt has been made to ascertain their value as sources of supply to the Indian tribes, and it is hence very easy to condemn the *whole* of both reservations as irredeemable and of no account whatever to Indians, should it suit the purposes of some speculating white man to do so. If any portions of the Reservations are ever withdrawn, it should be those por- tions which after years of development are found to be utterly worthless for Indian purposes, and which, *topographically considered,* will not interfere with the future prosperity of the Reservation.[16]

Thus, he accused previous agents with not furthering the Bureau's educational policy, not using the land for the benefit of the Indians, and actively scheming to transfer the reservation to Anglo use, if not ownership. Douglas' insistence that an effort to develop the reserva- tion precede talk of its abandonment was unusual for its bluff hon- esty and staunch support of Indian interests.

Douglas was not long the agent at Pyramid Lake, and his succes- sor, Reverend Bateman, immediately recommended reduction of the land area of the reservation. His report of 1873 pointed to the small amount of acreage suitable for cultivation out of the very large re- served area, before stating, "Now, a portion of each lake near the mouths of the rivers that flow through the reservations is important to the Indians for fishing purposes, but the larger portion is entirely worthless for the Indian service; in fact, it is a burden, as it only requires an expenditure of time to guard. I respectfully recommend that all that portion of Pyramid Lake reservation north of a due east and west line from the north side of the [Anahoe/Goat] island be cut off. It is of no use whatever, as I have said, to this service. This will give the Indians and this service, after said reduction, more than twelve miles of the Pyramid Lake—all that can ever be made available for fishing purposes."[17]

This suggested halving of the reservation found popular support in the Reno area and it reappeared under different guises for many years. Sometimes such rhetoric took the form of urging that Indians should be neighborly. Having already given up nearly all of Nevada without treaty settlement, they should now share with their white co-residents the benefits of rich fishing and farming potential at Pyramid Lake. More often, white proponents of division simply said Indians did not have a right to all those rich resources. On the other hand, some Bureau officials perceived the danger of such a division. For instance, once operating legally on one part of the lake, white fishermen could not then effectively be contained within that section. From such an initial limited entry, agents foresaw the final loss of the entire reservation land-base. So, we suspect, did the local Anglo supporters of the plan.

The litany of abandonment was not chanted only by local interests and corrupt agents seeking land for their own use. Several high-level officials, inspectors, and special commissioners also advocated the reduction or abandonment of the reserve. Such a one was John Wesley Powell of the Smithsonian Institution, who headed a special commission to investigate the condition of Indian tribes of the Great Basin in 1873. Fearing the imminent acquisition of all the best agricultural land along the Truckee by the Central Pacific Railroad, and believing that this would seriously hinder the usefulness of the reservation, he sought other locations for the Paiutes. He saw no prospects in the area because, as Dodge had noted in establishing Pyramid and Walker reserves 14 years earlier, there simply were no other areas where a large amount of unoccupied but fertile land was still available. So if the railroad claimed the bottomlands, Powell recommended removal of the Paiutes to the Malheur Reservation in Oregon: "Doubtless the Indians themselves would raise very serious objections to the removal, but they are industrious, intelligent, manageable people, and it is believed that if the necessities for the removal were properly represented to them ... they will eventually consent to the removal. ... The Commission deem it wise that an effort should be made to consolidate all these [Northern Paiute] Indians."[18] In the interests of bureaucratic efficiency, he consistently suggested that the scattered bands of Nevada Indians be collected at a few points where full services of the Indian Bureau could be offered to them.

Federal inspectors, periodically sent out from Washington to check up on the administration of the reservations, also recommended reduction of Pyramid Lake during the 1870s. Inspector Vandever, in his report of 1875, advocated the Bateman line to cut off the northern half of the reservation above Goat (Anahoe) Island, saying that "The Indians are not at all benefited by any of the lands situated north of this line, and that part of the reservation could be abandoned."[19] Another inspector two years later devised a slight modification of an old plan, recommending that Walker River be abandoned and the two groups be combined at Pyramid Lake. He argued that "Farming will, doubtless, always be a failure here [Walker River Reservation], and in view of the small appropriation for these Indians, I am inclined to think it would be better to abandon this reservation and remove the Indians to Pyramid Lake."[20] He maintained that there was sufficient good land at Pyramid for both groups, and that in this way the Indian Service could save the expense of a farmer at both locations. Further, in a clear expression of the paternalistic and manipulative administrative style of the BIA at that time, he said that it would be easy to accomplish this plan, as there were no strong chiefs at Walker River to object.

Some agents, in anticipation of potential clashes over as yet unthreatened resources of the types coveted by whites, recommended immediate abandonment in order to avoid trouble. Such a policy was voiced by the agent at Walker River in 1879, who expected increasing encroachment by miners in the more remote areas of his reserve. He feared that trouble might develop between the miners pursuing gold and the Indians who felt that the reservation was for their exclusive benefit. He suggested "that the Ind. Dept. send out a special agent for the purpose of reporting upon the expediency of resurveying these

Reserves [both Pyramid Lake and Walker River] with the view of throwing out all Mineral lands. Such a survey can be made without loosing [*sic*] a single acre of agricultural land or anything else that is of material benefit to the Indians."[21] Mineral rights were, of course, not seen as of material benefit to Indians. He confidentially asserted that once Anglo cupidity was appeased, there would be no trouble with maintaining the remainder of the reservation.

Justifications for abandoning all or part of one or both of the major Northern Paiute reservations ranged in a continuum from the covetous to the cowardly. Official suggestions to do so were certainly a far cry from the staunch defense of Indian resources and property rights that one would expect from federal employees charged with their protection for the progress, betterment, and education of the Indians. In only a few isolated, and therefore the more laudable, cases, such as Bateman and Douglas, did agents actively defend Paiute persons and property. It would be an oversimplification to say that no agents were honest or that none had the best interests of the Indians in mind. But it would not be an oversimplification to say that the attempts to force reduction of the reservations in western Nevada were continuous, and that in several cases the federal administrators were in active collusion with local interests.

The state legislature reflected those local interests in a series of memorials to the U.S. Congress. First in 1869, and again in 1877 and 1886, Carson City petitioned for prompt abandonment of either Pyramid Lake or Walker River or both. In the second petition, the legislature stated "that said territory is rich in mineral and agricultural resources, and that already on said reservation, and adjoining the same have been discovered three mining districts, rendering it of great importance that the same should be opened to settlement as other government lands . . . and that by continuing the said reservation a large and fertile region of country is withdrawn from settlement by white citizens, and at the same time is useless to and unused by the said Indians."[22] This was an unusually open statement of the priority given to white settlement in the thinking of the state officials of Nevada. The 1886 petition not only repeated the same arguments, but utilized as weapons some agents' public declarations that the reserve was larger than necessary.

By the mid-1870s, a clear pattern had developed. Local citizen interests coveted the land reserved at Pyramid Lake, and the elected state legislature supported those desires. Assigned Indian agents were convinced that the land base was too large and underutilized. These were indeed powerful threats. But yet another force loomed on the horizon—the Central Pacific Railroad. Its right-of-way would pass right through Pyramid Lake Reservation. The challenge presented by this huge corporation threw agents into a flurry of letter-writing. Intricate negotiations formed a maze of proposals and counterproposals. Agents saw this complex episode as the most dangerous of the nineteenth-century land-grabs, although it did not prove to be so in the long run.

The transcontinental railroad was a massive construction project undertaken jointly by the Union Pacific and Central Pacific railroads with heavy government subsidies. The Railroad Act of July 1, 1862, provided free grant of the right-of-way for the roadbed, free building materials, lenient government loans for each mile of rail laid, and, most important for our purposes, extensive grants of land flanking the tracks.[23] These land-grants were of alternate sections of land for 10 miles on each side of the right-of-way wherever it passed through public lands which had not yet been homesteaded and which the government had not already designated for federal purposes. The railroads were then able to sell this land to fund their enterprise. Hopefully, farmers would buy the acreage, and towns would spring up, providing passengers for the railroad and produce to be freighted. The West would be settled, satisfying government goals, and a steady and permanent market would develop for railroad services.

This dream of frontier progress became a nightmare for Pyramid Lake. The right-of-way crossed the Truckee in the valley extension of the reserve, cutting through the narrow band of arable land. When the agency was sent a map outlining the anticipated railroad grants in late 1873, Agent Bateman immediately saw their importance. "I feel heart-sick over the news contained in said letter relative to the Pyramid Lake reservation," he wrote, "for according to the showing every rod of tillable land with all the improvements, buildings, ditches, fences and in a word every thing pertaining to the service is included in the area belonging to the Central Pacific Rail Road Company. Here in the moment of our hope every thing is frustrated, I could weep over it if it would do any good."[24]

Bateman's initial emotional response had some justification in fact. In this region of strictly limited areas of productivity, the precise location of the one-mile squares which would fall to the railroad became the critical question. If the mile encompassed the valley bottom at the mouth of the river, containing the broadest extent of arable land as well as the fishing sites, it would be a tragic blow to the reservation economy. Other vast areas on the higher terrace levels were of limited value. In any case, the grid pattern assured that some good land would fall to their claim; and because that claim extended 10 miles to the north and south of the actual roadbed, significant portions of the reservation would be taken. A well-controlled survey had not yet been done in this area, and it was not at all clear which acreage was involved.

Regardless of which locations were directly lost, the effect of the railroad claims would be substantial. Once the land was sold to whites, there would be interracial residence within the reservation bounds. In view of general frontier history and the events at Pyramid Lake itself, agents feared that such inroads would then form bases for further encroachments. The checkerboarded grid pattern would also make Bureau development projects difficult, if not impossible. None of the Indian sections would have common boundaries, so irrigation ditches could not be designed to flow from one to the next. Grazing could not be easily pooled, and a single section was far too small to be economical in the dry uplands.

But equally important was the threat to the fishing sites on the Truckee shore, where Indians gathered a necessary portion of their food supply. Bateman feared that "The R.R. Company according to the diagram marked ownes [*sic*] all that portion of the Pyramid Lake as well, that is worth any thing as a fishery; for not one acre of land north of the lines of said company is worth any thing for cultivation and balance of Lake is too remote for profitable fishing purposes."[25]

Dreading these events, Bateman did not wait for them to occur, but devised practical alternatives. He proposed that the government buy out the Central Pacific claims to the Pyramid Lake sections. He pointed out that there really was not much land involved, not over

1000 or 1200 acres, and yet if that were lost the reservation would be valueless for BIA purposes. With minimal expense, the government could buy out the railroad sections and secure the reservation as a consolidated, useful body of land. The clinching argument was this, of course: "It is idle to look for, or think of, another reservation. There is no unoccupied land within hundreds of miles worth any thing."[26] Thus, it was cheaper to retain the reservation land through purchase than it would be to relocate the Indians elsewhere, even ignoring the loss of labor investment and resource potential. This was a telling bureaucratic argument, and Bateman was permitted to pursue negotiations with the railroad.

By March, he had spoken with the head of the Central Pacific Railroad's Land Division and its Board of Directors. They agreed to sell back to the government any of their sections within reservation boundaries at the same price they would get from settlers, about $5 per acre. Furthermore, they agreed to post the land as unavailable for entry and to refrain from sales until a survey was completed and Washington had decided on the purchase.[27]

This agreement was not necessarily altruistic on the part of the company. Since their grant did not legally apply to lands the federal government had previously reserved for its own purposes, including Indian reservations, much of the dispute centered on the date the reserve had been established. If the company were found to have claimed and then sold to settlers any lands to which it was not entitled, it would be subject to a massive federal lawsuit. By graciously offering to sell to the government at market value lands which it might already own, the company stood to lose absolutely no money, had a guaranteed sale, and protected itself from lawsuit at the same time.

During this period, five dollars per acre was considered a very high price for farming land in the West, and the government was visibly balking at what it considered an exorbitant price. But as agents pointed out, these lands were the key to the rest, controlling irrigation potential, protecting ditch rights, and providing fishing shoreline, all critical to the mixed economy being practiced or planned at Pyramid Lake.

Rather than meet this cash price, the government counterproposal was to exchange federally retained sections skirting the reserve for railroad sections within it. The Central Pacific rejected the offer, pointing to the great disparity in value between the river bottoms of the reserve tract and the higher mesas of the surrounding countryside. The next offer was to trade an equal number of sections of government land south on the Truckee below the reserve, but the railroad still held out for a better offer.[28] The next proposal was for federal sections around the railroad's own terminal and maintenance yards at Wadsworth. The company refused. Then the Central Pacific offered to exchange the Pyramid Lake property for government sections elsewhere in Nevada or California having an equal appraised value, but insisted on retaining the right to choose each section themselves. Thus they stood to gain rich California mineral or Sierra timber land in the booming "Land of Opportunity" for relatively poor agricultural acreage isolated in Nevada.[29]

Meanwhile, the reservation was in an uproar. Indians were unsure if their lands would be taken from them, so they lost interest in investing further effort in improvements. The agent did not know if a compromise would be effected in time. When a survey was ordered, local whites thought that the long-desired opening of the reservation was imminent, and scouted sections they wanted to homestead. Bateman telegraphed Washington in desperation: "Is Pyramid Lake reservation abandoned or to be? White men are rushing upon it and I am powerless through ignorance of facts to prevent them. Indians are full of anxiety which I can't allay. I beg for instructions. Answer."[30]

Finally, late in 1875, the Commissioner of Indian Affairs wrote that he supported the idea of exchange of lands, if mutually acceptable sections could be found and if Congress would pass enabling legislation. The Nevada State Legislature, in an effort to block that contingency, petitioned Congress to abandon Pyramid Lake Reservation altogether.

It was not until March 1878, five years after Bateman had received the first map of the railroad claims, that the Commissioner of Indian Affairs, in writing to the Secretary of the Interior, expressed the opinion which finally settled the issue. He recounted how the reservation had been withdrawn from the public lands for federal purposes originally in 1859. The Monroe Survey of 1865 had established its extent. "The subsequent order of the President, of March 23rd, 1874, defining the boundaries of the reservation, should, in my opinion, be held merely as a reaffirmation of the reservation made December 8th, 1859."[31] Thus, the government claim preceded that of the railroad; in fact, it preceded the existence of the railroad act itself. The commissioner's opinion was accepted by the Secretary of the Interior, who ruled that the Central Pacific was entitled to the right-of-way only, and not to alternate land sections on either side of the track. No exchange of land would take place; the railroad had no claim. The reservation remained intact.

In contrast to the Indian Bureau's prevailing record of abandoning resources that white men claimed, here it had successfully defended access to land which was vital to its plans for Northern Paiute culture change. The situation could easily have ended otherwise, judging from the Secretary of the Interior's willingness to yield to the railroad claim without question as early as 1865. Had it not been for Agent Bateman's determination in forcing the issue with every passing inspector and Washington official, in negotiating directly with the Central Pacific Board of Directors, and in pressing for a solicitor's opinion, the results might easily have been the loss of both the agricultural land and the lake.

However, the problems brought by the railroad were not over. While this whole land dispute was under negotiation, the line had established its regularly spaced repair and maintenance shops to service the neighboring stretch of track as permitted by law. These were located unchallenged on the reservation's southern tongue. This incipient village soon grew into the town of Wadsworth. Legal difficulties which Wadsworth created mushroomed over the years to plague the BIA and the Pyramid Lake tribe until well into the twentieth century.

During the first 20 years of the reservation's existence, newspapers, local interests, and their elected officials in the state legislature and the governor's mansion had called for the abandonment of Pyramid Lake Reservation; Indian agents concurred, some scheming for their own private profit, others claiming naively that it would benefit the Paiutes. Inspectors, special agents, and military observers also agreed, while the Bureau in Washington vacillated. Extremely powerful corporate interests then wanted their fair share of the spoils.

The attack came from many different directions and the rationale was uniformly inconsistent. Indians did not use the land the way that white interests believed it should be used; therefore, they did not deserve it, did not need it, or would never use it to its optimal extent; it should be taken away from them and given to those who would capitalize upon it, bringing Progress and Prosperity to the State. The land was desert and useless; it was too good for Indians. The reservation was too far from town to benefit the Indians; it was too close to the railroad.

Raised against this chanted litany was the thin voice of defense. Men like Douglas asked: If the land is valueless, why do these white men crave it? If it is of value to a white man, why can it not also be of value to an Indian? But even Douglas did not issue the ultimate challenge: Why reduce the reservation at all? Other agents like Bateman fought long and hard to salvage whatever scraps powerful forces overlooked; sometimes they got lucky and won. But these few men struggled against overwhelming odds. Bateman once despaired, "I have to say, strange as it may appear, anything that is forbidden seems to be always coveted. Though there are millions of acres of good lands in the territory of the United States that can be had by simply occupying them, yet the disposition to encroach upon reserves seems to be a mania. And lands never so rugged or remote from civilization are not exempt."[32]

It seemed that the forces against the reservation were numerous, powerful, and persistent, while those supporting it were few, weak, and sporadic. Paiutes stood firm and uniform in their outcry against any attempt to take the last of their lands and their bounteous lake away from them. But they were powerless and unheeded.

However, the government had asserted its 1859 priority and laid claim to the reserve. Covetous forces, blocked for the time being, shifted to other tactics. Not able to possess the land openly and legally, their alternative was to trespass covertly and illegally against the resources of that land.

This strategy they pursued voraciously for the next hundred years.

SIX

Grazing Trespass

During the early reservation period, local whites not only challenged the legal existence of the Pyramid Lake reserve and tried to have it reduced or abandoned, but also questioned the physical location of the boundaries. Large portions of Nevada, and indeed of the whole American West, remained unsurveyed for many years because of its sheer vastness. Homesteaders, miners, and other land claimants commonly had to have isolated plats made which were not tied into a regional grid. In many areas, the first large-scale surveys accompanied the railroads, when they became necessary for corporate township claims and land sales. Therefore the initial lack of a survey of the Pyramid Lake reserve was not unusual, but it did constitute a considerable problem for Indians and agents alike. Without a survey, without fences, without even boundary monuments to firmly establish the reservation periphery, it was hard to tell which actual acreage lay inside and which out. Cattle drifted across the open range, from one sweeping valley to the next, blind to all boundaries. Their owners always claimed that they were outside of the reservation limits.

In November 1859, when Pyramid Lake was first set aside as an Indian reservation, only a sketch map recorded its boundaries. The General Land Office removed lands from public sale as indicated by that map. Copies of it were forwarded to the Nevada Land Office upon statehood in 1861, where they were available to interested parties. There should have been no question of the reserve's location, to the extent that this map depicted it, but unfortunately it was vague. Clearly the entire lake was contained within it, as well as a considerable slice of surrounding land. The portion of river valley included was explicitly described in a boundary sign Agent Dodge posted in August 1860:

To All Whom It May Concern

In a communication received at this office from Hon. A. B. Greenwood, Commissioner of Indian Affairs, Washington, D.C., I am instructed to give Public Notice to the Citizens of Utah Territory, to refrain from trespassing upon the following Lands, the same being reserved by the United States Government for Indian purposes, viz.:

All the valley of the Truckee River from the Great Bend, or one mile above what is known as the Lower Emigrant Crossing, to the mouth of said River, including Pyramid Lake and contiguous lands on both sides of the River and Lake. . . .

Notice is further given that the "United States Intercourse Law" will be in full force on the above Reservations, and that the commanding officers of the United States Troops will be called upon for assistance to execute them if necessary.[1]

The Trade and Intercourse Acts to which Dodge referred were a series of laws based on constitutional authority which delegated to the federal government exclusive regulation of commerce with Indian tribes. Upon this foundation was constructed the entire edifice of federal control of Indian affairs, including jurisdiction of federal courts for white crimes in Indian country, authority of the U.S. Army to remove trespassers, and authorization of Indian agents to arrest trespassers and confiscate their property. The 1834 version, which was in effect through the late nineteenth century, contained the following pertinent provision:

> That if any person shall drive, or otherwise convey any stock of horses, mules, or cattle, to range and feed on any land belonging to any Indian or Indian tribe, without the consent of such tribe, such person shall forfeit the sum of one dollar for each animal of such stock.[2]

The existence of the 1834 Intercourse Act, together with the withdrawal of Pyramid Lake Reservation for Indian purposes, gave any assigned agent the power to confiscate cattle, arrest their drovers, and fine their owners. He had the power to protect the pastures and prevent trespass for grazing purposes. The agent need only have proven that the cattle were intentionally herded across reservation boundaries. But to prove this, the agent first had to know where the boundaries were; this raised the problem of the Pyramid Lake survey and accurate ground markers.

Dodge's map was not enough, and the posture taken by Territorial Governor Nye, as the *ex officio* Superintendent of Indian Affairs, did not help the situation. He wrote, "The trouble is not in their [Pyramid Lake and Walker River reservations] sufficiency or in their adaptation to the wants of the Indians in regard to productiveness of wood[,] crop and grain, but in respect to definiteness of boundary and their exact locality. Indian Agent Dodge established while here in charge two reservations, one on the Truckee River including Lake Pyramid (which is the Sink of the Truckee River). How far from the river each way or how far up we are unable to ascertain. . . ."[3] His question on the width of the valley portion of the reservation was understandable, but his doubts on how far upriver the boundary lay were odd in view of Dodge's very explicit statement that it was to be one mile above the Lower Emigrant Crossing, certainly a landmark well-known at that time.

Was Nye creating confusion where none existed? His position, that the reservation was ill-defined, became popular among white Nevadans, for then their incursions could be justified. They could rationalize that trespass was not their fault. They were confused. No one knew, after all, where the boundaries really were, they could say. If this were once admitted as a valid argument, the field would be ripe for continuous nibbling at reservation resources. The Governor continued:

> Both of said reservations are admirably adopted and located (if we can find where they are) to the occupancy of the Indians; and both can be well defined by natural boundaries except the end up the River which will have to be surveyed. . . . I shall take such measures as you have directed to put these reservations in such a condition as that there shall be no mistake as to where they are and have such boundaries marked and well defined.[4]

If natural barriers had in fact been adequate indicators of the lakeside borders, there would not have been the great controversy over white squatters on the western shore nor of cattlemen encroaching on the eastern lands. If the survey of the river portion were properly "marked and well defined," the reservation would have been spared the profusion of squatters in that area as well. The ineffectiveness of the Governor's actions in this regard eventually served the best interests of at least some of his Anglo constituency, but resulted in loss of land for the Pyramid Lake Paiutes.

Early in 1864, the Nevada Indian agent was instructed to have the boundaries of the Pyramid Lake Reservation surveyed. He employed one Eugene Monroe, who recorded the bearings and chain distances between thirteen stations and completed the survey in January 1865. Although the lines on the eastern boundary were later found in error and adjusted, this original Monroe survey became in essence the official boundary of the reserve. This was the description filed in the General Land Office and later quoted in the Executive Order of 1874. However, the boundary problem was not over.

Because the Central Pacific Railroad right-of-way crossed through the southern part of the reservation, it was thought for a time in the mid-1860s that that corporation was entitled to alternate square miles for 10 miles in either direction from the tracks. The resulting checkerboard of land would have been administratively unmanageable, so the Commissioner of the General Land Office issued an order in August 1865, briefly returning to the public domain 10 miles of the riverine tongue of the reserve. This proposed reduction was intended to remove administrative problems that, it was assumed, would accompany the still-contested railroad claim to alternate odd-numbered sections. This withdrawal action clouded title to that important portion of the reserve for years to come. Although the section was again withdrawn from public sale and returned to the reservation only four days later, and although the railroad was finally ruled not to have a claim to the land, the status of that sector remained in doubt for so long that white men subsequently entered and settled on it and, as we shall see, were later able to make good their claims on grounds of long residence.

There were other sources of confusion over boundary lines. Almost a year after the Monroe survey, the Land Commissioner was still not sure that the work had been done.[5] The agency itself was not provided with a copy of the Monroe map. Because agents were changed often, the lack of a record in the agency office explaining the extent of the jurisdiction caused no small administrative confusion. Douglas explained the problem to Washington:

> The boundaries of the Truckee River Reserve are not marked, and there is no evidence whatever that it has been surveyed and its limits fixed. There is no record of any survey in this office to refer to, in case any man chooses to locate and appeal to law to sustain him. I have succeeded in suppressing the fishing by white men; but my success was more owing to their ignorance of my weakness than to any other cause. The original boundaries are said to have included the town of Wadsworth, but the land office records show that one township has been laid off on the Truckee river north of Wadsworth, by what authority I know not. . . . I have no means of knowing why that portion of the reserve was withdrawn, or whether there was any color of authority for its withdrawal. It is certainly not now considered a portion of the reserve, and is settled by white men.[6]

Watchful white men had taken advantage of the confusion generated by the proposed railroad withdrawal and had located on the best farming land of the reservation.

A year later, an inspector still could find no record of its boundaries. "I endeavored to ascertain the limits or boundary of the reservation," he wrote in his report, "but as there was no official data of that nature in the hands of any person, as far as I could learn, I was compelled to rely on the mere verbal statements" of the previous farmer. This information was vague and unsatisfactory. He concluded, "I will here remark, that until the metes and bounds of the reserve are authoritatively established, it will not be free from the encroachments of a bad class of white men, who seldom believe in according any rights to Indians."[7]

In 1873, eight years after completion of the Monroe survey, there was still no map of Pyramid Lake Reservation in the agency office. The agent again requested one, and elaborated that there was not "a single surveyors mark on the lands and thus it is almost, yes, quite impossible to tell who may or may not be encroaching."[8] Even after the arrival of a map copy, the agent complained, "This difficulty to a certain degree, still exists, though modified somewhat since the transmission to this office of the diagram of the original survey; and in fact no further safeguard would be required if the points marked on the map had been definitely established by stakes or monuments distinctly marked. But this was not done, especially in the Lake district, and for this reason we are subjected to annoyances."[9] Two years later an inspector reiterated this view when he said, "The exterior lines of Pyramid Lake Reservation have never been definitely established, and it is important that they should be."[10]

Both agents and inspectors were acutely aware of the relationship between lack of physical markers on the ground posting the boundaries of the reservation and trespass by white men. They all believed that as long as they could not actually show markers to interlopers, and therefore lacked hard proof which might serve as evidence in court prosecutions for trespass, they and the reservation lay helpless against incursions. The agent in 1878 specifically said, "If I am required to show the boundary lines to these parties or others that are liable to locate upon this reserve, I cannot do so for the reason that the monuments erected by Eugene R. Monroe when he made the survey in 1865, if any were erected, have been obliterated and no trace of them can be found, except perhaps one or two, that would afford a starting point for a surveyor to establish the red lines as indicated by the said Monroe's map."[11] Until a firm boundary was established which would constitute acceptable court evidence, the U.S. Marshal was reluctant to remove trespassing whites. Without his support, agents in turn hesitated to proceed on their own authority, as, they believed, removal would cause much community ill-will to no avail. That Anglo community, of course, denied that the agents had any authority to exercise.

It would seem to have been a simple matter to rewalk the boundary and build some permanent and visible monuments. However, there were problems associated with even this simple expedient. Surveys at that time typically began at a prominent geographic landmark or an immovable manmade marker. From here, a specified distance was pursued at a given angle to a second point, where a new angle was followed another distance, and so on until the circle was closed. Western Nevada was not yet surveyed into the national grid pattern, so there were no benchmarks. Therefore a special monument of some kind was necessary to mark the beginning and turning points of any isolated survey such as Monroe's. Several reports similar to the one above mentioned the existence of wooden markers on the ground. Governor Nye and others stated that they were putting up such markers, without benefit of formal survey. Any of these would be of dubious validity and could not serve as court evidence. The one real survey performed during this period, Monroe's, did not solve the problem, as "plat of this survey, giving metes and bounds, is on file in this [Commissioner of Indian Affairs] Office, but it does not appear that any return of field notes has ever been made, and there is, therefore, great uncertainty existing as to the initial point and lines of such survey."[12] Without the field notes and without a permanent monument marking at least the beginning point, it was difficult if not impossible for another surveyor to duplicate Monroe's work.

If any further confusion were needed, it was supplied by the doubts an inspector expressed in 1886. He questioned the validity of the survey itself, saying, "I have examined Monroe's Map which Shows the line to be near the tops of Mountains and it also shows very long lines between changes of variations [of angle] and all lines are represented as being on or near the tops of mountains. I know Eugene Monroe cannot run any Such lines and give the chains and links that he represents on his map. No living Man can do it."[13]

The boundary issue had become such a morass that one inspector stated that "unless a person is found trespassing upon the waters of the Lake in a boat, it appears impossible to convict any one before a Court of Justice, of trespassing, on the Reserve."[14] As the next chapter will show, some people even questioned that.

Indians joined agents and inspectors in complaining about the survey, but they were concerned with its accuracy. According to oral tradition, Dodge had originally intended that Winnemucca Lake be included when he had set apart the reserve. Paiute elders told an inspector in 1886 that "in 1861 Governor Nye Surveyed this Reservation and it included Winnemucca or as now called Mud Lake[,] that in 1865 Eugene Monroe claimed to Survey the Reservation and left out Mud Lake."[15] This Indian belief of a valid claim to Winnemucca Lake persisted a long time, reappearing, for instance, in Senate hearings in 1932.[16]

Everyone was unhappy with the survey situation, except the white trespassers and poachers. By 1880 the office copy of Monroe's map had once again disappeared and the agent was requesting a replacement.[17] The local newspaper was describing the reservation as "an indefinite tract of land. . . . The word indefinite is used because no one knows just where it begins or where it ends."[18] Inspectors were calling for a resurvey. Finally Washington agreed, but for reasons of its own. Secretary of the Interior Schurz wrote (after a visit to Nevada as a result of which a town on the Walker River Reservation was named after him), "The boundaries of the reserve will have to be resurveyed, as there is much doubt about them, and encroachments are frequently happening."[19] However, protection of the reserve was not his only motive, for he was a strong supporter of allotment. This program, which became official BIA policy in 1887, entailed the breaking up of reservations, then held by the government in trust for the tribes as wholes, into small plots to be owned individually. Any land left over after the allotments had been filed would then be opened for sale to non-Indian homesteaders. In order to pass title to individual Indians in this way, an accurate survey was needed. The Secretary continued, "I told [the agent] Mr. Spencer to make preparation for a division of land among those of the Pi-Utes who are in the habit of residing on the reservation."[20] With this purpose in mind, the General

Land Office completed a second survey and sent map tracings to the BIA in 1889. This survey changed very little, as only a few areas east of the lake were altered from Monroe's survey lines. This 1889 survey was the final one until the 1940s, when minor sections were once again remapped.

For over a generation the Pyramid Lake Indian Reservation had lacked an authoritative survey and boundary markers; agents were uncertain of the territorial extent of their charge. The legal status of this executive order reservation was questioned. Agents not familiar with their own authority over whites trespassing on Indian lands hesitated to act forcefully. There were white men who quickly perceived the ambiguity of the situation and pressed in on the weak defenses of Pyramid Lake. They came to graze livestock, to fish, to settle, and to farm upon the lands reserved for Indian use.

One of the earliest forms of such illegal exploitation was trespass on grazing rights. Cattle were mobile and the periphery of the reservation was unfenced. It could always be argued that the stock had wandered over the unmarked boundary without the owner's knowledge. Furthermore, such trespass did not need to involve the owners at all, since it was common practice in this area to leave large herds of cattle unattended for prolonged periods of time. Beef-raising had become a lucrative business in Nevada ever since the mines had lured in a large population of men seeking quick fortunes. They were not interested in investing time to raise crops for their own support and were capable for the most part of paying well for food supplies. Not only were there major cattle-owners, but nearly all small farmers kept a few head of cattle for meat; and of course everyone, farmer, rancher, miner, or Indian, kept horses for transportation. Arid Nevada provided few lush grazing areas. As a result, extensive acreage was needed for each head and herds were moved frequently, primarily over public land. When it became known that the reservation was unguarded, stockmen moved rapidly to exploit this grassland available without grazing fees or permits, apparently free from prosecution.

The free grass was one attraction which drew stockmen there, but as much of Nevada was also open range, this was an insufficient reason. A second motivation was actually the presence of the Indian villages. Cattle-owners soon learned that they could make claims against the government for cattle lost to Indian "depredations." By declaring that Indians had killed them, owners could be reimbursed for natural losses of stock. This would substantially increase their profit margin.

As early as 1861, Indians at Pyramid Lake complained that the Overland Stage Company, delivering mail on a federal contract, was pasturing its horses and cutting hay on the reserve.[21] The army too was grazing horses on Indian lands.[22] Indians objected because they had already become aware of the financial value placed on grass by the horse-using and nomadic whites. More than ten years earlier, the cutting and selling of grass for emigrants' horses had become a lucrative seasonal occupation for Paiutes on the Humboldt.[23] They saw the benefit of catering to this market and sought to control the income-producing resource as much as possible. For this reason, they objected to stockmen entering reservation lands and taking the grass without payment.

During the winter of 1859, as narrated in Chapter Three, there were over 3,000 cattle grazing on the range around the lake. Winnemucca came into Virginia City to complain of trouble with their owners. "He said that the country was his," a citizen recorded, "and that when the herders had come in the fall to ask leave to put their cattle on his ground they had asked him to protect the cattle and prevent his people from killing them and they would pay him money for doing so, but now they broke their promise and would give nothing and he had ordered them to remove their cattle for he wanted the grass for his own ponies which were very poor. The herders had destroyed all his [grass] and paid him nothing for it and they must leave." However, when he tried to evict them, they threatened him with violence, claimed that his people had stolen several head, and "threatened to bring down a heap of white men from Virginia City and kill all the Indians at Pyramid Lake." At that juncture, Winnemucca went into town to seek support for his case. In that he was unsuccessful as "no one at that time supposed anything of a serious nature would grow out of it, in fact, but little attention was paid to it or to Winnemucca's visit."[24]

This grass, a notable human food resource in pre-contact times, now necessary for the Indians' own horses and a source of cash income, was being unjustly taken from them. They protested the moral right to protect their private property, but Indians could not gain a hearing in Virginia City. White disregard of Indian property rights and also of just complaints at their violation, was certainly a frustration contributing to overt conflicts. At least one local Anglo, John Reese, had no doubt of the connection of grazing trespass to the outbreak of the Pyramid Lake War. Reese declared that "in laying out these reserves he [Agent Dodge] assured the Indians that the Whites should not come upon them either to graze their stock[,] to mine or for any other purpose. The Whites did go there to graze and to dig for gold, the Indians demanded protection. . . . the Indians killed and eat [*sic*] several head of cattle belonging to the Whites, and said it was done to get their pay for the use of their lands because the whites have driven their game away and were eating up their fish. The Whites shot some of the Indians, and the Indians retaliated which brought on the war."[25] Paiutes, it appears, not only resented the grazing of stock on their lands without permission or payment, but also the accompanying hunting and fishing carried on by the stockmen, their employees, and others entering the area. The Indians made many efforts to lodge protests similar to Winnemucca's but they were ignored.

After the conflict, the cattle trespass continued; in fact, it increased. Governor Nye, *ex officio* Superintendent of Indian Affairs for Nevada, struck to the heart of the matter when he noted: "These Reservations cover a large portion of the best grazing lands in the western and middle portions of the Territory." Then he clearly expressed his point of view when he complacently continued: "The increasing [white] population, bring in their train a large increase of stock, and the great scarcity of forage in the Territory makes it almost a necessity for them [the whites] to occupy a portion of the Reservations."[26] When the person in charge of Indian affairs stated that it was "almost a necessity" for whites to encroach on Indian resources, it could come as no surprise that trespassers were numerous and were not prosecuted vigorously for their offense. Cattle interests even tried to have one of their numbers appointed agent at Walker River in order to expedite the exploitation, but mercifully this maneuver was blocked.[27]

Paiutes refused to be complacent about the situation, however, and they stated their opinions publicly. Even the Governor was aware of their position, noting that "The Indians are exceedingly sensitive to any infractions upon their supposed rights, and a series of trespasses makes them testy and uneasy."²⁸ Nevertheless, the trespasses continued throughout the 1860s.

Occasionally agents objected to the presence of white-owned cattle, especially when they were driven brazenly into the river valley within sight of the agency house.²⁹ Cattle were removed only after threat of military intervention, but they soon returned. Eventually they were simply tolerated if discreetly kept in a remote area of the reserve.

In 1870, Agent Douglas had a plan. If cattle were to graze on the reservation anyway, why not capitalize on it? "There is another method, besides agriculture," he explained,

> by means of which the reservations [Pyramid Lake and Walker River] may, in my opinion, be made almost self sustaining. I allude to the grazing resources of the reserves. The amount of arable land on both reserves is very small, compared to the very large tracts of land, not susceptible of cultivation, but upon which grows a nutritious grass, suitable for the grazing of stock. Many citizens have desired to graze their stock this winter on the reserves, and are willing to enter into articles of agreement, placing themselves under bonds to pay a stipulated sum of say 50 cents per head per month if they herded the stock themselves—or $1.00 per head per month, if herded under the direction of the Indian Bureau. Limiting the number to 1000 head for each Reserve, would bring $1,000 per month to the Indian fund for at least six months in the year, without any cost or outlay on the part of the Indian Bureau, and without interfering in any measures with Indian interests—and by this means a large amount of land now utterly useless to the Indians would be converted into an abundant source of revenue.³⁰

In this way, the agent believed, "vast tracts of waste land" could be converted to profit. Of course, this plan assumed that Indians did not use the hinterland of the reservation for any purpose, that it was in fact wasted land. However, Paiutes did continue to use the wild food resources throughout this period, which made this assumption doubtful. Further, the agent asserted that leases would not interfere with "Indian interests," in other words with the limited arable land— for it was assumed that Indians were to be farmers. Paiutes were to be protected in their farming, but not encouraged to enter the occupation of ranching, which was so very lucrative in the territory at the time. Thus the opportunities for Indians to use the resources of their lands were limited for them by the management policies of the Bureau of Indian Affairs. It was not suggested that they should be subsidized in cattle purchases in order to use their grazing land themselves, although farms, irrigation, and milled lumber houses were so funded. The proposed policy was blocked in Washington, and not until 1891 was it legal to lease Indian lands at all. Not until 1894 was the BIA authorized to issue leases for farming purposes.[31]

Agent Douglas also charged that a previous agent had been in the habit of making private grazing contracts with local ranchers for winter pasture, from which that man had personally profited to the amount of $15,000. Ranchers approached Douglas himself several times, apparently believing that this practice was standard and would be continued. Although the charge of private profit was never substantiated, the illegal presence of cattle not owned by Indians continued uninterrupted.

Eight years later, they were still there. The agent mapped the illegally exploited pastures, took a census of the number of cattle there, and recorded the owners of the herds. He claimed that all these cattle were grazing illegally, "for all of which not one dollar is received either by myself or the Indians, with the exception of Mr. J. Gregory, who occasionally kills a beef for the Indians for the privilege"[32] of running his cattle there.

The Indians frequently objected to this trespassing and were vitally concerned with protecting the grassland, which they wanted to use themselves; the availability of grazing was one important consideration in their decision to live there. One agent, bemoaning the failure of his agricultural policy, proclaimed that "these Indians have gradually been leaving the reservations for the past five years, caused by the failure of crops, for the want of irrigating ditches, encroachment of white men upon the fisheries, and an inadequate appropriation. The larger portion of the Indians that reside upon the reservation during farming season are those that are the owners of ponies, that stay for the purpose of guarding pasturelands from white men's cattle."[33] Paiutes were annoyed by the loss of revenue and also by the damage caused by the cattle and drovers. From an early date, these white men supported themselves by shooting wild game which Indians considered by rights their own. And as Paiutes complied more and more with the agency agricultural policy over the years, they became vulnerable in yet a new way. An inspector recorded in 1886, "The Stockmen allow their Stock to come here and break into their [Indians'] fields. When Indians complain the cattlemen tell them to show the lines, which they cannot do."[34]

The leasing idea cropped up again in 1889. "There are a large number of Cattle + Sheep grazing on these lands, the property of white men, who are located, some of them within the borders of the Reservation," the inspector noted. As a matter of expediency, he suggested, "Either Some arrangement should be made to Collect a grazing Tax from these people or else they should be removed. . . . If they were made to pay, I don't think the Indians would object to the Cattle, but the Sheep ruin the range. Thousands of acres could be grazed over by Cattle, without interfering with the range needed for the Indians or their farms, as the mountains + Lake, form a basin, which could be made the limit—A good revenue from this Range Could be secured these people from the Cattle men, who would be willing to pay rent of grass."[35] Here the inspector not only recommended tying land up in leases, which would then have limited Indian opportunity to go into commercial stock-raising themselves, but he also dictated the types of leases to be let, reflecting a typical cattleman's prejudice against competing sheep.

By now, several large commercial herds had been entrenched on the little-traveled eastern side of the lake for prolonged periods of time. Some of the ranchers had even made improvements in the form of shacks and corrals which they brazenly claimed should be paid for by the government if they were evicted. A federal commission cited as examples "Wheeler and Ridenour, who keep 10,000 sheep on the reservation summer and winter. Their improvements are valued by them at $5,000, but the Commission expresses the belief that they are not worth more than $1,000. They have grazed the reservation for nine years without paying any rent for the privilege, which Mr. Wheeler, one of the owners of the sheep, says has been worth $1,000 a year to them." These operations were not small, and the effects of

this intensive grazing on the sparse desert vegetation can only be estimated. The Commission continued, "All of the intruders on this portion of the reserve have always known that they were trespassers."[36]
After all the correspondence and complaints, it could hardly have
been otherwise. Yet the BIA did not prosecute, and local opinion con-
doned this overt theft of Indian grazing rights.

A few years later, when Indians were still complaining to their
agent about illegal cattle on the Winnemucca Lake side of the reservation, another inspector gathered the Indians together and advised
them to rent the land out to lease, "setting forth the advantages of
renting said land and getting some revenue from it, rather than having it a bone of contention and getting nothing from it." The Indians
agreed to let the lease. He rationalized his role in legalizing this trespass by arguing, "The Indians at Pyramid Lake do not own all told
one hundred head of cattle, if they owned any to amount to anything
and could profitably use this land I would not advise its rental; as it is
they are deriving no benefit from it." He still did not take the next
logical step and recommend that stock be acquired for the Indians so
they could utilize this obvious resource themselves rather than relinquish it to Anglo use. Instead, he explicitly pointed out that the funds
derived from leasing would be adequate to provide subsistence payments to the indigent. He said, "If it is thought advisable to act upon
the foregoing recommendations, not a dollar in my judgement, will
have to be expended upon the old and infirm Indians, by issuing rations, +c, +c. The money obtained from the lease of the land above
mentioned, and the ground rents in Wadsworth could be set aside for
their support. The sale of fish would furnish abundant revenue to the
able bodied."[37] It was significant that he acknowledged by omission
that farming could not provide a subsistence base. Land used for
grazing, however, could be valuable and converted to Anglo use, and
the income pirated for services that the BIA had previously provided.

Leasing was finally instituted by 1911 to generate income for the
"benefit of the Indians."[38] However, the results were not those recommended by the advocates of the plan. These men had persuaded Indians to support leasing by stressing that the funds would be used for
assistance to the old and infirm, or by making vague promises of direct benefit to the Paiutes. However, once the policy was instituted

and leases signed, the Bureau called into effect one of its regulations which stated that any profit from reservation enterprises had to be used first to meet the administrative costs of operating the reserve. They argued that agency policies and programs did in fact generally benefit all the Indians, and that therefore they were fulfilling the promises. Some Paiutes might have disagreed with that line of logic. Grazing-lease funds were placed in the "proceeds of Indian labor" category and used to pay white agency employees.[39]

The basic problem of business dealings by trustees of any kind was not long in rising over Pyramid Lake. Was the federal trustee making every reasonable effort to get the best lease possible, with protection for tribal interests as well as maximal profit?[40] In 1919, after only five years of leasing, the Special Supervisor in Nevada was outraged at a lease giving grazing rights over the entire reservation to sheepmen at a rate of $3,750 per annum. After talking to the lessors, he reported, "While they are not shouting over their success, I could see that they were a long ways from sorry. You will note, upon making a slight calculation, that the acreage price is $.015, as the Reservation contains 240,000 acres. Had the superintendent been on the job and had this been on an acreage basis, as we have our range, the outcome might have been very different especially as the same parties are leasing railroad lands adjoining the Reservation, which are much poorer in carrying capacity, at 3¢ and over per acre."[41] Apparently the Bureau was not driving hard bargains for the use of Indian resources. In the twentieth century, whites could no longer use the reservation grazing for free, but it was still cheap.

Even so, there were those who wanted to avoid paying this minimal rent. Cattle trespass continued, primarily by those white squatters maintaining small, illegal farms on the southern river portion of the reservation. In the spring of 1920, during the annual reservation round-up for branding, Indians discovered over 150 head of cattle belonging to neighboring white men, including a few owned by a state senator. Nearly 130 were owned by one white man whose cattle had been on reservation lands for years. The agent had notified him ten days before the drive that he should remove his stock from the Indians' range, and he admitted that he was so warned, but refused to remove his stock. The agent failed to use that power to fine which was granted him by the 1834 Trade and Intercourse Act. He returned the cattle to their owners without fee or penalty. He then complained to the inspector present that "'the office ties his hands.' Your inspector discerns no thongs used in restraint, and is for himself not conscious of thongs, bracelets or hobbles, imposed by 'the office' on his official actions."[42] The inspector recommended prompt prosecution in court of the two major and most habitual offenders. His recommendation was not followed.

White men's cattle had grazed illegally on the reservation since at least the 1860s without prosecution or financial penalty. The leases when finally issued were at extremely favorable rates. Even when caught in blatant violation, owners were not subjected to the legitimate impounding fees. It was indeed a favorable situation for white trespassers.

While concerned with leases and trespassing, the BIA did not seem as interested in helping Paiutes utilize the rangeland to their own benefit. Of course, individual Indians had horses, and some had a few head of cattle, but these were small-scale holdings. Although an agent suggested buying a herd of cattle for Indians in 1872, his suggestion was ignored by Washington.[43] In 1891 a presidential commission negotiated the release of the southern part of the reservation in exchange for cattle, but the agreement was not approved by Congress.[44] No cattle were forthcoming, despite repeated warnings from various federal officers that the reserve lacked sufficient farmland to provide agricultural subsistence.[45] Until the end of the nineteenth century, Paiutes bought their few head of stock on their own initiative and they had only about one hundred all told. An inspector observed during the early years of World War I, "The reservation has considerable grazing land, which has been leased to outside stockmen and an effort should be made to increase the number of cattle belonging to the Indians looking to the time when they will use all their range themselves."[46] In 1916, Paiutes were grazing over 175 head at Pyramid Lake, but the largest individual herd was 36 head and most owners had fewer than 10.[47] Wartime demand and the postwar boom encouraged Paiutes to expand. By 1930 they had built their herds to over 630 head, utilizing money from the forced sale of reservation land to squatters; in 1934 there were over 800 Indian-owned cattle there.

In that year a Senate investigating committee came to Pyramid Lake for testimony on BIA administration, and the cattle issue was raised by the Indian witnesses. They asked what could be done about stock still trespassing, some owned by the same white men mentioned in the 1920 report. Senators replied that they could impound the cattle, drive them off, or file suit against the owners. One Senator pointed out that "it is the duty of the Indian Bureau to protect the Indian reservation from trespassers. This is an Indian reservation and you can keep trespassers off the reservation. The superintendent can refuse to permit white men to come on the reservation. He can go so far as to oust any white man on here. You have absolute power, as a matter of fact. . . ." The agent, when asked about this problem, replied, "What we need, it seems to me, are a couple of line riders, and that is what the Indians have asked time and time again. We have put it up to the office and so far we have not got far."[48] He suggested that it was best not to press the issue, because the reservation was still not completely fenced and occasionally Indian cattle wandered outside. Local whites, he said, might retaliate with countersuit. As late as 1938, wire fencing was still being cut in remote sections of the reserve in order to drive Anglo-owned cattle onto Indian land.[49]

The Paiutes, however, refused to acquiesce in the matter. Ever since Winnemucca's visit to Virginia City in 1860, they had objected to stock grazing freely on their range. They did so again in 1947, shortly after they had acquired a legal consultant. One of the first questions they asked her was what could be done about the trespassers. She suggested immediate legal prosecution through the district attorney. She did point out that they would need to prove that the cattle had been intentionally driven onto the range and had not simply strayed. Despite her suggestions, the agency continued to tolerate illegal cattle presence, as it had for 90 years. Into the 1950s it was writing letters to the white owners: "This is to advise you that if you do not immediately cease and resist [*sic*] from trespassing upon the Indian lands, in accordance with the request heretofore made upon you, it will be necessary for this office to take the proper action relative to any violations which you continue to incur."[50] Court suit was never filed.

Beginning at the very founding of the Pyramid Lake Reservation, cattle owned by white men grazed illegally there. Initially permitted entry by the confusion over the boundaries of the reserve, whites exploited the opportunity to pasture livestock free upon Paiute lands. Agents were weak and ineffective in defending Indians' right either to use the lands for their own stock or to gain maximum financial benefit from the white population. Paiutes never flagged in their concern over this trespass, constantly drawing it to the attention of agents, inspectors, newspapermen, and congressmen.

Grazing trespasses have persisted throughout the more than 100-year history of the reservation. They continue even to the present.

SEVEN

Fishing Trespass

When Fremont first traded for trout on the shores of Pyramid Lake, Anglos learned what Indians had known for centuries—that this lake teemed with fish, large and small, abundant at different seasons. Masses of discarded fishbone had formed the archaeological sites dotting the shoreline, places where prehistoric Indian men had brought their catch to feed their families. Before the coming of white Americans, Northern Paiutes had fished extensively at the mouth of the Truckee River and for several miles upstream. Late in winter and through the spring, they had pursued a series of important species, especially Lahontan cutthroat trout and cuiui. Paiutes had developed an elaborate fish-catching technology—willow weirs and fishing platforms, special basketry traps, floats and sinkers, prepared fields of white pebbles for night fishing, harpoons, fish poison, hooks for single and set lines. Tribesmen from distant areas had brought their tackle to share the rich harvest. They had filleted and dried fish by the ton for later seasons.

When the BIA began casting about the arid West for suitable locations in which to concentrate the mobile Paiute bands, it looked at river valleys. Only in areas with permanent streams could agricultural colonies be established in accordance with federal policy. However, in western Nevada the Bureau reserved two of the three great lakes in their entirety, along with their fertile riverine valleys. This was a clear recognition of the importance and value both of the water, for future Indian development, and of the fish in Indian economic life. The Nevada Federal District Court declared in 1879: "We know that the lake was included in the reservation, that it might be a fishing ground for the Indians. The lines of the reservation have been drawn around it for the purpose of excluding white people from fishing there, except by proper authority. It is plain that nothing of value to the Indians will be left of their reservation if all the whites who choose may resort there to fish."[1] Even the BIA, after in practice denying the financial value of fishing for decades, reversed itself in a 1969 memo which stated unequivocally, "The reservation was established to provide the Indians with control of the Pyramid Lake fisheries as their primary food source."[2] Throughout the historic period, Anglos have dipped into the waters of this lake to take the rich fish resources, despite their legal retention for exclusive native use. The resulting dispute over control of the Pyramid Lake fishery began early and has continued to the present.

When the reservation was first established in 1859, the agents' primary concern was to concentrate Indians on it. Their interest focused on that problem for several years and they issued no complaints concerning the fishery, but apparently trespass on Indian fishing rights began this early. Such trespass was so well established by 1869 that a federal inspector, Jesse Lee, reported, "Upon my arrival at the reservation I was soon convinced that it was nothing more nor less than a rendezvous for white fishermen, men engaged in prospecting for mines and self-constituted fishermen and traders and others." When he asked a meeting of Indian elders for their complaints, their very first protest was against this incursion on their fishing grounds. Lee duly reported: "The Indians very justly complain of interference with their fisheries by parties of white men who have been located on the reservation for some time—from one to two years—near the mouth of the river."[3] Lee found white-owned fishing nets and lines stretching completely across the river in more than 20 different places on the lower two miles of river, well within reservation boundaries. Fish were caught as they began their spawning runs, so that far fewer reached the river pools where Paiutes habitually operated. Native techniques were well adapted to the shallows of riverbanks and lakeshores, but these areas were now dominated by Anglos. Indians complained that those fish that escaped Anglo nets were driven back deep into the lake by noise and boats. Once there, they were beyond Paiute reach, for the Indians did not traditionally have boats for deep-water work and lacked the money to buy white-manufactured wooden ones.

Lee found four white men fishing near the mouth of the river, two of whom were not only fishing on their own but buying fish from the Indians. Like all concessions operating on federal property such as national parks or military bases, Indian traders were required then as now to be licensed and bonded by the government. Therefore these men were not only trespassing and poaching but also violating federal trade regulations. Lee issued notices for all to leave the reservation within 20 days, but no legal action was taken against them.

In the course of their trespass, whites introduced new techniques of fish capture, using nets stretched completely across the river, boats for use on the open lake, and an implement locally known as a "grab hook," a hooked metal gaff for raking fish ashore. The competition provided by these new methods forced Indians to alter their own techniques, though they were hampered in this effort by lack of money for boats and tackle for deep-water work.

Further, and perhaps more important, the white fishermen were working for maximum commercial harvest. While the concept of trading off one's surplus was old in native culture, it was a new idea to specialize full-time in any single product in order to earn cash, to convert in turn to basic subsistence needs. Paiutes had never participated in a market economy before. But shrewdly, they soon perceived the mechanics of this complex system and discovered where the profit lay. They asked the inspector for control of the production base through enforcement of reservation boundaries and of existing federal laws on bonding and licensing Indian traders. Further, they recognized that white men were trying to force them into a producer's role only, while keeping the lucrative middleman position themselves. Therefore the Indians requested "to have the fishing for their exclusive benefit, that the pecuniary profit realized therefrom shall accrue to them;—also that only one man be designated or allowed to buy their fish on the reservation, and that it be optional with them to sell their fish to him or take them to market themselves."[4]

Despite the difficulties which white competition placed in their way, Indian commercial fishing was already substantial. The nearby mining towns were food-short and inflation-ridden, so it would have been remarkable indeed had Paiutes not expanded their fish trade into commercial marketing. A military observer commented in 1868 that the Pyramid Lake Paiutes "subsist upon the profits of the fish trade, carried on between Virginia City and the Reservation,"[5] indicating that this trade provided most of their cash income. That income was not inconsiderable, for only three years later the official trader bought 10 tons of fish from the Indians for over $2,000.[6] Since Anglos would not eat cuiui, nearly all of these tons of fish must have been cutthroat trout, undoubtedly increasing even more the Indians' reliance upon the sucker for their own subsistence.

Prices for trout ran about 10 cents per pound, and the resulting potential profit encouraged a small group of white men to enter the reserve to harvest fish. As Major Douglas, an early agent at Pyramid Lake, realized, "The fisheries at the mouth of the river are excellent, and of immense value as sources of subsistence, quite a large income is derived from the sale of fish caught at these fisheries, so much so, that the cupidity of white men has been excited, and they have endeavored to appropriate the fisheries and realize the profits, which of right belongs to the Indians."[7] By 1870, Douglas and Inspector Lee managed to "break up a rendezvous of white men, who for some time had been monopolizing the fishing, much to the injury of the Indians."[8] But local whites did not stop at simply expropriating a portion of the fish harvest. They also tried to eliminate their Indian competition by political pressure to have one or both of the regional reservations abandoned. Agent Douglas, one of the few early agents who recognized the lacustrine nature of Paiute adaptation in this area and the value of fish in their diet, noted:

It has been the design of some citizens of this country to break them [the reservations] up on the pretext that they are valueless to Indians. As it would be a matter of small importance to such persons whether such was or was not the case, unless the reserves, in case of withdrawal might be made valuable to themselves, I am inclined to believe such designs were not conceived in an honest spirit. The reserves are not valueless, for without man's assistance, nature has endowed them with fisheries, which afford the Indians a bountiful supply of food; that they have not been valuable in other respects is owing to official neglect and maladministration, and not to any lack of inherent value.[9]

Douglas was aware that fishing could potentially add to Indian income if protected and that it could develop as a viable occupational specialization. He was also very cognizant of the raw economic basis to self-serving Anglo arguments, which favored abandonment of reserved lands. The presence of resources, and the rights to exploit them, have never been separate from an advocacy of abandonment of reservation lands in the West.

One such proposed reduction came in 1865, in association with the Central Pacific Railroad claim. If successful, such a claim would have taken large portions of the available agricultural land on the reserve, and the Paiutes did not particularly object to this. However, when two more miles of river valley were suggested for removal the Indians protested vigorously to their agent, who reported: "You will therefore See that one of their Most favorite fishing grounds lies within the two Miles additional Survey. They would yield it reluctantly, and it would doubtless become a fruitful Source of trouble and great dissatisfaction to them. They declare themselves entirely Satisfied with the first, or ten Mile Survey, but the two Miles additional lacks much of meeting their approbation."[10] Although this attempt to withdraw land failed, as was seen in Chapter 5, it was not the last attempt to be made on those reservation lands which controlled fishing access. Throughout this period Indians firmly defended the Pyramid Lake fishery, although their means to protect it from white men were slight.

All of these issues of new technology, commercialization, disputed access to the fishery, and attempted reservation reduction were intertwined in the most serious challenge to Indian fishing rights in the nineteenth century. This major contest began as a case of trespass by white fishermen. As early as 1869 Inspector Lee found white men fishing on the lake, in violation of the reservation boundaries, and had them removed by the military. These men immediately returned and resumed fishing, some on the lower river shores and others in the lake itself. After repeated removals of the offenders, Lee claimed in 1870 that he had suppressed such trespass; he was a bit premature in this judgment.

Once the inspector left with his supporting military troops, Anglos returned to fish the lake and river through the ensuing years, with, if anything, increasing rapacity. By 1877, Agent Barnes at Pyramid Lake wrote in despair that the white fishermen were a nuisance "almost beyond endurance."[11] Throughout that summer a number brazenly established themselves on the river within sight of the agency buildings. Barnes gave them notice that if they did not leave in 20 days they would be liable to arrest. Although the agent's control over Indian lives was nearly complete, he did not, in the nineteenth century, have any direct authority over non-Indians, either on or off the reservation. He certainly lacked any police powers, and his only available force was the U.S. Marshal or that of his own personality and six-gun, which he used at his own risk. Proper channels required the cooperation of other federal agencies—the military for policing and the U.S. Attorney's office and federal court system for legal prosecution. Therefore Agent Barnes, restrained by the limited power of his office, went through appropriate channels when, instead of following up directly on his threatened arrests, he wrote to Washington for advice and for explicit authorization to proceed.

Barnes knew that any action he took would lead to a heated confrontation. Local whites viewed Paiutes as a conquered people after the so-called war of 1860, and believed that as such the Indians should yield all their goods and resources upon demand. They interpreted any attempt on the part of the agent to do his job and build or save anything for the Indians as an intrusion on their claimed rights of total confiscation. By enforcing the boundaries of the reservation against fishing trespass, Barnes incurred local hostility. On the other hand, the Paiutes had a vested interest in protecting the fishery.

Barnes wrote, "The Indians *are very much excited* concerning this matter and are making complaints to me daily that these white men will supply the market with fish from the lake and thus deprive them of their *only means of making a livelihood* during the fishing months (commencing in October and ending in April)."[12] Indians were not passive observers at any time during the subsequent struggle, and constantly tried to pressure agents into more aggressive action.

The BIA in Washington advised Agent Barnes to have a U.S. Marshal remove the trespassers from the reservation. But Barnes soon telegraphed the Commissioner of Indian Affairs: "Am unable to remove the trespassers from Reservation. The Marshal has been fired on and declares his inability to clear the Reservation without military assistance. The Indians are enraged."[13] A military detail from San Francisco was authorized to aid the agent and the marshal, but before it could arrive the fishermen notified the marshal that they would not resist removal. Nor did they, but neither did they stay off the reserve; by mid-January they were fishing again. The marshal returned to the lake and read them the law. While aware of the law and not disputing it, the white fishermen then escalated the stake by changing the issue from their own trespass on federally reserved lands to the existence of the reservation itself. They were very much aware, as was Agent Barnes, of the vague definition of the reserve and the ambiguity of its boundary markers. Further, as the case developed, they raised the question of the very legality of the reservation.

No treaty had been formally signed with Pyramid Lake Paiutes, as was customary in carving out a small portion of a tribe's previous holdings to restrict them, while opening the rest to Anglo appropriation. Rather, Pyramid Lake Reservation was created by administrative withdrawal of public lands for Indian purposes in 1859, followed by Congressional appropriations for an agency there and a Presidential order recognizing the status quo 15 years later. Local whites challenged this method of creating Indian reservations by the executive branch, although the practice has since been recognized as legal and became common in late nineteenth-century and twentieth-century federal dealings with Indian tribes.

The white fishermen initially maintained that the northern half of the lake was beyond reservation limits, since there were no markers in that remote area and they saw no reason why they should not be able to fish there. As Barnes quoted the marshal, "They [the fishermen] also informed me that in case I should have warrants for their arrest at any time, I need not bring any military to assist me, as they would come peaceably, that all they wanted was to have the case decided in the courts and have lines of the reservation established."[14] Without permanent markers, the local Anglo population refused to accept the total inclusion of the lake within the reservation. Further, Indians did not maintain a large number of permanent residences on all shores of the lake and therefore, to the Anglo way of thinking, did not possess it. Agents continued to press, as we have seen, for an accurate survey and clear boundary markers in order to protect Indian resources. But such action would only forestall future difficulties, and Barnes was aware that his confrontation would be a turning-point in the relationship between the Indians and the local white population. At the height of the crisis in 1878 he wrote:

> I do not hesitate to express the opinion that unless all these questions that have been sprung by these white men fishing in the lake are settled by the proper authorities, other white men will, very soon, come in and locate upon the lands of the reserve for the purpose of farming for a livelihood, and when that is commenced I am almost certain it will not be in my power or any other agent, to control the Indians and prevent them from fighting for what they believe to be their rights.[15]

Now new battle lines were drawn which replaced those of open warfare. This was a new kind of battle, fought with words in a courtroom, with weapons stemming from a foreign cultural tradition. The warriors were men of another society and the Paiutes could take no active role, for they were without power, lawyers, or even the legal right to testify in courts, as they were not citizens of that new country. But the prize of this battle was their land and their last remaining means of earning a livelihood. The stakes were high, and the helpless Paiutes had to rely on the unproven advocacy of the federal government and its officers to protect them from the proven acquisitiveness of the local white citizenry. This new form of battle would soon become all too familiar, for Pyramid Lake people would have to fight it over and over again in the years to come.

The Bureau finally took positive action in March of 1878. The Commissioner authorized the local agent to call on the U.S. Marshal to protect a half-mile perimeter around the entire lake. While the Commissioner recognized the executive order which established the reservation and the Monroe Survey on which it was based, he was also aware of the persistent lack of boundary markers. He realized that without them it was hard to prove to whites where the boundaries lay or to evict trespassers. The arbitrary half-mile zone was a stopgap measure at best, but Barnes promptly placed wooden markers along this bound in the sections along the river and up the lake as far as he thought practically useful. These were the first markers actually on the ground. However, the most important aspect of the Commissioner's order was his recognition of Indian fishing rights as requiring and deserving protection: "The territory embraced within the above limits is believed to be considerably within the boundary defined in the Executive Order of March 23rd, 1874. It will, however, be sufficient to protect the fishery rights of the Indians until such time as more definite action is had."[16] This provided the all-important charge for agents to assert Indian fishery rights and defend them with military force if necessary.

All too soon it did become necessary. At the beginning of the winter fishing season of 1878–79, posters appeared in the mining camps: "WANTED: 100 MEN TO FISH ON PYRAMID LAKE WITH OR WITHOUT FLOATS AND FISHING TACKLE."[17] Substantial profits were guaranteed. Several competing commercial fishing companies recruited men. A local paper reported that there were 75 white men with 45 boats operating on the lake and lower river, with sales of over $5,000 a month during season.[18] In early January the situation reached a climax. White fishermen were operating on the shores of Pyramid Lake itself, and the agent called in the military to remove them. They had to evict six companies plus 20 more independent fishermen and confiscated 73,740 pounds of fish in hand, worth more than $7,000.[19] The fishermen left without resistance, but returned and began fishing once again as soon as the soldiers had departed, in direct violation of federal authority. The challenge was flung down.

Most of the fishermen were from the Reno area, where popular opinion stood firmly behind their attempts to break the authority of the reservation. For instance, the editor of the Reno *Journal* steadfastly refused to admit that the reservation was valid and that it actually included all of Pyramid Lake. He spoke about "the imaginary line of the precious reservation," and perpetuated the idea that only a portion of the lake was enclosed. The *Nevada State Journal* reflected the confused state of public knowledge when it reported the fishermen as planning to "take immediate steps to ascertain just where the reservation ought to be and to have those limits properly designated. The Reservation agents, they [the fishermen] assert, claim several hundred thousand acres, while the Act of Congress creating this Reservation only allow[s] 5,000 acres. They claim further that the original location was near Glendale, but that the agents have gradually worked it down until now it is located on the shores of Pyramid Lake, 35 miles away. They also assert that there never has been a survey of the Reservation made. . . . "[20] Of course, these claims were all untrue. On the other hand, the *Territorial Enterprise*, out of Virginia City and a bit more distant from the problem, researched the issue more thoroughly. Its editor corresponded with the U.S. Surveyor General's office and discovered that the Monroe survey had been properly recorded. Moreover, a copy of the map, showing clearly that all of Pyramid Lake lay within the reservation boundaries, had been on file in the surveyor's office in Reno for over 12 years. The *Enterprise* concluded, "It will be seen from the foregoing that if the fishermen at Pyramid do not know the boundaries of the reservation, it is not the fault of the Government. . . ."[21] This paper was willing to defend a claim on the part of the Indians, if it were a legal and valid one, but advocated negotiation so that whites could share those fishing rights. Agents feared such a compromise settlement. In the face of overwhelming Anglo public opinion, once a crack were admitted to the exclusivity of Indian rights the numerical and technical advantage of the white population would overrun native use.

Not only did the local white citizens favor Anglo fishing rights on the lake, but even the military, charged with enforcement of the reservation boundaries, were not impartial. When the military once again arrived in January 1879, their enforcement was noticeably lacking in fervor. As the *Reno Weekly Gazette* reported, "they discovered four or five harmless fishermen and marched them over what they believed to be the line, and turned them loose."[22] "At the north eastern end of the lake the above parties [nine fishermen who were subsequently arrested] had their camp; two soldiers came to their place and led the fishermen to a point which they presumed was off the government agency. But the fishermen thought that they were not in the reserve and returned to their camp, the soldiers soon rejoining them and accepted an invitation to supper."[23] That menu undoubtedly featured fresh fish. The lieutenant of the troops was quoted by a local paper as saying, "It really seemed too bad to molest them."[24] Such lackadaisical enforcement of the boundaries was not destined to inspire respect for reservation limits.

The white fishermen had, in fact, no respect for those boundaries. They asserted that the boundary markers were arbitrary and bore no relation to the survey map. They even hinted that the agents had extended their domain far beyond congressional authorization for reasons of personal benefit. Further, the fishermen claimed that the northern part of the lake was so far above the agency buildings, and even the last of the stakes, that they must surely be well off the federal reserve. When the nine fishermen whom the troops had escorted beyond the half mile limit returned to the lake, they openly flaunted federal authority. They were charged with trespassing on an Indian reservation, and a grand jury found that there was sufficient evidence to hold them over for trial.[25]

The main issues in this case remained those of the entire frontier history—the size of the reservation and inclusion of the entire lake, the white frontier population's refusal to accept Indian control of valuable resources, the American belief of "proper use" (which meant intensive agricultural use) as validating possession, and the legal status of an executive order reservation.

From March until June tensions mounted. Newspapers throughout the area stoutly supported the fishermen, giving great publicity to their avowed intention not to "stop until the Reservation is destroyed and the thousands of acres of land now wasted upon a few dozen Indians, thrown open for occupancy as farms."[26] The press praised the "peaceful," "intelligent," "law-abiding" citizens who had lost their "just livelihood" through the self-serving actions of "empire-building" agents, and declared that the fishermen were "not infringing upon the rights of two or three dozen Indians who draw rations from Uncle Sam."[27] Anglo opinion was so anti-Indian that the agent took an unauthorized leave of absence and fled in fear of his personal safety. He wrote to Washington to justify the adandonment of his post: "It is my sincere belief that if I had remained on the reservation until this [court] decision had been announced, that it would have been at the risk of my life, having been the principal instigator and prosecutor in the actions."[28]

When the new agent arrived, he immediately discovered the degree of cooperation he was to receive from the U.S. Attorney, a federal appointee charged with providing counsel to government agencies and their officials. When the agent wrote the lawyer inquiring into the current status of the case, he received in reply: "I am not your legal adviser relative to reservation matters unless requested by the Indian Department. The Department would not like any interference with its plans. You must consult your superiors in office and if they refer you to me I will then advise you."[29] Rebuffed by such insistence on formal channels, so uncharacteristic of frontier politics and so unwieldy in this remote area, the agent wrote Washington:

> I have had your hearty moral support for which I sincer[e]ly thank you, but have had poor 'backing' and little aid, as facts go to show, from the Department of Justice. Whether they *could* not or *would* not heartily second my efforts I do not know, but the *results* have certainly been very unsatisfactory. I do know that the statutes are seriously at fault and I know this also, that, the trespassers are all Reno men, the U.S. Atty. is a Reno man, the citizens of Reno as a rule are covetous of the reservation and while they would not perhaps advise their fellow citizens to defy law, yet when Reno men are caught in its violation they give them their hearty sympathy.[30]

Contrary to popular opinion in the area, the overwhelming amount of actual evidence supported the existence of the reservation. The federal court found that the reservation boundaries totally included Pyramid Lake and that therefore the nine fishermen were guilty of trespass on federal property. One was further convicted of trading on an Indian reservation without a permit. However, sentence was indefinitely suspended while the arresting marshal, the prosecuting attorney, the judge, and the governor all signed a petition for presidential pardon.

The public, while relieved that penalty would not follow trespass, was still outraged by the evidence of reservation legality. One Reno paper proclaimed:

> The decision of the United States courts, that the Pyramid Lake reservation is valid and binding, is of great importance to Reno and the whole coast. It ties up the lake from all but the few lazy Indians who will have a monopoly of the fine fish which have hitherto been shipped to all parts of Nevada and California, within the reach of the railroads. This will not only deprive people everywhere of a real luxury, but, what is of more importance to us, it will kill a valuable industry, which would in time add materially to our resources. ... It is simply monstrous, that such a vast tract of land, enclosing the largest sheet of water in four states, where the largest ships could run easily, should be held in reserve for a couple of hundred Indians, who do not have use for a thousandth part of it. If the matter were put in i[t]s proper light before the department, we have no doubt but that it would be cut down at once.[31]

The editor here added a new argument to the old familiar ones of maximal resource use (according to American standards), the necessity of progress, and forthright appeal to profit and commercial self-interest. He suggested that fishery resources had previously been enjoyed by the white population, and that insistence on the legal boundaries at this late date would constitute a *deprivation*. Thus the weak BIA defense of Indian resources had permitted initiation of a usufruct claim. This pattern of weak federal defense, allowing local whites to develop vested interests, was to be repeated many times in the history of Pyramid Lake resources.

By October of the following year, sentence had not yet been passed on the convicted trespassers. The Indian agent was outraged: "This delay has had a most demoralizing effect on the community at large and especially on those having an interest in catching fish in the lakes. It is interpreted as impotence on the part of the government to punish offenders, or as a lack of inclination to enforce the few defective statutes that exist. Those whose interests prompted them to engage in this unlawful pursuit have been watching carefully the result of that suit and now conclude that there is nothing for them to fear, no penalty to be paid and now say 'I go a-fishing'."[32] He recommended that a squad of soldiers be sent to the lake to destroy the boats, tackle, and shacks of the trespassing fishermen who were gearing up for full-scale operations in the new fishing season.

One of the convicted but unsentenced fishermen returned to the lake with a horse-drawn seine net and proceeded to guarantee legal immunity to his employees; he kept a caravan of wagons hauling trout to Virginia City and Reno. Another enterprising soul, not willing to invest capital in his own transportation system, brought his loads to the stage station illegally maintained on reservation lands and posted his fish to market by U.S. Mail.[33] The agent appealed to Washington that "if a reservation is to be maintained here, I pray that it may be so conducted as to command the respect of all law-abiding citizens, by compelling an obedience to wholesome and just laws from vagabonds, drunkards, and common poachers. The meanest Indian of this Pah Ute tribe has more true manhood than these hoodlum invaders, and common justice demands that his moral and legal rights should be secured to him by the strong arm of the government." This had to be through federal agency, as "the civil power is ineffectual, in fact, to protect these Indians from the lawless."[34] His recommendations were ignored. The President pardoned the convicted fishermen late in 1880, an election year.[35]

The results foreseen and feared by the agents came to pass. White men continued to engage in commercial fishing at Pyramid Lake. In 1884 the military was called in again; three white commercial fishing operations were removed, their boats confiscated, and six boats owned by private parties in Reno, kept at the lake for occasional pleasure-boating and sport-fishing, were seized.[36] Thus it seemed that the agents were continuously unable or unwilling to keep the lake clear of whites interested in encroaching on Indian fishing rights.

Not only were the actions of white men on the reservation affecting Indian fishing, but so also were events far away in the California Sierra. Beginning about 1872, an extensive lumbering industry was developing in the forests of northern California, with eager markets in the boom towns of California and Nevada. In the high reaches of the Sierra, owners found it easiest and cheapest to dispose of sawdust and shavings by simply dumping them into the rapid streams which rushed downhill. These carried the waste out of the mountains, but it only reappeared farther downslope where the more gentle incline slowed the rapid rush of the waters. Reno began to complain of sawdust visible in the Truckee River. But the wood particles did not stop. Eventually they floated down-stream to lodge in the slow waters of the Truckee delta at Pyramid Lake. There the mass accumulated until a spring or summer flood should break it loose, etch a passage through the artificial sediment, and drag sawdust, by some reports, a mile or more into the lake itself. If it did not sink immediately to the bottom, wave action washed the sawdust back onto the shore, building a soggy, unsightly deposit around the southern edge of the lake. By 1875 the sawdust deposit had grown to such an extent that it closed the channel to Pyramid Lake entirely, rerouting water flow into shallow Winnemucca Lake to the east. It was evident to agents and inspectors that there was damage to the free swimming of fish into the lower river from the lake, and thereby danger to spawning. Inspector Vandever reported in 1875, "One of the chief means of support for the Indians on this reservation, is the trout fishery of the Truckee River and Pyramid Lake, the value and production of which is being impaired, and may ultimately be destroyed by the saw dust discharged into the river from the mills situated higher up the stream in the State of California."[37] Further, by damming the water flow the artificial delta also threatened agricultural use of the primary area of flat arable land, the shores of the lower valley.

Indians complained to the agent about the sawdust, and the agent wrote to the Bureau and to Washington newspapers. He also invited several prominent Nevadans, including Governor Bradley, to inspect the situation. The Governor reputedly exclaimed, "I never had an idea that there was so much saw dust in the world,"[38] and proceeded to lead the Nevada Legislature in requesting that California issue regulations to restrict the dumping of sawdust and other offal into the interstate river systems. Nevada further memorialized Congress to issue interstate pollution regulations. California mill-owners quickly developed an effective lobbying effort to defeat any such regulation by their own legislature. They were aided in this by the untimely occurrence of one of the periodic floods characteristic of the desert West, at the very time observers from California were inspecting the delta. This flash flood ripped out a bridge and a water flume in the lower Truckee before chiseling a narrow and shallow trench through the sawdust delta. The flood left a sizable deposit of sand and silt which then covered the sawdust from view, confusing the situation still more. The observers reported back to the California Legislature that the reported damage was an exaggeration, thus eliminating any hope of cooperation from that state.

If the mill-owners were to be required to burn their waste products instead of dumping them, it became evident that voluntary cooperation would not be forthcoming and that congressional intervention would be necessary. Agent Bateman took the issue to the Nevada delegation, but Congress did not act. By 1888, Senator Stewart could still report damage to the Pyramid Lake fisheries due to the "large quantities of sawdust that are constantly being sent down the river. . . . This is killing the fish in the Indian Reservation and filling up the entrance to Pyramid Lake, thus causing the water to flow off into Mud [Winnemucca] Lake. This is a very injurious to the Reservation."[39] He referred the matter to the Commissioner of Indian Affairs, defining it as an Indian problem even though the BIA, with no authority off-reservation, certainly did not have the necessary interstate powers to effect a solution. By this late date, periodic floods had covered much of the deposit of sawdust, and the new agent denied that there was any significant damage. Nevertheless, he documented the presence of large numbers of cuiui dead on the southern shores of the lake, floating sawdust a mile into the lake, and at least 8 inches of sawdust in the very channel of the riverbed. Further, he reported on the river branch leading to Pyramid Lake:

> On arriving at this point, we found what water there was in the river all running into Mud Lake branch. The river is very low, and if there was ten times the amount of water running in the stream as there is at the present time, not a drop would flow into Pyramid Lake. This evil should be remedied at the earliest possible moment; if not it will most

certainly prove disasterous [*sic*] to the fish in Pyramid Lake in the near future, as the waters of these lakes are strongly impregnated with alkali and unless they receive a supply of fresh water they will soon become so brackish that the fish cannot survive. This would be a great loss, not only to the Indians, but also to the citizens of this coast.[40]

His solution was to initiate a large-scale construction project, to build a dam across the Winnemucca Lake branch of the Truckee and force water into Pyramid. This alternative, within the power of the BIA, would not require authority over white citizens of either state, treating the symptom without affecting the cause. This initial request, in the name of preserving the fishery for both Indians and whites, was not acted upon until years later, and was at that time justified on the entirely different grounds of agriculture. Meanwhile, BIA personnel who were in a position to actually observe the conditions of Indians on the reservation continued to report, even until the turn of the century, that "Fish are and must be their chief support."[41]

After the trial and conviction of the nine fishermen in 1879, it became clear that the BIA did not intend to allow commercial Anglo operations on the lake. Large-scale poaching was ended there, but this was not the only trespassing problem. As early as the 1880s, private parties were in the habit of maintaining small boats at the shore for pleasure outings and occasional sport-fishing. While each party might only catch a few fish, individually constituting no threat to the Indian commercial market, the cumulative effect of the many such trespassers became substantial.

In 1884, when the military were making a final sweep of large-scale commercial operators, the lieutenant in charge noted "six [rowboats], belonging to parties living at Reno, and other distant points, who have been in the habit of bringing their families here for a few days fishing and pleasure."[42] The owners volunteered to remove these boats since, they said, the agent had never told them that they were violating any regulations. Agents for the next 30 years made minimal effort to protect the fishery from this persistent form of trespass. They did not consider it a threat; however, Indians did, and there was a steady stream of protest. In 1913, for instance, a meeting of the tribe drew up a petition for the BIA stating five major complaints. One was: "The white people come down from City of Wadsworth and Fallon, Nev. + some other place[s] and haunt [*sic*] and fishing on the reservation. we want this stopped and fish and games saved for the Indian."[43]

Younger Paiute men were less willing than their elders patiently to ask the agent to fulfill his duty and protect their rights. Two years after that unavailing petition, a group of youths went to Sutcliffe on the west side of the lake, where white-owned boats were still being stored, and carried them up into the sagebrush. The deputy sheriff was called from Reno and the agent ordered the young men to their homes. When the sheriff arrived and found the furor over, he proceeded to spend the rest of the afternoon fishing with one of the white boat-owners, after the craft had been retrieved from the hillside.

The Carson City *News* seized this opportunity to issue a racist article entitled "Indians in War Paint at Pyramid Lake."[44] It reported that 30 "bucks" displayed an "inclination and desire to destroy property belonging to white persons on the reservation and lake," and yet it did not ask by what right such property was on the reserve in the first place. A headline insinuated pointedly that the "braves" were "unarmed." While a destruction-crazed mob was implied, a careful reading of the article indicated that no damage to private property was actually committed. In fact, the only specific verbal threat was against the sole motor-driven boat. As early as 1869, Paiutes had complained about the noise of white fishing methods as detrimental to the fish and to native competition. Their deeply rooted value of peaceful fishing was especially insulted by this new innovation, the motorboat. Despite Paiute outrage, their protest was suppressed by the agent and flouted by the sheriff. The local press displayed the same scornful disregard of legitimate Indian protest as had the nineteenth-century papers.

Although the agent wrote a few years later, "I have had some trouble with the Indians by giving a permit for a white man to fish only for a day for the sport of catching a trout or two,"[45] he did not stop the practice. An inspector, visiting the reservation in early summer of 1920, recorded that

> there were probably forty automobiles at The Willows [Sutcliffe] and in that vicinity, and fishing boats were widely scattered on the adjacent

waters of the lake. . . . from such trespass more serious trespassing is developed and your inspector believes that the right of the Indians should be jealously guarded. The material point is that there are as many trespassers on Indian fishing rights as care to trespass. The squatter above "The Willows" has boats for hire. No notices against trespassing are observable anywhere. The superintendent does not appear to make any effort to abate this trespass. . . . Your inspector believes that Superintendent Oliver habitually and illegally gives permits (even if oral) to acquaintances to fish on the reservation. He believes that the trespass is encouraged by Special Agent L. A. Dorrington.[46]

The inspector recommended enforcement of the law against these trespassers but apparently was not heeded, for two years later a special agent reported that the situation was unchanged. This official again recommended confiscation of all boats on the lake not owned by Indians. He specifically mentioned the presence of that same motorboat which the youths had kidnapped seven years before.

By 1924, the agency had instituted a day-use fee to be purchased by non-Indians using the lake. This bureaucratic action simply validated and legalized the omnipresent trespass, thus abdicating any Indian claim to exclusive possession of the lake. Although the fee was minimal, it was continuously avoided by whites who believed that they had a just right to fish anywhere they pleased. The Superintendent wrote in 1924, "I hear that there are a number of people fishing and boating on Pyramid Lake without permits. . . . you [agency farmer] should 'drop in' frequently at Sutcliffe's and White's and ask to see permits; taking up all one-day permits, and collecting from all without permits and reporting their names and addresses to this office."[47]

The problem with this plan as a revenue-generating effort was its lack of enforcement, for at this time there was one agency farmer at Nixon and one tribal policeman. Neither had authority against non-Indians. Should a trespasser choose not to comply with BIA regulations, there was little they could do. Further, the perimeter of the lake was very large and several roads approached it from various Anglo towns. The two men simply could not patrol all these locations in addition to their regular duties. Tribal members complained of these problems to a Senate investigating committee in 1934, and as late as

1944 the tribe was still asking for "a court whereby we can prosecute non-Indians who poach illegally upon our domains."[48] It became clear that the tribe could pass all the fishing regulations it chose, claim legal rights to the fishery, or hold a reservation under federal trust relationships, but they had no power to enforce their rights or their rules. Without the cooperation of the BIA and other federal agencies, they could not control the lake.

The history of Anglo trespass on the Pyramid Lake fishery clearly shows that the federal government was reluctant to protect Indian use of these resources. Anglos were tolerated in direct trespass. They entered the reserve from its earliest moment in order to exploit the fishery on a commercial scale. When some of these men rashly flouted federal authority by returning to fish under the very eyes of the military, they were arrested and reluctantly convicted, but pardoned, much to the jubilation of the white community. In the course of this case it became clear that other federal officials, particularly the U.S. Attorneys, were unenthusiastic about defending Indian rights, and that even the BIA would defend federal property only under utmost provocation. Small-scale sporting trespass was tolerated throughout the nineteenth century and finally encouraged by the issuance of permits. Anglos encroached on the Pyramid Lake fishery in indirect ways as well. Polluting sawdust from timber cut and sawed in California prevented water from flowing into the lake and blocked fish from reaching the spawning beds in the upper river.

With the technological advances of the twentieth century, Anglos would find even more imaginative and more efficient ways of preventing Paiutes from enjoying their heritage of fish in Pyramid Lake.

EIGHT

Land Trespass

White men came to Pyramid Lake, drawn there by the rich natural products of the waters and of the pastures. They also came to take the land itself. While much of the Pyramid Lake Indian Reservation had value only for grazing, there were isolated pockets in the river valley where irrigation was possible. Along the western lakeshore a few small streams entered at infrequent intervals. These patches of arable land were the next quarry of Anglo exploitation. To further their ends, whites recruited the assistance of Congressmen and Senators who brought to bear all the power of their office. From the nineteenth until well into the twentieth century, official Washington aided and abetted the seizure of lands which had been promised to Pyramid Lake Paiutes as reserved tribal property.

When Agent Dodge first recommended Pyramid Lake as a prospective Indian reservation, only one white man lived in that district, with a cabin in the center of Truckee Meadows. In all likelihood he was the very same Williams at whose homestead the Pyramid Lake War began. Whoever he was, the man immediately left the area after the outbreak of hostilities.[1] However, this was not the end of white occupancy of lands set aside for Paiutes. As soon as the actual fighting was over, Dodge requested military assistance to exclude from the reservation "all persons except those authorized by law."[2] He specifically mentioned that non-Indian residents were committing "outrages" against Indian women. Such behavior was, of course, one of the accusations local whites made against Williams and his hired hands to explain the outbreak of the so-called Pyramid Lake War. Within a year, Dodge again requested that "the most stringent orders be sent to the Commanding Officer of the U.S. Army stationed here to assist in removing all intruders from the reservations when called upon by the Indian Agent. Trespasses and depredations of every conceivable kind have been committed on these Indians. They have been personally maltreated, and their property stolen, and even now, the miscreants are not satisfied, but are resorting to the most damnable intriguing to provoke a war."[3] Whatever assistance he received at this time was apparently insufficient. In the following year, 1861, the first permanent white settler, Joseph Fellnagle, established a 120-acre ranch on the prime bottomlands along the Truckee in the southern part of the reservation. In subsequent years agents repeatedly warned Fellnagle to quit federal lands and abandon his improvements. However, by 1890 his holding had more than tripled in size.

Fellnagle was not alone in this encroachment, for as soon as the railroad right-of-way was laid out in 1864 local whites swarmed over the reservation. They did not accept the existence of the reserve, established as it was by administrative fiat. Despite the Central Pacific's written promises neither to issue title nor to encourage entry until the legal status of the reservation was clarified, land-hungry whites assumed that here, as elsewhere along the tracks, alternate sections of land would soon be sold. The Indian agent, who in his own corruption was plotting the removal of Goat Island for private profit, did not put up stout resistance. Whites trespassed freely, and over the next two years a wave of settlers attacked the agriculturally usable bottomlands of the southern reservation. Between 1864 and 1865, at least 840 of these acres were occupied by white men, in violation of all legal authority. This seemingly small figure gained significance when compared with BIA estimates that only 12 –1500 acres of the entire reservation were arable with nineteenth-century irrigation technology.[4] Thus whites controlled over half of the agricultural lands at Pyramid Lake by 1865. All of these Anglo land holdings later grew rather than shrank, as the squatters gradually expanded onto the lands surrounding those first fields.

Not all of this trespass was the benign absorption of vacant and unused agricultural land. At even this early date, several Indians, among them Truckee John, were attempting to conform to agency farming demands. Truckee John fenced in a piece of property on the lower river, built a house, and raised horses, grass, grain, and vegetables. Local whites thought of him as a very "industrious" Indian, and agents held him up as an example which they hoped other Paiutes would copy. However, Truckee John's very attempt to meet Anglo cultural demands led to personal disaster. "His prosperity," a contemporary account reported, "it seems, aroused the jealousy and hatred of a mean, worthless and villainous white man 'Fleming' who brutally murdered the Indian near his ranch July 4th, 1867."[5] The situation was not quite that simple, however. Another source noted the important detail that "The Plan was concocted at the House of one Mr. Gates living near the Ranch of Truckee John By Alec Fleming and Edward Payne."[6] While Payne and Fleming disappeared from local history, Gates was the one who ended up in possession of Truckee John's ranch. So it seems that Gates, already squatted on Indian land, desired to increase his holding at minimal effort to himself by simply taking it away from a prosperous neighbor.

He took it by violence. The crime was committed on the 4th of July at about one o'clock in the afternoon and, one white neighbor wrote, a "more *Cold* Blooded Thing has never transpired here."[7] In a haze of patriotic drunkenness and directed by Gates' avarice, Fleming and Payne murdered Truckee John in a particularly ugly way which even offended the sensibilities of rather hard-bitten Nevadans, not normally repelled by the killing of Indians. The pair then proceeded toward the Comstock, killing at least two other Indians along the road.[8] The murderers openly proclaimed their actions and boasted that they were going to Virginia City, Gold Hill, and other places to raise a company of men to "clear out the Indians."[9]

Meanwhile Truckee John's widow, in the appropriate Paiute fashion, burned the house, fencing, and other personal possessions of the deceased and vacated the property. A government official later reported that the "tract of land has been abandoned, the Indians being afraid to locate on it, lest they meet with the same fate as its first occupant." This left the field open for Gates, who was undoubtedly delighted with the outcome. The government source continued, "No cognizance [has] been taken of the dastardly murder by the civil or the other authorities."[10] This murder made it clear to local white men that land could safely and profitably be taken away from Indians at Pyramid Lake. Paiutes perceived the threat and their resentment was intense, so intense that it lasted for generations. Over 70 years later, in 1937, when another land swindle was being discussed at a tribal meeting, at least three councilmen repeated the story of how Truckee John had "lost his life and his land." They had heard of the murder from their fathers, who had heard it from their fathers. These twentieth-century descendants knew clearly that, as in their own time, the cause of nineteenth-century trouble was "over the possession of land of the Indian."[11]

In the year 1867, when Truckee John was killed, white men had already begun to locate not only along the river bottoms but also at the small creeks and streams entering Pyramid Lake along its western shore. The long and dishonorable histories of several of these properties profoundly affected the economic development of the reservation, and for this reason warrant retracing. One such was a plot of land in a side canyon about 11 miles from the agency house. A man named Mullen drew water from a spring there, built a small house, planted a few fruit trees, and claimed a ranch of 10 acres in approximately 1864. He then utilized the surrounding 100 acres or so for grazing and soon became comfortably prosperous. About five years later, a military patrol warned him that he was illegally located on federal property. Mullen asserted that he had never heard this before, that no Indian agent had ever told him to leave or even visited him. This might have been inaccurate or it might have been a self-serving attempt to legitimize his actions. Two Indians, Numaga and Captain Jim, were Mullen's nearest neighbors and had a seasonal fishing station a few miles north along the lakeshore. A white neighbor reported that several years before the army arrived he had seen Numaga carrying Mullen an order from the Agency Farmer to quit the reserve. Despite this probable demand by the agency and the definite warning from the military that he leave, Mullen continued to reside there. After passage of the Desert Land Act in 1877, he filed for a patent title but was denied on the grounds that the land had already been within a designated Indian reservation at the time of his entry. Despite this, he sold out for a substantial profit to another Anglo, and the property was thereafter bought and sold numerous times without ever being legally challenged.

About 15 miles north of Mullen's ranch and directly across the lake from the famous pyramid, a character known locally as "Doc" Woods established a ranch on a small stream, fencing in 50 acres and using another 110. The creek provided not only reliable drinking water but also irrigation, which made the property desirable to whites. Since time immemorial, the spot had been used as a Paiute fishing camp. The Paiutes charged that Woods had "ejected members of the band who had settled there in order to enable him to establish his ranch."[12] This, like the case of Truckee John, was a reminder that the Pyramid Lake area was not vacant land, a wilderness, or an empty desert. Northern Paiutes had lived here long before whites arrived and continued to do so afterwards. If whites were to appropriate valuable locations, they of necessity had first to displace the previous inhabitants. Such displacement was resisted, resented, and remembered. Nevertheless, Doc Woods operated a stage relay station, planted an orchard and, in fact, made permanent settlement.

Thus, bit by bit, white men took land until, in 1869, they controlled no less than 80 percent of the usable river bottomland on the southern tongue of the reservation. At least two major ranches were established on the western side of the lake where probably no more than three or four additional inhabitable sites existed. Further, a large number of white men were fishing in the lake itself.

In 1865, the BIA agent at Pyramid Lake inquired from his superiors in Washington what authority he had over trespassers. He was reminded that the Federal Trade and Intercourse Act of 1834 stated "That the superintendent of Indian Affairs, and Indian Agents and Sub Agents, shall have authority to remove from the Indian Country all persons found thereon contrary to law, and the President of the U.S. is authorized to direct the military force to be employed in such removal."[13] The agent could forcibly remove squatters who were participating in any unauthorized activities on reservation lands, including, of course, farming and fishing. Naturally, the white trespassers refused to acknowledge this authority. The Commissioner of Indian Affairs then requested and received authorization for military assistance to clear the squatters from the Pyramid Lake Indian Reservation. In his annual report, the Commissioner related that "Upon their [the squatters] being notified by the superintendent to leave, and their refusal to obey the order, a small detachment of soldiers accompanied the superintendent to the reservation, and the intruders were compelled to leave it; since which no further difficulty of the kind has occurred."[14]

However, this military action did not sufficiently impress the local whites, for during the following year they made additional inroads onto reservation lands. Several of the original trespassers simply sold out to other white men, who also undoubtedly had full cognizance of the illegal nature of the title thus acquired. In 1869 the military was once again called out. The lieutenant in charge, J. M. Lee, reported a wide range of illegal activities, including many white fishermen, a few illegal traders, several squatters, and extensive grazing interests operating on the reservation. He warned that continued toleration of such trespasses "would lead to greater and more considerable impingements on the rights of the Indians."[15] He issued notice to the squatters to quit the reserve.

The following year the squatters were all still there, and in March 1870 Lieutenant Lee returned once again to Pyramid Lake. Primarily concerned with fishermen, Lee again warned off one George Frazier, who had a home and extensive property holdings. Frazier declared his intention to leave; yet later he reappeared as the licensed reservation trader with extensive ranching interests, conveniently (and legally) centered at the agency house. Another Anglo named Belknap Bowers, also warned off the year previously, had resumed fishing by the time Lee made his second visit. When faced with stiff military threats of his immediate bodily removal and subsequent court prosecution, Bowers replied that he would now abandon his illegal enterprise. Nevertheless, he apparently simply ceased fishing and turned to farming instead. He later sold his 80-acre spread at a considerable profit. Thus, as the Lieutenant and the Indian agents had foreseen, one form of encroachment did lead to greater and more offensive trespass.

On his return trip to the lake, Lieutenant Lee removed a white man from Truckee John's property, the second to so occupy it since the Indian's murder. Doc Woods was conveniently not at home when the Army called, but they tacked a notice on his door demanding that he leave federal property within 20 days; this threat was never followed up. Lee pleaded special consideration in the case of Mullen, who contended that he had received the permission of his neighbor Numaga to settle there, a power which no native headman would have had in reality. Mullen further argued that he had not known he was on reserved lands until the patrol the previous year, that his land was near the still-ambiguous borderline, and that he was clearly off the lake and not fishing. Lee suggested that he be either bought out or permitted to lease his ranch from the Indian Bureau. Federal financial records reveal that Mullen neither paid any rent on the ranch nor did the government purchase the land or foreclose on it.[16]

Time and again, both squatters and fishermen simply acquiesced to the demands of the military, waited quietly for them to leave, and then peaceably returned to their own private pursuits on federal property.

Having gone as far as military threats, it might seem odd that Indian agents failed to pursue the matter with the next logical action, court prosecution. But the reason was simple: they despaired of any hope of success. One of the more active agents of this period bemoaned, "If I were satisfied that the juries of this state would sympathise [*sic*] and see the justice of my action, I would promptly act. — but such is not the case, they rather feel kindly disposed toward such violations of law and will accept nothing but the most positive legal proofs."[17] He and his fellow agents observed the attempts to prosecute fishermen who had openly operated on the lake itself, indisputably within the reservation, and the delays and defeat which those cases met, despite a favorable court ruling. It was only with utmost effort that such token protection of Indian rights could be attained in face of prevailing Western public opinion, even within the federal court system.

Thus trespass continued. By 1873, a new agent reported that Doc Woods still occupied his 200-acre ranch. Woods told him that "he had been there nine years, and have been ordered off the reserve by every Agent that had preceeded me during that time, but he had convinced them that he was not on the reserve at all. Then he went on to tell me that there was no Pyramid Lake or Truckee reservation, that one was once laid out including lands where Wadsworth now stands and down the river for six miles but under the Nye administration [about 1861] it was broken up and lands sold off."[18] Either local whites did firmly believe such rumors, or they were trying to convince gullible eastern agents, who found themselves without knowledge of their own authority or even a map of the territory in their charge, that there was in fact no trespass. Fishermen were using the same excuses to justify their illegal activities. In addition, the local white population questioned the legal existence of the Pyramid Lake Reservation on grounds of its ambiguous founding and its as-yet undeclared executive order status. Ever since 1864, the situation had been further complicated by the potential railroad claim to right-of-way across the southern portion and to a 20-mile belt of alternate sections of land. In that year, as we have seen, a rush of white men entered the reserve to establish claims which they hoped would later prove valid as soon as the federal survey reached the area. Frontiersmen believed that Indians and whites could not live together, that Indians had to yield to white claims, and that inevitably therefore Indians had to remove from the proximity of the railroad and Pyramid Lake. This ideology constituted the hope of these squatters.

In the early 1870s, the Commissioner of Indian Affairs stated in his annual report that the railroad claims might be valid. Local squatters, of course, were overjoyed. Rumors of imminent success of the railroad claim led to additional major land entries along the river, including seizure of a 320-acre plot by a man named Olinghouse. On the western shore, white men moved in, anticipating abandonment of the entire reserve. There in Hardscrabble Creek Canyon, where Numaga and Captain Jim had previously lived, "the Whiteheads took the land and water and forced these Indians to abandon their holdings."[19] The resident agent himself was scheming to remove Anahoe Island, purportedly as a goat farm. Rumors escalated until, in 1875, the new Indian agent telegraphed the Commissioner in panic: "Is Pyramid lake reservation abandoned or to be? White men are rushing upon it and I am powerless through ignorance of facts to prevent them. Indians are full of anxiety which I can't allay."[20] Belknap Bowers, many times warned of his trespass, told a great number of Indians that "the reserve was broken up—sure—and he was glad of it as he would get his old ranch and fishing ground." Another habitual offender declared to a Paiute that "the reservation was broken up and [he] was glad of it—and that he had come to jump my [the Indian's] ranch and *hold it this time*—he said—he would claim it, but I might stay and work it. He didn't care what came of the other Indians as they would all be driven off from their land, and we would go too if he hadn't 'jumped it' as other white men wanted it and he 'jumped' to keep them off." Yet another Anglo threatened that "he was going to build a house on my claim and was going to buy fish."

A whole regiment of white men were eager to enter the reserve and were doing all within their power to intimidate the Indians. Nevertheless, Paiutes remained firm in their desire to remain on their land. When the agent asked Captain Jim, an Indian leader and near neighbor of the squatter Mullen, "What do you say about this matter?" he spoke for many: "I want this reservation to stay. I want to live here and do what the Government tells me. Don't want any white men on the reserve."[21] The Indians asked the agent to protect the integrity of their reserve. The military was called out again while the agent entered into extensive negotiations with the railroad over possible land exchanges. It was not until 1878 that the Commissioner of Indian Affairs and his legal counsel firmly asserted the priority of the reservation over railroad claims, putting an end to white rumors and hopes of legal entry. The Commissioner ordered the Army to remove trespassers from a minimum of one-half mile of the lakeshore and requested a resurvey of the reservation perimeter.[22]

Meanwhile the white fishermen had lost their case in the courts, and yet their punishment was still pending. The new Indian agent found himself without any cooperation at all from the U.S. Attorney and was unsure how to proceed. He was confused by the ambiguous authorization that he could use "all available force at his command" to remove trespassers. "I have," he wrote, "pen and tongue, muscle and employees. Shall I use these? And if they fail, then What? Please send me *explicit instructions* what to do in the *various contingencies* that may arise. I want to be ready to act *promptly, legally, effectually.* These men want *delay*."[23]

And delay they got. The situation became even more complicated in 1874 when a presidential proclamation recognized the reservation as an executive order reserve. Many local Anglos and Indian agents interpreted this to be the first official creation of the reserve. Therefore, it appeared that many of the squatters' claims, dating back as they did into the mid 1860s, preceded the federal withdrawal of this land for Indian purposes. If such were the case, virtually all the arable land and much of the valuable grazing would be legitimately held by white men.

Much of the subsequent controversy focused on the claims of "Doc" Woods and the Whitehead brothers. Woods had been denying for years that the reservation existed at all, and the Whitehead brothers had been ignoring agents' nearly annual demands to abandon their claim.

A post road from Fort Bidwell, Oregon, traversed the western shore of Pyramid Lake for about 20 miles before running over the pass at Mullen's place and heading for Reno. It was apparent to the company which held the U.S. Mail contract that somewhere along the lakeshore stretch they needed a relay station. Doc Woods obligingly took over this duty and cooperated with the local white fishermen by accepting shipments of illegally caught trout to be mailed to the Reno market. When challenged about his right to squat on this land, Woods justified his claim on grounds of his service to the community and the necessity of the U.S. Mails to continue.

The Whitehead brothers, on the other hand, had a far more elaborate defense. J. W. Whitehead wrote:

> It seems that as early as 1859 a tract of country was set aside as an Indian Reservation but the boundarys was never established very definitely, and in 1865 one Eugene Monroe made a survey of a tract of land at the mouth of the Truckee river, and run a base line, and made a

triangular sketch of the whole lake, from one mountain peak to another, at a distance of some two miles from the lake shore, but there was never any monuments set up at the North end or the West side of the lake, and no one knows where the reservation line runs on those two sides. . . . S. D. Wood[s] made his location in 1866 and has paid taxes on it for fourteen years. In April 1871 I made my location which is two and a half miles from the lake shore and twenty miles from the reservation house. . . . The land had not been surveyed and there was no chance to get a title to it until 1877, when the Desert Land law was passed by Congress. So in 1878 I had an isolated survey made of two hundred and twenty seven acres and duly entered in the Land office at Carson, and some three weeks ago I went to Carson and made my final payment of one dollar per acre. Although I live half a mile outside what they call the reservation line [the Commissioner's make-shift half-mile perimeter], and have got the Receivers receipt for my money, I was notified by Mr. Spencer [the Indian agent] a short time ago to leave the reservation or all my buildings and fences would be confiscated and destroyed. . . . we have made our location in good faith and all we have got is here, and it would work a terrible hardship on us to be put off at this date. If the Government had extended the survey at the proper time, I could have taken a homestead claim for twenty dollars and now I have paid out over three hundred dollars to the Government and I am still annoyed by the Indian agent.[24]

Issuance of the patent title was denied to the Whiteheads on the grounds that this land was within a legally designated federal Indian reservation. They were once again served notice to quit the reservation posthaste.

A variation on the Whitehead argument was to have damning effect upon Indian land rights at Pyramid Lake. The *Reno Weekly Gazette* enunciated this posture on February 5, 1880:

Some of the old white dwellers by the shore [were served] notice to quit, on the ground that they are within the limits of the Indian reservation. Dr. Woods, the Whiteheads, and Mullin [*sic*] have lived there and cultivated their farms for many years in undisturbed possession. . . . On proper representation of the facts it is probable that [Interior] Secretary Schurz will agree to narrow the limits of the reservation. At any rate, he will see that no injustice is done to the respectible white citizens who have lived so long at the lake.[25]

That vested interest once established did legitimize the initial trespass was an argument which would be raised again and again. The BIA's inability to root out the trespassers at the very beginning enabled the development of an established financial investment, which, in the eyes of the American legal system, had to be acknowledged and perhaps even protected. Initial inroads, once tolerated, gained legitimacy.

The cause of this lethal delay was easily discovered. Following the precedent of the fishing case, in 1880, the Pyramid Lake agent requested the U.S. Attorney to file suit against certain trespassers, among whom was a fellow named Watson. The Attorney soon reported, "Nothing has been done in any of the cases, except I had Watson brought up for judgment when he satisfied the judge that he had not taken fish, but was simply keeping a stage station on the mail road. It seemed a very hard case, and we all concluded to let the matter stand over with the other cases, hoping a final disposition of them at Washington. I can't help thinking that Watson must have been misrepresented to you. He has a wife and a young family, and I confess my sympathies are awakened in his behalf."[26] The agent was outraged by the attorney's statement and reacted with biting logic:

> Here the matter stands, and plenty of others, present and prospective trespassers, watching the result of these cases, and by this decision, decide what mischief they may or may not do with impunity. Watson lives where [he] has lived for nearly or quite two years. Notified repeatedly to vacate the reservation, he hides behind a mail bag and evokes pity on account of a "wife and young family." His "wife and young family" occupy today a ranch which belongs to the Indians. More than a score of Indians with each a "wife and young family" are exiles from this reservation today—vagabonds turned loose on the scattered community simply because there was no irrigable ranch to give them. This one is easily irrigated and is large enough for two families. "I confess that my sympathies are awakened in behalf" of those who have been wronged and robbed by this man and others like him. But Watson "satisfied the judge that he had not taken fish"—did he satisfy him that he had not robbed two Indians, with a "wife and young family," of their only home and driven them out into the desert to dig wild potatoes, hunt ground squirrels, or starve? Did he satisfy the judge that he was not appropriating to his own use the legal, moral, rightful prop-

erty of others? The quoted letter informs us that "the entire sentiment of the community is against the enforcement of the penalties in these cases." No doubt of it; for every trespasser on Pyramid Lake, so far as I know his citizenship, is a member of that "community." It seeks, I am informed, by petition and congressional representation, to have the entire reservation thrown open to sale and the Indians crowded off from the farthest end of the log. It demands the *whole*, but *would* take, say half, but in any event is "averse" to enforcing U.S. Statutes against a dozen of their community who "don't take fish", or even those who do. As I said above, other trespassers are watching the result in these cases. If those found guilty are allowed to escape the penalty of law, a whole band of law-breakers will invade this and Walker River Reservation and flaunt their defiance in my face. I dread the result. ... I say let the lawless know that the Indian has rights—some small rights at least—which white men must respect. This man Watson has invaded those rights, has been found guilty, has acknowledged his guilt, has had the sentence hanging over his head for months, continues to break a just law, refuses to cease its violation, is daily and hourly perpetrating a serious wrong on the innocent and unoffending, taking bread from the mouths of others as hungry as those of his own family, to feed his own wife and children; and thus allowed to trample on law and good order, on justice and right he is a living example to encourage others to do all the wrong that he is doing.[27]

In 1884, the military once again removed large numbers of fishermen from the lake, but they did not dislodge the squatters, since they had no specific orders concerning land trespass. The stage stations were still being operated. Whitehead, Mullen, and Woods's successor-in-interest Mr. Symonds all assured the patrol that they never caught any fish, not even for their own use, and therefore they were not fishing trespassers. They continued their occupation, and Paiutes continued to ask for the undisturbed possession of the reservation which had been promised to them 20 years before. The agent wrote, "One thing that they (the Indians) do not just understand is why the trespassers are not removed from the reservation. ... they think the law is all for the white man and none for the Indian."[28]

Trespassed holdings passed from one white man to another as valuable real property. Titles to these lands were accepted, legal documents drawn up concerning them, and taxes paid to local and state entities. New entries were still being made and tolerated by the administration. In 1886, James Sutcliffe fenced off 30 acres along the lakeshore where the Reno road branched off. There he built a fishing center and today, still held by whites, this is probably the most valuable piece of property on the reservation. Whites grabbed the last scraps of land in the Truckee bottoms by the end of the 1880s, leaving only the delta and river mouth, directly under the windows of the agency house, in Indian hands. Not only did these white squatters dislodge Paiutes and fence off parcels of land, but they proceeded to utilize a wide range of other reservation resources without compensation. Their cattle grazed far from their homesteads on Indian lands. The white men fished. They cut the scarce timber for cabins and firewood, especially from the cottonwood groves in the Truckee canyon where so many of them were settled. They took water from the river for irrigation as necessary to their farming. Some even drew water out of the BIA ditch built by Indian labor. It was not simply a matter of land, but of total, illegal exploitation of the resources of Pyramid Lake, reserved in the name of the Paiutes by the federal government.

Large-scale interests were not to be outstripped by the nibbling of petty entrepreneurs. The Central Pacific Railroad held 773 acres for the actual roadbed, maintenance dock, and assorted other purposes. The State of Nevada itself withdrew and platted an entire township of 120 acres in 1867. Within five years it successfully laid claim to an additional 421 acres for highways, schools, and other purposes.

In 1890, the Indian agent at Pyramid Lake summarized the situation:

> Upon Pyramid Lake Reserve tillable lands comprise only about 2,000 acres, and fully one-half of that amount is in possession of and cultivated by whites. The last mentioned are also far more valuable than any other bottom lands on the reserve, being easily irrigated and at the same time safe from serious damage by overflow of the river, while those bottom lands held by the Indians are almost all submerged [in times of spring flooding]. In consequence applicants for homes on the reserve can not be furnished with lands upon which to establish themselves and make a living. The railroad town of Wadsworth is built upon the southern end of the reserve and about one-fourth of the reservation Indians make that place their home. . . . Some of these would

locate near the agency school and send their children to it, but there is no land available for such purpose. . . . The validity of the claims of whites to the lands within the boundary of Pyramid Lake reserve should be tested and the vexatious question of the title set at rest.[29]

Not only had Paiutes been reduced from a large aboriginal holding to a delimited reserve, but they were being squeezed off even that. The BIA appeared to be helpless in the face of white encroachment. Paiutes were indeed strangers in their own land.

Bad though this situation was, it was destined to become worse. A new and unexpected threat soon loomed over the reservation. Hidden within the BIA budget bill of 1891 was a rider stating that a presidential commission should be appointed to "enter into negotiations with the Indians of Pyramid Lake Reservation for the cession and relinquishment of the southern portion of their reservation, such cession and relinquishment not to extend farther north than the north line of township 22 north, or the extension of the same."[30]

This apparently sudden move was related to other changes in U.S. Indian policy. A few years before, in 1887, Congress had passed the General Allotment Act, which had proposed to break up reservation properties as then held in trust for the tribes as wholes. Rather, lands were to be consigned in small parcels to individual Indians, and any land discovered "excess," thus freed, would be opened to Anglo settlement. The BIA would thus in a few years become superfluous, as trust properties requiring its administration gradually diminished. Many Congressmen believed that the government should "get out of the Indian business," for by now active warfare with tribes was over in most areas and Indians no longer posed a military threat. The majority of tribes had been subdued and restricted to reservations. Anglos had taken over the great bonanza of Indian land, but the West was already filling up and yet more whites wanted cheap Western land. Strong pressures were therefore put on the now militarily and politically helpless tribes to accept reduced reservations or individual allotments. In this way, a few more scraps of land could yet be transferred to white ownership.

The position of the new presidential commission to Pyramid Lake in this general historical movement was made clear in its own final report:

> Whereas whites have settled upon and made claim to considerable portion of the improved and improvable lands in the southern portion of said reservation; and whereas the village of Wadsworth is located within the boundaries thereof and the land and title thereto, in that portion of the reservation, is complicated and somewhat uncertain; and whereas the rights of the Indians to that portion of the reservation, namely, the southern portion, have been invaded, and they have been thereby deprived of the benefit and advantage of these lands, although justly entitled thereto; and whereas it is considered and deemed best that a cession or relinquishment of a portion of the southern part of said reservation by the Indians aforesaid to the United States upon just and equitable terms and conditions, and fair compensation to be paid therefor by the United States be made, that justice be done and further complications in the matter be avoided. . . .[31]

It was obviously the purpose of these negotiations to legalize the trespass of whites on that section of the reservation which they already so thoroughly dominated, to justify continued Anglo occupation, and to invalidate any Indian claim to these properties.

Toward these ends a commission was duly appointed, to be headed by Ebenezer Ormsbee. When these men arrived at Pyramid Lake in early September, they found that a large number of the Indians were off working in the harvest fields of the surrounding countryside. The proposed meeting was postponed until the end of the month when they held two days of discussion. The commissioners' report could not conceal the Paiutes' reluctance to relinquish this large land parcel:

> We were forcibly reminded by the Indians that not only the valuable lands on the southern portion of the reservation were occupied by whites, but also those around Pyramid Lake and those between Pyramid and Winnemucca lakes on the north, and within the proposed limited reservation, were in possession of white ranchmen, and that as a condition precedent to considering the proposition to relinquish the southern portion they, the Indians, must be guaranteed the peaceable possession of the proposed diminished reservation, and that all white intruders must be removed therefrom by the Government.[32]

After investigation, the commission substantiated the Indian complaint. "We found," they said, "every tract of improvable land thereon [in the southern portion of the reservation proposed for reduction] occupied by whites."³³ This southern portion had a total of 18,700 acres. The commission reported that 1,300 of these acres were actually under cultivation, and that in their judgment only 2,100 acres more were improvable under existing technology. Thus 3,400 acres in this zone had any value agriculturally, and of these, they stated, over 3,000 were already possessed by white men.

On investigation of the Indians' claims of intruders on the western portion of the reservation, the Ormsbee Commission again documented extensive white landholdings. They reported that white men "make claim to and are in possession and enjoyment of substantially every available acre of the reservation on the west side of the lake that is improvable. With the exception of two very insignificant patches occupied by the Indians, not an acre is left for the Pah-Utes, although there are many families of them wanting a place, just such places, too, as these ranches would furnish."³⁴ The commission estimated that white men in this area removed an aggregate income of at least $5,700 per year, a sizable amount of money in those days. Not only were these men directly benefiting from the property of the Paiute Indians, but they were also preventing the rightful owners from making a comparable profit. What is more, the commission said in condemnation, "all of the intruders in this portion of the reserve have always known that they were trespassers."³⁵

In addition to the downstream and the lakeshore trespassers, the commission discovered large herds of cattle and sheep grazing between Pyramid and Winnemucca lakes. Some of these cattle belonged to the Truckee River squatters, but others were part of large-scale grazing operations based off-reservation. The commission estimated that these illegally grazed cattle ate off at least $1,000 worth of pasture annually.

Paiutes refused even to discuss a reduction of the reservation until they had a full commitment from the government to enforce trespassing laws against all these squatters on their remaining land. Such a promise was given and written into the agreement.

Negotiations then began over a new line of demarcation for the southern, riverine portion of the reserve. The line agreed upon was the northern edge of T21N. This boundary, the commission explained, "was fixed at this point rather than farther north for the reasons that all white settlers on and along the Truckee River were located south of said line; and the next ranch north, adjoining thereto, is claimed by an Indian, and valuable to the Indians for wood growing thereon; and also this line secures to the Indians valuable fishing interests on the river between this point and Pyramid Lake."[36] This line thus satisfied the purposes of the commission.

The piece of land to be cut off included the town of Wadsworth, where many Indian families were residing. The government had recently built a school there for their children, who had been rejected by the Anglo public-school board in town. To protect this federal investment, the commission exempted from withdrawal a plot of 110 acres around the school. This would remain in government hands and be administered as part of the Pyramid Lake reservation. The commission reasoned that Paiute families then living in Wadsworth could remove to this oversized schoolyard and there remain under government supervision if they so chose. The school would thus become a tiny, isolated reservation in and of itself. Contrary to their explicit instructions, the commission made no plans to compensate these Indians for improvements they had made in the relinquished portion of the reservation, homes and gardens which would have to be abandoned in their removal to the school plat. The double standard was clear. While white property rights, developed in trespass on lands to which they had no legal claim, were to be protected and legitimized by a presidential commission, legitimate Indian property rights, developed on lands guaranteed them by presidential executive order, were to be sacrificed freely and without compensation.

In return for the estimated 18,700 acres of land to be yielded, the government agreed to pay the Pyramid Lake Paiutes $20,000 worth of cattle, to be purchased for them and delivered to the reservation within a year of congressional approval of the agreement. This was slightly more than $1 per acre, an evaluation below the homestead fees charged by the government even for unimproved lands. If only arable acreage was considered, the amount was approximately $6 an acre, at a time when agricultural land was drawing a far greater price in land-short Nevada. Based on commission estimates, the total value of the proposed cattle herd was significantly less than the value of the crops removed illegally from the reservation by these squatters in any two-year period. Thus by any rational measure, this real estate transaction, proposed and arranged by the Indians' own trustee, was a very poor business deal indeed. It hardly constituted the "just and equitable terms and conditions" with "fair compensation" and "justice" which the commission had so rhetorically proclaimed for itself. There was apparently very little negotiation with regard to the terms of this agreement. Indians were presented with a package which they were told they could either accept or reject. The commission secured the consenting marks of the majority of the adult males at the conference. Lacking a census of the reservation population, and therefore having no idea whether this represented a majority of the Paiutes who actually resided at Pyramid Lake, the commission then took "considerable pains to visit scattered members of the tribe at Reno and elsewhere who were not present at the general council held at the agency."[37] The commission asserted that these persons "belonged" at Pyramid Lake rather than at one of the other Paiute agencies or to the portion of the tribe attached to no reserve. The agreement was once again translated and additional signatures obtained. In this way, 133 marks were affixed to the agreement and it was returned to Washington with the appropriate report.

The Ormsbee Commission was appointed to further a policy designed for administrative convenience, to avoid anticipated difficulties, and to accommodate the trespassing Anglos. Through its actions a way was opened for squatters to acquire legally through homestead purchase from the United States government those lands which they illegally occupied in an Indian reservation. The commission did its work well.

By this time, 1891, treaties, which required only Senate approval, were no longer being negotiated between the United States government and any Indian tribe. The Ormsbee negotiations, therefore, produced an agreement, entered into with participation by both parties, which needed approval by both houses of Congress before it could be binding on the federal government. Therefore the Ormsbee Agreement was duly submitted to Congress but there failed of passage.

The tantalizing hope which the Ormsbee Commission held out to the squatters, of actually obtaining the most valuable portion of the reservation, only whetted the appetites of desirous local whites. Thwarted by congressional rejection, these interests sought a new spokesman, and found him in the senior senator from Nevada, William Stewart. Stewart was eager to serve his constituency and seized the opportunity. He openly proclaimed his advocacy in an 1892 letter written to a lawyer for the squatters. "We can then secure a release of the lands on the north side of the Lake which would be of no use to the Indians. There would then be no excuse for retaining them. Tell Mr. Calligan [who at this point held the Whitehead Ranch] that I will use my best endeavors to get his land and others similarly situated released. . . . I will look into the matter further and see if I can get the Reservation reduced as Mr. Calligan desires."[38] It was very clear that throughout the late nineteenth century Senator William Stewart of Nevada actively served the interests of the trespassers on the Pyramid Lake Reservation and exercised all his power and influence, which were considerable, to legalize their cupidity.

Seeing the vulnerability of Pyramid Lake lands, Stewart proposed a new scheme. Arguing that it was too inefficient to continue administration of two large reservations so near each other as were Pyramid and Walker River, and that development of both would be far too expensive, he urged that the entire Walker River reserve be abandoned. Further, he suggested that the portion of Pyramid Lake Reservation north and west of the lake itself should be relinquished, as well as the southern riverine lands. He asserted that Paiutes did not live in these areas, although clearly they did not do so simply because whites had already seized all the possible living sites. Here Senator Stewart, serving not only the narrow special interests of whites on the lower river but those of all squatters on the reservation, proposed Indian surrender of all lands already illegally appropriated. Therefore he proposed a bill for a new commission to renegotiate the agreement with the Paiutes, this time relinquishing the north and western shores of the lake as well as the southern portion of the reservation in the Truckee Valley and all of Walker River. His proposed bill was approved for passage by the Indians' only voice in Washington, the Commissioner of Indian Affairs, and by his superior, the Secretary of the Interior. This bill failed when Congress feared that Indians would not accede to such a massive land swindle. Taking this problem into consideration, Stewart submitted a new bill[39] the following year in which no commission would be sent, but rather the same land transfers would be dictated by unilateral decree of Congress with or without Indian consent. Again the highest authorities in charge of Indian affairs approved this bill. If it were to become law, the Walker River Paiutes, stripped of their own lands, would be moved to Pyramid Lake. Under the guise of benevolent Progress and to provide pragmatically for the survival of this increased population on a reduced land base, Stewart's new bill allowed a quarter of a million dollars for construction of an irrigation project at Pyramid. This plan would be ten times more costly than the Ormsbee Agreement, although Stewart argued that the sale of Walker River lands would partially compensate the government for the expense.

The Indian Agent at Pyramid Lake was outraged by this proposal and spoke out for the rights of the Indians. He immediately wrote Washington in protest: "Indians of both of the reserves are unanimous in their opposition to the propositions contained in the bill and it would require the strong arm of the Government to *force* them to change their opinions." He outlined the areas of opposition, primarily the extreme reduction of the land base and the loss of control over the fishery. He said that this bill would

> make these Indians forever a burden upon the Government and subject them to poverty and servitude the rest of their lives. It would crush out of them the present spirit of progress and civilization, and make them idle, worthless paupers, as are many of the other tribes. . . . To, now, by a selfish piece of legislation, solely to gratify the whims of a few clamorous tresspassers and the interest of a souless corporation, undo all the good that has been accomplished during the past twenty years; place a chain of slavery about their loins and tell them that from now on they must live in poverty and shame. . . . [This] would be the blackest blot on the pages of Indian history.[40]

The agent believed that the initial defeat of the Ormsbee Agreement had been engineered by the Carson and Colorado Railroad, which passed through Walker River and had very strong interests in breaking up that reservation. The corporation was joined by cattlemen, ranging in the deserts to the north of Pyramid Lake, who wanted to get in on the windfall of easily acquirable title. Thus, he said, vested Anglo interests, hoping to get a share of the spoils, had opposed the initial limited agreement, increased the stakes, found a spokesman in Senator Stewart, maneuvered Indians out of the process entirely, and resubmitted their requests for a now-massive land grab.

The United States Board of Indian Commissioners, an advisory policy board without any political power, also opposed Senator Stewart's bills. They pointed out that the Carson and Colorado Railroad was at the time violating its agreement with the Walker River Paiutes by means of which it had acquired a right-of-way in return for free passes. When the passes turned out to be a more expensive habit than originally envisioned, the railroad hoped to free itself of the bonds of the agreement by getting the reservation eliminated. One commissioner wrote, "It is my belief, which is shared by nearly all the people I conversed with in Nevada, that this railroad company is responsible for the attempts to remove the Walker River Indians from their valuable lands, and thus free themselves from their contract and open the Indian lands to white settlers."[41] He also pointed out that the Walker River and Pyramid Lake Paiutes had never been particularly friendly, and that each group desired to retain its own separate reservation. The Indians, therefore, would oppose the merger. Perhaps most damning was the objection that while Senator Stewart's bill required the abandonment of Walker River and the removal of those Indians to Pyramid Lake within a year of passage, the irrigation system needed to support this tremendously increased population on a reduced land base had no stated date of construction. Thus, Indians might have to endure for many years before they received the water promised them. Considering all these facts, the Board of Indian Commissioners opposed the Stewart bills, saying, "The main features of Senate bill No. 99 are, in my opinion, very injurious to the interest of the Government and the Indians."[42] Stewart's plans once again failed to win congressional approval.

When the Ormsbee Agreement had been rejected, the government's specific promise to clear the reservation of illegal squatters had also failed to become obligatory. No further attempts had been made in the 15-year interim to solve this problem. In 1905, Numaga, the man who in his youth had made war against the whites unsuccessfully, wrote a petition to Washington:

> The Indians have not much left—and it makes my heart sick, when I see the injustice done my people. If the land in question had been held by white people, and white people were the intruders,—How long would it have been kept out of the courts? The White man would call for some kind of settlement, and would get it.—but the Indian—no—. Friend Commissioner I am an old man, my hair is gray with age, maybe I will not live long, (nobody can tell), I respectfully ask you to help us people to get the land unlawfully held by the Whites, and either eject them from the Reservation, (which the Agent here ought to do, according to law), or give us settlement for the land of which we are being robbed with the full consent of the Govt officials in charge.[43]

While Numaga hoped, forces beyond his control were trying yet another scheme to acquire lands for the white trespassers. A rider was tacked on to the BIA budget bill in 1904, extending the general allotment policy specifically to the Pyramid Lake Indian Reservation without the consent of the residents.[44] Couched in the benign terminology of providing irrigation for the reserve, each Indian was to be allotted the munificent sum of 5 acres of land. The remainder of the reservation was to be sold to white settlers under federal homestead laws to pay for the irrigation project which Paiutes had never requested. In this way, Indians were to be restricted to uneconomical parcels of land, while the squatters could easily legalize their claims to far larger pieces of the remainder by filing for title. Such a plan was certainly not in the best interests of the Paiutes for, as the agent wrote in 1905, "Five acres of land is not enough to support the Indian allottee. In many cases upon this reservation Indians have from 15 to 25 acres of river bottom land under a first-class irrigation system. They have cleared and acquired this land by years of labor. It does not seem right to deprive them of it now, and if the new proposed reclamation ditch is to cover this land the act should be amended so as to give these Indians at least 25 acres under the new system. Neither Indian nor white man can make a living upon 5 acres of land in Nevada."[45] Fortunately, no specific date for implementation was ever stated.

While a survey was made in preparation, the actual division was never made final. Nevertheless, this bill remained hanging over the heads of the Paiutes until 1934, threatening imminent doom to Indian land title at Pyramid Lake. Once again the friends of the squatters had placed weapons in the hands of the enemies of the Pyramid Lake Paiutes.

Meanwhile those enemies enjoyed possession of lands at Pyramid Lake. For the 20 years after the Ormsbee negotiations, any federal pressures against the squatters remained in abeyance. Lands passed from hand to hand as the original settlers sold their land to other whites or passed it on to heirs. This continued undisturbed until 1910, when a seriously concerned Indian agent named Creel was stationed at Pyramid Lake. He gathered data on the extent of Anglo holdings and documented in detailed reports the exact location, date of settlement, and legal transference of all Anglo-held lands on the reservation. He wrote letters to the Commissioner of Indian Affairs demanding governmental action to deal with the squatters.

Creel's agitation forced the hand of the Indian Bureau, which then sent out an inspector to survey the trespasser issue. The inspector's lengthy report substantiated Creel's evidence but differed in interpretation. Much as the Paiutes had been wronged, the inspector believed, the Anglos who had invested money and effort in these lands would also be wronged if they were summarily removed. He advocated a compromise, but a compromise requiring immediate federal action:

> I presume, however, since the government is somewhat at fault in allowing these people to remain on the reservation for so many years that ejectment would be the proper action as this would allow the parties to present a defence, and give them a day in court. They could probably be summarily removed from the reservation without a proceeding in court, but this would probably be not advisable under the circumstances of this case. . . . I will therefore, respectfully recommend that proceedings be instituted against all parties holding land on this reservation without title, and that they be dispossessed and removed from all unpatented land, and if necessary enjoined from further interference with the property of this reservation.[46]

The inspector was not alone in his views. Colleagues in the Indian Bureau, particularly in the Irrigation Engineering Department, found that the squatters' location on the reservation interfered with development plans which they had for it. For many years squatters had been tapping federal irrigation ditches intended for Indian use and had been applying that water to their illegally held land. Many Anglo-held plots stood between the ditch heads and Indian lands downstream. To construct a new rational and efficient irrigation system at Pyramid Lake, all applicable lands had to be consolidated into a single system. Such a major development project was then under Bureau contemplation, so the Irrigation Department recommended that "the question of the claims of the white settlers now occupying some 5000 acres of the most valuable agricultural land of the reservation be determined as early as possible."[47]

Indians, too, keenly felt the need to remove squatters from their land. They had persistently complained to agents of trespass ever since the 1860s, and their outcry continued. One of their numerous petitions shortly after the turn of the century stated: "There is plenty of good land up around twon [*sic*] of Wadsworth, Nevada, and [illegible] down river where them Italians is now. they are making considerable money on [illegible] We poor Indian rec'd nothing. Now We all Indian who are occupied here for living wanted whole reservation, an allotment of 40 acres or more of land for the head of every family of our tribe."[48]

From Indians, its own field agents, and development staff, the Indian Bureau received pressure forcing it into action. Late in the summer of 1909 it passed a request to the Secretary of the Interior, who then wrote the Attorney General: "It is requested that the United States Attorney of the District of Nevada be instructed to institute suits to eject the trespassers named from the lands illegally used and occupied by them, and to enjoin them from further use and occupation of the land."[49] Court action was finally to be initiated.

The U.S. Attorney in Nevada received his instructions in September of 1910, but he took no immediate action. As an agency report blandly observed, "for one reason or another, the matter has been delayed." The Paiutes were not pleased, as the report went on to say: "The Indians know the condition and are disposed to doubt the interest and activity of the Office in determining their right to the land which is in dispute."[50] It was not until seven years later that suits were actually entered against eight of the squatters and three corporations claiming land at Pyramid Lake. The defendants in only five of these suits bothered to answer the charges. In other cases, squatters denied United States jurisdiction, saying that only the Pyramid Lake Paiutes themselves could file suit, as they were the ones claiming property. In this way the squatters hoped to escape opposition by the powerful Department of Justice and to force the inexperienced and poverty-stricken Indians to file suit in their own behalf. Tribes at this time in history could not legally hire a lawyer, nor did they have funds to pay one. Individual Paiutes would have had to pool scant private monies and to sue as individuals. Further, their likelihood of finding a lawyer anywhere in the state willing to represent them was most slim. The Paiutes would stand virtually no chance at all in court under such circumstances.

A second major issue in the squatter defense was the court system's jurisdiction. The U.S. Constitution states that when the federal government is a party to a suit, all cases must be tried in federal courts—from the U.S. District Courts, to the federal Circuit Court of Appeals, and eventually to the U.S. Supreme Court. If the federal government were successfully driven out of the suits and denied the right to represent the Paiutes, then the cases would descend from federal to state courts. These were far more easily influenced by the attitudes and the political power of major white landholders. The legal issues would also then be decided by state law, far less mindful of Indian interests and not cognizant of the peculiarities of Indian trust status. The squatters' arguments to eject the federal government from the suit were rejected by the district court because the Paiutes, along with other Indian tribes, were legally defined as wards of the federal government. As with any trustee, the government was not only able but required to file suit to protect the property of its assigned wards.

The preliminary issues then settled, the suits finally proceeded in 1918. The U.S. Attorney was confident of success and wrote: "In my judgement, there is absolutely no legal defence to the government's case, and there is no question whatsoever but what the government will prevail. Undoubtedly these lands will be restored to the government for the benefit of the Indians, unless Congress intervenes by passing a bill giving title to the various occupants of the land."[51]

The Attorney's fears proved sound. Having lost their preliminary attempt to have the cases thrown out of federal courts, and having every fear that they could not win in open adjudication, the squatters shifted tactics. In a new attack against federal court jurisdiction, their attorney went to Washington in May 1917 to lobby the other U.S. Senator from Nevada, Key Pittman. Squatters hoped for a piece of special-interest legislation which would grant them title to the land without risking a court settlement. Pittman duly submitted a bill to Congress which would recognize the squatter title on ground of lengthy possession. The U.S. Attorney in Nevada said that "in his opinion our contention [in the lawsuits] was absolutely correct; that the defendants knew it and for that reason were afraid to go to trial and were therefore now endeavoring to procure title through special legislation by Congress." The Indian Agent at Pyramid Lake wrote, "Unless prompt and positive steps are taken, the defendants will no doubt defeat justice and obtain title to lands, which they have no right."[52] He urged the Commissioner of Indian Affairs to oppose passage of Pittman's bill.

While Congress was considering this bill in late December 1918, the decision came down in Nevada Federal District Court against the first of the squatters. James Sutcliffe, owner of the fishing station on the western shore of the lake, had situated clearly within reservation bounds and obviously after the reservation's founding. All of the motions in his defense were denied and he was given 20 days to file an appeal, which he failed to do.

The court unequivocally stated that he had no just claim, and it would have seemed logical that the BIA's next action would be to issue ejectment proceedings against him. However, three years later Sutcliffe was still there. Explanation for this was in a letter from the Secretary of the Interior to the Senate Subcommittee on Indian Affairs. This high official felt more than subtle sympathy for the Anglos at Pyramid Lake and clearly favored their claims. He wrote, "As to the lands immediately here in controversy, the equities in favor of the

Indians are far from strong. Prior to cultivation by the whites these lands were desert, and as such had a nominal value only. . . . Here this value has been materially enhanced by improvement, cultivation, and in many instances by long-continued irrigation by the whites. Clearly, therefore, if the equities thus created in the whites are to be recognized, the Indians are not entitled to the present value of these lands. Again, it should be born in mind that the most valuable asset attaching to these lands is the water right."[53] Thus he asserted that the Anglo squatters had a vested interest which deserved recognition by the federal government and that their investments were not sufficiently compensated by the years of subsistence and profit which they had enjoyed while resident on the reserve.

The Secretary laid a great deal of the blame upon the government itself for allowing these men initial entry and subsequent development of vested interests. "A predominant feature of the entire situation," he wrote, "is the fact that apparently the Government stood by for a long period without protest or effective objection against the occupancy and improvement of these lands by the whites, and it is difficult, therefore, at this late date to deny the equitable rights so created."[54] This statement was inaccurate. It was clearly documented that agents, inspectors, and even officials in Washington had complained about the trespasses on many, many occasions. They had posted squatters and the military had forcibly removed them. The government had been delinquent, however, in not pressing for court settlement, the most effective and permanent action in such a situation. This delinquency had permitted a vested interest to be established which was now being asserted with the aid of the most powerful political parties. In comfortable inaccuracy the Secretary continued:

> Apparently the matter then slept more or less peacefully until 1909, when the Attorney General was requested to institute proceedings to eject the alleged "trespassers" from the reservation. A new survey was called for, to relocate the boundaries of the reserve and to determine the extent of the claims therein hostile to the interest of the Indians. The survey was made and thereafter suits instituted against the white claimants. In some of these the issues are still pending before the trial court, while in others judgement has been obtained by default, the

defendants or their attorneys admitting that from a legal standpoint their claims are practically hopeless. Writs of ejectment have not yet been issued, however, and as bills to relieve the situation have been pending within recent years (S. 2658, 65th Cong., and S. 5033, 66th Cong.), on March 15th, 1921, I requested the Attorney General to suspend further action in court until the matter of additional legislation effecting a settlement could be considered.[55]

Once more in the history of land at Pyramid Lake the wheels of justice ground to a halt. While it had been essentially empty of Anglo settlers at the time of its initiation, Pyramid Lake Reservation experienced progressive encroachment over the years. Some of this was permitted by the reserve's uncertain legal status, denied by local settlers and untested in court. The date of its establishment, and hence priority, was confused by the late declaration of the executive order. The railroad made claim to some of the most valuable land on the reservation, and the validity of this claim lay undecided for many years. Weak and scheming agents, inefficient and uninformed of their powers and duties, tolerated the encroachment of whites who flooded in to exploit the ambiguities of the situation. Whites not only took the best unoccupied lands but also coerced Indians to yield established ranches and favored campsites by threat, by physical force, and occasionally even by murder. Once entrenched, whites absorbed further resources, grazing their cattle on surrounding pasturelands, withdrawing irrigation water from the river, and cutting timber from the limited supplies in the Truckee bottoms. For many years these men drew profit as well as subsistence from their illegal occupancy. They sold hay and cattle and fish. They ran trading posts and stage way-stations. In innumerable ways, their presence denied directly or indirectly the benefits which Paiutes could have justly expected from undisturbed possession of these promised lands.

Paiutes were denied the potential profits which they, not the whites, should have received. They were denied the right to use their reserved lands in a way of their own choosing. From the inability to consolidate the valuable lower river holdings, they were denied the opportunity for rational and efficient development of the critical irrigation system. All observers acknowledged that Paiutes of Pyramid

Lake were poor, that their lands were underdeveloped, and that they had few prospects for profit in the immediate future. In 1922, after the Secretary's decision to discontinue federal prosecution against the squatters, the annual agency report for Pyramid Lake stated that "owing to gross mismanagement on the part of somebody, this reservation has been allowed to run down, the fine boarding school was abandoned, the Indian stock interests have been reduced to little or nothing and many Indians have left the reservation in order to make a living and find better prospects."[56] While the power of Congress and the federal administration worked actively in the interest of the Anglo land squatters, Paiutes were being forced off their reservation for lack of economic opportunities.

All voices were not stilled, however, and some rose in outrage at the federal decision to protect the trespassers. During this period, an inspector perceived the paradox:

> These trespassers, by commission of an illegal act, and by daily and hourly repetition of that act for more than thirty years past, have not, in the belief of your inspector, made that act legal. . . . Your inspector does not believe that, because these people [Paiutes] are poor they can well bear to be so magnificently robbed; but he recognizes in the porposed [sic] legislation the fulfillment of the prophecy: "From him that hath not shall be taken away even that which he has." This ecclesiastical riddle was not solved until nations declared wards, gave them property that they never were allowed to enjoy and then allowed the property to be taken from them because they could not enjoy it.[57]

While the federal posture might have been self-contradictory, it became a political reality. White trespassers had begun with simple individual occupation of the valuable portions of the Pyramid Lake Reservation. They had attempted to acquire title by assertion, by denying agency demands, and by ignoring military warnings. However, having no shadow of a legal title and fearing that court decisions would turn against them, they had sought out powerful friends. They had turned to the senators from Nevada, who were inextricably politically allied to major land interests. These congressmen were committed to protect white land claims over native ones in a state which lacked historical transfer of Indian title by treaty. Further, Congress, having asserted the power to create reservations, logically also had the power to reduce or abandon them. It was to this congressional power and these political commitments that the trespassers turned. In these legislative chambers their words were heeded and their senatorial friends led the battle to wrest lands from Pyramid Lake Reservation. This battle was fought in Washington, invisible to the Paiutes, far beyond their political or financial ability to compete.

The struggle for possession of land which had begun at Pyramid Lake in 1860, and which had continued there ever since, was now relocated to a distant battlefield where the rules were unknown, the warriors unfamiliar, the opponents faceless. Paiutes were forced to rely on the uncommitted and transient support of Indian agents and Bureau officials. They could not defend themselves.

NINE

Squatters and Their Friends in the Senate

Like many Western states, Nevada characteristically reelected its congressmen year after year. Advancing through the seniority system and gaining assignment to important committees, these men became increasingly more efficient in advancing the interests of their constituents. Since Indians did not vote in Nevada until 1924, this constituency was largely white, the same Anglo population which was encroaching so persistently upon Paiute resources.

Nevada Senator William Stewart had 27 years' seniority when he retired in 1905. Because he sat on and later chaired the Indian Affairs subcommittee, he was in an excellent position to influence Indian legislation; his actions and opinions exerted a significant effect on the Northern Paiutes. Long ago he had taken part in the so-called Pyramid Lake War and, as we have seen in Chapter 4, he enthusiastically reminisced about his "indian fighting days." It was Stewart who acquired congressional reparation for expenses which victorious whites had incurred in that contest. Stewart firmly believed in the frontier philosophy that Indians had to yield to the onrush of American civilization. One historian described him as a "member of that class of pioneer exploiters of the public domain who considered their great fortunes as legitimate rewards of aggressive industry and opportunism."[1] As such, Stewart made an ideal representative for Nevada public interests.

Stewart held a clear opinion about whether Indians had any right to reserve portions of their previous territories:

> I am and always have been opposed to the dedication of any portion of the territory of the United States to barbarism. The recognition of the tribal relations of Indians was a mistake in the beginning and is now a sham and a fraud. ... Lands should be allotted to them in severalty. ... Every acre of land not allotted to the Indians should be opened to settlement. The reservation system pauperizes, demoralizes and degrades both Indians and white men. ... No Indians on this continent are so worthless and degraded as those in the United States—all the result of the vicious system of feeding them in idleness. In answer to your questions I am in favor of opening the whole of the Indian Territory to white settlement as fast as possible.[2]

In short, he favored the forced breaking of tribal relations, individual assimilation of Indians, and unbridled competition for the resources of the continent. Since Indians had suffered military defeat and occupation in Nevada as elsewhere, surely they were in a disadvantageous position for any subsequent Darwinian struggle for land. Stewart proclaimed his laissez-faire policy with the certain knowledge that the results would not be unfavorable for his Anglo constituents.

Senator Stewart coupled pragmatic opportunism with loyalty to his political allies and friends. An incident which illustrates his skill and power involved H. M. Yerington, a partner in the railroad which had gained a right-of-way through the Walker River Reservation in return for perpetual free passage for Indians. To his dismay, Yerington found that Paiutes adapted quickly to rail travel, visiting distant relatives, transporting game, and costing him money. To circumvent this contract, he enlisted the aid of his one-time attorney and friend, Bill Stewart. In reply, Stewart told "My dear Yerington" of a successful visit to the Commissioner of Indian Affairs. As a result of that meeting, the BIA ordered the Department of Justice to "let the matter rest until other arrangements can be made."[3] These other arrangements, Stewart proudly explained, were "to have the Walker River Reservation abandoned and all the Indians transferred to Pyramid Lake Reservation. . . . I have no doubt that I will succeed, to have Walker River Reservation thrown open to the public. There is no sense in having two reservations for Indians that could just as well live on one. . . . In the meantime you [Yerington] will not be troubled any more about your contract. The Commissioner admits that it would be unreasonable . . . but he prefers to stop proceedings and wait for some arrangement to settle the whole matter."[4]

It was William Stewart again who proposed the amendment to the Ormsbee Commission agreement, suggesting renegotiation to relinquish not only the river-valley portion of the Pyramid Lake Reservation but also the north and west sides of the lake and all of Walker River reserve as well. He later substituted an amendment calling for seizure of these lands without consent of the tribes. It was again Senator Stewart who, failing to inflate the Ormsbee land cessions, sought to use a large-scale irrigation project to increase the carrying capacity of Pyramid Lake reserve and thus justify relocating all the Walker River Indians onto it.[5] It was more efficient, he asserted, to invest development funds at Pyramid Lake than at Walker, because farming in Nevada was impossible without well-controlled water sources, and the Walker River was unpredictable. But then, so was the Truckee. Nevertheless, Stewart inconsistently proposed to sell this useless, unirrigated Walker Reservation land under homestead laws to white settlers who apparently could be expected to farm it. Further, the projected irrigation project at Pyramid was to include 17,000 acres for the expanded Indian population, and nearly 14,000 more acres in a sector of the reservation which would then be sold off to pay for the Indian project. The lands Stewart proposed for Indian irrigation were the high mesas, which he described as "all the Land between the mountains and the river from Wadsworth to the Lake, the Indians would be provided for and Walker Lake Reservation might be abandoned."[6] Stewart well knew that this land had porous, sandy soil and was far too high above the river to be irrigated practically. On the other hand, Stewart explained to a group of his Wadsworth constituents how they would benefit directly: "I have a measure in hand to set aside a part of Pyramid Reservation and as the mesa above Wadsworth is very fertile, its thousands of acres would, with irrigation, make this a farming community. I would apply the township law to Wadsworth and give every man occupying ground here a title to the lot upon which his house is built."[7]

It was clear that Stewart did not have the best interests of the Indians at heart. Like Senators to follow him, he was a formidable foe.

In presenting his irrigation scheme to the Department of the Interior, Stewart argued the inevitability of Indians' yielding to Anglo desires, asserting that "he can see no reason why the bill should not pass; that on the contrary it seems to him very necessary that it should; that the town-site will never be used for Indian reservation purposes, and that the inhabitants of the town-site will be greatly benefited to get title to their homes." Stewart's advocacy for the white squatters was forceful and effective. The Commissioner of Indian Affairs, buckling under that pressure, concluded that "the people of Nevada desired further reduction of the reservation than that provided in the said [Ormsbee] agreement and the restoration to the public domain of the entire Walker River reservation in that State."[8]

This plan was so obviously in the interests of the Anglo citizens of Nevada that the Pyramid Lake agent and the federal inspectors wrote a series of increasingly critical reports of it. Even the irrigation development, intended to allay the fears of liberal organizations favoring Indian rights, was perceived for what it was, an impractical political ploy. One member of the U.S. Indian Commission, an advisory policy board, wrote, "The scheme of furnishing water is a very wild one— the Truckee river is to be carried in an open ditch over 45 miles through a porous soil. The Indians are to receive water at the *end* of this improbable ditch after furnishing Wadsworth with water and irrigating 17,000 acres of white man's land. I think the Indians would never get any water. Moreover, the ditch would take away the water the Indians now have." He concluded that these bills were "wholly in the interests of the whites."[9]

The field agent in charge of Pyramid Lake protested strongly and argued with sound logic that if the northern section of the reserve were opened to Anglo ownership, control of that section of lake would be lost also. In view of the record of Anglo fishing trespass, it was highly probable that white control would then expand to the whole lake and river. This would mean ultimate loss of the one resource still of significant benefit to the Paiutes, the fishery, and negate forever the purpose for the reservation's creation. "The Indians," he reported, "view the taking of this lake from them in the light of a bold robbery, as they were promised when they settled here that this body of water would be reserved for the exclusive use of themselves and children for all time to come." The Walker River Paiutes would be abandoning homes and improvements made painfully over the years, and he labeled the irrigation scheme "absurd." In short, the agent said of the plan, "The Indians do not want it, do not need it, and would not take it as a gift."[10]

Despite these warnings from subordinates and advisers, the Commissioner of Indian Affairs and Secretary of the Interior, administratively charged with protecting Indian interests, obligingly favored passage each time the plan reappeared; the congressional committee, under Stewart's sway, voted for it. However, the bill repeatedly failed passage on the floor, for the injustice of this special-interest legislation was simply too raw for even a callous congressional conscience. Not discomfited, Stewart repeatedly resubmitted the rank measure. In its last reincarnation, the bill did not even protect the property interests of those Indians who, complying with Indian policy and Stewart's own assimilationist thought, had already established residence in Wadsworth. Balking at this contradiction, the Commissioner of Indian Affairs insisted that these Paiutes should, like the neighboring Anglos, acquire title to their Wadsworth lots. However, unlike white titles which would be free and clear, he suggested that Indians' titles should be held in trust with the federal government for a period of 25 years, as were individual Indian titles under the General Allotment Act. The Indian school, built by the government when Wadsworth whites had refused to admit Paiute children to the public school system, should be retained in trust by the government as well. Further, the Commissioner insisted that the bill, once passed by Congress, should be submitted to the tribe for acceptance before going into effect.[11]

Even with these ameliorating amendments, the bill was unacceptable to Congress. While Stewart schemed in Washington, the squatters stayed in Wadsworth. In 1894, a federal inspector was still objecting that these trespassers were located on reservation lands without legal justification. He once again recommended that they either be summarily removed or pay some form of rent, either to the tribe or to the federal government.[12] No action was taken on these recommendations.

Stewart, blocked in his blatant attempts to give away large portions of Indian reservations in the now-fading nineteenth-century fashion, and yet clearly pressed to some action by the illegality of Anglo presence there, tried a new tack. In a time-honored ploy much used in Congress for forcing through legislation which could not win approval on its own merits, the Wadsworth township question was attached as a rider to the BIA appropriation bill in 1898. Fearful that disapproval of the rider would interrupt necessary funding for the entire Bureau, congressional opponents to the Wadsworth provision let it pass. Thus the following regulation became law:

> That the inhabitants of the town of Wadsworth, in the county of Washoe, State of Nevada, be, and they are hereby, authorized to proceed, and acquire title to the town site of such town under the provisions of section twenty-three hundred and eighty-two of chapter eighty of the Revised Statutes of the United States, relating to the reservation and sale of town sites on the public lands, and on compliance with the provisions of such town-site laws the inhabitants of said town of Wadsworth shall acquire title in manner and form as provided by the statutes aforesaid: *Provided*, That the proceeds of the sale of the land in such town site shall be paid into the Treasury, and be used by the Secretary of the Interior for the Piute Indians of Pyramid Lake Reservation. . . .[13]

The rider continued, reserving the school lot and declaring that Indians might acquire title under the same regulations as white citizens. Thus Paiutes as individuals, not as a tribe, were given the right to purchase pieces of what was previously their own reservation.

Anglos in Wadsworth had no intention of paying for their lots if there was still a chance to get them for free. Their advocates were still in Washington, so they maintained hope of ultimate victory. Five years later they had made no effort to comply with federal provisions for title acquisition. The BIA then inquired whether title could not revert to the government in the interest of the Indians. The General Land Office replied, "I am directed by the Secretary [of the Interior] to advise you that it is believed under all the circumstances that it is not necessary or desirable that the Secretary should at this time proceed in this matter under the latter section."[14] Thus any action on the Wadsworth question was forestalled for an indefinite period of time.

During these intervening years, the Southern Pacific Railroad materially changed the situation. In 1904 it decided that the roadways approaching Wadsworth's bustling maintenance station were too steep. Accordingly, it moved its tracks several miles to the south, using another river crossing, and changed its division headquarters from Wadsworth to Sparks, just outside of Reno. The railroad removed all its maintenance shops and offices which had been to a large extent the town's sustenance.[15] From a modern industrial town with a promising future, Wadsworth deteriorated overnight to a minor agricultural village with dubious land title. It had no railroad artery for its crops and no commercial importance. Anglo population declined until only about 100 whites lived there, along with an equal number of Paiutes. It was ironic that despite this radical change in Wadsworth's importance—which after all constituted a great deal of their validating argument—Nevada's senators continued to strive for the legitimization of Anglo claims to this property.

The BIA continued to monitor Anglo absorption of reservation land. The 1910 inspection documented in great detail the location and extent of white landholdings on the western side of the lake, down the river, and at Wadsworth, where a permanent Indian village with 100 residents had grown up on the northern edge of town. Of course it had been for their children, locked out of public schools, that the government Indian school at Wadsworth had been constructed. Facing the realities of this situation, the inspector recommended that the lower river zone, including the townsite of Wadsworth, be released from the reservation. In compensation, he thought, the white squatters on the western shore of the lake should be evicted in order to provide homesites and fishing stations for the Paiutes of the reservation.[16] In short, he was suggesting that the BIA continue its appeasement policy in the case of the town, where Anglos were most insistent in their demands for Indian land and such a seizure held most promise of profit. Against the scattered, rural ranches, of value only to their individual holders, the BIA should proceed to do its duty. This compromise between yielding and minimal defense was characteristic of the BIA's hesitancy throughout Pyramid Lake's history.

Ten years later, another inspector, representative of the recurrent but ineffective voices protesting this policy, again looked into the claims and counterclaims over land at Pyramid Lake. He was appalled by the extent of trespass, particularly in the Wadsworth area, of which the "chief part" was located on trespassed lands: "Insofar as lots have been sold in that part of the town of Wadsworth, Nevada, located on such trespassed lands, your inspector must record his belief that illegal traffic in the property of these Indians has resulted." His inquiries revealed that some of these squatters sought to defend themselves by claiming leases or title purchase from previous Anglo "owners." The inspector could only conclude that "leases for Indian lands have been made by those having no authority to do so, not bonded officers representing the Indian Bureau . . . contrary to law and for the purpose of defrauding enrolled Paiutes of Pyramid Lake Reservation, Nevada, of revenues rightfully theirs and that should be, for their benefit. . . ."[17] He staunchly recommended that the government confiscate any lands sold or rented to non-Indians in the Wadsworth area. Should the squatters remain recalcitrant, roads, highways, and other access routes to the community should be shut down and the town put to siege. Needless to say, such drastic action was never undertaken.

This 1920 inspection uncovered yet another abuse of Indian resources. The Wadsworth Power and Light Company, a locally owned corporation, had obtained "the consent of the entire tribe and the agent" to construct an eight-acre reservoir and install power-generating equipment near the town. Indians living on the site were removed. Construction was completed in 1897, and the reservoir was filled from a ditch whose head was off-reservation but which flowed on reservation land through most of its length. This withdrawal of river water infringed on Indian water allocations. Paiutes alleged that in return for use of this land they had been promised free electric lights for their homes in Wadsworth, and the inspector discovered that they had not received any such power. Similarly, the reservoir was designed for multiple use, piping unpurified water for the community's lawns, gardens, and sewage disposal. Once again, despite promises, the Indians had been bypassed in the development of this water system; whatever water they had from this source they carried themselves in pails.

In 1907, after only ten years of operation, the power plant was shut down because, as Wadsworth dwindled in size, it was not clearing a profit. The public service commission refused to allow dismantling of the plant, and therefore leased it from Wadsworth Power and Light for a token dollar annually. The town continued to use the reservoir and, to forestall federal seizure, argued that to shut this down would constitute a deprivation. Federal suit for trespass on Indian land was filed against the company in 1918 but never actively pursued. In 1920, the inspector concluded that the power company promoters had not complied with their promises to the tribe; no further governmental action was taken on this matter.[18]

By 1920, Anglo-Americans had entered the Pyramid Lake Indian Reservation, laid hold to its most productive lands, and utilized them without legal title for over 50 years. Nevada's congressional delegation, led by William Stewart, had made valiant efforts to acquire free title for them by cutting off sections of the reservation, but had failed. An appropriation rider had separated Wadsworth from the reserve. As we saw in the last chapter, the Department of Justice had instituted suits against some of the ranchers trespassing on Pyramid Lake reserve in 1909. When these cases finally reached court in 1917, several of the trespassers neglected to defend themselves at all, knowing full well that they had no legal justification for their actions. They were then automatically found guilty of trespassing on federal property. Nevertheless the next logical step, suits to actually eject them from the lands, had not yet been entered by 1921. At the urging of the Nevada delegation, the Secretary of the Interior ordered that proceedings against the squatters cease, pending certain legislation then in Congress.

Since Congress continued to resist all Stewart's attempts to grant the trespassing Anglos title to the lands free of charge, Nevada's representatives tried a new tack. In 1921, Senator Key Pittman introduced a bill proposing the transfer of title to these trespassers at Wadsworth as well as those at ranch sites along the river and lake, but only upon payment of the minimal homesteading fee. This bill would allow the Secretary of the Interior to sell up to 640 acres of reservation lands to each of the illegal squatters who had seized and occupied them and could now buy them at a rate of $1.25 per acre. They only had to have maintained possession for ten years or more. In other words, ten years of effective trespass, held by force against the interest of the rightful owners and their trustees in the federal government, was now the qualifying criterion. If they had settled "in good faith," meaning that they had actually resided on the land and intended to occupy it as a family farm rather than as a commercial speculation, their claims would be permitted under this bill. Any patents acquired from the railroad were automatically confirmed. The township of Wadsworth would be surveyed, platted, and sold, excepting only the Indian school. Any Indians residing in the town would have the "same rights of purchase under the said statute as white citizens," thus permitting those for whom the reservation had been held in federal trust to purchase the right to continue residing on it. Any monies from these sales would be held in the federal Treasury to "be used by the Secretary of the Interior for the Piute Indians of the said Pyramid Lake Indian Reservation."[19]

Lower-echelon BIA officials, particularly field personnel familiar with the Pyramid Lake situation, protested against the proposed legislation. In 1920, when World War I had just recently ended and many of its prejudices were still very much alive, an inspector declared that to take land "from wards of the government, without compensation, and bestow it, without known and admitted price, upon those who were lately subjects of the kingdom of Italy," was a gross miscarriage of justice. He emphasized that the Paiutes had no voice in this matter. "These Paiutes, wards, have their hands tied while their property is wrested from them. . . . The case seems to be in the hands of spoilers."[20] He objected to the basic logic of the bill, that a persistent illegal action should be made legal post hoc, that the brazen seizure of someone else's property should result in compliance to that demand without stout challenge.

The inspector was not alone in his outrage. "Unless prompt and positive steps are taken," the Reno area agent wrote, "the defendants will no doubt defeat justice and obtain title to lands, [to] which they have no right." He did not yet know that his superior had already tacitly and later would overtly approve this legislation. Futilely, therefore, he recommended pressing on the suits to eject the squatters, actions which both he and Nevada's U.S. Attorney felt were a certain success. He urged that "every honorable means [be] employed within reach as will prevent the acquisition of these lands through other than a court of justice, where only the rights of all parties concerned can be presented and proven."[21] He warned the Commissioner of Indian Affairs that the trespassers' attorneys were lobbying in Washington. His telegrams and letters exhorted action on the part of the Bureau, repeatedly warning that "The passage of said bill is not considered would be [*sic*] in the best interests of the Indians concerned."[22] All memos, letters, and telegrams failed to stimulate any action on the part of the Commissioner, who had no intention of supporting the claims of the Indians against the trespassers—for he had already, in fact, sent his approval of the bill to the Senate committee. The Secretary of the Interior also approved the philosophy of the bill, but thought the fee too low; he insisted that it be changed to an amount designated by his office, and the amendment was made. Nevertheless, the bill did not pass Congress on its first appearance.[23]

The Department of the Interior then requested time for its own field investigation of the squatters' holdings. In July of 1921 Interior Inspector Trowbridge therefore arrived at Pyramid Lake, to gather specific information on the extent and duration of trespass and make a preliminary estimate of the value of the properties in question. His resulting report was very thorough, but its greater significance lay in the nature of his recommendations, the logic of his arguments, and his unstated assumptions, all of which reflected the attitudes of official Washington at the time. This report was to serve as a basis of much federal thinking and some federal action on the squatter issue in years to come.

Trowbridge effectively recommended that this land be sacrificed to Anglo cupidity. His review of the reservation's history stressed the brief removal and reinstatement of the ten-mile railroad claim and subsequent confusion over title in that area. This was a transparent attempt to justify the initial entries. In view of the long-standing white occupation of these lands and the subsequent complex land transactions, it was, he said, neither "advisable or practicable at this late date to attack these titles which have passed through various hands."[24] Since this line of reasoning had the hollow ring of a convenient excuse, the inspector had to marshal further rationale.

Thus he asserted that these lands had been practically worthless at the time Anglos had originally settled them. Their present value, in an Anglo-dominated market, lay almost entirely in improvements made by the squatters, especially leveling and ditching for irrigation. The squatters loudly proclaimed that since they had improved these lands by their own work, they therefore should not have to pay the federal government for the value which they had themselves created. If they had to pay at all, they wanted to pay only the $1.25 per acre homesteading fee which the government charged for unimproved land. Trowbridge agreed with their basic logic; however, he did not feel justified in allowing the sale for a mere $1.25, since some of the better lands were admitted by the trespassers themselves to be worth $150 or more per acre. Trowbridge thus proposed a compromise evaluation, not charging the squatters the full market value, but rather taking into consideration their own labor investments. He suggested that the Secretary of the Interior assign specific evaluations, but that these should be a maximum of $30 per acre for irrigated land and $5 for grazing grounds. One by one he listed the Anglo-held lands outside Wadsworth, a total of over 3,800 acres, 1,000 of which were irrigated and 700 of which were prime, scarce river bottom. In nearly every case he recommended that the squatter be permitted to buy the entire holding then in his possession—in some cases, even more. In all, he proposed sale of nearly 3,500 acres at an aggregate price of slightly under $38,000, or roughly $10.10 per acre. The squatters were to be given 30 days to file their request for title and to place one-fourth of the evaluation as a down payment, the balance of which they had to pay within a year.

He made absolutely no attempt to evaluate homes, barns, fences, or other properties which had been erected upon the land. In fact, if squatters defaulted on payments he thought that they should be allowed to remove these superficial improvements from the acreage. No consideration was given at all to the value of the agricultural products which had been removed from the land over the years, nor of the profitable subsistence from which the squatters had benefited.

Trowbridge's justification for this abdication of reservation land is exemplified by his discussion of the Whitehead property on the western lakeshore:

> But considering the fact that valuable improvements have been placed on this area; that the present occupants and their predecessors have remained all these years unmolested; that the present occupant controls the water supply for the area in question; that the occupants perhaps had confidence in the possibility of securing title on the entry of John Whitehead; that the disposal of this land to the present occupants will not injure the Indians on the reservation, this [family] corporation should be given the privilege of purchasing the lands occupied by them and embraced in the legal subdivisions described below....[25]

He also accepted as valid justification that the squatter was a hardworking family man, that he had children to support, that sons were veterans, or that he had never been overtly hostile to the Paiutes. A squatter could dispossess Indians of their land as long as he was amicable about it and later proved to be a good neighbor on the reservation. If the land was either very remote or "not adapted for allotment for Indians," Trowbridge considered it expendable, even though in some cases the plot was 700 acres or more and could easily have been subdivided into several workable farms.[26]

Rationalizing that the railroad title confusion had allowed a loophole for justifiable initial entry, Trowbridge said the government was now faced with a de facto situation which it must admit, and by admitting must condone. Both this premise and conclusion were most dubious. Nevertheless, he argued that these men had settled in "good faith," with all the brazen appearance of a serious seizure. They had made improvements and wrested profit. However, the telling blow had been the federal reaction. Through bureaucratic mixups in the state tax and federal land offices, a shadow of a title had been established. Agency powerlessness and federal apathy had tolerated the squatters' presence. So once again there reappeared the now-familiar argument: This has been going on so long, we *cannot* justifiably do anything now. This in spite of the fact that each and every one of the squatters admitted freely under oath that he had known that these lands were within a federal Indian reservation at the time he had established and built his improvements there. Trowbridge specifically recommended that no retroactive measures be levied against the trespassers for their prior use of the land.

The inspector's assertion above that the Indians would suffer no injury if these lands were separated from the reserve seemed strange at first, in view of the extreme shortage of arable land there and the government's persistent efforts to make the Paiutes into farmers. This peculiarity dissolved once the hidden assumptions underlying the statement became clear. Trowbridge elaborated upon his remark:

> Damage to the Indians by occupancy of the present claimants is not of large proportions, as five of these holdings are located in remote parts of the reservation, far from the usual haunts of the Indians. The farm lands on the "Truckee Bottoms" would be of value to a few of the energetic Indians, but they certainly would never have shown the results accomplished by the present settlers on these lands, after great toil and thrift, and this is partially demonstrated by results shown on the Indian Reclamation Project, located north of these settlers, where tentative allotments had been made ranging from 1 to 20 acres.[27]

Here again was the familiar mercantilist logic that maximum use of land, as measured in dollar value of agricultural produce, justified possession against all other claims. The inspector totally subordinated any Indian rights in the land to the profit motive. He never observed that the Indian farms of 1 to 20 acres were far smaller than any of the Anglo farmlands, most of which ranged from 50 to 700 acres. Nor did he consider that Indian farms might well have been larger if historically, by the time Paiutes had begun effectively to enter agriculture, all of the arable reservation lands not directly under the gaze of the agency house had not already been taken up by white squatters. These trespassers had then proceeded to absorb water claims, further limiting the Indians' ability to expand their agricultural commitment. The resulting Indian plots were simply too small to support a family; perhaps some of the desultory nature of Indian farming sprang from this reason, but the inspector never considered this as an adequate explanation. The Secretary of the Interior observed that "Being somewhat destitute, they are without means to purchase stock and necessary implements with which to properly cultivate the soil." But neither bureaucrat really credited simple inability to acquire the proper tools as a sufficient reason for lack of agricultural production. They could comfortably write off Paiute efforts with the Secretary's blithe utterance: "These Indians are not agriculturalists."[28] Since farming was still one of the few defensible uses of land in Anglo eyes, this declaration to a large degree undercut Paiutes' claims on governmental interest in them, and hence their practical chances for defense of their land.

Trowbridge exemplified another tacit assumption of his age when, while tolerating individual exploitation of federal trust property by yeoman farmers, he rejected corporate enterprises. Corporations, legal fictions created for "pure profit," had been excluded from nineteenth-century homestead laws and were still, in 1920, viewed with some suspicion. The purpose of the government land policy had been to get stout men of good character onto the land to work it. This policy was continued in the Pyramid Lake case. If the squatter had resided for a substantial period of time, built a home, made improvements, and proven his competency by digging a ditch and taking water from the Truckee River to irrigate his crops, then he was considered a settler in "good faith" and qualified for title to Indian lands. In other words, if he had seized federal property energetically and without any hesitation, then he would be rewarded with ownership. If, on the other hand, he had approached the acknowledged Indian title with caution and for security had established residence off-reservation or had incorporated, then he was considered as not acting in good faith and was disqualified.

Although many of Trowbridge's biases and unstated assumptions militated against Indian interests, one worked in their favor. He declared without equivocation that under no conditions should lakeshore property be entitled to whites. "Pyramid Lake is the most important part of this reservation," he said, "in fact it is the keystone to the situation, and becoming the bone of contention between the Indians and the white inhabitants of the region. To give any rights to individuals on any part of the shore of this lake will be the entering wedge for dispossession. If this lake had not existed, the reservation would doubtless never have been established in this region."²⁹ Like Agent Dodge who 50 years before had fought white fishermen, Trowbridge realized that Anglo entry onto any portion of the lake itself would swiftly lead to absorption of the entire surface for white interests. Thus he thought that any foothold on the lake should be denied, although he was not similarly defensive about water rights in the Truckee River.

The local Indian agent was, however. He recognized the close connection between the squatters and the water problem which was to grow acute in coming years: "There are twelve ditches taking water from the Truckee River between the Derby Dam and the Indian reservation. . . . it is the custom for the owners of these ditches to leave the head-gates open night and day throughout the irrigating season; and what water is supposed to reach the Indian reservation has to run the gauntlet of all these ditches. . . . It is simply a case of each one helping himself, which leaves the Indian reservation at the mercy of all the water users between them and the Derby dam."³⁰ Since the eight miles between Derby and the reservation boundary was mostly narrow, uninhabited canyon, the vast majority of these water users were located on the reservation. These were the self-same trespassers who had been found guilty of illegal occupancy by the federal courts and whose land Trowbridge was now evaluating for abdication by the federal trustee. Trowbridge thought bottom lands could be given away with minimal dispute, but the lake should be protected.

Trowbridge's assumptions were compatible with federal policy of the time; the Secretary of the Interior found his work thorough and accepted his recommendations. Therefore when Pittman's bill to allow transfer of title to the squatters at Pyramid Lake was reintroduced into the next Congress, it moved rapidly through committee. The Interior Department requested only that, should the squatters not file for title or not make their first payment within the designated 90 days, the land would revert to the government for reservation purposes. The Paiutes would get back their lands if the squatters did not deign to take it. With this minimal protection, the bill was passed on June 7, 1924.[31] Squatters' claims on the Pyramid Lake Indian Reservation were now legalized by the legislative branch of the federal government, with full concurrence of the executive branch.

However, transfer of title to the Anglos was not as simple as anticipated. The law provided for the survey, plat, and sale of any unpatented land in Wadsworth township under specified regulations. When the survey was completed and filed, the General Land Office rejected it because it was in the format of the wrong federal provision. A second survey had to be made to comply with the appropriate federal standards. Thus a federal snafu postponed for an additional eight years the actual enactment of this law. It was not until October 1932 that the town of Wadsworth became available to the roughly 100 Anglos there and sales began.[32] Since the legal status of the Pyramid Lake Paiutes was now very soon to change, this delay proved significant.

Once the bill was passed, formal appraisal began. Using Trowbridge's careful investigation of the history of each claim as a foundation, assessors went to Pyramid Lake in the summer of 1925. They evaluated the 3,800 acres to be released for sale, ranging from $3 per acre for non-irrigable land to $75 per acre for improved and irrigated land. This was a higher reevaluation than Trowbridge's preliminary work, in which maximum value had been $30. As a result, the aggregate value according to the second appraisal rose to approximately $57,000.[33] This became the official price to which the white claimants were statutorily liable. They were then required by law to submit one-fourth of the amount within 30 days and pay the remainder in three equal annual installments, along with five-percent interest on the deferred payment.

The Mullen, Hardscrabble, Sutcliffe, and Bonham ranches were promptly bought; an initial payment was made on the Simmons property. The other 13 claimants outside of Wadsworth made no payments at all. Since the government was under no continuing obligation to allow them to purchase the land once the time period expired, this latter group became subject to eviction. In the town of Wadsworth itself, 8 families filed application for city lots and made total or partial payment, while an additional 16 families there ignored the law, failed to file applications or fees, and continued to occupy the town lots as squatters. As the deadline stated in the law passed, all were left in undisturbed possession. The land should have automatically reverted to the reservation, but in no case did the federal government file suit to have any of these squatters evicted.

Instead of meeting these minimal federal requirements, the remaining squatters raised a hue and cry to their senators. Answering this call to forward the interests of his constituency, Nevada's Senator Tasker Oddie asked the Secretary of the Interior to reconsider the land evaluations. Still another inspector was sent to Pyramid Lake, and in February 1926 he obediently reported that, after careful examination of the lands, he was satisfied that the appraised prices were too high. He recommended reinstatement of the earlier, lower Trowbridge evaluations. Since the Secretary did not have the authority to reevaluate property once terms had been fixed by his office, additional legislation was now necessary; therefore Senator Oddie filed a bill in Congress which would have removed the distinction between irrigated and unirrigated land, reduced the evaluation on all classes below Trowbridge's $3.00 minimum for open grazing land, and charged a flat $2.50 per acre. If payments had already been submitted, Oddie's bill proposed that squatters be reimbursed by the federal treasury for their "excessive" payments. The government would then reimburse the tribal account for the difference between Trowbridge's evaluation and the amount actually charged the squatters. In this way Anglos would acquire title efficiently, quickly, and cheaply.

Even this blatantly special-interest legislation failed to rouse official Washington. The Commissioner of Indian Affairs reaffirmed that the squatters' "equities are unquestioned" and that "not one of them may be charged with bad faith." He continued: "The Indians were not in possession when the white settlements were made, the boundary lines of the reservation were not clearly established, the Government offered no opposition to the settlers, and that their claims were bought and sold much in the manner of privately owned lands. The new purchasers took possession, and no objection appears to have been raised by the Government. As a matter of law, the

Indians occupy the same relative position as the white settlers." Thus did he abdicate any power to oppose this transfer of land to squatters. However, he did object to the flat rate of $2.50 per acre, claiming it was unjust to the Indians "because of the wide difference in the values of the areas involved."[34] Therefore he was maneuvered into suggesting the compromise desired by the clamoring white settlers and Oddie in the first place, that the Trowbridge evaluations be reinstated and the privilege of filing claims on Indians lands be reopened. New calculations of balances due were submitted to Congress.

As time passed, it was the Great Depression which ultimately provided the justification for fee reduction, even though this financial disaster did not strike until years after final payments were delinquent. If the trespassers had complied with the provisions of the original bill, they would have held clear title before the Depression hit. By 1930, four people had paid off these reduced Trowbridge evaluations. Several more had made partial payments. However, five had submitted only the initial payment required in filing for title and had assiduously ignored further deadlines.[35] Nevertheless, they enjoyed undisturbed occupancy until the 1950s, when Nevada's congressional delegation once again rose to the occasion. A Nevada senator would then again propose legislation allowing these squatters to acquire Pyramid Lake Reservation land free of additional charge.

From 1890 to 1930, Anglo interests at Pyramid Lake clearly found powerful allies in Nevada's congressional delegation. After initial failure to simply have large portions of the reservation lopped off, Nevada's senators moderated their demands to individual squatters' specific holdings. The town of Wadsworth was removed because of a rider on an appropriation bill. Its residents were given a second chance in Oddie's 1924 bill. When squatters refused to pay even moderate fees, their champions in Washington blocked eviction proceedings, contrived price reductions, and assured new opportunities for filing on Indian land. Throughout, the BIA appeared helpless before aggressive white demands.

The fight over Pyramid Lake land had shifted from Nevada to Washington. There it proceeded, all but invisible to Paiutes. Without either political power or the active advocacy of the Bureau of Indian Affairs, they were helpless before the attack.

TEN

New Challenges, New Strengths

Any response which the Paiutes could make to the challenges posed by Anglo-American society depended to a large degree on the nature and position of their leadership. In the earliest days of the reservation, community leaders were headmen, many of whom had served their people long before the arrival of whites. Informal, without power of force, guiding by suggestion and example, these men used their skills as best they could within the new situation. As they eventually grew old and were not replaced, the last of these "captains" or "chiefs" left a leadership vacuum. Some new men arose, like Numaga, men with new skills demanded by the shifting conditions of life. However, as the Bureau of Indian Affairs gradually consolidated its control over the reservation, it demanded the right to make and execute those decisions which, as an independent community, the Pyramid Lake Paiutes had previously made for themselves. Paiutes could no longer gather food where they chose, because Anglo concepts of private property were enforced by wire fences and rifles. When white fishermen invaded the lake, Indians were told to let the military take care of it for them. When horses were stolen, government inspectors urged reliance on white courts for satisfaction. Personal insults could only be ignored, for if an Indian took offense and sought retaliation himself, the mercurial violence of his Anglo neighbors soon brought disaster.

By the turn of the century there was a genuine crisis in indigenous leadership. Without power to make meaningful decisions, community leadership no longer had any function and so withered. Despite its promises and assumed role, the BIA did not provide an adequate substitute, because it was not concerned with the survival of the Indian community, but rather with the assimilation of individual Paiutes. The community was left with no organization to combat the machinations of local Anglos and their senators, whose pressures increased as the structured defenselessness of the Paiutes became increasingly obvious. Individual Paiute protests, appeals, and petitions, which streamed forth over the years, were for the most part ignored since they did not come from any organization which Anglos recognized as representing the community.

Traditionally, important community decisions had been made in council meetings at which all adults had spoken their opinions until a consensus had formed. The BIA continued to find it convenient to call such meetings whenever Anglo legal forms required titular tribal approval. For example, a group meeting was called when the Ormsbee Commission needed endorsement to release valuable parcels of reservation land. In other cases, if the Indian Bureau did not want to veto Anglo requests for certain favors itself, it called tribal meetings. Then it could say that the Indians resisted the project. For instance, in 1929 a Renoite requested a lease on a piece of the Pyramid Lake shoreline to construct a hotel. Rather than openly oppose this plan itself, the BIA held a special meeting of the Indians, where, it claimed,

> most of the Indians were in attendance, they expressed themselves unanimously as being opposed to the lease of any tract of land on the reservation for hotel purposes. . . . The Indians of the Pyramid Lake Indian Reservation have fresh in their minds the memory of lands obtained by squatters on the reservation, and they are much opposed to leasing any of the reservation lands for hotel purposes.[1]

Meetings were also called for administrative convenience, as an agent in 1913 explained: "On questions of importance to the Indians I deem it advisable to call a meeting of the Indians. This meeting includes all the Indians that care to come, and generally I consider it a help in handling some of the questions that come up."[2] Those questions were ones the BIA deemed important, and meetings served as conduits for information about projects it was instigating on the reserve. These might include group work projects, ditch-cleaning, fence-checking, or lectures on "progressive" agricultural methods. Since information on these topics originated solely with BIA personnel, and since other topics were not allowed on the agenda, the BIA necessarily controlled discussion; it had made all necessary decisions before the gathering ever came together.

Meetings to discuss issues of interest to the Indians, such as fishing, or to contest BIA decisions, were suppressed. The agent in 1923 explained this selective toleration of councils very clearly:

> One of the great draw-backs to Indian progress is the desire on their part to "hold councils" and spend practically three-fourths of their time (if allowed to do so) in talking about ancient history, what was "promised" them years ago, what they ought to have, etc., etc., but very little about their own shortcomings, the need of their doing certain work, obeying the laws, supporting their families, improving their home places, etc. In this connection it is quite proper to have frequent meetings, when such meetings do not interfere with work, to arrange for local improvements, farm or road improvements or giving them directions as to sending children to school, health, or other matters of the kind. But, as I stated, the "talk habit" should be discouraged.[3]

Meetings, the BIA thought, were for its issuing instructions, which the Paiutes were then to follow obediently.

Pyramid Lake Paiutes were not satisfied with this unilateral use of council meetings. Over the years they made several attempts to organize permanent councils which would be more responsive to their interests and needs. These, if recognized by the BIA, could then bridge the gap between Washington and tribal members. Thus, in late May of 1920, the Indians of Pyramid Lake organized a council of 12 members, including a chairman and an interpreter. This council was presented to one of the periodic inspectors, who then recommended to the Commissioner of Indian Affairs that he should recognize it as "representing the will of the people of the Reservation and entitled to participate in an advisory capacity, in the affairs of the Reservation."[4] This was truly a community council, as indicated by the wide range of social and political information it asked for: health care, household maintenance, crop planting, control of the liquor traffic, the Indian position relative to state game laws, the extent of their legal rights in the reservation lands, water rights, and educational matters. Since this was exactly the kind of information which the agent should have been providing automatically, the BIA structure was apparently ineffective in carrying out its own policy. The Paiutes selected fellows whom they believed best exemplified their concepts of leadership. If their list of inquiries is a fair indication, their concerns were very much in line with BIA policy. Nevertheless, the BIA agent labeled this group "not progressive"—perhaps because, as it was an indigenous movement, he had no control over it. The BIA refused to recognize the council and it fell immediately into disuse.

However, the Indian Bureau held more frequent meetings to discuss those Indian-expressed concerns of which it did approve. The University of Nevada at Reno was contracted to provide agricultural experts for frequent farmers' meetings. Other gatherings discussed the growing problem of state fishing regulations in the 1920s. The agent could soon report that "The spirit of cooperation in all matters, industries, social affairs and religious work is dominant. From a discontented and turbulent group of Indians and employees the change has been so marked. . . ."[5]

Nevertheless, as Paiutes became more irritated with BIA policy and ineffectiveness, they demanded a greater voice in the regulation of their own reservation. In 1930, ten years after the first abortive attempt, the Pyramid Lake Indians organized another council. The elected chairman wrote immediately to Washington expressing the tribe's great concern over irrigation matters, water rights, and agricultural advancement. Paiutes were clearly concerned over their lack of valid choice in reservation management, and asked specifically that the "Government [might] recognize some one person as a Captain or Chief of the Indians at Pyramid Lake Indian Reservation, and that this practice should be resumed. . . . at this meeting it was the unanimous wish of all present that the undersigned so act, as such a personage as between the Government and the Indians to clarify and get a better understanding of all question[s] involved for the betterment of the Indian and harmonizing them with the Government."[6] Soon the nominated council protested about Anglo cattle trespass and the Bureau's lack of support for the aged. Again the BIA stonewalled this council, and its communications soon ceased. But the idea of a community council did not die, for in 1934 a Paiute testified before a senatorial subcommittee: "The main thing that we want now and what we are trying to form is a sort of council to represent this reservation, and if we could get the approval of the Indian Office or the Commissioner or the subcommittee from Washington for that, we would be glad to have a committee chosen as a business committee and to work as a council."[7]

In 1934 the BIA experienced a major shift in policy. For the last 50 years the BIA had tried to individualize Indian relations with the federal government. The General Allotment Act had been designed to break reservations down into small private farms. Tribes as wholes were denied legitimacy, authority, or power. Further, each Indian was encouraged to spin off on his own in imitation of Anglo individualism. He was to use modern agricultural methods to enter the market economy. He was to be ambitious, to achieve, to get ahead—presumably ahead of his friends, kinsmen, and neighbors. Such a federal policy met with decided lack of enthusiasm from many Indians; this was certainly the case at Pyramid Lake.

Change from this policy began in 1928, when a major federally funded report, *The Problem of Indian Administration*, severely criticized the BIA for mismanagement of Indian resources; the progressive alienation of land from Indian control; the astoundingly high levels of poverty, disease, and poor housing found on reservations, and the exceedingly low levels of educational achievement there; and the general failure on the part of the BIA to achieve its own stated policy goals. The report showed that Indians were becoming increasingly more unlike neighboring whites rather than assimilating. It strongly urged Indian participation in policy formation, since in any democracy, such as the United States claimed to be, self-determination and real choice between political alternatives was declared an inalienable right.

As a result of this report, a bill was introduced into Congress which was soon to be known as the Wheeler-Howard Act, or the Indian Reorganization Act of 1934.[8] This was an attempt to remedy some of these glaring problems by a basic restructuring of Indian policy. The pressure to split Indians off from one another was reversed, and tribes as wholes, not recognized since treaty days, were once again acknowledged as legal units. Reservation lands were again managed as large tribal units, rather than splintered into family-sized holdings, in the hope of consolidating valuable economic units on a scale competitive in twentieth-century agriculture. In order to manage these properties, tribal councils were set up for the first time. Although decisions remained subject to the veto of the Commissioner of Indian Affairs and ultimately the Secretary of the Interior, the councils had limited but legally specified authority. The Wheeler-Howard Act expressly forbade further sale or allotment of land by either the BIA or tribal councils, thus stemming the tide of land loss. In fact, tribal councils and the Secretary of the Interior were actually empowered to purchase land, often allotments located within existing reservation boundaries which had been previously sold to non-Indians. The tribal councils could enter into business transactions in the name of the tribe, including, for the first time indisputably, leases and contracts for land, resource extraction, or services. Rotating loans were made available for the development of irrigation systems, purchase of agricultural machinery, educational scholarships, and other projects. Thus for the first time reservation groups, including those on executive order reserves such as Pyramid Lake, could have a recognized, albeit limited voice in the management of their own affairs.

The law gave tribes the right to accept or reject the formation of such tribal councils and business committees for their reservations. The BIA sent out model constitutions, simplified versions of the United States government structure, but these models differed in many ways from traditional Paiute political forms. The new councils were based not on consensus but on majority vote, thus always compelling acquiescence by some minority who still disagreed. Such council structure assumed representation of the many by a few empowered to make decisions for all, rather than the traditional form of direct political representation of each person for himself. BIA councils were hierarchically constructed, with chairmen of greater importance and power than ordinary tribesmen. Despite these formalized and alien political structures, many tribes adopted constitutions.

In February 1934 the BIA called a meeting of all adult Indians of Pyramid Lake. An official explained the provisions of the Wheeler-Howard Act and asked whether they wanted to organize such a tribal council. While most Paiute speakers were initially favorable, they decided to adjourn until community members had had a chance to discuss among themselves the advantages and disadvantages of such an organization. At a second meeting they chose to form a tribal council under the act and elected a slate of councilmen. Throughout this and the following year, Pyramid Lake Paiutes held many meetings to draw up a formal constitution, establish bylaws, and organize a business committee. The tribal constitution was finally approved by Washington on January 15, 1936.[9]

The Pyramid Lake Tribal Council specifically had the power to manage any tribal property and funds, negotiate with all government agencies on behalf of the tribe, regulate tribal membership, provide social services, coordinate community labor projects, and generate tribal ordinances to regulate internal matters. Further, the council, as successor to the independent native tribe, claimed any reserve powers not explicitly abdicated over the years to other agencies and governments through treaty, agreement, or contract. Nevertheless, any council decisions were subject to the approval of the Agency Superintendent and the BIA.

The Pyramid Lake Tribe became a legal corporation, with duly elected officers, clearly stated duties, and explicit bylaws. Unlike the loose collection of individuals which they had been in the past, they could then act as a legally recognized group to serve their own interests and to manage their own properties. This was a corporation which the BIA acknowledged as having authority. For the first time, the Paiutes could make their voice heard in a forum which the government could not ignore.

Perhaps it was for this reason that Nevada's Senator Patrick Mc-Carran proposed the first of eight bills specifically denying reservation groups in his state the right to organize under the Wheeler-Howard Act.[10] In each case, the Pyramid Lake Tribal Council issued resolutions calling for defeat of these bills, uniformly opposing any legislation which would undercut their right of domestic self-government.[11] McCarran's petty special-interest legislation was defeated, and the council survived. The problem was then to put it to work.

The new political form called for new ways of thinking as well as for skills long unused. Councilmen were clearly uneasy with their new authority and unfamiliar with bureaucratic intricacies. In a community with a long history of consensus politics, they feared to exercise their power, for friends and neighbors might view their actions as dictatorial. They were cautious about the responsibility now placed on their shoulders for managing the affairs of an entire community. At first they relied on their Superintendent, Alida Bowler, to suggest actions and tactics. Squarely in favor of the reorganization policy, she saw her role as one of guidance while they gained familiarity with the new governing powers which they had undertaken. She respected the right of the tribal council to make their own decisions, even at the risk of making their own mistakes, for, she said, "it is through such unhappy experiences that the Indian councilmen learn how to manage their affairs in better order."[12] Nevertheless, she exercised her support in a selective fashion, for instance discouraging commitment to the revolving credit fund and other long-term debts. In some matters she was even willing to utilize her veto power as granted in the Wheeler-Howard Act. For the most part, however, she stood behind the decisions of the tribal council and gave positive encouragement, much needed in these early formative years.

The first concerns of the tribal council were traditional economic questions: grazing trespass, land squatters, and water rights. A few of these problems were solved simply by their organization under the Wheeler-Howard Act, which protected against the allotment of tribal property, thus removing the five-acre threat posed by the old 1904 legislation. In addition, the council had veto power over any proposed land sales. Senator Stewart's dream of unilaterally dissecting the reserve also came to an end. Nevertheless, other land issues remained—the squatters, Wadsworth, and active development of tribal property. As time went on, the council dealt with a rapidly expanding range of problems. When the Western Pacific Railroad wanted to build a spur line up the western side of the lake, the council had to cope with complex land leases.[13] Nationwide organizations such as the National Congress of American Indians (NCAI) brought to the council's attention issues of more than local scope, as well as pending federal legislation.[14] As the Pyramid Lake council joined these organizations, their interests expanded from provincial reservation matters to problems common to all Nevada tribes, and eventually to Indian peoples everywhere. In this way, councilmen became increasingly sophisticated. They gained skills in effective political techniques and broadened their perception of threats against them.

An early test of these skills came in a conflict over the right to legal counsel. The Wheeler-Howard Act explicitly empowered tribal councils "to employ legal counsel, the choice of counsel and the fixing of fees to be subject to the approval of the Secretary of the Interior."[15] Previously unincorporated tribes, as groups of mere individual wards of the government, could not employ lawyers in behalf of tribal interests. As individuals, Indians with private funds could, of course, hire attorneys. However, in this capacity they could only defend private interests, not those shared by the group as a whole. The BIA, as with any trustee, was under legal requirement to provide protection to its wards' property. Since it was a government agency, the BIA had access to attorneys from the Department of Justice. However, Justice Department attorneys were reluctant, and in later years expressly forbidden by internal regulation, to defend tribal interests against those of other government agencies within the same department, such as the more prestigious Bureau of Reclamation or the Forest Service. Further, political pressures from Nevada senators, as we have seen in the fishing and squatter cases, stalled and blocked effective use of federal attorneys to defend the Pyramid Lake Reservation against local Anglo interests. Therefore the explicit provision of the Wheeler-Howard Act establishing the tribe as a legal entity with the right to hire an attorney was extremely important for Pyramid Lake. This useful privilege soon became a point of conflict between the new tribal council and the Bureau, as the BIA tried to exercise its regulatory privilege to control the relationship between the tribe and its attorneys.

The dispute focused on a tribal suit against the federal government.

From the time of the founding of the United States until the mid-twenti-
eth century, Indian tribes, like other parties, could not directly sue the
federal government because of its ultimate sovereignty. Such cases
could only begin through the federal court system after Congress legislated special permission for that specific suit. Several tribes took this
option over the years, and in 1936 Pyramid Lake joined a proceeding
on the part of the previous Malheur Reservation Indians for land lost,
violation of treaty obligations, and other damages resulting from federal actions. Such cases were becoming so frequent that Congress
sought a general solution to settle tribal claims against the United
States government once and for all. Toward this end, Congress in 1946
passed the Indian Claims Commission Act,[16] establishing a commission to adjudicate grievances of the tribes against the government. The
amounts of land involved were vast and the stakes high. Many tribes
immediately took advantage of this act and filed suit.

The very special relation between tribes and the government is
based on individual treaties, specific court decisions, and particular
arrangements which vary from tribe to tribe; the benefits guaranteed
to one tribe do not automatically pertain to any other. Thus Indian
law is highly specialized and intricate, and it is virtually impossible
for a general attorney to handle Indian cases effectively. Over the
years a small number of specialists had developed the expertise to
plead such suits. Passage of the Indian Claims Commission Act encouraged more attorneys to enter this field, among them James Curry.
The Pyramid Lake Tribal Council met Curry through the NCAI,
which provided free legal advice to member tribes. In 1948 the Paiutes retained Curry to manage their claims case, and soon signed a
private two-year contract with him for general legal services. Furthermore, the council knew that a successful claims case required an attorney in Washington. As other problems, such as the squatters and
water rights, became more a matter of federal legislation than of local
conflict, it was critical to have a Washington-based lawyer permanently on retainer to protect tribal interests.

The Pyramid Lake claim against the United States derived from
the fact that before the arrival of Anglo-Americans the Northern Paiutes had occupied extensive lands beyond reservation boundaries.
They had never signed a treaty relinquishing control of those lands to

the federal government. Nevertheless, the United States had proceeded to sell much of that area under homestead laws, without having actually acquired the legal title itself. In that sense, all Anglo land
holdings within the traditional boundaries of the Northern Paiute
tribe were in trespass. The land had simply been seized without bill of
sale or act of condemnation, and therefore without transfer of title.
The Pyramid Lake Paiutes were suing for the lost value of their traditional section of that land.

When the Wheeler-Howard Act gave organized tribes the right to
employ counsel, it specified that "the choice of counsel and the fixing
of fees [were] to be subject to the approval of the Secretary of the
Interior." Through this provision the BIA, in the person of its Commissioner, attempted once again to manipulate and restrict the incipient power of the Pyramid Lake Tribal Council. Attorney Curry knew
that the new Indian Commissioner, Dillon S. Myer, was a close friend
of Senator Pat McCarran, who was the initiator of many bills that
would abolish tribal councils in Nevada, give more liberal terms to the
squatters on the Pyramid Lake Reservation, and interfere with water
rights there. Fearing collusion between Myer and McCarran, Curry
warned the tribe in 1950, "I am afraid, when it [his contract] expires,
that McCarran will try to get rid of me."[17] Indeed, shortly after his
appointment, the Commissioner moved to revise the regulations under which attorneys' contracts would be approved by the Bureau. In a
paternalistic memo, he justified his actions as "for the protection of
the tribes and for the protection of the Federal interest in them. . . .
Underlying all of these restrictions is one fundamental premise,
which is that Indian tribes *need* Federal protection because they are
not always able adequately to look after their own best interests."[18]
The more stringent new regulations resulted in the denial of nearly
10 percent of the contracts then outstanding with all tribes. Curry's
fears had been justified; eight of the contracts were his.

One was that with Pyramid Lake. They had already signed a ten-
year agreement which the tribe could terminate for any reason on 90
days' notice. The Commissioner insisted that this term was far too
long, and wanted to substitute a two-year contract. According to his
format, the tribe could not break the agreement without consent of
the Commissioner of Indian Affairs. However, he retained the right

to fire the attorney at any time without notification or cause. Curry and the tribe both perceived that such action would make the lawyer more accountable to the Commissioner than to his client, the tribe, and Curry wrote to them: "I cannot do good work for you with the threat hanging over my head that if I displease the Commissioner by taking your side against his, he will fire me."[19] Next, the Commissioner was concerned about reportability. Curry had always submitted quarterly reports to the tribe, detailing the manpower, time, and expenses incurred in pursuit of their case. Myer now demanded that these reports go not only to the tribe, but also to him. The lawyer considered this a violation of attorney–client confidentiality. The Commissioner also objected to Curry's being in Washington, and so unable, he said, to deal with local matters. This statement ignored the fact that Curry had for over a year subcontracted with several local lawyers to take care of such problems. Finally, the Commissioner turned to the issue of incurred expenses, for which attorneys were traditionally always reimbursed. He suggested that these expenses should not be guaranteed by the tribe, but be contingent upon successful conclusion of the suit. The attorney would have a vested interest in the litigation, Curry objected, and this would lead to a basic conflict of interests and violate the American Bar Association's ethical standards.

While other attorneys renegotiated their contracts and capitulated to Bureau demands, Curry refused to sign either an interim agreement or to compromise. The Commissioner continued to refuse to sign his contract or to reject it overtly. As time dragged on, both the lawyer and the tribe demanded an immediate decision.[20] John Collier, the ex-Commissioner of Indian Affairs and now President of the Institute of Ethnic Affairs, issued a press release accusing the Bureau of inactivity. To refuse, he said, either to deny or approve the contract, to simply allow it to expire, "will seriously endanger the Indians' capacity to defend themselves against predatory interests."[21] The NCIA declared: "Myer is attempting to dictate to the Indian people what attorneys they may hire with their own money, or whether they shall be permitted to have any attorney at all."[22] In February 1951 the Pyramid Lake Indians' contract with Curry lapsed. They were left without the attorney's services upon which they had come to depend.

To protect the continuity of its land-claims case, the tribe retained Judge Carville, previously one of Curry's locally subcontracted associates. However, not content with such defensive action, the Paiutes also sent a delegation to Washington to voice their objections to the proposed revision of Curry's contract. "We think the objections to the contract," they declared, "are trivial and that they are not important enough to justify you in interfering with the Tribe's own agreement with its Attorney. This is an interference with tribal democracy, which should not be made except for the most important reasons. The contract should be approved as written."[23] The Commissioner retorted: "If the trusteeship [of the U.S. Government over Indian tribes] means anything at all, it certainly means that we are called upon to safeguard the tribes against unwise or improvident expenditures."[24] This extravagant concern over financial matters seemed hollow to the delegation, in view of the Bureau's record of unconcern over actual resources. They accused the Bureau of inactivity in guarding water rights, failure to protect them against McCarran's machinations to alienate land, and neglect to buy out the squatters' now-expired claims, as permitted under the Wheeler-Howard Act. The Paiutes then tried to go over the head of the Indian Commissioner and see the Secretary of the Interior. Curry, mobilizing the power of the NCAI, appealed his case to President Truman, all to no avail.

All this controversy did lead to a Senate investigation, however. The special subcommittee concluded that Curry's 26 general tribal contracts and 30 claims-case contracts constituted an overload for the staff which he retained, such an overload that he could not possibly provide quality service to all clients. They criticized his practice of subcontracting the work to other attorneys, who might or might not have the necessary specialized expertise in Indian law. Both the Senate Ethics Committee and the American Bar Association censured his techniques for recruiting contracts. The investigation supported the BIA's authority to regulate contracts as stated by law.[25] This hearing essentially ended Curry's contract with the Pyramid Lake tribe.

Thus the Bureau of Indian Affairs won. It proved its power over the tribe's legal representation, precisely when so many matters were pressing that their Superintendent declared: "Developments of the past months, and particularly in more recent time, have convinced me that you cannot afford to be without a lawyer, who is in a position independently to fight your battles."[26] The tribe immediately sought new counsel and has never been without a lawyer since. As the tribe has acquired more control over reservation resources, the assistance of such an attorney has become increasingly critical.

In addition to the struggle over attorneys' contracts, the new tribal council early faced the persistent challenge of Wadsworth. As we have seen, in 1898 the residents there had received congressional permission to file for title to lots within the townsite. The Wheeler-Howard Act of 1934, however, radically restructured the relationship between tribal entities and land.[27] Property was no longer to be handled simply at the discretion of the federal government, but rather the tribal councils were entrusted with its management. Specifically, Section 4 of that act read: "Except as herein provided, no sale, device, gift, exchange or other transfer of restricted Indian lands or of shares in the assets of any Indian tribe or corporation organized hereunder, shall be made or approved." Effectively, this put a stop to all alienation of Indian lands without the specific approval of tribal councils. However, Section 3 of the same act protracted any previously authorized sale of tribal property:

> The Secretary of the Interior, if he shall find it to be in the public interest, is hereby authorized to restore to tribal ownership the remaining surplus lands of any Indian reservation heretofore opened, or authorized to be opened, to sale, or any other form of disposal by Presidential proclamation, or by any of the public-land laws of the United States: *Provided, however,* that valid rights of claims of any persons to any lands so withdrawn existing on the date of the withdrawal shall not be affected by this Act.

In the Pyramid Lake case, since Congress had already authorized sale of the Wadsworth townsite, that authorization was still valid. Any filings which had already been made could be completed, but those townsmen who had not bothered to begin this legal process would be barred from initiating purchase. By 1936, only 8 of the families in Wadsworth had actually purchased their lots; another 16 families had made no effort to comply with the law and were illegally occupying a total of 58 lots in the town of Wadsworth, valued at over $8,000.[28]

Since the tribal council was now the manager of tribal lands, and since the unsold lands would, by law, revert to the tribe, it was reasonable for the tribe to handle the actual transfer of title. Alida Bowler, the Superintendent for Pyramid Lake at the time, thought this was an excellent opportunity to school the Paiutes in bureaucratic procedures and administrative skills which they would need later. She favored the tribal council's taking over these land transactions, and supported them in their efforts to understand the legal technicalities.

Some Paiutes feared that council involvement in these land transfers might constitute tribal acknowledgment of the squatters' right to acquire tribal land on the reservation.[29] The council, however, soon realized that the Act of 1898 had already given the trespassers at Wadsworth a legal, if not a moral, claim. The Wheeler-Howard Act did not give them power to retract that right of purchase. It was far better, they thought, for the tribe itself to oversee the orderly transfer of title than to let the BIA proceed with its customarily casual adherence to time limits and its less-than-enthusiastic defense of Indian property. Therefore in April 1939 the council unanimously approved resolutions that unsold Wadsworth lots should revert to the Pyramid Lake Reservation as soon as legally possible, and that, in accordance with the powers granted by the Wheeler-Howard Act, no provision should be made to sell additional lots.

They relied on the BIA for technical advice on how to proceed, for, as Bowler wrote, "It is their desire that we [the BIA] assist them to determine a reasonable rental, and that they be instructed through us as to exactly how to go about leasing these lots in the proper fashion."[30] In meeting after meeting they wove through complex questions of application, of sale, and of leasing to delinquent squatters those lands which they occupied in the township of Wadsworth. Ground rules were set. Wadsworth residents appeared at tribal council meetings to petition for time extensions, for increase in allowable size of lots, and for reduction of the minimal $25 fee.[31] The council attempted to restrict the number of lots each individual could purchase. There was further delay when Washington demanded a new survey of the township before the disposal could proceed.

Finally, in 1948, the sale began, and by February 1949, 14 town lots had been transferred to white ownership and the question of the

Indian school settled. Nevertheless, in 1951 there were still 11 purchasers delinquent and unpaid. Eventually the evaluations of the land became so outdated that the tribe closed off the sales, which were not reopened until 1958.[32] By this time it was very clear that the tribe had lost effective control over the Wadsworth township. Their attempts to facilitate an orderly withdrawal of reservation lands had absorbed a great deal of the council's time and effort in the preceding ten years. This effort had brought them information and experience and produced increased sophistication in the hierarchical complexities of the U.S. legal system; it may also have diverted their attention from other issues of greater importance over which they did have some real control—squatters elsewhere on the reservation and encroachment on water rights.

Wadsworth was primarily a residential area, limited in extent and of relatively minor importance. However, nearby lay the fertile bottomlands along the Truckee River which were capable of productive output and of great importance to the tribe. Before 1934 there had been no tribal entity to resist encroachment on these lands, and the BIA had been negligent in protecting Indian interests there. During its first ten years of organization, one of the tribal council's earliest and most persistent concerns was the issue of title to these 3,800 acres of reservation land illegally held by non-Indians.

At first the council approached the question gently in its letters to the Commissioner of Indian Affairs, John Collier.[33] They expressed concern over the squatters' use of this land and of water from the Truckee River. They noted that Indian farms then averaged only 7¼ acres, far smaller than the Anglo landholdings in question. They suggested an official investigation into the matter, or perhaps exercise of the Wheeler-Howard authority to purchase the land. In short, they asked for any solution, rather than continued sufferance of the current ambiguous state of affairs.

As the situation stood, those squatters had been given the opportunity to purchase title from the federal government by the Act of June 7, 1924. Some of the squatters promptly paid off their assessments; others clamored for a reduction, which came in 1926. Nevertheless, a small number, particularly the several Ceresolas, their half-brother Depaoli, and the incorporated Garaventa family, refused to pay even this reduced fee. Long after the payment period had expired, these intransigents were still delinquent. The new tribal council soon pressured the government to do something about it.

In response to the squatters' disregard of federal authority and to the tribe's urging, the Commissioner of the General Land Office formally notified the trespassers in May 1936 that their right to purchase the land was canceled. He demanded that they vacate at once. The delinquent Garaventa Livestock Co. and the Depaoli family immediately went to the Federal Land Office in Carson City and offered to pay off their accounts. The Garaventa payment was duly rejected, but through a clerical error the Depaoli monies were accepted and deposited. In October the tribal council, along with the Pyramid Lake agent, met with the U.S. Attorney to discuss legal procedures, but it was not until February 1938 that the federal government finally filed eviction suits against the remaining squatters. The tribe supported prompt prosecution, and the council passed a resolution vowing to use whatever funds it had "to fight this case."[34]

Nevada's indomitable congressional delegation geared for action. Senator Pat McCarran and Representative James Scrugham asked the Department of Justice to postpone prosecution, on grounds that once again they had legislation pending to give squatters the land scot-free. The Nevada State Legislature urged congressmen to "pass legislation permitting the white settlers who have made homes on lands in Pyramid Lake Reservation in Nevada to obtain title to said lands and remain thereon."[35] The legislature, like Pat McCarran and other prominent Nevadans, again harped on the founding date of the reserve, refusing to accept any evidence that the reservation had been established before the 1874 executive order. Of course, if this were true, it would mean that Anglo entries onto the lands now in question would have preceded reservation withdrawal. As these claims were sold and resold, the title would then have remained valid.

The tribal council protested both this ahistorical logic and the delays in prosecution urged by Nevada's congressmen.[36] The Secretary of the Interior supported them and asked the Department of Justice to pursue the eviction suits against the white squatters with all deliberate speed.[37]

But such speed was not very swift, and by 1938 the tribal council wearied of the slow pace. Since the government put the suits "off and on," they resolved to hire a private attorney to "get them off of our land." Accordingly, they filed a request with the BIA to release tribal funds to hire lawyers for this case "like our Constitution says."[38] The Bureau refused. This would be a waste of money, it argued, since the tribe was entitled to free legal counsel from the Department of Justice, through its connection with the BIA. This reply outraged the Pyramid Lake Superintendent, who protested that according to the constitution, already approved by the BIA, the council had the power to expend tribal funds "for any other purpose approved by the Tribe."[39] She had assumed, she wrote, that this

> meant just what it said and would be inclusive of attorney hire. It is hard for anyone except a legal mind to see how such an all-inclusive term could fail to cover attorney hire. May I ask that in order to clear this matter up you [Commissioner Collier] obtain a ruling on this matter *immediately*? If the ruling is adverse, I am sure that the Pyramid Lake Paiute Tribe would appreciate your undertaking immediately to obtain such legislation as might be necessary to make it possible for them to hire attorneys if they deem it necessary because of continued delays or if they should find themselves not satisfied with the handling of the case. This would seem only fair in view of the promises extended to them in the Indian Reorganization Act [Wheeler-Howard] that they would be given the power to manage their own affairs.[40]

The tribal council expressed their lack of faith in Justice Department attorneys to the Commissioner:

> We hope you will get this legal opinion for us from some place else than from the Attorney General. The way that the Attorney General has acted about our eviction suits has robbed us of all our faith in his fairness to us. It is a very long time since the action of the Secretary gave us back these lands. Had the Attorney General been fair to us those white settlers would have been off of our land long since and fifteen or twenty of our own young men would now be supporting their families by using that land.[41]

However, the ruling was never forthcoming. The BIA persistently refused to allow the tribe to use funds for attorney hire in the eviction suits. Once again the Paiutes were stymied from active resolution of the squatter problem and thrown back on the Justice Department. They could only await the slow pace of these cases through the courts. Tribal patience was growing thin.

When the eviction suits, placed on the court calendar for early October 1938, were once again postponed, the tribal council passed the following resolution:

> We are told, by people who know, that the legal title to that land is ours. Is it not then the duty of the United States Government, as our guardian and trustee, to evict the people who now occupy that land illegally? The entries covering these tracts were cancelled by the Secretary of the Interior on May 13, 1936. Already one, -two, -three summers have come and gone. Squatters have gathered and eaten or sold the crops that should rightfully have been ours to tend and to harvest. They do not even pay us ground rent. . . . So far our guardian, the Government, has failed to fulfill its sacred obligation to the Pyramid Lake Paiute Tribe. . . . Due to the failure of the United States Government to protect our property we have had no use of these same lands since 1870 or a little earlier. Think how many hundreds of thousands of dollars that has meant in lost crops. Think how much it has meant to the white people who have had the free use of that land, without legal title to it. Our people believe that they have a valid claim against the Government for some of these losses, and that we should ask Congress to authorize us to file a claim in the United States Court of Claims, to cover all, or at least part, of these losses. . . . But we want our land more than we want money. Money is soon spent, and gone forever. The land stays, growing food for the people, down through the generations. That is what our Tribe wants. Under the Indian Reorganization Act our land is protected. We have the right to veto any sale of it. Our Tribe has adopted a constitution which prohibits the sale of any Tribal land. That is how our Tribe feels about it. But we seem helpless to get the use of these lands. . . . We earnestly beg that no further delay be allowed. There must be some way to get action.[42]

In the midst of this difficulty, Pyramid Lake faced yet another challenge, the loss of Superintendent Bowler. She had always been outspoken in support of tribal council self-assertion, and for this she had earned the intense dislike of Senator McCarran. In some 1937 hearings, he described her as "the most unfair officer of the federal government"[43]—unfair for siding with the Indians against the claims of the whites whom he represented. He slandered her among the bureaucracy of Washington and poisoned the minds of the Senate committees against any evidence she might present. In December 1939 she was transferred from Pyramid Lake, where she had successfully battled for tribal council autonomy and active pursuit of the squatter cases. Gossip on the reservation was rife that Senator McCarran had something to do with her sudden removal.[44] Although she denied this rumor, like the loyal government official that she was, her transfer did in fact remove from the tribe an active and effective ally. In her place was sent first Ralph Gelvin and shortly thereafter E. Reeseman Fryer. As perhaps few other Indian agents at the time, Fryer would continue Bowler's policy supporting independent tribal action in reservation matters.

In March 1941, action finally came in the first of the eviction suits. The U.S. District Court found in favor of the Garaventa Land and Livestock Company.[45] By accepting the executive order of 1874 as the founding date of the reservation, the court argued that the squatters' claims existed prior to federal withdrawal of the land for Indian purposes. In addition, the court maintained that while the land purchase bill of 1924 specified that squatters had the right of purchase, it did not specify that the government had the right to cancel those purchases once the process had begun. It only gave the government the right to reclaim any land upon which squatters failed to initiate a filing. Since the Garaventas had made an initial payment, they were safe, as far as the District Court was concerned. Government policy during the Depression offered leniency to people financially distressed; on these grounds, the court argued, the government should not foreclose even though final payments were not yet entered.

On appeal, the Circuit Court rejected this suggested limitation on federal power to cancel the delinquent purchases. It also rejected the proffered 1874 date for establishment of the reservation. All the settlers and their successors in interest, the higher court ruled, had been well aware that this was federal reservation land; they had invested in improvements at their own risk. The court thereby rejected the argument, long used by Nevada's senators, that these squatters had valid, vested property interests which commanded legal protection. To the contrary, the court held that the squatters had legal obligations which they were shirking. In making initial payment, the squatters had formed an implicit contract. They had accepted the terms of payment that they should pay one quarter of the principal each succeeding year, along with interest on the balance. Since they had defaulted on this obligation, their action, like any contract violation, had canceled any future responsibility between the two parties. Nevertheless, in yet another act of government leniency, the court gave the squatters 30 days to complete payment. Failing this, they would irrevocably lose the right to purchase the land.

The Depaoli case was a slight variation on the Garaventa theme. In 1935, when evaluation of the land was reduced, the family was given 30 days to complete payment. They were again notified in March of 1936 that in 30 more days all the interest and one quarter of the delinquent principal were due. Six months later the Depaolis still had not made the payment, and their application to purchase the land was canceled. In August, the Depaolis appeared at the U.S. Land Office in Carson City with the full balance plus interest and a petition for reinstatement of their right to make payment. The Commissioner of the General Land Office in Washington denied this petition and returned their proffered final payment. Nevertheless, their down-payment of over $2,500, made years previously, was still resting in the federal Treasury, and this the government refused to return. Despite the expiration of the time limit, rejection of their final payment, and denial of their petition for reinstatement, the Depaolis argued that they held a vested interest in the land on the basis of their initial down-payment. In 1943, the Circuit Court of Appeals issued a summary judgment that the Depaolis' case did not differ substantially from that of Garaventa.[46] As with any other credit purchase, the Depaolis' failure to make final payment within the allotted time period resulted in forfeit of the down-payment and cancellation of the contract. The U.S. Supreme Court refused to review the case, thus letting the judgment of the lower court stand. There could be no further appeal. The squatters had been given their day in court, and the facts had been found against them.

Now the Department of Justice ordered the U.S. Marshal to serve eviction notices on these remaining squatters. However, Senator Mc-

Carran once again asked the Justice Department to withhold the writs, suggesting "That eviction proceedings be delayed to a date not later than January 1, 1945, and he, Senator McCarran, will endeavor to obtain an appropriation from Congress with which to buy for the use of the Pyramid Lake Tribe the interspersed patented lands owned by whites."[47] Out of congressional courtesy, the Department of Justice complied. Although the evictions were postponed far beyond 1945, McCarran never actually introduced the promised legislation to purchase land for the tribe. Rather, once BIA acquiescence to his stalling action was won, he offered much more characteristic legislation by which Congress would give the squatters this land without further payment. Once again the wily senator outmaneuvered the Indian Bureau and rendered the Justice Department ineffectual.

Like their loyal ally in Congress, the squatters did not stand by idle. Long before, they had dug irrigation ditches onto these Indian lands and diverted a portion of the water allocated to the reservation to farm them. In retaliation for the judicial denial of their land claim, they opened negotiations with other landowners in the area to sell the water rights to these ditches.[48] Sale of water off the land would make it utterly worthless should the Indians actually ever repossess it.

The tribal council's reaction to all this was remarkably restrained. Since the Department of Justice had not actually managed to pry the squatters off the land, the council decided to make the best of a bad situation. By March 1944, when McCarran thwarted the evictions, it was almost too late in the agricultural year, a councilman observed, for the white squatters to find other lands to substitute for those now decreed to the tribe. It was also very late in the season for the tribe to get the needed equipment to utilize the land effectively. So rather than spitefully harm the squatters when the tribe itself could not benefit, the council suggested that the Anglos be permitted to continue their use of the land under a bonded lease agreement for the coming agricultural year, as long as they acknowledged the recent court decisions against them. The BIA prepared the leases, effective through January 1, 1945, when McCarran's moratorium on evictions should cease. Although the council went out of their way to cooperate, they still insisted on their legal rights. They urged the Department of Justice not only to proceed with the eviction notices, but also to investigate, under Wheeler-Howard Act authorization, reacquisition of any land which Anglos held legitimately within the reservation boundaries. Meanwhile the tribe continued to authorize leases. By November 1947 the Ceresola brothers were delinquent in their payments and the BIA had to force collection.[49] In December of 1948, when the Depaoli three-year lease expired, the family refused to renegotiate the terms. They also refused to leave the land. The Agency Superintendent observed that the lease fee was well below the prevailing rates for land rental in the area and that the tribe very badly needed the land for their own people: "You should, if you approach the Council on another lease, be prepared to meet the prevailing rental rates for land. It seems that your present lease was a special concession because your son was in the Service and that you might have ample time to move your buildings, from Indian to your land, without being subject to the inconvenience or extra expense because of the pressure for time."[50] Nevertheless, the Depaolis were entrenched and refused to leave. During the next season they began an active program to damage the value of the property by not maintaining the ditches which irrigated it.[51] This not only damaged the land, but also threatened extensive Indian acreage below on the same ditch.

The Pyramid Lake Tribal Council had recently joined the NCAI. In 1947 an NCAI attorney visited them, very much concerned over the tribe's land problems. She pointed out that the writs of removal were still sitting in the U.S. Marshal's office and that, contrary to normal procedures, Nevada's congressional delegation had made no attempt to expedite the serving of these warrants. She suggested that the council escalate the fight for possession by filing suit against the federal government for its delay. Such legal advice as this, at a time when the council had extremely limited experience with such matters, stimulated their exploration of new strategies and their own new powers. The Superintendent reported to the Commissioner of Indian Affairs that "The Tribal Council and a Mrs. Bell [NCAI attorney] have suggested that if there is apt to be a delay in this action that the Tribal Council employ the legal services of the National Congress of American Indians to take the matter into the appropriate courts for action."[52] It was this threat that apparently brought action from Washington. In September the Secretary of the Interior requested the

Attorney General to proceed with the writs evicting all the squatters except Depaoli, whose case was considered ambiguous. The Commissioner of Indian Affairs reassured the Pyramid Lake Superintendent that "If and when the settlers attempt to interfere with the use of the ditches, any necessary legal action will be recommended."[53] This promise would not be kept.

By April 1949 the Superintendent began making arrangements for the Paiutes to utilize that land which the courts had decreed to them.[54] The tribe did gain control over some of the now-dry riverine lands, including Truckee John's homestead and some of the previous Olinghouse properties. These were quickly assigned to tribal members. One member of the Depaoli family appeared before the tribal council, pleading that some agreement be reached. The Superintendent pointed out that his interference with the ditch was hurting everyone. Unabashed, Depaoli boldly asked for a long-term lease in exchange for his permitting the water to flow through his holding and on to Indian lands below. The council, continuing to cooperate, agreed to negotiate, but refused to condone his illegal occupancy of tribal land, attempting instead to form an agreement for joint maintenance of the ditches and to reestablish the lease at prevailing rates. Depaoli neglected appointed meetings and rejected both offers through his attorney. Finally, in frustration, the tribal council outlined their grievances to their own lawyer in June of 1949:

> We find, however, that agreement is impossible. He [Depaoli] has repaid our effort to be more than just and fair by: 1) Entering our own lands to build dams across ditches to prevent water from reaching our land. . . . 2) Moving two buildings, which we believe were decreed to us by the courts, from our lands to his. 3) Taking some 1000 board feet of heavy redwood timbers, which were pulled out of the ground by tractor, from our land to his. 4) Maintaining in trespass on tribal lands, despite a notice to remove them, livestock varying in numbers from 30 to 90 from January 1, 1949 to the present time. 5) Occupying and using, in trespass, houses, barns, and other improvements held to be the property of the Tribe, without compensation of any kind. 6) Interfering with the use of water from Proctor Ditch to irrigate tribal land, thus causing the loss of at least one crop of alfalfa, and endangering, if water is not applied to it very soon, all of the alfalfa now grow-

ing on tribal repossessed lands on the east bank of the Truckee. . . . Our
attempts to settle this matter in a friendly way have failed.[55]

The Superintendent believed that the only realistic way to get the
squatters actually off this so-called repossessed land was to pay them
for their improvements. He feared, a bit late, the growth of interracial tensions:

> Should the Congress take this land away from the Indians and force
> the Secretary of the Interior to sell the land to the settlers, there would
> be a feeling of bitterness between the Indian people and the settlers
> that would remain from here on out. In effect, by winning the settlers
> would be losing. On the other hand, if the Indians moved onto the so-
> called repossessed land, there would be a terrible bitterness between
> the settlers and their Indian neighbors that would also carry on from
> here on out.[56]

The fact was that the squatters had been in possession of this land for
nearly 80 years. Had this not engendered a bitterness in the Paiutes
when coupled with all the other wrongs history had piled upon them?
The only new bitterness that could now arise would be that of the
whites, who had previously consistently had their own way. In this
one case they might be thwarted. Was this perhaps the origin of all the
editorial outrage, bureaucratic concern, and senatorial intervention?

There were yet other economic sources of tension. Like other federal land holdings such as national parks and military bases, Indian
reservations were not subject to local land taxes. In areas heavily im-
pacted with federal ownership, such as Nevada, local citizens and
state legislatures saw this as an imbalance in the tax base and a threat
to their economy. Although the 600 acres still unresolved in this dispute was miniscule in terms of the county tax-base, the Pyramid Lake
Tribal Council made a desperate and unprecedented gesture to attempt to overcome Anglo resistance. They offered to allow these
lands, if repossessed by the tribe, to remain on the tax rolls.[57] They
asked the federal government for funds to buy out the squatters' interests in the lands already awarded them seven years before by the
U.S. Supreme Court, as well as small amounts of patented land within

reservation boundaries. The tribe would then continue to pay taxes on these properties. This was a completely voluntary abdication of the unquestioned right of Indian tribes to tax-free reservation land, in recognition of their once-sovereign aboriginal status. Such a waiver of tribal land tax-exemption would have profoundly affected Indian tribes throughout the country and restructured much Indian law. Perhaps fortunately, Congress balked at the third of a million dollars the Ceresolas greedily asked for their small property. Local resistance remained adamant against any Indian land purchase. The tribal offer was rejected.

Because of its association with the NCAI, the tribe had an attorney of its own by this time. Although concerned with a broad range of issues, he took particular interest in this question of land repossession. He encouraged the tribal council to adopt a resolution which urged the federal government to do its duty and repossess the lands and improvements as soon as possible. The government was far stronger than the tribe both financially and politically, he said. Therefore the government, acting as tribal trustee, was more likely to succeed than was the tribe acting independently. "Only if the United States refuses to do its duty, should the Indians then proceed. . . . Also, of course," the lawyer noted in passing, "I have in mind to sue the United States for its past neglect and to sue the squatters for the value of their past use of the land."[58]

The new structure of the tribal council, coupled with the legal expertise of independent counsel, led to an increasingly self-assured and aggressive stance which could not be ignored. In 1950, the BIA asked the Attorney General to enforce the six-year-old Supreme Court decree. There was no longer justification for delay. Ever since the court decisions, the memo observed, squatters had waged a war of retaliation against the Indians.

> The defendants in the case have cut wires and destroyed fences erected by the Indians to protect the lands, and have refused to permit the Indians to use the available ditches to deliver water to irrigate the lands. Indians who have attempted to clean the ditches and restore them to a condition which would permit their use in irrigating the lands have been frightened or driven away. The Depaoli family has

been particularly troublesome. . . . It is accordingly recommended that appropriate proceedings be instituted (1) to enforce the writ of assistance against the Depaoli family and to restrain them and the other defendants in the *Garaventa Land and Livestock Company* case from trespassing on the lands awarded to the Indians; (2) to quiet title to the buildings on the land unlawfully occupied by the Depaoli family; (3) to quiet title to the irrigation ditches,[59]

and to adjudicate the still ambiguous water rights.

Finally it appeared that the squatters would actually be removed. However, just at this juncture, Superintendent Fryer was transferred from Pyramid Lake. There was no question that Fryer, like Bowler transferred before him, had been active in pursuing the Paiutes' claim to the land. Fryer had "taken definite steps," the tribal attorney wrote to a colleague, "as required by law, to restore to full Indian possession and use the lands that were illegally taken by the Ceresolas, Depaolis, and Garraventas [*sic*]. This is the reason that Fryer is being transferred. My information, in which I have full confidence, is that [BIA] Commissioner Dillon Myer is taking this action at the direct behest of Senator McCarran. Myer was personally confronted with this charge. He said that the transfer was made, not at McCarran's, but at Fryer's own initiative. This was checked with Fryer, who denied it."[60] The *Washington Post* concurred in the lawyer's suspicions and proclaimed that "the public should know the relationship between Fryer's removal and McCarran's efforts to grab the Indians' lands."[61] But suspicion was hardly necessary, for McCarran himself had written to a friend, "I have no use for this fellow Freer [*sic*] who is Superintendent of Indians. I am laying the groundwork toward getting him removed, but I don't know if I can get him out before September [when McCarran went up for primary re-election]."[62] Once again the menace of Nevada's senator was raised against the Paiutes.

Fryer appealed his transfer to the Secretary of the Interior, who refused to act on his behalf. Eventually, with the support of the Institute of Ethnic Affairs, the NCAI, and other Indian advocacy organizations, Fryer went directly to President Truman. The President found evidence for Fryer's complaint and countermanded Myer's order of transfer. Then and only then did Fryer resign from the BIA. "Like any superintendent worth his salt," Fryer told reporters, "I would remain in Indian Service only if I knew I could do creditable work. This requires the support of the Commissioner."[63] If the Commissioner of Indian Affairs were to buckle under political pressure from the Nevada delegation, Fryer, as a subordinate, could accomplish nothing. In the past, such interference had repeatedly blocked his efforts. While investigating the feasibility of constructing a duplicate ditch system to replace the one now blocked on the repossessed lands, Fryer had begun an irrigation survey in 1950. The survey had been stopped by order of Dillon Myer at the request of Pat McCarran. Again, when the tribe had suggested buying out the squatters, McCarran attached a rider to the BIA appropriations bill that monies therein could be used for land purchase in any state except Nevada. In the year after Fryer's removal, McCarran was to pressure Myer to cancel Attorney Curry's contract with the Pyramid Lake tribe. Thus Nevada's Senator McCarran was attempting systematically to strip the tribe of their activist agents and their independent attorney. Once they lost these allies, he hoped they would also lose their ability and willingness to fight the insidious legalistic war he was waging against them in the halls of Congress.

By the early 1950s, the Paiutes were losing patience with the Indian Bureau. When they sent a delegation to Washington to protest the cancellation of Curry's contract, they also protested against the delay in reclaiming the land. A 1952 council resolution declared that "Various Federal officials, in cooperation with Senator Pat McCarran, have been trying for years by the foulest means to prevent the Pyramid Lake Indians from retaking possession of said lands and the waters appurtenant to said lands."[64]

This growing irritation did not prevent the squatters from brazenly proposing to trade the lands which the court had already awarded to the tribe along with their patented acreage, in exchange for tribal lands located along the outside boundary of the reservation. In considering this proposition, the council was soon bogged down in a morass of technicalities over the value of the respective acreage, water rights, pasturage, and improvements. All of this delayed and distracted the tribal council while McCarran launched yet another flank attack from Washington.

Senator McCarran was fond of reminiscing about his childhood spent along the Truckee River and his later active membership in the Truckee River Water Users Association. He was also fond of publicly proclaiming his repeated election successes in Wadsworth, the Anglo town, and his proud losses in Nixon, on the reservation. This self-portrait coincided with his political position in a series of nearly identical bills introduced between 1937 and 1954, from the time of the first federal eviction suits against the squatters until the time of his death. Each bill yielded complete free title to those remaining squatters who were still delinquent in their final payment for Indian land at Pyramid Lake. In all its reappearances, McCarran's bill was essentially the same as in the first edition. It simply said:

> Be it enacted by the Senate and the House of Representatives of the United States of America in Congress assembled, That the Secretary of the Interior is authorized and directed to issue, to each person who entered lands under authorization of section 1 of the Act entitled "An Act for the relief of settlers and townsite occupants of certain lands in the Pyramid Lake Indian Reservation, Nevada," approved June 7, 1924, or to the successor in interest of such person, a patent for the lands so entered for which part of the purchase price has been paid, without requiring that any further sum be paid on the principal of such purchase price or the interest on the unpaid part of such principal.[65]

At the hearings for this and subsequent versions of his proposal, McCarran's arguments reflected the opinions of many Nevada Anglos, loaded with diagnostic assumptions, errors, and intentional oversights. For instance, he refused to acknowledge the 1859 establishment of the reservation, a date which federal courts had accepted as both accurate and legally binding years before he held his first bill's hearing. The senator consistently referred to the "so-called Indian reservation" because, he said, "There is merely an Executive order creating that as a reserve for the Piute [sic] Indians."[66] This was certainly a false issue by this time, for executive powers to establish Indian reservations had been acknowledged by Congress in 1884 and explicitly validated by an opinion of the Attorney General in 1924.[67]

The reason McCarran took this untenable position was once again to open the possibility of recognition for those squatters' rights

taken up between 1859 and 1874. Many of the present settlers, Mc-
Carran declared in public hearings, "are families or descendants of
the early first settlers."[68] This assertion was simply untrue, since none
of these Italian-surnamed families were such descendants, and none
had purchased claims before 1900. Nevertheless, McCarran still
claimed that "their ancestors came in here as pioneers. They are the
sons and daughters of pioneers."[69] In his most ringing senatorial rhetoric, McCarran painted fields cleared of sagebrush and leveled, with
water flowing in ditches: "They stand up like little green gems along
the river."[70] Upon these lush pastures, he portrayed the squatters,
"born on some of these tracts of land. Here they gave their young life,
they were married, they gave in marriage, they buried their dead."[71]
In contrast to this glowing prose, he declared disparagingly "these
Indians are not inclined to be agriculturalists. They never were agriculturalists. . . . They are fishermen. They are nomadic. They are a
rambling tribe."[72] Such assertion flew boldly in the face of the facts,
since the Paiutes had been resident on Pyramid Lake Reservation un-
interruptedly for 70 years. They were certainly no longer nomadic in
any sense of the word. But through this misrepresentation, McCarran
could then argue that "No Indian ever took possession of these lands
in any way, form, or manner. So you are taking nothing whatever
from the Indians. What they never had they never lost. . . ."[73]

Here of course was the old frontier argument once again, that possession made right and that maximum agricultural use of the land
justified its possession against any "lesser" use. McCarran glossed
over the cause of the Indians' nonpossession, that white men had
forcibly seized all the arable acreage and steadfastly refused to yield it
despite legal right, administrative action, and Supreme Court decision. McCarran then observed that Indians were farming less acreage
than their formal water allotment allowed, insinuating that they
would not use the lands well if they should regain them. He again
ignored the cause of Indian behavior, that they could not use their full
allotment of water because it was being diverted onto these squatted
lands upriver. Long-term possession and subsequent vested interest
justified, McCarran argued to his legislative colleagues, yielding of
title to the squatters.

Committeemen, eager to prove their bureaucratic acumen, inevitably asked about those payments still outstanding according to the 1924 bill. Unlike the others who paid off their debts, McCarran replied, the remaining five squatters were unable to do so as a result of the Depression. "From 1925 or 1926 on, the farmers of our entire community were hard hit," he said. "These farmers—and they are real farmers—were heavily mortgaged. . . . They were trying, during all those years, to refinance themselves so as to pay this obligation, if it were possible, and get through with it, although always they were protesting that the price was too great."[74] Why the Depression should have affected these five more than others, he never explained.

This illogic gave Commissioner of Indian Affairs John Collier opportunity to launch an attack with information on the yields and prices for alfalfa, sheep, and livestock in northern Nevada during those years.[75] He proved that these ranchers, if they were financially pressed, should not have been. In fact, these same ranchers were actually purchasing off-reservation land during this period, building barns, and engaging in other expensive activities. In short, Collier argued, these squatters were not in nearly as bad a financial situation as McCarran wished Congress to believe; they could have made payment according to the law if they had so chosen.

Surely it would be harsh, McCarran then pleaded, to throw these squatters "out into the cold world, [from] where they and their families have lived and paid taxes for years, and where no Indian ever set foot upon that land, either in private or in public ownership."[76] This patently untrue assertion gave Collier yet another opening. He searched the county records and showed that no taxes had been paid for most of the lands in dispute.[77] At this juncture the Secretary of the Interior suggested a compromise, that the principal designated by the bill of 1924 should be paid, but the interest waived. McCarran amended his own bill to this effect.

Despite the errors of history and fact in McCarran's presentation, congressional committeemen bowed to the will of their powerful colleague. On July 22, 1937, the amended bill passed the Senate and moved on to the House, where the congressman from Nevada, James Scrugham, a political foe of McCarran, objected on the floor. As is customary with special-interest legislation, the House assumed that the local representative was more knowledgeable of the circumstances and followed his recommendation; the bill died in the House.

The next year McCarran was back with S. 92, simply a duplicate version of the same bill. The committee report reprinted a sample of the material from the earlier hearings.[78] The new Secretary of the Interior, however, recommended against any further relief for these squatters. He observed their recalcitrant rejection of the repeated opportunities to acquire Indian land; he felt that they did not deserve to have ownership virtually forced upon them. Nevertheless, McCarran's bill was approved out of committee over departmental objection and it passed in the Senate. Again Scrugham objected, and it died in the House. Undaunted, McCarran came back with S. 13 in 1941 and S. 24 in 1943. Again attesting to McCarran's seniority and his ability to influence his colleagues, committee and Senate again approved the bills over the objection of the head of the Interior Department.

Paiute defenses were dangerously thin. They rested solely on the unstable political infighting of domestic Nevada politics. It was not the justice of their position or their own allies which shielded them. Rather, they were benefiting from personal hostility within the Nevada delegation, enmity rooted in other causes. This could evaporate without warning.

As they gained in strength and political awareness, the Pyramid Lake Tribal Council was no longer content to risk being defended solely by the ineffectual BIA and uncertain congressmen. They passed resolutions stating their opposition to McCarran's bills, and sent delegations to his Nevada offices, and later, with limited tribal funds, to the hearings in Washington. Through the cooperation of the National Congress of American Indians and advice of politically sophisticated Washington attorney Curry, they began a series of letter-writing campaigns. Refusing to be defeated by McCarran's repetitious tactics, the council generated a flurry of activity every year as the Pyramid Lake bills came up in Congress. They contacted the chairmen of various congressional committees, congressional delegations from other states, the American Association on Indian Affairs, Indian Civil Rights Association, Daughters of the American Revolution, and eventually even Eleanor Roosevelt. To President Roosevelt the tribal council complained about "Senator McCarran's bill to take away our lands without our consent. That seems to us to break solemn promises made us by the New Deal in our Indian Reorganization Act [Wheeler-Howard Act]. Our people have been learning how to hope after many years of despair. To you they now look to keep that hope alive and to show them that our Government at least through its leaders means to keep faith with them."[79] In a letter to Indian Commissioner Collier they said, "All Indians must know whether the promises in it [Wheeler-Howard Act] will be kept by our Government or whether they are just like old time promises made to be broken when white people want what we have and what we need so bad."[80] They won the support of Indian rights organizations, which themselves added to the massive correspondence.[81] The tribe placed notices in Reno newspapers presenting the facts and asking for public support,[82] but local opinion was not to be changed, and the state legislature once again passed a joint resolution urging Congress to approve McCarran's proposal.[83]

By the time of the full-scale House hearing on McCarran's 1943 version, the tribe was well aware of the immense threat the bill posed and was organized to resist. The tribal council sent its chairman, Albert Aleck, and secretary, Albert Mauwee, to testify. They pointed to the judicial decisions which consistently had come down in favor of the tribe. The Circuit Court of Appeals had just decided against the last of the squatters, and the Supreme Court later reaffirmed that opinion. The tribal representatives reviewed for the congressmen the squatters' persistent heedlessness of the opportunities offered them. They explained the tribe's immense need for this land. Chairman Aleck enumerated the 21 Indian families who were now without land and, as soon as the war was over, the nearly 40 more young men who would return to the reservation and need a place to earn a living for themselves and their families. "All we ask is justice," the tribal representatives said, "not as wards of the Government, but as free, self-respecting patriotic Americans."[84] Despite their testimony, the committee recommended that the bill be approved and sent it out onto the floor. There Nevada Congressman Sullivan led its defeat in the House.

At the 1949 reincarnation of McCarran's bill, the new Secretary of the Interior suggested that the government buy out the squatters at current prices. If that failed, the government should simply acquire the land and water rights by condemnation, he said. This proposal ignored the prior judicial decision which had opened the way for far less drastic techniques. McCarran quickly blocked this proposal with his rider denying the use of BIA appropriations to purchase land in Nevada. The committee then suggested yet another reappraisal of the land values and one more chance for the squatters to buy the land. Attorney Curry, tribal representative Avery Winnemucca, and the BIA could marshal no evidence to convince the committee otherwise. Nevertheless, the bill again failed to win approval on the floor.

Year after year the tribal council urged members to send telegrams protesting the McCarran bills. Whenever hearings were held, their Washington attorney alerted them in time to send representatives. The BIA consistently presented evidence on their behalf, all seemingly without effect. At the same time, there was trouble in Nevada with the repossessed lands themselves, over water rights and grazing trespass. Interracial hostility was vented through slander and gossip.[85] By 1950 the Nevada political scene had changed, and the sole state representative could not be relied upon to object to the land-stealing bill. Former Superintendent Bowler advised the tribal council, "Your rights will have to be defended in the House by some one from another State, devoted to the cause of Indian rights."[86] The tribal attorney warned the council of the dangers of the consent calendar. This was a means for bills, if not objected to by at least one congressman, to pass quickly and automatically without a vote being taken. A single protest drove the bill through the whole committee procedure and floor debate. Each time the McCarran bills had come up, the NCAI had mobilized such an objection.[87] But it was increasingly difficult to call in pro-Indian congressmen, and in 1949 Curry wrote that he was sure that McCarran's bill would pass that year.[88] However, it failed to slip through when Minnesota's Hubert Humphrey rose against it.

In 1952, at the height of the tribe's problems over attorneys' contracts, McCarran introduced S. 2. Nevertheless, the tribe managed to send a delegation to Washington for the hearings and again passed resolutions opposing the bill. The NCAI again organized floor resistance and defeated the bill.

For over 16 years the Pyramid Lake tribe had been constantly on the defensive, fearful lest some day McCarran's bill might slip through when their friends in Washington were not looking. Like a bulldog, McCarran refused to let go. He kept up the attack, utilizing his very broad and effective congressional contacts to attempt to wrest these lands from the tribe. As late as 1954, he proposed a bill for a supplementary appropriation of $31,000 for Depaoli's patented land within the reservation. Both houses approved this bill, which was signed by the President on August 27th of that year. By then Garaventa had sold out to Depaoli and the Ceresolas had failed to negotiate a reasonable price. Shortly thereafter, Pat McCarran died. This battle was finally over.

In the 20 years between 1934 and 1954, many changes had affected the Pyramid Lake Paiutes. They had formed a tribal council, a legal corporation to represent them and to manage their affairs. Councilmen had gradually learned their own powers and had become familiar with large-scale political processes involving distant federal officials. The tribe had fought with the BIA over the right to hire and control their own attorney. They had won court battles against the squatters and pressed the government to issue evictions. They had faced the insidious challenge of Senator McCarran's nine bills. With the aid of their attorney, national Indian organizations, Indian Commissioner Collier, and supportive superintendents, they had launched successful letter-writing campaigns and lobbying efforts to block passage of these bills. In the end, the squatters had won a titular victory when the government had purchased Depaoli's property.

The land trespass problem was not yet over at Pyramid Lake. In 1948, for instance, 81 head of cattle and horses had to be removed from the repossessed lands. As late as 1963, the tribal council minutes noted in irritation, "Several cases of trespass were brought to the attention of the Council. The gravel pit by DePaoli (Dodge Brothers) has been extended onto Indian land. Ceresola is expending [*sic*] his feed lot onto Reservation property. The Philgrims are reported going beyond their boundaries. James said another trespass in Wadsworth is at the old place sold by Maller Crosby and that Marge McArthur has fenced in the land by the water by the school. The Council asked what happened about the Agency promise to investigate the Witty and

Hard Scrabble ranches' boundaries."[89] There were still patented properties within the reserve, most importantly the Ceresola and the Sutcliffe holdings. Whites with property bordering the lower end of the reservation constantly encroached on the rich bottomlands. Always tightly interconnected with this problem of land was the question of the indispensable water rights. This water issue had a history as long and as complicated as that of the land itself; it was, if anything, more bitterly fought. In Nevada, land without water was an empty victory. The tribe, now sure of their strength, plunged headlong into the dispute over this vital resource.

ELEVEN

The River and the Lake

Under the American legal system, the states normally administer water rights. There are two general patterns of water law which they follow: in Eastern states, the prevailing type is called riparian law; in the West, the dominant doctrine is that of prior appropriation. Both in logic and in results, these two types are very different.

Under riparian law, land and the water flowing through it are considered inseparable. Any property bordering on a stream automatically has rights to the water of that stream. The owner can use the water in reasonable amounts, proportional to the amount of frontage that his property controls. He can use any amount of water for his own profit, so long as he does not interfere with the similar rights of other users. Since the water pertains to the land, he can apply it only within that natural watershed, and the law forbids him to remove it to any other drainage system. In times of shortage, all water users have to reduce their water use by a common percentage. In short, water is treated legally as a tenancy in common among all the land-owners on that watershed.

In contrast, the Western doctrine of prior appropriations is highly individualistic. A basic premise of this legal concept is that land and water are separable. Therefore, water is not automatically acquired with land purchase; water rights are acquired when a person first uses water for a socially recognized purpose, and his legal right dates from that diversion and use. Thereafter he must utilize the water for his ownership to be maintained. His rights are to a specified amount rather than a percentage. If his needs increase, he must acquire additional water rights through new diversion or purchase. Since water is separable from land, it can be removed from the watershed and applied anywhere the owner chooses. In times of shortage, rather than all users reducing their diversions by a common percentage, the person with the earliest appropriation date uses his full amount. The next-oldest claim is then satisfied in full, and so on, until the water source is exhausted. Those with the most recent, and so the lowest priority dates may get no water at all.

Historically, the doctrine of prior appropriations evolved in the arid West to meet the requirements of commercial mining. Nevada and California, the archtypical mining states, pioneered this development. There water became a market commodity, in some respects similar to subsurface mineral rights. Each resource was bought and sold separately. Mine owners purchased whole streams and rerouted them to stamping mills for ore processing. Unused water lapsed into public ownership, again subject to individual diversion.[1]

The federal government, arguing on the basis of its ultimate claim to the public domain and its legal authority, superior to both the riparian and the prior appropriations laws of the states, could claim those water rights not owned by private citizens. An entire body of water law was developed to regulate such federal titles. Because tribal relations were an exclusively federal concern, and because Indian resources, including land and water, were held in trust by the federal government for the tribes, Indian land title and water rights generally fell under the jurisdiction of these federal, rather than state statutes. The overlapping jurisdiction of state and federal water law and the conflicting philosophies on which they were based became serious problems in the history of Pyramid Lake.

By the 1880s and 1890s, Nevada mining was in a depression. The production of ore declined seriously as surface strikes were exhausted; deeper deposits were more difficult and expensive to mine. Ores of more complicated chemical composition required more processing than had the earlier purer metals. Having expanded rapidly on the strength of mining alone, Nevada found itself losing population. To add to its economic woes, agricultural prices were declining all across the country. In response Populism grew as a national political movement, and it found strong support in Nevada. The Populist platform called for broader citizen involvement in the government and increased federal intervention in the economy. One such proposed federal economic measure was a series of major reclamation projects.

By the 1880s, whites had taken up most of the nation's easily farmed land under the various Homestead and Desert Land Acts. Only swamp and desert lands were left. The transformation of such marginal areas into productive agricultural property was extremely expensive, often beyond the means or willingness of individuals. As an economic stimulant, Populism called for the federal construction of large-scale regional drainage and irrigation projects. Such newly productive properties were then to be sold at homestead prices to depression-ridden farmers.

Nevada's Senator William Stewart proclaimed the Populist cause. In 1887, he declared to Congress that the Carson, Walker, and Truckee rivers wasted "at least ninety per cent" of their waters by running into their sinks and there evaporating.[2] This was an unconscionable waste in such a dry state, he said, and advocated reclamation. He encouraged John Wesley Powell, head of the infant U.S. Geological Survey, to perform preliminary hydrographic surveys. These he hoped would be quickly completed to clear the way for the immediate pork-barrel investment of government dollars within his constituency. Over the next decade the senator continued to press Congress for a reclamation bill. He chaired irrigation committees and ordered investigative reports, all to keep the reclamation issue before the Senate. Young Nevada Congressman Francis Newlands feuded with Stewart politically but joined him in his stance on reclamation. In January 1902, Newlands introduced a bill which authorized the massive government funding of irrigation projects and established the Bureau of Reclamation within the Department of the Interior to administer those funds. Eastern congressmen resisted such massive

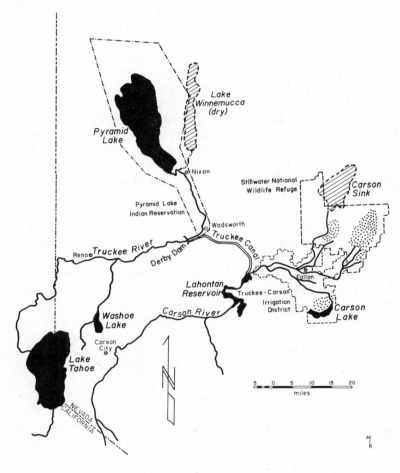

Figure 4. The Newlands Project

investment in projects which were of limited use to their region, but Western congressmen outvoted them, and the bill passed in June. Since Newlands was the author and the leading proponent of the reclamation bill, he acquired the right to have the first project in his district, according to congressional custom.

On March 14, 1903, the Secretary of the Interior approved the Newlands Reclamation Project. Anglo engineers and Western farmers asserted that the Truckee River had "excess" water, that which had previously flowed down to Pyramid Lake. The Truckee Valley, they argued, offered little arable land where this water could be used advantageously. The Carson Valley, on the other hand, was broad and level for easy irrigation. The Newlands Project proposed the construction of Derby Dam, 10 miles upriver from the Pyramid Lake Reservation boundary, to store these waters. From there the 32-mile-long Truckee Canal would carry a quarter of a million acre-feet of Truckee River water southward into the Carson River drainage each year. Since Nevada's water law was based on the principle of prior appropriations, this diversion was legal, although it would not have been under riparian law. Once in the Carson drainage, Truckee waters would rest behind Lahontan Dam until the summer irrigation season. In this way, it was said, 350,000 acres of land around Fallon and Carson Sink would be reclaimed from sagebrush desert and be put under intensive and profitable irrigation agriculture. The federal government would provide the funds for this initial construction, estimated at 5–10 dollars per acre, to be recovered through sale of the land to Anglo settlers and through irrigation fees. The resultant agricultural expansion would greatly increase Nevada's tax base and provide much-needed economic diversification.

The overall effect of this project was to redistribute water that normally would have flowed through Indian lands to Pyramid Lake within an Indian reservation. This water would be taken outside the reservation and into another river drainage where it could be utilized by white farmers.

In planning this massive diversion, engineers neglected several very important considerations. Only after Derby Dam was completed in 1905 were the soils of the proposed farming area tested, and only then did officials discover the unpleasant truth. Although this was a desert area, the water table was shallow. With irrigation, the level of highly alkaline desert groundwater would rise still further. When it reached the bottom of the root zone of the domesticated plants, the crops would die. The more irrigation water applied, the worse the problem would become. Alkaline flats and beds of toxic salts were the future of the Newlands Project unless expensive, deep drains were constructed. Fearing that news of the salinity problem would drive off prospective settlers, and fearing that the cost of the project would escalate if drainage had to be provided by the government, Reclamation officials denied the existence of this problem until 1914. Then they asserted that the government had agreed only to provide irrigation water; drains were beyond its contractual obligations. The settlers would have to finance any necessary drainage. The white entrymen raised such an outcry at this crass declaration that the Reclamation Service belatedly admitted its liability for drainage construction in 1916. Over the next four years, more than 100 miles of deep drains were installed, at a cost of nearly three quarters of a million dollars.[3] Even this did not solve the problem. No more than 60,000 acres have ever been farmed in the project area.

Drainage was not the only difficulty. Much of the soil in the Newlands Project area was sandy and infertile. As soon as the natural vegetation was disturbed, strong winds deflated the extremely shallow topsoil layer. Further, the unlined main canal lost 30 percent of the Truckee's water before it ever reached the Carson drainage. Ranches in the project area were not contiguous, and 20 or 30 miles of canal banks soaked up water every time flow was shifted from one allottee to the next. There was no geographically rational system to deliver the water. Inexperienced farmers overirrigated and wasted water, which then simply ran out the bottom of the ditch network. A certain headwater, as it was called, was necessary to carry the relatively small amount of water actually used to those plants at the far edges of a field. In 1919, headwater in the project area averaged 4.5 second-feet, all of which became wastage. Headwater loss, poor soil absorbency, and waste of various kinds allowed large amounts of water to escape through the Newlands Project. Travelers began to report pools of standing water east of Fallon. Soon these sprouted tules and turned into a bona-fide swamp. Migratory ducks and other waterfowl which used to inhabit Winnemucca Lake nested here. This artificial extension of the Carson Sink became so well established that it was later named the Stillwater National Wildlife Refuge and Game Management Area, heavily patronized by Anglo sportsmen.

Most farmers in the Newlands area raised pasturage, hay, and other low-yield crops, rather than the more profitable row crops envisioned by the project's designers. The original government estimate suggested annual production costs at $5 per acre for machinery, fertilizers, and water fees. Settlers found that their actual expenses ran as high as $100 per acre, including chemicals to control encroaching alkali. After this, they simply could not afford to invest in the extra machinery or take the risks of row crops. As a result of these crop decisions and the limited acreage planted, tax returns were never as high as local politicians had hoped. In all regards, the Newlands Project's economic benefits to the region were disappointing.

In contrast with the mirage of economic boom in the Newlands area, the effects on Pyramid Lake were both real and devastating. Even before construction of Derby Dam, Pyramid Lake had had a water problem. Local rainfall was roughly 5.4 inches per year, while the evaporation rate was 52 inches.[4] Nearly all the natural inflow to Pyramid Lake had always come from the Truckee River. Only insignificant amounts were from springs in the lake's floor or from the intermittent runoff of surrounding hillsides. A few springs along the riverbed below Derby Dam and water seeping underneath the barrier also provided minor amounts. The combined average inflow from the Truckee River and other sources was never enough to sustain the lake level against the constant evaporative drain. During normal flow years, the surface elevation actually lowered. However, this loss was more than adequately replaced when the Sierra Nevada got a heavy snowfall. Then the spring melt forcefed the Truckee into a roaring torrent. It disgorged water far above what the lake needed that year, recovering its losses. The lake surface fluctuated around a stable level only because of these periodic floods.

Derby Dam drastically upset this natural balance. By holding back and containing flood waters, the dam prevented this cyclical rejuvenation of Pyramid Lake. Furthermore, the diversion of 48 percent of the Truckee River's water to the Newlands Project eliminated any

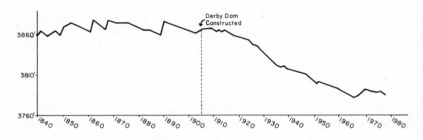

Figure 5. Pyramid Lake Surface Elevation, 1840–1980

hope of sufficient water to maintain Pyramid Lake. Of necessity, the surface level had to lower as evaporation took its toll. Because Pyramid was a deep lake, engineers suggested that it would shrink in surface area as it became more shallow, rather than disappear totally as a playa would. Then this smaller lake would have less evaporation. Sooner or later, Pyramid Lake would reach an evaporation balance with its reduced inflow, and thus stabilize at a lower level. Most estimates indicated a reduced lake roughly half to one-fourth its original area and a much smaller fraction of its original volume. This tiny lake would still contain all the mineral impurities of the previously much larger and deeper lake; the concentration of these toxic salts would eventually become lethal to all fish life. Within a few years after the dam was completed, Pyramid Lake began its decline.

Politicians and engineers accepted the inevitability of this scenario. Congressman Newlands declared that Pyramid and Winnemucca lakes existed "only to satisfy the thirsty sun"[5] and ignored their value to the Paiutes. None of the planning reports considered the effects Derby Dam might have on Paiute agriculture or on the reservation economy downstream, which still, at the turn of the century, depended heavily on fishing. The government did not warn the tribe of the effect that Derby Dam would have on their lands or of the effect that the removal of great quantities of water would have on their lake.

For years, the Indian Bureau had pressured Paiutes to take up family farms. In 1904 Congress had passed a rider providing for the allotment of five acres of land to every Indian on the Pyramid Lake Reservation. These plots, irrigated by a federally constructed system, were to compensate Paiutes for the loss of Pyramid Lake. "It can thus be seen," *Scientific American* asserted, "that the Indians will not suffer, even though Pyramid Lake does dry up on account of its main artery, Truckee River, being diverted from it."[6] Thus Congress and the Bureau of Reclamation dictated what the BIA had attempted for years. Irrigation was to become the foundation of a new agricultural economy at Pyramid Lake. However, there was no completion date mentioned in the legislation for this Indian irrigation project, and it would be more than a generation before Pyramid Lake saw BIA water development of any significant scope.

In 1907, shortly after the construction of Derby Dam, Reno quivered with a new excitement. The *Nevada State Journal* ran banner headlines on page one—Pyramid Lake Reservation was to be opened to white settlement any day. The source of this rumor was apparently the routine BIA census of the reservation. The Anglo public hoped that this was a preliminary enrollment in preparation for imminent allotment, as promised by the Act of 1904. Once each Indian had his five-acre parcel, there would still be lots of land to buy up. Further, some Anglos misunderstood the geography of the Truckee Canal and thought it fed its 250 acre-feet of water not to Anglo farms at Fallon, but to reservation fields at Nixon. The newspaper editor scoffed, "Certainly Uncle Sam did not do this for the Indian 'farmers', who, under government supervision, cultivate a few dozen acres of alfalfa back of the Indian agency buildings."[7] He thought that such expensive plans could be only for white homesteaders who would soon be given the area. Although the Department of the Interior denied these interpretations of the water diversion and the census, it could not discourage Anglo rumors of impending allotment.

Despite agency hopes and plans, farming never prospered at Pyramid Lake. Fishing, on the other hand, was always a dependable enterprise. It required little capital investment and was the Indians' preference. In 1922, Dave Numana, an elder at Pyramid Lake, told the agent, "This lake is my meat." He explained that the government had given other Indian tribes cattle for food, but had given Pyramid Lake to the Paiutes "from which we may secure our food for ourselves and families."[8] Some poor families relied totally on dried trout and cuiui, particularly in years when crops failed and there was consequently little work available on local white ranches. Until the 1920s, the majority of Paiute cash income was through sale of fish—7,000 to 8,000 dollars' worth annually.

The planners of the Newlands Project, sportsmen's groups, and Paiutes immediately recognized the threat to the Pyramid fishery posed by Derby Dam. As Agent Creel observed, "The plans of the Reclamation Service apparently are based upon the use of every drop of water in the Truckee River for irrigation purposes. If this assumption is sustained, this means the total extermination of the Pyramid Lake trout within a very short period of time."[9] Newlands Project Director Richardson informed him that indeed "the plans of the project were not based upon allowing any of the water to go into Pyramid Lake for the purpose of preservation of the fish."[10] As early as 1913, the Nevada State Fish and Game Commission reported, "Tons of fish have died at the Derby Dam. . . . It was shown that thousands of pounds of valuable fish food had been allowed to die through sheer neglect on the part of the Government."[11] The spawning fish, driven by instinct upstream, could not surmount the barrier at Derby and tried vainly to leap over it until finally, in exhaustion, they died. The state fish commission charged that fish could not pass the dam as a result of the poorly designed fish ladder. They did not face Derby's real threat, that to the lake itself, and with the lake, to the entire fish habitat.

As a result of the various complaints, Senator Oddie asked the Secretary of the Interior to call a conference to discuss the causes for the decline of the fish population at Pyramid Lake. In March 1924 representatives of the Bureau of Reclamation and the Indian Irrigation Service met with Senator Oddie. While all agreed that the fish ladder at the reservation irrigation dam was adequate, "the fish ladder at the Derby Dam of the U.S. Reclamation Service was very severely condemned by all those who voiced their sentiment relative to the matter, many stating that it was a joke."[12] Further, small fish were being flushed into the unscreened irrigation canals and out into the fields, where they died as the water soaked into the ground. "This loss," the conference reported, "is said to be especially large in the case of the Main Canal of the Newlands Project, which is diverted at the Derby Dam. It is said that large quantities of fish are carried down this canal and out into the laterals and ditches and thence on to the irrigated lands." Participants at the 1924 conference also discussed the pelicans who preyed on the spawning fish, vulnerable in the shallow water.

Most importantly, however, all of those at the conference agreed that preservation of fish life in the lower Truckee River required "a steadier and more uniform flow of water than has been obtained during recent years,"[13] especially in the section below Derby Dam. They suggested that the Newlands Project power plant, built near Lahontan Dam on the Carson, be moved to Derby. The electric generators ran year round and released large amounts of water through the spillways. During the agricultural off-season, this water simply washed down the main canals and out into the Stillwater marsh. On the other hand, if the power plant were operating at Derby Dam, this unneeded winter water would come precisely during the spawning season. It would also help maintain the lake level. There was no mechanical difficulty in the move to Derby, but the Reclamation Service later vetoed the suggestion. The fishery on the Truckee River was simply not worth the expense.

Members of the conference were concerned not only with the amount of water but also with its quality; "it was the sentiment of a large majority of those attending the meeting that stream pollution from the paper mill at Floriston, and by the sewage waste from the cities of Reno and Sparks, is the most serious menace to the fish life of the Truckee river."[14] They recommended immediate construction of sewage treatment plants and control of industrial wastes.

Although many of the participants in this conference did not favor Indian interests, its report did not accuse Indian fishing of contributing to the decline. Nevertheless, when Senator Oddie wrote the President a few years later to complain again about the decline of the Pyramid Lake fishery, Indian subsistence fishing headed his list of causes: "The fish go up this river to Spawn, but the Indians, who control the outlet of the river . . . slaughter the fish in a most wanton manner as they start up the river, with the result that they are becoming much depleted in number."[15] Only later did he note the inadequate fish ladders or lack of fish screens, and he never even mentioned the decline of water caused by the government's own reclamation project.

On the contrary, the BIA argued that the decline of the fishery was a direct result of the building of Derby Dam and the massive diversions down the Truckee Canal to Fallon. In a letter to Senator McCarran, the Commissioner of Indian Affairs stated:

> We believe that the large volume of water diverted from Truckee River for irrigation purposes is largely responsible for the recession of the lake and the increased alkalinity of the water therein. If this diversion of water continues and especially if it is increased in the future, it is probable that the alkalinity of the water will increase to the point where fish life in the lake will disappear.[16]

To forestall such a disaster, the BIA notified the Reclamation Service early in 1922 that "This Office, therefore, desires to do everything practicable to conserve and protect the fish and to this end earnestly solicits your cooperation so far as may be consistent with the activities of the Reclamation Service."[17]

In response to this memo, Reclamation instructed the Director of the Newlands Project, John Richardson, to investigate the matter. While Richardson had a genuine concern for fish life, he in turn blamed the situation on the state's scattered and piecemeal approach to the problem: an improved fish ladder here or a fish screen there would not solve the problem. Young fish could not be swept into the irrigation ditches unless the older ones had already managed to get upriver to spawn. Therefore he returned to the problem of water quality and declared that the greatest danger lay in the destruction of water purity, to which trout were very sensitive. In this he charged Nevada's congressional delegation with the responsibility for leadership, because they alone had the power and influence to force industry and urban areas to control their effluent.[18] As a secondary measure, Winnemucca Lake could be physically separated from the Truckee drainage in order to reduce the evaporative surface of the system. In this way, he thought, perhaps Pyramid Lake could be saved.

C. A. Engle, an engineer for the Indian Service Irrigation Division, brought attention to yet another problem in 1924. Like all rivers entering still bodies of water, the Truckee dropped its load of silt and sand at its mouth. This formed a sloping delta, normally under water, which angled down to the bottom of the lakebed. As the water level declined, large portions of the delta were exposed as a sandbar. Instead of flowing down a steady slope into a level lake, now the river had to wash across this short, steep delta. The new lower base level of the declining lake caused downcutting of the channel through its last several miles to the lake. This eventually damaged 600 acres of Indian agricultural land in the lower river valley, virtually all they had salvaged from the white squatters. At this early period, however, Engle was more concerned with the immediate effects on fish life. "At low stages of the lake or river," he reported, "when there is little or no water over the bar, the fish of course cannot ascend the river, and many are left stranded on the bar by the frequent fluctuations in the water level, and by wave action."[19] The fish gathered around the mouth of the river hoping to find enough water to ascend, but were blocked by the delta. If a north wind came up, as it often did in winter, four-, six-, even eight-foot waves rolled down the lake and threw the fish up onto the bar. When the waves receded, the fish were left stranded to die. The engineer saw no practical advantage in dredging an artificial channel, because the first spring flood would overflow the banks and carve a new riverbed, while leaving sand and debris to fill in the old. He recommended that "the cost of the channel construction would without a doubt be out of all proportion to the value of the fish it would conserve."[20] The main problem he saw was the simple one of insufficient water in the stream and progressive exposure of old river delta. He fell back on the cosmetic solutions of improved fishways, reduced stream pollution, and increased efficiency of water use.

At about the same time, Indian Agent Lorenzo Creel also worried about the threat to the fish posed by Derby Dam, but less for the sake of the fish themselves than for the Paiutes who depended on them. "It is decidedly to the advantage of these Indians," he argued, "as well as to the state and the Nation, to prevent a diminution [of the fishery]. To that end the establishment of Federal hatcheries along the Truckee is very necessary."[21] He recommended that such a hatchery be built on the reservation itself, since this was land already under government control and it had the requisite river and lake access. His suggestion passed through the BIA and the Interior Department and on to Commerce and Labor, where the Bureau of Fisheries was housed; there his memo died. In 1929, BIA field personnel again suggested the idea of a federal fish hatchery on the reservation, but again they were ignored.[22]

In the meantime, federal neglect allowed the fish population to reach dangerously low levels. Despite all the conferences, studies, and recommendations, nothing was done to solve the basic problems of the fishery. The annual catch by both Indian and white fishermen continued to decline. In 1935, yet another study was done, this time by M. J. Madsen of the U.S. Bureau of Fisheries. He reported extremely high alkalinity levels in both Pyramid and Winnemucca lakes. Nevertheless, he blamed the decline of the fishery not on the obvious concentration of lethal salts as the lake lowered, or on the equally obvious pollution, but rather on Indian fishing methods: "Without exaggeration no more than fifty percent of the fisheries resources of Pyramid Lake are being properly utilized. The lenient regulations governing fishing by Indians is probably the basic cause for this unnecessary waste."[23] He particularly objected to allowing any fish to be sold. While his first recommendation was for an adequate river flow to stop the disastrous decline of the lake surface level, his second was for the prohibition of sales of fish and the limitation of Indian subsistence fishing.

Full of generalizations but with very little data, Madsen's report was completely unsatisfactory to activist Superintendent Alida Bowler. She demanded an independent study, which was completed by Stanford University fisheries expert F. H. Sumner in 1938. After gathering data in the field for several seasons, Sumner proved that the number of trout caught by all categories of fishermen was falling precipitously. By the end of the study period, the catch was less than one-third of what it had been only three years before. Even more frightening was the doubling in size of the average trout caught. Delighted with their record-breaking fish, sportsmen did not understand that this indicated a remnant population. Only the grand old relics now survived in the lake, without younger, smaller generations to bring down the average fish size. Unless the situation were changed rapidly to permit active spawning, trout would die out in Pyramid Lake as soon as the last of the old specimens were brought in.

The state had propagated cutthroat trout artificially in its hatcheries for a number of years, and had returned some of the fry to the Truckee River. Apparently the replanting was unsuccessful, or the numbers of fry were inadequate to maintain the trout population. Sumner considered the artificial propagation of cutthroat as "probably impracticable," because its great market value led sportsmen to fish trout out before the fry had a chance to grow and reproduce. A further problem was the warmth of the shallower river and the salinity of the smaller lake. If water diversions were sustained at the current level, he said, Pyramid Lake would shrink to about half of its 1882 surface area before it reached a balanced evaporation regime. Even accepting this conservative estimate, the lake would have about half the density of sea water. Of course, freshwater fish could no longer live in it. He thought this diminution would take long enough that conservation efforts would be economically feasible, despite the inevitable doom of fish life in the lake.

Cuiui had peculiar difficulties, because they spawned early in May, about the time of the first irrigation withdrawals. At that time of year low water often made the delta uncrossable, and cuiui stood even less chance than trout to spawn successfully in the lower river. Further, the suckers spawned in water so shallow that the surface lapped their backs. Once deposited, the eggs could easily be exposed and dried out, if additional irrigation withdrawals were made. Sumner concluded that "if it cannot spawn successfully in the lake . . . its chances of survival are slim."[24]

The fish expert estimated that the exposed delta at the mouth of the Truckee had become completely impassable to the spawning cutthroat trout and cuiui about 1929. As a result, he said, "The Pyramid Lake trout fishery has declined to a point which makes its rehabilitation by any means dubious. The fact that the environmental factors concerned will probably become less favorable, particularly with regard to water diversions, is all the more reason for believing that the cutthroat trout of Pyramid Lake is doomed." Even if no trout had been caught for consumption or sale, the situation probably would have been about the same, he argued, because "diversion of Truckee River water has been the major cause of the decline of the fishery." He concluded that "the cutthroat trout of Pyramid Lake is well on the way to extinction." Based on Sumner's report, Superintendent Bowler protested to Washington: "The fish industry of the Pyramid Lake Indians is rapidly being destroyed thereby [by irrigation development]. Any further inroads must be protested at all costs."[25]

By the late 1930s, Winnemucca Lake was completely dry. The cutthroat trout reproduced only artificially through the intermittent and inefficient services of the State Fish and Game Commission. The cuiui catch was declining rapidly.

Damage to the fishery was not the only threat to Paiutes' livelihood that the construction of Derby Dam posed; it injured Indian agriculture as well. The most immediate problem was irrigation water. The reduced river flowed lower than the headgates of the Indian ditches, so whatever water entered the reservation was beyond the reach of the existing irrigation system. In 1908 the BIA built a small dam at the headgate to pool the water and raise it up to the level of the ditch heads.[26]

However, as the years passed it became obvious that the problem had not been solved. Complaints increased that Derby Dam was not letting down a fair allotment of water to tribal land and that there was no water in the Indian ditches. No new lands were opened up and put under irrigation; the lands already farmed were threatened in years of water shortage. By 1923, the agent reported, "Lack of water for irrigation, however, curtails farming operations, and further prospects of water shortage makes the outlook for the future rather gloomy."[27]

Indians complained to the agent and wrote petitions to Congress, but to little avail. The Pyramid Lake agent wanted Reclamation to declare what amount of water the Indians could reasonably expect from Derby Dam. The Newlands Project Manager replied, "As a matter of practice we have so governed the discharge of water at Truckee [Derby] Dam during the dry season as to give a minimum of about thirty second-feet for the watering of all these lands around Wadsworth down to and including Indian lands near the Lake." In addition to this, there was some seepage from the section of the Truckee Canal which flowed parallel to the lower river. Still more water came from the return flow of irrigated lands near Wadsworth and from springs in the lower river. From all these sources combined, "it is probable," the manager said, "that the Indians could depend upon receiving forty to fifty second-feet of water at their diversion dam during the dry season and of course during the spring season, when a greater supply of water is necessary." The engineer refused to assure any fixed quantity of water because "we are not in a position to set apart any portion of it [the water] for the use of the Indians and more properly the application for Indian water right should be made to the State authorities, and if it were so made we would probably object to it as an encroachment upon our priority."[28] He was suggesting that the Paiutes should be considered on exactly the same criteria as other water users, disregarding their aboriginal title, their first priority to water on the river, and the government trust obligation which led to federal jurisdiction over Indian water rights. By acknowledging state authority, Paiutes would be at a political disadvantage immediately, for Anglo water users were far more influential in the state than were Indians. Further, it was assured that they would have the full power of the U.S. Reclamation Service thrown against them if they should allow themselves to be forced into the state forum.

Not only did the Reclamation engineer suggest a dangerous appeal to state law, but he also mentioned another major source of Indian irrigation problems. In the minds of the Reclamation Service, the water below Derby Dam was a single entity; all water for both white and Indian lands was lumped together. Thus all the squatters in the Wadsworth area, holding Indian lands illegally and rapidly expanding their own ditches farther onto Indian lands, competed directly with Paiutes for a share of this single water allotment. Since the squatters were upstream from Indian lands, these people pulled off water before it reached the Indian ditch heads. In 1921, Inspector Trowbridge discovered that the Indian irrigation system could serve over 3,000 acres, but only 425 acres were being farmed that year because of inadequate water supply due to the Truckee diversion. At the same time, Anglo squatters were irrigating 1,100 acres of reservation land.[29] A few years later, the newly formed Indian Irrigation Service found Paiutes cultivating only 750 acres, in contrast to the 1,150 acres that whites farmed illegally on the reserve. The Indian

Service hoped to extend the Indian ditches to an additional 1,300 acres and considered nearly 20,000 acres potentially irrigable with simple gravity techniques, but it could not proceed until the water question was settled. To prevent continued water theft, it recommended to the Secretary of the Interior that efforts to settle the question of title to the trespassed lands should be pursued as quickly as possible.

However, those suits to evict the squatters stagnated for the next decade, while the water situation reached crisis proportions. In August 1920, the Indian agent walked along the Truckee River and found "that no water was coming over our weir, for the use of Indians at all."[30] This was not an isolated instance. Three years later, the agency farmer measured 5.5 second-feet arriving on the reservation, while the Reclamation Service asserted that Indians were receiving between 40 and 50 second-feet. Of the amount Reclamation claimed they were releasing, 90 percent either was lost to evaporation or was siphoned off by squatters.[31] The following year, a BIA fisheries expert commented: "During the low water season, we are informed the U.S. Reclamation Service passes only sufficient water through the Derby Dam to supply the Indian lands. The entire amount is frequently taken by these white settlers, leaving the crops of the Indians, who have the first water right on the entire river, to dry up."[32] Deprived of late summer water, Indians' crops did not ripen and harvests dwindled. Government tolerance of white squatters, its negligence in not removing them, its own actions in reclamation and water manipulation, and the subsequent damage to the fishery, all interlocked to create a crisis for the Pyramid Lake Indian economy.

To solve this problem, the government suggested not more water, but more construction. The original Newlands Project design had included a second stage, to be built after the main canal between the Truckee and the Carson river drainages had been completed. Stage two covered additional lands below Derby Dam in the lower Truckee drainage itself, including some reservation property. This so-called Spanish Springs Extension would permit enactment of the 1904 bill, passed through Congress shortly after the Newlands Bill itself. In the event of major governmental development of irrigation on the Pyramid Lake reserve, this bill authorized allotment of five acres of irrigable land to each Indian before the remainder of the reclaimed land was sold off to recuperate expenses. Sales of land plus water fees to new Anglo landowners would pay for the cost of the Indian section of the project. In late 1925, the Bureau of Reclamation notified the Secretary of the Interior that it was ready to begin construction of the Spanish Springs section. From the amount of available land and the number of Indians, the Secretary calculated what the sale price for the "surplus" land would have to be. In order to make the project self-supporting, he would have to charge $49 per acre, about ten times what land in that part of Nevada was selling for at the time. At this price, he observed, land was very unlikely to sell. Therefore, he concluded, "it is not believed to be profitable to include the Indian lands in this project."[33] He was unenthusiastic about reservation improvements on other grounds, as he believed "these Indians have not made the best use of the present irrigable areas under their project constructed under the jurisdiction of this Bureau."[34] He employed the traditional, Anglo best-use argument about "proper" land utilization, while at the same time blaming Paiutes for the troubles they had experienced. The theft of their best lands, the pilfering of their water, the inconsistent and insufficient assistance and protection which the Bureau had provided, were not sufficient justification in his eyes for their failure to embrace Anglo farming techniques. He did suggest that if they really wanted to farm, Indians should be offered the opportunity to buy the lands in the projected, newly irrigated areas at the market rate, that same $49 per acre which he knew Anglos would refuse to pay. Essentially, he was suggesting that Paiutes be allowed to buy allotments in their own reservation.

Despite these views, the Secretary ordered the Pyramid Lake Indian agent and a Reclamation field representative to reevaluate all parcels of land in this area so that the decision on the Spanish Springs extension could be based on sound, cost-efficiency analysis. In the winter of 1925–26, this reappraisal team evaluated each 40-acre tract very carefully according to levelness, soil type, proximity to existing irrigation ditches, need for pumps to lift water, alkalinity, and other factors. The 20,000 acres showed an aggregate value of $70,500, or $3.50 per acre. This land was simply not worth the investment to irrigate it.

While this field study was in progress, the Indian agent held a series of meetings with the Paiutes. He asked them whether they wanted this irrigation development and the increased value of irrigated land, but also the subsequent sale of large portions of it to outsiders. He stressed the advantages, what he called the "desirability of the development and settlement of a country, and how it helped any community." The Paiutes voiced their unanimous opinion through one of their traditional headmen: they were opposed to sale of any land of the Pyramid Lake Reservation to settlers under the Newlands Project or for any other reason. They declared that "they wished the lands reserved for the benefit of their children and their children's children."[35] They needed the grazing land for their own stock, they said, and even now did not have enough irrigable land for immediate needs. Over 150 adults signed a petition which protested any action involving the sale of reservation land. The Indians were "very positive," the agent reported, in their stance opposing the sale of land. They feared that any further reclamation construction would reduce still further the small amount of water available in the lower river and thus damage the supply of water to their present lands. While ample water was available theoretically, a series of water-short years had shown that, given the actual diversion practices of Nevada water users, Indian lands went dry. If still more land on the same river system were opened up for white settlers, the Indians feared it would be at their expense once again.

The Spanish Springs extension was never built. The cause for this cancellation was less likely Indian protest than the simple fact that the land once irrigated would be worth far less than the cost necessary to develop it. Without the cost-benefit failure of the project, it would certainly have proceeded despite Indian wishes.

Beginning with the Newlands Project in 1905, removal of water which was needed for farming and fish propagation doomed the Pyramid Lake economy to stagnation. The effects were soon apparent. When Paiute elders spoke to BIA interviewers years later, they recalled the period between 1910 and 1930 with nostalgia and bitterness. All were convinced that fish were unable to spawn because of the lessened flow of the river and the subsequent lowering of the lake level. They said that this "ended for all time their opportunity to gain a livelihood from fishing, deprived all of the Indian residents of the main staple of their diet, and caused many families to leave the reservation to seek a means of livelihood elsewhere." One white trader who had been the commercial middleman in the reservation fish sales commented, "There was never a hungry person on the reservation, they loved that kind of work—that way of making a living, and they had a dignity, which went away after the last run in 1937. Nearly all the fishermen went off to Reno, or somewhere, and never came back." The BIA representative summarized the testimony: "The restricted flow of the river, experienced after the construction of Derby Dam, finally resulted in the total destruction of the natural fishery in the 1930's—with a disasterous [*sic*] impact on lives of all the Indian residents, particularly those who found it necessary to leave the reservation for the cities."[36] The cost of the Newlands area development for the benefit of white settlers included decline of the Indian economy at Pyramid Lake. Apparently the Reclamation Service was not reluctant to accept this cost, and the BIA was obviously powerless to stop it.

Indians were not the only ones unhappy about the Truckee River situation; so were white farmers. Many landowners argued that under Nevada state law based on prior appropriations, the federal government could claim only specified diversions. Further, they contended, federal priority dated from construction of the Newlands Project in 1905, whereas the federal government maintained that its claims stemmed from public domain, thus antedating all private claims under state law.

In addition, the federal government claimed 6 vertical feet of water stored artificially in Lake Tahoe. When the Newlands Project was first suggested in 1902, the design envisioned Lake Tahoe as a storage area. Its level could be regulated through the use of headgates at the point where it overflowed to become the Truckee River. To control this, the federal government had to acquire an existing dam built by a lumber company in the 1870s in order to hold back extra water used to flush logs downstream to Reno. Since the company refused to sell, the government condemned the property in June 1915 and then replaced the old wooden 4.5-foot structure with a 6-foot concrete dam. The government planned to use this dam to drain the lake down to its natural level in winter. The water would run down the Truckee River, be diverted through the main canal, and augment supplies at Lahontan Reservoir on the Carson. Then spring and summer runoff from the Sierra would refill Lake Tahoe to the top of the dam in time for the tourist season. Thus, the government argued, the amount of water available for irrigation would be increased and landowners not be harmed.

However, California water law was based in part on riparian logic, rather than prior-appropriations doctrine. Release of this 6 vertical feet of government water required agreement with the more than 300 owners of lakeshore property on the California side of Lake Tahoe. Very few of these people were willing to let the government lower the water level, since this would create extensive mudflats on the lake side of their property. Further, the state of California saw this federal plan as an attempt to drain water from the two-thirds of Lake Tahoe which belonged to California, for the sole benefit of residents of Nevada. Therefore California itself strongly supported the private landowners in their resistance to federal plans.[37]

The federal government claimed a quantity of water, a priority date, and a right to manipulate the surface level at Lake Tahoe; white landowners challenged all three claims. In addition, the enormous size of the federal diversion for the Newlands Project complicated the water rights of individuals all up and down the Truckee. With water rights problems, of course, came ambiguity in land values, sales, and titles. Reno and Sparks were growing rapidly and absorbing water upstream from Derby Dam. Since all these problems became only more complex with time, the federal government filed suit in 1913 to settle the vexing question of Truckee River water rights once and for all. This was a friendly suit, it said. The government was not trying to take water away from anyone; it was just trying to discover all the legitimate existing claims under state law, so it would know how much unused water it could justly claim for the Newlands Project. Known as U.S. v. Orr Water Ditch Co. et al., after one of the major ditch associations around Reno, this suit sought to adjudicate all claims against the Truckee River, including some 2,000 private water users, 20 corporations and power companies, and several city water departments. Once the courts apportioned water among all existing claims and the federal government diverted the rest for Newlands, any new water users would have to purchase one of these adjudicated claims.

In pursuing the Orr Ditch suit, the Department of Justice treated the reservation water claim separately from the claim for the Newlands Project. Even though both were federal interests, one was an Indian property held by the federal government in trust for the tribe and the other was directly owned by the government. This legal separation of the claims avoided an otherwise direct conflict of interest between the project and the Paiute claims which would have been disastrous for the Indians. The difference in priority dates between the two claims, plus the direct competition between the Anglo water users in the Fallon area and the Pyramid Lake Paiutes for the same water, would have made it virtually impossible for Justice Department attorneys to defend both titles adequately. Once this division of claims was decided, the BIA was content. It calmly asserted that the "rights of the Indians are being looked after by the Attorneys for the Department of Justice."[38] The BIA did not directly intervene in the suit on behalf of the Indians at Pyramid Lake.

The Department of Justice position on the Indian claim was very clear; the Indian Office was told that the Justice Department had calculated "the *acreage* to claim water for on the Indian reservation."[39] The Act of 1904 alloted five acres of irrigable land to each adult Indian. Since there were roughly 600 Indians on the reservation, Justice considered that there were therefore 3,000 acres of potentially irrigable land to which the Indians ultimately had a claim. They ignored the potential claim to 19,000 acres of benchlands which the Reclamation Service anticipated developing whenever the reservation was opened up to white settlement. In addition, they said that 2,400 acres of already irrigated land lay along the Truckee River and the delta, although "a few farms further up the river were occupied by the squatters."[40] The Justice Department considered that the land already farmed plus the 3,000 acres of potentially irrigable land made a grand total of 5,400 acres for which Indians had a justifiable water claim. The lawyers initially prepared a defense for the priority date of 1874, accepting the executive order rather than the earlier 1859 withdrawal of the land from public sale as the founding of the reserve. In other words, the Justice Department sought water for the minimal amount of land and at a priority date least favorable to the Indians.

To justify even this degree of involvement in Indian interests, Justice lawyers felt compelled to point out that all the water necessary for the Indian lands could come from seepage from the Truckee Canal and return flow from Anglo irrigation in the Wadsworth area; the reclamation project need never refrain from diverting Truckee River water in order to provide the Indian allocation. Therefore, the lawyers asserted, there was no conflict of interest between the two government claims.

The Justice Department's decision to claim only enough water to irrigate farmland amazed Agent Creel, and he promptly proposed a new line of argument to the lawyers. Since the Pyramid Lake Reservation had been established for the use and benefit of the Paiute Indians, and since the only significant natural resource on the reserve was the Lahontan cutthroat trout, Creel concluded that the purpose of the reservation was to assure Paiutes a livelihood through fishing. Therefore, any action which damaged the trout population was a violation of federal interests in the reserve. Further, if the reservation had been established to provide Indians with a place for fishing, then, he argued, the Indians had a claim in the Orr Ditch case for water to maintain the fish supply. In reply to Creel's suggestions, the attorney in charge of the Indian section of the case reasserted that "he has made no contention for water to pass into the lake for the purpose of maintaining its level and preserving the fish."[41] When Creel checked with Reclamation, he found that they too accepted calmly the inevitable evaporation of Pyramid Lake and the destruction of the fishery. Furthermore, they already planned additional diversions to clean up any remaining "waste water," guaranteeing that there could be no permanent inflow.

Both the Bureau of Reclamation and the Department of Justice seemed to agree that beneficial use of water, like beneficial use of land, had to accord with Anglo ideals. Water was allocated and defended for agricultural purposes, but such nonagricultural use as the propagation of fish was designated as wasteful. That water would be given to other users. Of course, this water policy followed from the Anglo perception of fishing as a sport and not as a means of food production. The Anglo-American cultural prejudice in favor of agricultural usage, which had influenced BIA policy on the Pyramid Lake Indian Reservation since its inception, was here brazenly enforced. Few save Agent Creel and the Indians themselves challenged this assumption.

Creel pointed out that water claims could probably be made for fish propagation. It could be based on those special legal arguments applicable to any Pyramid Lake claim. Most important of these was the legal principle which applied specifically to Indian reservations known as the *Winters* Doctrine. It was founded on the general legal premise that Indian tribes, once aboriginally independent sovereign nations, retained any powers and property which they had not explicitly yielded to either the federal government or private parties. In other words, the loss of political control over the continental land base did not automatically imply the loss of all personal and property rights, unless these were clearly given up through treaties, agreements, or other legal documents. The *Winters* Doctrine concerned water rights specifically and got its name from the 1908 Supreme Court decision in the case Winters v. U.S.[42] In that decision, the court ruled that Indian water claims did not need to be expressly reserved in treaties and documents. Tribes had water rights based on their aboriginal sovereignty. The tribes retained those rights until they were terminated or passed on to other owners in some legal fashion. If they were not explicitly released, then implicitly they were reserved by the tribe. Thus the absence of specific assertions of water claims in the early treaties, often signed long before competition for water became an issue in the West, did not necessarily imply that water was unimportant to Indian lives or that they gave it up to white men. The presence of a statement manifestly reserving water rights did not need to appear in the treaties for there to be a tribal water right.

A second issue in the *Winters* case was the relationship of Indian water rights to state law. Since states acquired authority over most water when they joined the Union, did they gain control over Indian claims as well? Did tribes lose residual rights at this point? The *Winters* decision specifically denied that states could take over Indian water rights without explicit federal consent. Finally, the *Winters* decision argued that the federal government would not have established Indians on reservations if it had intended to deny them the means to earn a living there. Since the reservation in the *Winters* case was designed to provide a land base for a new agricultural economy in an area where irrigation was required, the government in all conscience could not yield the water rights required for the irrigable portions of that reserve. Thus in the act of authorizing any Indian reservation, the federal government implicitly created water rights for the "beneficial use" of that reserve for whatever purposes it was intended.

Later decisions clarified the principles first stated in *Winters*. Particularly difficult was the question of water rights priority, and whether this varied according to the way in which the reservation had been established. The case was clear with treaty reservations. The court said that "the treaty was not a grant of rights to the Indians, but a grant of rights from them [to the United States] and a reservation of those not granted."[43] Therefore, both the land claim and the attached water rights antedated the establishment of the United States and were by definition the earliest on the waterway. Even today, the situation is less clear in the case of executive order reservations. These may not date from aboriginal sovereignty, since they were not reserved from native territory by means of a treaty. Rather, such reservations may be seen as federal grants of land to the tribe from the public domain.[44] Therefore, the accompanying *Winters* water rights may hold a priority date only from the establishment of the reservation. Since Pyramid Lake was an executive order reserve, its actual founding date became a critical question. Whether it was legally established in 1859 or 1874 made considerable difference because of the number of Anglo squatters' land and water claims introduced during those intervening years.

A second area where the *Winters* decision needed clarification was on the issue of the amount of water which could be claimed. If the *Winters* Doctrine assured only enough water for the land actually farmed at the time of the reservation's withdrawal, or perhaps at the time of the first regional water suit, this might easily catch a tribe long before its adjustment to a farming life. If Indian water allocations were frozen at this early period, and Anglo users were allowed to absorb all the remaining available water, such action could deny Indians any chance to farm for all time. This would defeat the purpose of nineteenth-century BIA policy, stultify tribal economic growth, and further complicate already tense interethnic relations in the West.

Therefore, in order to give Indians a chance to gain familiarity with the new Anglo-European agricultural technology, the court acknowledged *Winters* rights to include all potentially irrigable property.[45] The Supreme Court later clarified that *Winters* rights included sufficient water for present and future needs in order to utilize the reservation for those purposes which had been intended by the government when it had originally set it aside.[46] This *Winters* Doctrine established a legal precedent which could have been used to strengthen Paiute water claims in the Orr Ditch suit; the Department of Justice chose not to employ the *Winters* argument for any but agricultural purposes.

To settle the Orr Ditch case, the federal District Court appointed a special water master to prepare technical recommendations. In 1926, thirteen years after the suit had been initiated, the court adopted the water master's suggestions in the form of a temporary restraining order. The temporary decree specified a water allotment and priority date for each of the water claims up and down the Truckee River. The court planned to let these temporary regulations stay in effect for a trial period, after which problems would be renegotiated and a final decree be issued.

The temporary decree designated two water allotments for the Pyramid Lake Indian Reservation. The first accepted a priority date of 1859 for the founding of the reservation. It allowed water for the 3,130 acres then accommodated by the Indian ditch system. With an application rate of 3.3 acre-feet per acre and a 15-percent transportation loss, the decree specified a diversion for this claim not to exceed 3.88 acre-feet per acre. Since the ownership of water rights on the lands held by squatters along the lower river was still very much in dispute, the decree forbade the transfer of these first Paiute water rights to "homesteaders, entrymen, settlers, or others than the Indians in the event that said lands are released from the reservation or are thrown open to entry or other disposal than allotment or transfer to the Indians."[47] Given the BIA's proven inability to protect land on this reservation, such a provision was probably sound policy.

The second allotment of water for Pyramid Lake Reservation was for the five-acre parcels guaranteed each Paiute under the Act of 1904. This claim carried a 1904 priority date. If the land already cultivated along the river bottoms and covered under the first water allocation was not counted toward the five acres per Indian, but rather the land was to be subjugated from the undeveloped and drier benchlands, the decree provided for the delivery of 4.1 acre-feet per acre. Allowing for evaporation and ditch loss, 5.59 acre-feet per acre could be diverted. The amount of land covered by this provision was unspecified, because it would depend on the size of the Paiute population at the time of allotment. Since the five-acre allotments were never made and the benchlands never developed, this water allocation was not used.

The Secretary of the Interior and the Commissioner of Indian Affairs approved the temporary decree. It then went into effect along the Truckee. No headgates or measuring devices were installed. Enforcement of the decree was solely in the hands of the water master and local custom.

Pyramid Lake Paiutes, unlike their bureaucratic guardians, did find fault with the water situation and the decree. They immediately complained that they were receiving far less than their allocated quantity of water. The Indian agent wrote his Commissioner that "something definite should be done about the protection of water and water rights of the Pyramid Lake Indians. ... each year the Indians lose more and more water. It would appear that their claims are not being properly protected. ... some effort must be made to stop the further looting of this water."[48] The BIA drafted a letter for the Interior Secretary's signature which described the informal local arrangements made by Nevada Anglos to circumvent the decree:

> It seems that the water master appointed by the Court has in the past held the Indian users to the maximum per acre quantity of water provided for by the present order and has arbitrarily determined that the upper non-Indian users may be furnished water early in the season considerably in excess of the amount provided for in the Court's order under the theory that such excess use during the early part of the season will provide a larger return flow later in the year. Such a distribution of the available water supply was not provided for in the decree nor does it appear that it was ever contemplated that such a division be included therein. ... In no circumstances should this obviously inequitable administration of the water supply be permitted to continue.[49]

The local Indian agent contacted Newlands Director Richardson about the water shortage on the reserve, and he defensively tele-graphed his superiors: "We are not guilty of depriving Indians of their water[.] There are many other appropriators on the stream nearly all of whom are diverting water in excess of their allowance under proposed decree. . . ." Of course, among these upstream appro-priators were the squatters who held Indian lands without title. Rich-ardson washed his hands of the matter, declaring, "Contractual obligations to water users on Newlands project must be fulfilled and any attempt by me to deprive them of their reasonable requirements under their contracts for the purposes of benefiting the Indians will be met by mandamus proceedings and other litigation."[50] He clearly saw his bureaucratic duty and loyalties to lie with the Anglo water users on the Carson drainage.

Inspector Trowbridge seemed to touch the core of the problem when he observed in his 1921 report: "The Indians have a water-right, but being at the tail-end of the river, so to speak, they are unable to obtain their proper share of the water, all other water users on the river having first chance and there is no one in authority to make a just and fair distribution."[51] In frustration, the Indian agent threatened to file suit through the U.S. Attorney's office, and this warning instigated bu-reaucratic attempts to reach an amicable agreement. Senator Oddie approached the Secretary of the Interior with some suggestions. Al-though the Secretary was the superior of both the Bureau of Reclama-tion and the Bureau of Indian Affairs, he replied that "in view of the decree, the matter seems to be outside the jurisdiction of this Depart-ment and I fail to see what we can do to change the existing condi-tions."[52] The solicitor for the Interior Department concurred "that the temporary decree should be made permanent before any stipulation is made concerning the rearrangement of the respective rights of other parties to the suit."[53] All the bureaucrats agreed that the entire water delivery system was frozen by the temporary decree.

This position was in direct contradiction to the avowed intent of the temporary decree, which was to establish a tentative allotment of water, allow it to operate for a few years, and see if it was adequate for everyone's needs. The temporary restraining order specifically stated that "Any person affected by this order may at any time present an application to the Judge of this Court for modification thereof in any regard."⁵⁴ Although Indians complained that the *de facto* distribution of water did not assure them their fair amount, neither the BIA nor the U.S. Attorney's office filed any official protest nor petitioned for redress under the decree. Neither the government nor any of the defendants ever asked the court to modify their allocations. All parties accepted the decree, and the federal government accepted tacitly for Pyramid Lake Paiutes.

Water decreed for the reservation was for agricultural irrigation and domestic water only. However, Paiutes believed that water should also be provided for maintenance of the fishery and fish propagation. By the late 1920s, the surface level of Pyramid Lake was dropping significantly, and Winnemucca Lake had dried up. Sections of the Truckee River delta lay exposed. Indians became very alarmed when fish clustered at the river mouth unable to get across the delta because of shallow water, and the spawning runs of cutthroat trout and cuiui were unsuccessful. A group of Paiutes declared to the agent, "Must have the water to save [our] fish; that is our water and should be turned down to us. We are under the Government and the Government should protect our rights to this water, and not allow the water [to be] taken away from us."⁵⁵ Agent Creel persuaded Director Richardson to release unneeded winter water in 1922, and a modest spawning run resulted. However, the immediate and intense Anglo criticism made Richardson reluctant to risk such cooperation again.

As soon as the temporary court order was issued, the local Reclamation agents asserted that they no longer had any options in the matter. The Superintendent of the Newlands Project wrote in 1926, "With the Truckee River being regulated under a court order by a Water Master, as is now the case, no independent action on the part of this office or the Bureau of Reclamation appears to be feasible. Apparently the situation is one which requires some action based upon agreement among all of the water users whose rights are affected unless water for the purpose desired was specifically provided for under the adjudication."⁵⁶ Obviously such permission for water to aid the spawning runs could never be acquired, he explained to the Commissioner of Indian Affairs: "As most of the ranchers consider irrigation more important than the raising of fish it is believed that it will be impossible to get the written consent of the ranchers."[57] Once the Department of Justice had begun the Orr Ditch suit in 1913 and had pursued it without ever making a claim on behalf of the fish population, it became very unlikely that any such claim could be successfully acquired later by consent of the Anglo water users. A fish specialist working for Reclamation declared that the only way to get water for fish propagation was a separate lawsuit instituting a claim on the part of the fish population, but the chief engineer of the Newlands Project chastized his suggestion: "Nothing can be accomplished by litigation or assertion of rights, except interminable delay, inordinate expense and final extinction of fish life in the river."[58] Instead, he recommended a redesign of the fish ladder at Derby Dam to require a lesser amount of water; he saw his responsibility as ending with the dam. On the other hand, his superior, Richardson, knew that a more efficient fish ladder was of little value without first solving the problems of the delta, water flow in the lower channel, urban sewage from Reno, and industrial pollution from California paper mills, because the fish would simply not get as far as Derby Dam to use it. His suggestion for a multifaceted attack on the problem was ignored. There was no bureaucratic consensus on what, if anything, could be done about the fish situation.

In 1931, the water master was forced to answer repeated Indian requests for more water to sustain river flow and maintain the lake level. He did a feasibility study of the water available in the Truckee in an average flow year and measured cubic footage stored in Lake Tahoe, return flows, springs, and other sources in the lower drainage, balancing all this against the contractual obligations with the Truckee River water users and the other assignees of the Orr Ditch decree. He reached the conclusion that it was impossible to "comply with the request of the Indians; that even if he were able to attempt to do so, that it would require a river water supply more than ten times the present supply to even make a small increase in the elevation of the water surface of Pyramid Lake."[59] It was impossible to save the lake, he said, and still meet the other obligations for water. The river was simply overallocated.

Meanwhile, the BIA procrastinated. Rather than file for additional water for fish and lake maintenance under the provisions of the temporary decree, they decided to wait until the final decree was issued. The Bureau of Reclamation declared that the whole fishery matter was outside its jurisdiction. The water master said that saving the lake and the fish was a physical impossibility. It seemed that the Paiutes could get no one to help them gain water for fish at Pyramid Lake.

However, the Indian Bureau was willing to press negotiations for irrigation water.[60] As the time approached for the final decree to be submitted in 1934, a flurry of correspondence passed between the BIA, the Secretary of the Interior, and the Department of Justice. Primarily, the BIA objected to the amount of water allocated to Indian lands in the temporary decree. At 3.3 acre-feet per acre actually delivered, their assignment was far below the 4.0 acre-feet per acre allotted to non-Indian tracts with comparable soil type. Given the predictable transmission losses, the BIA calculated that 4.71 acre-feet per acre would have to be diverted to assure Indians a water allotment equitable with that of white landowners under the decree. Secondly, the Bureau wanted the restriction on transfer of Indian water rights removed. By 1934, courts had found against the Garaventa Land and Livestock Company, Depaoli family, and other squatters. The BIA mistakenly presumed that the trespassers would soon be evicted. Thus they believed that the rationale for restriction against alienation was no longer relevant, and that the clause should be removed as an unnecessary infringement on federal and Indian rights. Thirdly, the BIA was concerned over possible ambiguity in the secondary claim for the five acres per Indian under the 1904 law. They wanted it clearly stated that these would be irrigable lands subjugated under future reclamation projects and not encompass those lands which Indians already had brought under irrigation by their own effort. This would assure maximum acreage allowable under the temporary decree and secure the second water right.

Commissioner of Indian Affairs Collier "formally protested" a simple continuation of the temporary decree because of these three issues. He also pointed out that the squatters had built ten dams across the river, with the result that, of the 28 second-feet of water sent down by Derby Dam, only 8.3 second-feet got to the reservation that year. His field agent reported that "Indians [are] unable to protect themselves against unlawful diversions."[61] Collier's appeal won Interior support for an Indian diversion to equal the water allotments given Anglos. The Truckee-Carson Irrigation District (TCID), the civil successor-in-interest of the government's Newlands Project which took over management of the delivery system in 1926, protested any such increase in the Indian allocation. TCID lawyers made it known in Washington that they would refuse to agree to equalization of the primary Indian allocation unless the federal position on the benchland acreage was softened and the no-transfer clause retained.[62]

When the final Orr Ditch decree was issued in 1935, it again recognized two water claims for the Pyramid Lake Indian Reservation.[63] In the first, the same 3,130 acres of existing bottomland farms received an allocation of 4.0 acre-feet per acre of delivered water, comparable to that allowed Anglo lands. With a 15-percent transportation loss, the actual diversion was not to exceed 4.71 acre-feet per acre. This claim still carried a no-transfer clause, similar to the one in the temporary decree. The second claim for benchlands was changed from the expansible five acres per Indian to one which allowed only a specified number of acres, 2,745. Four acre-feet of delivered water was allocated for each acre, with a maximum diversion of not more than 5.59 acre-feet per acre. This second claim applied explicitly to undeveloped benchlands, not to a general category of irrigable lands, and this provision protected future agricultural development. The second water claim also carried a no-transfer clause. There was no provision anywhere in the decree for water to maintain Pyramid Lake or its fishery.

Although the Orr Ditch decree was announced on July 1, 1935, it was placed in escrow for the next seven years. During that time many interests made last-minute attempts to change the water allocations it contained.[64] Only then did the California Division of Fish and Game declare that the fish in the Truckee River were a valuable resource for both sportsmen and small businessmen who catered to sport-fishing. It petitioned for a minimum year-round flow of 10 cubic feet per second in the natural channel of the Truckee River for fish-spawning purposes. The Bureau of Reclamation politely rejected their petition, as it had the similar Indian request decades earlier, pleading lack of jurisdiction. Truckee-Carson water users organized another attempt to have the temporary decree rather than the final one instituted, but this was denied by the court.

A far more serious disruption to the Orr Ditch compromise came in the form of a seemingly unrelated piece of legislation—the Wheeler-Howard Act. This of course was the law which permitted the formation of tribal councils and forbade unilateral federal sale of reservation lands. When the Pyramid Lake Paiutes organized a tribal constitution under this act, they gained the power to block the Act of 1904 and its planned allotment of five acres to each tribal member and sale of the remainder of the reserve. A lawyer working for the Indian Irrigation Service inquired how this might affect the second reservation water claim.[65] If Indians retained possession of all the benchlands which were potentially irrigable, could they then demand full irrigation and water allocation for 19,000 acres? If so, this water would have to come out of the allotments to upstream users, since the Indian priority date preceded many of theirs. If the government claimed this right to develop the whole bench in the final decree, the upstream water users would undoubtedly attempt to block it. If, on the other hand, the Indian claim were limited to a smaller acreage, this could severely limit the Paiutes' ability to develop these upper lands and to expand their agricultural base as guaranteed by the *Winters* Doctrine.

The TCID was immediately outraged at the suggestion that Indians might have the right to develop the entire benchland,[66] reasserting that the District had agreed to the decree only if the Indian claim was quantified in an "exact manner." If claims were made for additional acres of Indian land or left open-ended, the upstream users simply would not accede to it. In other words, non-Indians were using the concept of consent of all water users, which had successfully blocked a claim for the fishery, to limit Indian irrigation claims as well. Reclamation and TCID did not recognize these tribal irrigation claims as legally defensible, but only as negotiable with competing water users. Of course, these Anglo interests were politically much more powerful. Because the Paiutes had never been directly involved in the Orr Ditch case but had relied totally on the advocacy of the BIA, they were constrained in the ensuing negotiations. The BIA had never demanded legal water rights under *Winters* Doctrine to irrigate all arable land. Instead, it had allowed the already subjugated acreage to become the specified land base and, even more dangerously, had allowed the maximum water right to be quantified. This action circumscribed the amount of water available for Indian agriculture at Pyramid Lake.

The Newlands Reclamation Project benefited those very Anglo farmers in the lower Carson Valley whose opposition hampered Paiute hopes for development. That same Newlands Project brought massive destruction to Pyramid Lake itself. The original Newlands design assumed, and its construction realized, the decline of Pyramid Lake's surface level and the exposure of a dry delta at the Truckee River's mouth. These changes interfered with regeneration of the fish population which still provided a major portion of Paiute subsistence. The lowered lake created a new base level, and the Truckee channel began eroding down through valuable bottomlands. These damages to the fishery and to the agricultural base were brought about by a government project on which the Paiutes were never consulted and of which they never approved. Subsequent government attempts to readjust water allotments were also accomplished without Indian consent, although water users on the Newlands Project retained political veto power over Indian allocations. Paiutes had only indirect representation through the Department of Justice, which was limited by cultural biases concerning proper use of water and did not press Indian claims actively to the full extent of the law. As a result, Pyramid Lake Paiutes suffered. One officer of the state of Nevada later declared that "No private person of stature would have submitted to the loss of property values which the Reservation Indians of Pyramid Lake were to experience when the waters of the Truckee River were diverted by decree, with federal approval and direction, to the Newlands Project."[67]

As Pyramid Lake withered from irrigation withdrawals, the Paiutes faced yet another lingering threat to their fishery. Like most states, Nevada claimed authority over fishing and hunting licenses within its territorial boundaries. Beginning about 1890 and continuing for decades, the state made concerted efforts to control Indian fishing practices and seasons, both on and off the reservations. Indians saw this as an attack on their traditional livelihood. At the same time that fish populations were declining as a result of Anglo activities and the Orr Ditch case was coming to a peak, this dispute with the state was also reaching its climax.

Among the laws passed by the first Nevada Territorial Legislature in 1861 was its assertion of control over methods of trout capture.[68] Ten years later, the state legislature established the first fishing seasons by closing all waterways to trout fishing from January 1st to September 1st.[69] The Anglo idea reflected here, that fish should not be caught during their breeding period, directly conflicted with the Paiute tradition of fishing when the trout were spawning and hence were accessible to Indian shallow-water methods. As thousands of years of archaeological remains showed, Paiute fishing methods had not damaged fish populations in the days before dams and irrigation withdrawals. Nevertheless, by establishing fishing seasons, the state blocked use of these traditional practices in the name of conservation.

The first Nevada state law which specifically mentioned Indian fishing came in 1877. It promised that nothing in the law would "prohibit or prevent Indians from taking trout in any of the streams or lakes of this State, at any time, by the same means heretofore usually used and employed by them; *provided*, that the same are for their own use."[70] However, all fishermen were forbidden to fish at the base of dams, the modern and highly efficient version of Indian weirs. Since those Indian weirs were perceived in the same category and were explicitly forbidden, the state began its restriction of native fishing techniques, demanding conformity to Anglo ideas and Anglo technology. Since Indian fishermen still could use methods other than the hook and line permitted white men, section 10 of the law forbade Indians to catch fish for Anglos in any manner denied general fishermen. In other words, Indians were prohibited from capitalizing on their status under the law to sell their free labor as commercial fishermen. The state presumed that this law directly applied to all Indians, whether off reservations or on.

Although these early state fish laws established Nevada's intention to control Indians' fishing habits, they had minimal influence on Paiute lives because the state made little effort to enforce them. However, the situation changed in 1879 after nine white fishermen who operated illegal commercial fishing stations within the Pyramid Lake Reservation were arrested and tried before federal court. Despite their later pardon, interracial tensions mounted. The federal government asserted its jurisdiction over Pyramid Lake with military presence and blocked subsequent Anglo efforts to fish there on a large scale.

Actually there were few areas in Nevada where commercial fishing was possible. When shallow playa lakes periodically dried up, their fish populations were killed. There were only two large, relatively stable, deep-water lakes in the state, Pyramid and Walker, and by 1880 both of these were completely enclosed within Indian reservations. If the federal government insisted on denying Anglos access to these two lakes for commercial fishing purposes, then Nevada contained no waters suitable for an Anglo fish industry. As a result, the only politically active lobby interested in fish-related issues soon became sportsmen rather than commercial interests, and these Anglos grew rapidly in power. Their hand was seen in the legislature's 1885 petition to have Pyramid Lake Reservation reduced or abandoned. One of the arguments put forward was that Anglos were being excluded unfairly from reaping the benefits of the lake. Whites were being prosecuted in federal court, they said, while Paiutes fished and hunted game on the reservation "without regard to the fish and game laws of the State."[71] The sportsmen considered this outrageous. As with other resources of the state, Anglos wanted unrestricted access to natural game for themselves and wanted Paiutes to relinquish all their previous rights to hunt and fish on what had once been their land.

On the other hand, after competing Anglo trespassers were excluded from their reservation, Paiutes enthusiastically commercialized their trout surplus. Between 1870 and 1890, they sold not less than 50,000 pounds each year and sometimes twice that amount. According to agency reports, fish sales brought in $5–8,000 each year, an impressive sum in those days. This was especially important because the only other source of cash income Paiutes had was $2–3,000 in wage labor. Not only did fish sales provide the vast majority of cash on the reservation, but fish also were a winter food source of incalculable value.

Faced with Nevada's increasing attempts to control Paiute fishing, the agent at Pyramid Lake chose to avoid conflict with state authorities. He insisted that Indians on the reservation fish only in accordance with state standards. His bureaucratic superiors approved this decision, and the Secretary of the Interior wrote the Commissioner of Indian Affairs, "Your action in instructing the Agent at Nevada Agency to prohibit his Indians from killing or catching fish in the waters of said reservation, during the spawning season, and to forbid them from taking fish at any time except with hook and line, is approved."[72] By acceding to state demands on seasons and methods, the BIA abdicated Pyramid Lake Paiutes' implicitly reserved aboriginal hunting rights guaranteed to them under the general principles of Indian law. These should have stood independent of state law, certainly on reservation and perhaps even off. The Pyramid Lake Indian agent thus served as an agent for the state. Without legislative authority, he administratively extended the operation of state laws onto the Indian reservation, where they had no direct jurisdiction.

Receiving pressure from sportsmen and finding no resistance from the BIA, the state legislature passed a law in 1891 which was directly inimical to the increasingly profitable Paiute fishing industry at Pyramid Lake. Knowing full well that state law did not have direct jurisdiction on federal properties, including Indian trust lands, the state attempted indirect control. In order to sell fish, Paiutes needed two things. First, they had to have a source of fish, which they held in the form of Pyramid Lake itself and in the federal protection from Anglo commercial trespass. In addition, they had to have access to a market in which to sell. It was this market which the state attempted to cut off from them in the 1891 law, which stated:

> It shall not be lawful for any railway corporation, express company or other common carrier or private parties to ship or transport for sale, or to receive for shipment, or to have in their possession for transportation, any of the river or brook trout or land-locked salmon taken from the rivers, lakes, or other waters of this State, between the first day of October of each year and the first day of April of each year.[73]

Essentially this terminated commercial fishing in the state. Although the law did not specifically mention Indians in any way, it affected the Paiute economy far more than any other sector, because the accidents of geography and history had assured that only they held commercial fishing grounds in the state. The Pyramid Lake economy was devastated. In 1891 over $8,000 had been brought in through fish sales, but the following year, as a direct result of the new Nevada fish law, there was none.[74] Within a single year, two-thirds of the cash flow through the reservation economy evaporated.

Shocked at the unanticipated fruition of BIA appeasement policy, the Pyramid Lake agent inquired whether this law actually could apply to fish caught by Indians on the reservation. "The law is a wrong one in every respect," he protested, "and is solely in the interests of a few sportsmen."[75] In reply, the Commissioner suggested a test case. The agent submitted a box of fish to Wells Fargo and another to the Central Pacific Railroad, the common carriers servicing the reservation. He addressed the fish to California, in hopes of circumventing state jurisdiction by entering interstate commerce where federal law applied. In each case, the carrier refused to accept the shipments, citing state law. Unwilling to press the issue, Washington initiated no legal action.

If the state successfully denied Paiutes the right to sell winter fish, the agent observed, they would have no income during that season and would be thrown immediately onto federal relief. In 1894, an inspector confirmed the accuracy of this prediction. The Indians, he found, were "dependent for nine-tenths of their living from Pyramid Lake, which furnishes them an almost inexhaustible supply of fish. Under the fish law of the State of Nevada they are almost deprived of any revenue from this source." Although they continued subsistence fishing, he remarked, they were prevented from selling their surplus. "This law, as I have said, works a great hardship upon these Indians."[76] He joined the agent in calling for a test in the courts; the government continued to procrastinate.

While Paiutes were suffering from the state law and agents were protesting it, Nevada officials were also unhappy with the results of their handiwork. In 1896, a petition to the Secretary of the Interior signed by many high state officials complained that Indians were continuing to catch fish during the spawning season. Paiutes were still selling fish, they asserted, "in large quantities . . . in this State and California, thus violating the Statutes of this State and drawing great and illegal profits to the injury of the commonwealth; the State and County officers refuse to act, being doubtful of their jurisdiction in the premises, the offenses complained of being committed on an Indian Reservation."[77] The legislature had passed laws boldly intended to apply on reservations, but actual enforcement raised the question of jurisdiction. The petition asked that the federal government force Indians to abide by state laws on fishing methods, seasons, and non-shipment of fish. This indecisiveness on the part of the state allowed the development of a smuggling tradition, a common response among people who believe they are subject to unjust laws. While the agency reports showed no income through sale of fish during the next ten years, there was apparently enough individual clandestine sale of trout to offend state officials and local white residents.

The question of Truckee River fish was not simply a political problem but a real one, because changes were taking place in the fish populations themselves. By 1900, the city of Reno was dumping so much waste in the river that it created a dead zone where fish could no longer breathe. Irrigation agriculture had increased to such an extent that the dams and canals formed major threats to fish life. Spawning fish, trying to work upstream, could not scale the enormous slopes of dams such as Derby. Many of the fish ladders required by state law were inadequate. Fish on their return downstream were swept off into unscreened irrigation canals. Carried by the headwaters, they were flushed into the fields where they found shallow water; when the flow was cut off, they were stranded in the now-empty ditches. Irrigation diversion reduced water levels in natural streams, in some cases so low that fish could not pass. Anglo pollution, diversion of streams, reduction of water levels in the rivers, unscreened irrigation ditches, and dams made it increasingly difficult for fish to reproduce. The fish population in Nevada was dwindling.

As their quarry became more elusive, Anglo sport-fishermen became more outspoken about the "slaughter" of fish by Indians. Whites were outraged that Indians on reservations, outside of state jurisdiction, fished publicly during the spawning season and dried the catch for their own subsistence. Letter followed letter to state and federal fish officers demanding stricter controls over Indian fishing. At the same time, the Pyramid Lake agent was trying to have the state law ameliorated. He argued that the depressed reservation economy was a direct result of the state law which denied Indians access to a market for their fish. In 1911 the state legislature responded. Ignoring the far greater effects on fish life caused by Anglo behavior and construction, it blamed the decreasing number of fish on the "slaughter" by Indians. It retaliated by passing a new law which declared that all large fish species except cuiui were game fish and hence under state jurisdiction. Then it said that no one could possess more than 10 game fish or 10 pounds of game fish on any one day at *any* time of the year. However, the fisherman could use these limited numbers of fish either for his own use or for sale. To control sales, shipping companies were forbidden to transport, warehouses to store, or restaurants to buy more than the daily limit from any one individual. The law required all game wardens and sheriffs to enforce these regulations actively. Officers were empowered to search cars, barns, camps, and homes anywhere in the state and to seize discovered fish and violators. The discriminatory law specifically stated that if *Indians* "shall be in such large numbers as to be beyond the reasonable power of any fish or game warden of the state fish commission to control, or in case of forcible resistance," he could call on all civil authorities for assistance. The law continued: "It shall be no defense in any prosecution for violation of any of the provisions of this act that the trout or other fish in question were taken or killed outside the State of Nevada; nor shall it be any defense . . . that the trout or fish were taken or killed by any one other than he in whose possession said trout or fish were found."[78]

The law permitted a limited resumption of the fish trade. Small batches of fish, the daily catch of a single Paiute, were shipped by common carrier to markets in the Reno area. Under the law, any sale had to be made directly from the fisherman to the consumer. This meant that fishermen had to have a known buyer to whom they could ship, drive to Reno themselves to hawk their catch individually, or rely on the flooded local market in Wadsworth. Such small-lot marketing was cumbersome and not very profitable.

More importantly, the basic question of whether the state had jurisdiction over fish which Indians caught on the reservation remained unchallenged. Therefore the agent at Pyramid Lake and the U.S. Attorney convinced a trader at Wadsworth named Crosby to initiate a test case. In the spring of 1914, Crosby accepted the 10-fish limit from a number of Paiute fishermen. Each batch was wrapped separately and labeled. He tried to ship this combined package from Wadsworth, where the state game warden came onto the reservation without a warrant and arrested him. When the case came to court, Crosby argued that he had not been in the State of Nevada when arrested, and therefore the state game warden had had no jurisdiction to arrest him. Secondly, the fish had not been caught in Nevada state waters, and therefore were not a matter for state law. Since the lake was totally contained within a reservation which was itself under federal jurisdiction, in a sense Pyramid Lake was a federal fish hatchery. As a hatchery, it was not subject to state law. Finally, he explained, the fish did not belong to him but to the original fishermen, for whom he was merely transporting them on consignment. Despite these arguments, the State Supreme Court found him guilty under the second clause quoted above, and sentenced and fined him.[79] The BIA never again attempted to challenge the state's jurisdiction.

Orders came from Washington that state game laws were to be obeyed on the Pyramid Lake Reservation. In 1917 the local agent pronounced that "it is the intention of this office to observe the state fish and game laws as closely as possible." The state regulation against fishing at or near the base of dams was enforced. "A few of the Pyramid Lake Indians," the agent reported, were "caught fishing near the [reservation irrigation] dam and they were punished for this." Such voluntary cooperation with the state laws, he hoped, would win future concessions from the state legislature. Nevertheless, he did observe dryly that "most of the objections to the Indians fishing and marketing his catch is from a class of people that are sore because they are not allowed to fish on the reservation." When several carloads of Anglos were told to leave the reservation on the opening day of the fishing season, they became very angry. "Threats have been repeatedly made," the agent reported, "that they [the Anglo fishermen] would stop the Indians from selling their trout."[80]

Pyramid Lake Paiutes protested the agency's policy of submission to state demands. They smarted under the state restriction of their profitable trade and resented BIA unwillingness to defend them. The Indians objected to the Superintendent's habit of giving personal passes to friends and other white men to fish on the lake for pleasure. Some Paiutes established a policy of their own, to deny Anglos such access to the lake for sport-fishing and increasingly to withhold cooperation with state spawning activities. As related earlier, some young men removed Anglo pleasure boats from the lake and carried them up into the surrounding sagebrush. Despite the unsavory press reaction and agency punishment for their civil disobedience, Paiutes refused to knuckle under. They sought support from a Bureau inspector, who recommended that "the right of the Indians to dispose of the product of their labors, according to their own will and their own advantage be fully defended by the United States in justification of its office and obligations as guardian and sovereign power."[81] Washington ignored this suggestion.

Although the Indian agent blamed Paiutes themselves for their growing problems with the state, he admitted that the BIA was also at fault. In 1922, he said that the state was forced to pass repressive laws "because of the lack of interest on the part of reservation officials in stopping Indians engaged in the wholesale slaughter of fish, violations of laws relative to the taking of fish with nets, grab-hooks, etc., illegal sales during closed seasons and disregard of the efforts of State authorities to assist in the conservation of this important industry."[82] He did not ask whether there was any logical reason why Indians should conform to the state's designation of fish as sport rather than food. He did not ask whether there was any legal reason why the state should expect to have its laws apply on a federal Indian reservation. He believed that it was Indian resistance which drove the state to yet further restrictive measures.

In 1921, the state forbade the sale of game fish completely:

> It shall be unlawful for any person or persons, company, association, or corporation in the State of Nevada to buy, sell, or offer or expose for sale, any river trout, lake trout or brook trout, salmon, whitefish, or large-mouthed or small-mouthed black bass caught from any of the waters of the State of Nevada at any period of the year.[83]

This regulation completed the destruction of Paiute commercial fishing, as it was intended to do.

After years of negotiating with the state to have the restrictive laws removed, the Pyramid Lake agent saw that this new law terminated any hope of leniency. He reciprocated immediately. In the middle of the fishing season, the Superintendent instituted a permit system for the general public to fish at Pyramid Lake, charging a fee for the first time. He was immediately removed by Washington for his initiative. Oddly enough, the *Reno Gazette* supported his action.[84] The newspaper conceded that the state should not have passed the law without first consulting the Indians who would be so profoundly affected. Then the paper offered a classic solution to the jurisdictional conflict posed by Indian fishing: eliminate the reservation—immediate allotment of five acres per Indian, break-up and sale of the rest of the reserve to white men, and open access to the lake without restriction, would solve the whole problem.

The new Superintendent reinstated the conciliatory approach to the state in hopes that cooperation would lead to concessions. He required Indians to comply with the state laws and forbade fish sales. Nevertheless, the resident Farmer-in-Charge reported persistent smuggling of fish off the reservation and the arrest of several Paiutes in surrounding towns. However, he assured his superior in Reno, reports of Indians slaughtering fish were exaggerated beyond truth. When storm winds blew fish up onto the dry delta, Indians captured them rather than let them die and rot. The press quickly publicized this highly visible salvage process, the Farmer declared, and sportsmen's outrage was out of all proportion to the facts. Furthermore, after he himself was served fresh Pyramid Lake trout at an off-reservation restaurant, he inquired whether the Anglos buying the fish could not be prosecuted as well as the Paiutes selling them.

Of course, this was not the way the law was structured. The Superintendent rejected the Farmer's moderate position and employed his full power to control Indian behavior. His letters threatened that "those who persist in violating the law will be prosecuted under the law and will be deprived of their rights to fish on the reservation."[85] On the other hand, he did forward a Paiute petition to the Governor and the legislators which requested repeal of the fish law because it worked undue hardship on the Indian people. While admitting that there might be some Indians violating the law, the petition protested that this was certainly not true of all Paiutes. Nevertheless, all were suffering. The lake was totally within their reservation, they noted, and "therefore belonging to us," but the law "deprives us of a means of livelihood from this source."[86]

The BIA brought out of retirement an experienced and dedicated administrator, Lorenzo Creel, to investigate the fishing situation at Pyramid Lake. Politically astute, Creel observed, "While I am not subservient to political influences when it comes to adjusting matters between the whites and Indians, yet I am far from insensible to their great value in accomplishing desirable ends through this medium."[87] Creel argued that Nevada was then in the depths of a major agricultural depression which cut off Paiutes from their primary source of wage labor, harvest jobs on nearby Anglo-owned farms. This coincided with passage of the law strictly forbidding all sales of fish. These two factors combined to effectively remove all cash income from the Pyramid Lake economy, throwing it into a double decline. He offered the state legislature a compromise. Indian-caught fish would be tagged as such and sold; in return, the public would have access to the lake. To compensate Paiutes for the competition of Anglo sportsmen on their lake, Indians would be guaranteed the monopoly to rent boats, crew them, and guide white fishermen. Creel's plan gave Indians control over the lake, but at the same time the public gained access to it for recreation. He enlisted the support of fishing associations, government agencies, and legislators for his plan. Creel called meetings on the reservation to gather data to justify his requested modification of the fish-marketing law,[88] asking each of the 40 household heads present whether they wanted to be fishermen. Five men replied that they wanted to fish full-time on a commercial basis, and another 19, nearly half the population, wanted to fish as a part-time source of additional income. Of course, all the men wanted to fish for subsistence. The Paiutes voiced overwhelming support for any plan which would again legalize fish sales.

As the legislature considered the compromise bill, the agent tightened control over Paiutes at Pyramid Lake:

> Indians who violate the regulations will not be allowed to fish at all, or to sell fish; and their names will be posted at the Agency as law-

violators, in addition to such other penalties as may be imposed. . . . In other words, if the Indians are disposed to be 'square' and help carry out the new law in the right spirit, assisting the officers to prosecute offenders, etc., they will have no trouble; but if they are disposed to cover up law violations, do not report violations of the law, night fishing, improper sales, etc., they cannot expect to carry on a business which, properly observed, will mean so much to them and their future prosperity.[89]

Although the Paiutes were deeply concerned over the fishing issue, the agent discouraged them from acting directly. When they attempted to send a delegation to Carson City, he ordered them to return home. He had the situation well in hand, he told them, and their interference might upset all his work. He ordered the resident farmer: "In this connection, you must discourage 'meetings' of Indians that take them away from their work and do nothing but unduly excite them. Explain to them that you are not there to hold councils, but to direct work. The 'talk habit' must be stopped wherever possible."[90] He told Paiutes that it was in their own self-interest to inform on anyone selling fish. Indian police were ordered to arrest fellow Paiutes for violation of the state law. Understandably, these men were reluctant to alienate their friends and neighbors by enforcing an unpopular regulation with which they did not agree and which had dubious application on the reservation at all. This left enforcement up to the small agency staff.

Paiutes continued to act independently of agency wishes. Since at least 1914, Nevada had been fishing at the Indian dam in order to gather trout spawn for artificial propagation in state hatcheries. Indians claimed that fish were being killed by the process and they objected repeatedly to this "wanton slaughter" of fish. Tired of being ignored, Paiutes forced closure of the spawn-gathering operation in 1923. Believing that this might jeopardize relations with the state legislature just when negotiations were most delicate, the agent forced them to allow reestablishment of the spawn-taking program.

That year a revised fish statute was passed which provided for the tagging of Indian-caught fish in accordance with Creel's plan. These were marketable in season up to the standard 10-fish or 10-pound limit. Although this provision applied only to Indians, the law nowhere recognized fish selling as a legal or aboriginal right. It was seen as a privilege which the benevolent state was granting to Indians.

The Pyramid Lake agent took it upon himself to make sure that fish were tagged before they left for off-reservation markets. He monitored Paiute compliance with state laws which forbade fishing at the base of dams, because he feared that such violations would once again lead to the complete prohibition of fish sales. This enforced "cooperation" won concessions from the state. In 1925, the season was lengthened and the daily sales limit increased to 25 tagged fish or 25 pounds of fish.

Despite agency policy, Pyramid Lake Paiutes themselves resented Nevada's assumption of authority and interference with their lucrative trade. Paiutes insisted that they had aboriginal rights to fish as their people always had on those lands reserved for them.[91] Their irritation spilled over onto other state actions, especially spawn-gathering. On the basis of thousands of years of history, Paiutes argued that the trout reproduced in the river without artificial propagation. The handling technique was killing fish, they said, and the whole procedure was wasteful and unnecessary. In their assessment of the situation, they overlooked the effects of dams, irrigation withdrawals, and the emerging Truckee River delta, all of which posed real but novel obstructions to fish migration. In fact, the entire fish habitat was changing very rapidly. Nevertheless, acting on ancient perceptions which they believed to be true, Paiutes again forced the state to stop gathering spawn in 1926.[92] Although this closure was only temporary, it immediately elevated tensions between Paiutes and the state fish and game authorities.

In hopes of overcoming Indian resistance to the spawn-gathering program, the state employed Indian assistants in 1926 and paid the tribe a fee for camping privileges. However, when the state tried to move its camp from the dam to the mouth of the lake, right in the heart of the residential area of the reservation, Indian opposition arose. Paiutes wired Washington, asking that headquarters rescind the agent's permission for this highly visible state activity. In conformity with Indian wishes, the Commissioner of Indian Affairs reluctantly ordered the agent to revoke authorization for state spawn-taking.[93] The state Fish and Game Commission retaliated with allegations that Indians were selling more than their quota of fish, using grab hooks, fishing out of season, and violating other state laws on a massive scale. There were dire predictions that the cutthroat trout would soon be extinct because of Indians' violation of state regulations and their resistance to spawn-taking.[94] There was no suggestion that the federal irrigation projects, upstream pollution, or failure to allocate water for fish in the Orr Ditch decision had anything at all to do with the decline of the fishery. The Indian agent at Pyramid Lake began to see a definite correlation between cooperation with spawn-gathering and leniency in enforcing catch limits. "I am reliably informed," he wrote, "that at such times [as the Paiutes allow the state to gather cutthroat trout eggs] the game wardens in the various counties are instructed to allow the Indians to sell fish with impunity, but when the Indians have hesitated to allow spawn to be taken they have been threatened with arrest and punishment."[95]

In 1928 the state resumed egg-harvesting, but tensions were still high. The number of fry which survived replanting in the Truckee River were not sufficient to maintain the fish population at Pyramid Lake. As the fishery declined, both state personnel and Paiutes became more worried and angry. Beginning to believe its own propaganda about fish slaughter during the spawning run and excessive waste by the Indians, the Nevada Fish and Game Commission became increasingly reluctant to restock the lower Truckee. The Commission notified the Indian agency that "if the Indians on the Reservation hold the matter of conservation of the spawning fish at Pyramid Lake in their own hands, and they are permitted to continue to impoverish that body of water by taking those fish at breeding times when they are gathered close together and are easy prey, that *no* demand should be made upon this Commission to attempt to replenish that body of water in the face of such demoralizing procedure by the hands of the Indians."[96] The agent rejected this argument and countered:

> While there has been a pretended interest on the part of the State in keeping up the supply of fish in Pyramid Lake, in reality there has been no evidence of any sincerity in doing so, as the State has not planted any fish in the lake for years, although generous promises have been

made when they have taken millions of eggs in the spring time. What the State apparently wishes is the privilege of taking spawn from the reservation for its hatchery at Verdi and disposing of the young fish to its own advantage in any manner it wishes without any regard to the interests of Pyramid Lake.[97]

Although the BIA admitted that Indian fishing was a minor cause of decline, the real root of the problem, it said, was Derby Dam, which lay off the reservation and totally outside the jurisdiction of the Indian office. Meanwhile, some Indians were demanding short-term economic benefits from state spawn-gathering in the form of higher campsite fees and higher wages for more Indian employees, all very minor issues in comparison to the potential long-term impact of the program. It seemed that none of the parties could agree on what the issues actually were, let alone reach a solution.

After an abortive attempt to have the Washoe County hatchery take over spawn-gathering in place of the hated state personnel, the U.S. Bureau of Fisheries joined the program in 1930. Meeting Indian resistance, they eventually ignored Paiutes and gathered spawn anyway. The federal program returned 75 percent of the cutthroat trout fry it raised to Pyramid Lake, a far greater percentage than had the state, although the government did not bribe Paiutes with fees and employment. Indians protested this arrangement, and the agent asked for a federal marshal to contain the tense situation at the reserve.[98]

As the spawning year began in 1931, Pyramid Lake Paiutes and their agent wrote to the Commissioner of Indian Affairs: they "resent very keenly the fact that the waters of the Truckee River are not allowed to flow into the lake."[99] Clearly Indians connected the decline of the fishery with the lack of inflow to the lake. The agent's field investigation confirmed that no water was passing Derby Dam and that only seepage and spring waters were reaching Pyramid Lake. However, the focus of contention remained on the decline of the fishery itself. One Indian telegraphed Senator Oddie: "Very serious condition Pyramid Lake Indians. Due [to] Government and State action, seining. While hatchery is in possession of lake and river, depriving Indians, forcibly, of fishing[.] Stop. . . . Imperitive[.] Indians need fish to live."[100] State fish authorities complained to their federal counterparts that Indians were overfishing, selling spawn as bait, and deliberately destroying the fish population. The Indian agent defended Indians by protesting, "This charge is absolutely false and is nothing more than advance propaganda in the annual effort to get the Indians to agree to the taking of large quantities of spawn by the state." He perceived that the ultimate goal was to make Indians on the reservation comply with state game laws, despite lack of legal jurisdiction. "To gain this end," he said, "they do not hesitate to deliberately falsify."[101] The U.S. Bureau of Fisheries believed their professional colleagues against the protests of the agent and threatened to withdraw from the program unless they got full Indian cooperation.

The situation reached a crisis in 1932, when Paiutes accused the Bureau of Fisheries' operations chief at Pyramid Lake of being drunk on the job and being abusive toward Indian residents. Their drive for his removal was successful.[102] Later the same year, a young Anglo employee accidentally drowned. The public reacted immediately and angrily. The federal Bureau of Fisheries withdrew its spawning program, claiming shortage of funds, increasing salinity of the lake, and pressure on its hatchery capacity, but primarily lack of Paiute cooperation. The following year, the state refused to return to Pyramid Lake the high percentage of spawn which the federal program had offered. For a number of years thereafter, Nevada made very little effort to stock Pyramid Lake at all. Fish populations declined further.

Not until the establishment of the Pyramid Lake Tribal Council were any further negotiations held on this issue. Reflecting Paiute concern, however, the tribal council met with the Nevada State Fish and Game Commission during its first year to discuss the fishery problem. The effort was unproductive. The council unanimously decided that "the seining should not be allowed, because the Nevada Fish and Game Commission would not restock Pyramid Lake or pay for the spawn."[103] It was to be another 10 years before an amicable agreement could be reached between the state and the tribe.

Throughout the 1930s, the sale of fish became steadily less profitable. A number of factors combined to cause reduction of the fish population: failure of restocking efforts, inefficiency of fish ladders over the dams, pollution from industry and urban areas, irrigation systems, evaporation of the lake, emergence of the delta, but primarily reduction of the water levels in the river so that it was not only shallow and warm, but also periodically dry. Fish simply could not get upstream to spawn. By 1940 the tribe had to accept the reality that fishing was now a sport rather than a viable subsistence base or commercial enterprise.

The state changed its fish regulations very little in the 1930s and 1940s. Through World War II, Indians remained the only Nevadans who could sell fish, and then only if they were marked as caught on the reservation. It was not until 1955 that the state repealed the tagging law.[104]

On the other hand, during these years the tribal council made major efforts to establish a working relationship with the state. One of the first actions of the council in 1937 was to declare tribal fishing regulations.[105] Because Nevada law was not in effect on the reservation, to avoid confusion the tribal council drew up regulations closely parallel to those of the state. Since the Wheeler-Howard Act authorized tribal councils to assess local taxes, the Pyramid Lake Tribal Council imitated agents' passes of earlier days and required a subsidiary tribal fishing license, in addition to the state one, for non-Indians fishing on the reservation. In 1950 the state recognized the validity of these and also acknowledged the authority of tribal game wardens over white men fishing on the reserve.[106] In 1948, the tribe allowed cuiui to be declared a game fish.[107]

Despite increasing agreement between the state and the tribe over regulations, licenses, and authority, trouble persisted on the issues of spawn-gathering and return of live fry. Formal contracts followed one another, but the tribe remained convinced that the state returned an insufficient number of fish. Nevertheless, the major obstacle to the restoration of the fishery was simply lack of water.

In the 1950s, the federal government was making plans for another massive regional reclamation project which would absorb still more water. This Washoe Project involved construction of Stampede Dam on the upper Truckee River and Watasheamu on the Carson. These would trap, control, and store the seasonal floodwaters which escaped the ditches of the Newlands Project and which had previously been "wasted" in Pyramid Lake. An additional 72,000 acre-feet of water would be captured each year to irrigate 40,000 acres of new farmland in the Carson Valley. The dams would protect against periodic dry cycles, provide additional water for growing urban areas, and offer recreational use of reservoirs.

Northern Paiutes of Pyramid Lake sent representatives to the congressional hearings on the Washoe Project. They itemized the damage done to their fishery by previous reclamation projects. For the first time, a congressional body officially admitted that the federal government was largely responsible for the crisis at Pyramid Lake. This major political victory was followed by compensation; 2 million dollars were specified in the Washoe Reclamation Act for the development of fish and wildlife resources in the area, in particular the "restoration of the Pyramid Lake fishery,"[108] but the committee called for approval of the project nonetheless.

Since the Washoe Project was designed to develop regional agricultural productivity, the tribal council passed a resolution asking for development of the benchlands allocated water under the Orr Ditch decree.[109] The BIA began a resurvey of the Spanish Springs section. Years before, Paiutes had rejected subjugation of this area when it had become apparent that irrigation then would result in loss of the rest of the reservation under the 1904 allotment act. However, by 1950 the Wheeler-Howard Act protected them against such alienation of land without tribal consent. This time plans for expansion were not blocked by tribal fears, but by Senator Pat McCarran. Among his vocal constituents were the squatters, who feared scrutiny of their illegal and wasteful water practices if Indian lands were developed. McCarran pressured the BIA to stop the survey, and Indian benchland was dropped from the Washoe Project.[110]

When the Washoe Act passed Congress on August 1, 1956, there were no plans to develop Paiute agricultural lands or extend the reservation ditch system. The only direct benefit to the Pyramid Lake Reservation was a vague promise to make efforts to restore the fishery.

The Bureau of Reclamation could not proceed until it cleared title to the water. Since the Washoe Project involved land in two states as well as the flow of an interstate stream, the legal situation was complicated. Long ago, in 1925, the federal government had filed a friendly suit comparable to the Orr Ditch case to quiet title to water in the Carson River.[111] Powerful landowners in the Carson River valley resisted this Alpine suit, since it might result in headgates, measuring devices, and water masters to interfere with their traditional overuse of water. The case lingered in federal court for 25 years. Then it became obvious that the Washoe Project could not progress until the Alpine case was settled. Pyramid Lake Paiutes argued that the filling of Watasheamu Dam would necessarily increase diversions from Truckee River, which would affect their water rights. On these grounds they attempted to intervene in the suit, even though they had not been a party to the original filing. Acting for the Reclamation Bureau, the Department of Justice opposed their entry and Paiutes lost their bid to join the case after appealing to the Supreme Court.[112] Thus they could not participate directly in the Alpine case; the federal trustee refused to acknowledge that they had a legitimate concern in it, and therefore it did not actively protect their interests. When the Alpine temporary decree was issued in 1949, it failed to recognize any right to water for the Paiutes, for Pyramid Lake, or for Truckee River fish populations.

The tribal council gave tentative and suspicious support to the Washoe Project. By then they had learned to be cautious about federal projects which promised great benefits, since time after time those benefits had gone to others but not to Paiutes. However, because of the clause in the Washoe Act supporting the Pyramid Lake fishery, they encouraged sportsmen's organizations to request a water allocation for trout maintenance. Further, they sought support of the business community. By 1960, commercial interests perceived that Nevada's economy was never going to be based on agriculture. From the booming resort areas of Lake Tahoe and Reno, recreation seekers overflowed into the surrounding countryside. Chambers of Commerce throughout Nevada had discovered that a dollar invested in recreation gave greater financial return than the same dollar invested in either farming or ranching. Utilizing this purely economic argument, the tribal council accentuated the regional benefits which would result from development of Pyramid Lake's recreational potential, particularly its fishery.[113]

It was not until 1964, after the plans for the Washoe Project had been finalized and Congress had authorized funds, that the Department of the Interior finally asked whether in fact enough water existed in the Truckee and Carson river systems to provide for the needs of the new Washoe Project, as well as the existing Newlands Project, present irrigation users on both rivers, migratory birds at Stillwater Wildlife Refuge, and Pyramid Lake Indian Reservation. Interior's preliminary investigation showed that only with strict compliance to the Orr Ditch and Alpine decrees was there any hope of meeting all these needs. It recommended that the new Washoe Project take as much water as possible from the Carson River to satisfy the needs of the TCID. Then most of the water from the Truckee could be used for "every effort to maintain the greatest practicable flow of water into Pyramid Lake."[114] Such terminology promised only that an attempt would be made; it carefully avoided recognizing any right of water for Pyramid Lake. While other water claims were carefully specified and quantified in the draft report, the water for Pyramid Lake was left conspicuously vague. The government promised to salvage excess water, eliminate waste, and impose regulations on the Newlands Project area. These controls would reduce the 250,000 acre-feet diverted down the Truckee Canal, an amount which greatly exceeded beneficial use. According to Nevada's requirement that water be used for beneficial purposes, TCID was not justified in its water withdrawals and under state law should lose the excess portion of its water claim. The powerful TCID absolutely refused to comply with any suggestion to cut down its water allocation or to institute water-saving practices. On the other hand, TCID offered to increase the acreage under production until it matched the water allocation.

As plans for the Washoe Project solidified, the tribal council remained worried about where all the water would come from, and specifically asked the Secretary of the Interior whether the project would increase or decrease the inflow to Pyramid Lake. He assured them in writing that the Washoe Project would vastly increase the amount of water which the lake received. On the basis of this secretarial guarantee, the tribal council passed a resolution in 1964 supporting the Washoe Project.[115]

Despite the stated intentions of the Bureau of Reclamation, there were real problems. The reservoir behind Watasheamu Dam would have to fill, cutting off much of the Carson River for long periods of time. Some of this water normally flowed downstream to Lahontan

Dam for use in the TCID area. To compensate for this loss of Carson River water, a maximal diversion from the Truckee would be required. This in turn would stop any chance of extra water reaching Pyramid Lake. Stampede Dam also would have an effect. Designed to control high spring runoff and prevent damage to valuable property on Lake Tahoe, Stampede would cut off the natural floodwaters which were the only remaining major source of inflow to Pyramid Lake. As these facts gradually became apparent, and as Reclamation showed no intention of negotiating its position, the BIA and the Pyramid Lake Tribal Council in 1966 withdrew their approval of the Washoe Project.

Over Paiutes' objections, Anglo water users of the Truckee and Carson rivers approved the Nevada sections of the Washoe Project on November 3, 1964. By then the courts had decreed title to the waters of the Carson River and allocated the unutilized portions to federal ownership. The Washoe Project was poised to begin.

As with the histories of farmland, fish, timber, and pasturage, Anglos had long encroached on the water resources of Pyramid Lake Indian Reservation. Earlier attacks on those resources had been accomplished by individual white entrepreneurs, albeit with the aid and assistance of public officials. However, in the case of water, the federal government itself led the way. The construction of the Newlands Project, Derby Dam, and the diversion of Truckee River waters to the Carson drainage, initiated a series of changes which soon threatened the very existence of the Pyramid Lake fishery. As the lake level lowered, the dry delta emerged to block off fish from their natural spawning beds in the now-shallow Truckee.

Governmental action resulted not only in environmental deterioration, but also in legal handicaps. In the adjudication of the Orr Ditch decree, the Department of Justice presented requests only for Indian agriculture. It ignored any potential *Winters* claim for the fishery, that purpose for which the reservation apparently had been intended. White squatters, not yet evicted from the reservation, continued to use Indian irrigation allocations. Paiute agriculture suffered because Reclamation refused to make allowance for this illegal use of Indian water. Later the proposed Washoe Project still further closed the noose on any natural river flow reaching Pyramid Lake. The federal government intentionally misled Paiutes on the effect that this development would have on their lake.

In contrast to such decisions by other bureaus, the BIA often supported the Indian position. Local-level BIA agents, such as Creel, Bowler, and Fryer, were often concerned with the problems of the fishery. In 1942, the Indian Irrigation Service stoutly declared, "It would appear that their [Paiutes'] right to water to maintain their food supply from fish is as valid as their right to water to produce food on land. It was so intended when their rights to the resources of this area were restricted to the reservation set aside for them."[116] The Commissioner of Indian Affairs often agreed and sympathized, but found his hands tied, for the BIA had control over only the reservation itself. There it made major irrigation improvements in 1915 and again in the 1940s; the fishways and fish ladders built into these irrigation systems were so effective that they satisfied even the hostile state Fish and Game Commission. However, the BIA found that it could not compete with its more politically powerful sister bureau within Interior—Reclamation. Most of Reclamation's projects benefited the non-Indian population, which in Nevada not only controlled most of the land base but also comprised the vast majority of the voting population. Therefore the Nevada congressional delegation threw its support onto the side of the non-Indians and hence the side of Reclamation. Intense bureaucratic pressures were brought against the BIA. It crumpled. It failed to assert *Winters* rights for any purpose other than agriculture. Even then it made claim to irrigation waters only for those lands actually used or specified by Congress. Although the BIA voiced concern over the decline of the fishery, it never moved forcefully to defend Paiute water rights when these were challenged by Anglos. The Pyramid Lake Paiutes were overmastered in the high-level power plays of Washington.

Federal interests were not alone in their threat to fish at Pyramid Lake. Nevada state fish law, by attempting to control Indian access to a sales market, broke the incipient development of a Paiute commercial fishing industry. Although Anglo irrigation activities guaranteed that fish populations would decline below commercially viable levels, the federal government was still duty-bound to challenge the legality of these state actions; but it failed to do so. Senator John Tunney, in an investigation of BIA administration of the Pyramid Lake Reservation, summarized:

> The entirety of the Paiutes [economy] has centered on the once-flourishing fishing industry, which has been severely damaged as a result of neglect by the Federal Government. . . . In short, the Federal Government has reneged in its fiduciary relationship with the Indians by not protecting their rights, and the Indians have continued to go unrepresented or underrepresented, many times deliberately, when their rights were being adjudicated. . . . I feel that Pyramid Lake probably stands as one of the most flagrant examples of the disregard of Indian property rights and misuse of a great natural resource.[117]

Two more decades were to pass, another generation of Indians were to be born and grow to adulthood at Pyramid Lake, before the BIA would begin to use its power actively to support Paiute water rights.

TWELVE

"As Long as the River Shall Run"

Before the coming of Anglo-Europeans, Northern Paiutes controlled a vast land. Undisturbed, their small bands utilized the many resources of this territory, moving from place to place with the seasons and with the availability of food. This lifestyle changed irrevocably when fur trappers and immigrant wagons crept into the Great Basin. White men brought death in battle. As their lands filled with white miners and ranchers, many Paiutes were driven to seek refuge on the government reserves.

There agents tried to change their basic way of life, to transform these people into agriculturalists and to limit their mobility in order to free additional land for new white neighbors. Not satisfied with seizing the vast majority of Paiute lands, Anglos soon sought to have Pyramid Lake Reservation abandoned. When the federal government refused forthright relinquishment, Nevada Anglos sought by piecemeal and often illegal means to utilize the remnant Indian resources.

White-owned cattle grazed freely across unfenced boundaries onto reservation pasturelands. Anglo fishermen set their nets at the river mouth and violated the lake itself in flagrant flouting of federal jurisdiction. Insecure government Indian agents, their limited police powers repudiated by Anglos, were unable to keep them out. Only after military eviction and prosecution in federal courts were white commercial fishermen ejected from Pyramid Lake, thus allowing Paiute fishermen to develop a marketable resource.

Land control was an even more persistent issue. Although the reservation was quite large, farmland was limited to the narrow strip of valley floor along the Truckee River from its mouth to the southern border of the reserve and even these bottomlands were marginal and required irrigation. It took many years to devise a system to accommodate the wandering and seasonally surging flood pattern of the Truckee. Agency pressures on the Paiutes to adopt an agricultural way of life were most successful immediately around the government compound, where the Indians were safe from hostile Anglos upstream. In all other areas, white men forcibly evicted earlier Paiute residents and usurped the small but rare and valuable arable lands. These white squatters then bought and sold land to each other while agents stood by helplessly. By the turn of the century, the Anglo settlement in the Wadsworth section had grown so powerful that the Nevada congressional delegation gained legislation to separate it legally from the reservation. Squatters who desired free transfer of title spurned the privilege of purchasing this Indian land. Other squatters along the river saw this initial abdication of federal title as a potential opportunity which might yield them significant profits. Although the U.S. Supreme Court denied their claims to ownership, they managed to have a law passed which gave them the right to purchase title. While some promptly bought out federal interests, others ignored the law, still hoping to acquire title free. The federal government virtually enticed them to buy up reservation lands with reduction of fees and extraordinary extension of deadlines year after year.

Thus far, the story is the common one of frontier avarice. Rugged individualists systematically and illegally encroached on the resources of Pyramid Lake Reservation, yet without loss of federal title to any but small portions of the land-base. This encroachment did not end with the turn of the century. Anglo exploitation of Indian resources at Pyramid Lake intensified as time passed. Private white entrepreneurs learned to mobilize national political institutions to increase the scope and profitability of their trespasses. Nevada's congressional delegation lobbied for legislation to divide and sell the reservation, leading the floor fight for land giveaways. Above all, congressional spokesmen for their Anglo constituents engineered legislation to seize water from the Truckee River, so much water that Pyramid Lake was foredoomed. Although administratively charged to protect Indian interests, the Bureau of Indian Affairs was ineffective against private intrusions and consistently succumbed to political pressures from Nevada's congressional delegation.

In the 1930s, when new legal tools were available to them, the Paiutes of Pyramid Lake began to defend themselves. Their tribal council, in partnership with nationally based Indian rights organizations, defeated Senator McCarran's numerous attempts to give their land to white squatters. Through their lawyers they pursued successful suits against the federal government. They spoke out on water allocations and the gathering of fish spawn on their own land. In short, they began to assert the right to decide their own community's economic future.

But their battle was not yet over. An early BIA agent at Pyramid Lake once wrote that it was "the determination of the whites to either wrest the reservation from the control of the Indians, or avail themselves of all its resources and benefits."[1] History proved him accurate. Old Anglo patterns of pressure for reservation abandonment, land removal, grazing trespass, denial of fishing rights, and seizure of water did not stop in 1880 or 1900 or 1920. They continued through the first half of the twentieth century, and they continue to this day. Indeed, there is nothing to indicate that such infringement on Indian rights and property will cease so long as there remain resources at Pyramid Lake that either Indians or white men can use.

Denial of the validity of the reservation, and attempts to remove portions of land from it, were among the oldest problems at Pyramid Lake. Calls for total abandonment of the area as an Indian reservation have not ceased even in the latter part of the twentieth century. One such movement came in 1954 after federal policy shifted toward termination of special federal–Indian relationships. Indian tribes were struck with fear, but Western whites were jubilant. Expecting the demise of the BIA within a five-year period, many groups began to plan for the wholesale seizure of Indian reservations. The history of Indian land loss after the General Allotment Act of 1887 convinced many whites that Anglo wealth would quickly acquire Pyramid Lake if Paiutes were given outright ownership during the termination proceedings. A group of Reno citizens, led by an active ladies' auxiliary, began investigating alternatives.[2] State administration of properties was inefficient, as proven by the poor condition of state parks, and the record of state defense against local special interests was also abysmal. The Reno group thus thought that the only way to avoid sleazy commercial development of this potentially rich recreational area was to keep it under federal control as a national park. In this way Pyramid Lake would not be spoiled, and the public would have free and undisputed access to it. The Indians' home would be transformed into an enormous outdoor recreational park for Anglo pleasure-seekers. Fortunately, the Northern Paiutes were deemed unready for termination and the policy soon lost favor in Washington. Pyramid Lake remained an Indian reservation.

In addition to attempts to have the reservation abandoned totally, the piecemeal removal of land from it was another recurrent problem. By the 1880s it had become obvious that such encroachment could be successful only with federal consent or when the intruder was the federal government itself. In this way a 1913 executive order removed the 247 acres of Anahoe Island from the Pyramid Lake Indian Reservation for the use of another government agency.[3] This island in the middle of Pyramid Lake was one of only a small number of rookeries in the United States used by the Great White Pelican, and the island was transferred to the Department of Agriculture as a wildlife preserve. However, construction of Derby Dam by a federal reclamation project in 1905 assured significant decline of the water level of Pyramid Lake. As the waters declined, a spit began to emerge between Anahoe Island and the mainland. Still growing as the waters fall, it will not be long before this forms a causeway for natural predators, such as coyotes, to cross over to the island and eat the eggs and fledglings. Thus the usefulness of one federal project is threatened by another; both damage Indian interests.

Despite the record of unabated Anglo encroachment, Pyramid Lake Reservation lost surprisingly little of its land-base, compared with the relatively massive reduction of many Western reservations. However, only a very small percentage of the land at Pyramid Lake was valuable for agriculture and other Anglo economic enterprises. Of that portion which was profitable to Anglos, a significant proportion was successfully removed. Anglo-owned properties stretched along each of the permanent streams entering Pyramid Lake from the west—Hardscrabble, Mullens, and other creeks. Of the arable lands in the lower Truckee River valley, much was successfully preempted by white farmers. Some was patented land, its title gained through the Nevada state cessions. The federal government gave the transcontinental railroad subsidies of land for maintenance stations and, as a result, the entire township of Wadsworth was legally removed from Indian control. Squatters were given the right to buy up title to the lands they had seized. Nevertheless, the Pyramid Lake Tribal Council wrested back the unpaid portion of such lands eventually and assigned them to Indian farmers. Even though the vast majority of the original Pyramid Lake Reservation is still in Indian hands, a high percentage of the agriculturally valuable land has passed irrevocably into Anglo ownership.

To increase the productivity of remaining Indian agricultural land, the BIA constructed new irrigation systems in the 1940s and again in the 1960s. Coupled with the settlement of court suits and reacquisition of some of the previously trespassed land in the Truckee bottoms, the value of Indian agricultural output doubled in the 1970s. Most Paiute farming has remained the extensive type, consisting primarily of hay, fodder, and alfalfa, rather than the more capital-intensive but more profitable row crops.[4]

Much of the remainder of the reserve, not susceptible to irrigation agriculture, was good for grazing cattle. Historically, this pasturage tempted Anglo trespass, but such violations have been stopped. Early Anglo hostility was forestalled when the BIA opened the way for whites to range their cattle legally on Pyramid Lake land. Shortly after World War I, passage of a new law finally settled the question of whether the BIA had the authority to let leases on reservations in Nevada.[5] Not legally required to obtain Indian consent, the BIA began issuing large-scale grazing leases to local Anglos. It used the funds to meet its own administrative expenses at Pyramid Lake, particularly salaries for agents who had negotiated the agreements. It was not uncommon for the entire reservation to be let to sheepmen at a flat fee of $5,000 per year. Such fees were characteristically far less than those for similar-quality off-reservation land in the area, but the collection of even this small amount was not rigorously enforced by BIA personnel. There was no effective control over the number of animals run on the range and overgrazing was common, with subsequent destruction of the pasturage.

Once the Pyramid Lake Tribal Council was established, the situation changed. The council demanded fees comparable to the regional standard and required lessees to be bonded.[6] It was not uncommon for the tribal council to refuse to reissue a lease, and they gave priority to Indian bids. Toward the end of the 1930s and into the 1940s, Paiutes bought cattle with personal money and with tribal loans from funds generated by the sale of Wadsworth lots, the squatters' purchases under Oddie's bill, and the Wheeler-Howard reimbursable fund. Soon there were over 800 Indian-owned cattle needing pasturage.[7] Paiute livestock owners formed the Pyramid Lake Cattlemen's Association, which took over several of the large-scale leases from white holders by 1946.[8] Although the tribal council continued to let leases to non-Indians through the 1950s and 1960s, these were fewer in number, more restrictive, and routinely scrutinized by the tribal attorney. Nevertheless, years of uncontrolled overgrazing had done great harm, and in 1961 the tribal council described the grazing lands as "in deplorable condition."[9] Maintenance of this damaged pasturage posed a problem, and the council sought assistance from the BIA and the Agricultural Extension Service of Nevada for range management and range development. The old trespass problem and Anglo claims of unknown boundaries and wandering cattle were overcome when the tribe completed fencing the perimeter of the reserve. In remote areas, there was still an occasional report of trespassing cattle, and fences did go down between the visits of the tribal fence-rider, but these were minor compared to the flagrant violations of the past. In sum, the tribe has gained control of the hinterlands of the reservation.

The role of the tribe as its own economic manager extended beyond grazing leases to the letting of many other resources as well. The tribal council began to lease small areas for pipelines of various kinds, state highway maintenance stations, guano mines, even a gambling hall.[10] Leases for mineral exploration, including several for uranium, discovered no ores of marketable value and did not lead to major extraction. During World War II, the Navy sought a location away from the coast to train pilots in over-water bombing for Pacific operations, and the tribe leased them the right to fly low across the lake, as well as a small plot on the lakeshore for collection of their dummy bombs and storage of supplies.[11] Leasing of all kinds has become a routine process.

Like the questions of grazing access and land title, the problem of fishing rights at Pyramid Lake did not disappear with time, but became even more complicated and more bitterly fought in the second half of the twentieth century. Although individual Anglo fishermen were successfully routed from free trespass, the state and the federal government remained locked in combat over control of the Pyramid Lake fishery. Nevada struggled for many years to regulate the sale of Indian-caught fish from Pyramid Lake and won. Later both the state and the federal government asserted the right to gather spawn on the reservation, for conservation of endangered species. In the 1930s the tribe managed to shut down such operations completely. The issues of sale of fish and gathering of spawn merged with the question of public access to Pyramid Lake in the 1940s and 1950s, as the newly organized tribe entered into a series of delicate negotiations with the State Fish and Game Commission.

After many years without any fish-stocking at Pyramid Lake, the Nevada State Fish and Game Commission approached the tribal council in 1948 with a proposal to resume planting. In return for this public investment, they demanded general access to the Pyramid Lake fishery. The BIA firmly supported this suggestion. "I have read a draft of the proposed agreement," the agent wrote, "and to me it would mean the only salvation for fishing in Pyramid Lake. . . . I believe an arrangement of this kind would be one of the finest things that could be worked out in order to bring back the fishing in Pyramid Lake."[12] He pointed out that there would be many indirect benefits to tribal members through boat rental, concessions, and tourist-oriented enterprises. Succumbing to this pressure, or perhaps seeing the wisdom of it, the tribal council signed a ten-year agreement with the State Fish and Game Commission in May 1950.

In that contract, the Commission pledged an effort to maintain the original cutthroat trout as well as other game fish populations, promising to stock the lake whenever fish were available and it was financially feasible. This phraseology gave the state a notably flexible commitment. Nevertheless, the state did acknowledge the importance of fish to the Indians as a source both of food and of income, and the contract stated that the Paiutes' "reasonable needs shall be met before the surplus is available for sport." [13] The state further agreed that Indians could fish on the reservation without a state license, but that non-Indians would need a reservation license as well as a Nevada one before fishing there. The state admitted the tribal power, which had been given to the council by federal statute, to make and pass regulations regarding on-reservation fishing. In addition, the state promised to enforce those regulations against non-Indians, while tribal game wardens were responsible for Indian compliance. The tribe acquired a monopoly of guide services and boat rentals. Although tribal permit fees were low, this income soon became the major source of funds for the tribal government.

In 1960 the contract was renewed in essentially identical form. The State Fish and Game Commission promised to plant at least 5,000 pounds of trout every year, again if the fish were available and the agency had sufficient funds. There were a few changes in the area of enforcement. Specifically, the tribe agreed "that the representatives of the [Nevada State Fish and Game] Commission are hereby given special permission to enter on the lands and waters of the reservation to perform such duties as may be properly assigned them under this agreement." [14] On the other hand, tribal game wardens were deputized by the state with authority over non-Indians as well as Indians. This arrangement improved the efficiency of enforcement of both state laws and tribal regulations at Pyramid Lake.

During the term of this agreement, major changes took place. The BIA granted the tribe $500,000 to construct a small fish hatchery on Hardscrabble Creek above Sutcliffe. In 1975, this research center and hatchery began raising one million trout and cuiui fry each year.

The Pyramid Lake Indian Tribal Enterprises (PLITE) administered the facility and trained the 15-person staff in hatchery management and fish physiology, biology, culturing, and diseases through programs both at the regional community college and at tribal seminars. PLITE acquired additional grants to add holding ponds and holding nets to float in the lake.[15] This project was designed to remove any portion of the fish life-cycle from state jurisdiction, thus putting it completely under tribal control. Instead of having to travel up the Truckee River, over dry deltas, across dams, and through polluted waters to spawn, the trout now do so in ponds along the creek and in protective nets in the lake itself, completely within reservation boundaries. All the fry produced are released in Pyramid Lake. It is hoped that these developments will permit restoration of the fishery at Pyramid Lake, despite ever-increasing problems of lake level, salinity, and river flow, while avoiding interjurisdictional disputes with federal and state agencies.

Throughout the 1960s and early 1970s, the tribal council voiced complaints that the fishery agreement with the state was not being fulfilled. The state either did not deliver the promised number of fry or they were not healthy enough to survive transplanting. Tensions mounted in 1976 as the agreement's expiration date approached, and the tribal council refused to renew. In rejecting contractual agreement, the tribe withdrew permission for state wardens to enter the reservation and for the state to gather spawn there. They totally repudiated state authority over the reservation, in accordance with the general principles of federal Indian law so long neglected. They denied that the state fishing license could be required in addition to tribal license, and tribal game wardens were given orders to check only for tribally issued permits.[16] The tribe has now broken all contractual relations with the Nevada State Fish and Game Commission. In so doing, they have moved toward solution of the long-standing and bitter disagreements over licenses, collection of spawn, and ultimately jurisdiction over the reservation itself.

For the plan of tribally controlled fish propagation to work, one critical factor remains unresolved—water. Steady supplies must be maintained to the hatchery. The shoreline must be stable for the holding-net and lake reproduction cycle. The lake must stay at reasonable salinity levels. In the long run, the lake itself must remain a viable fish habitat, and that viability is threatened by long-standing patterns of Anglo water withdrawals.

In 1955, the Paiutes desperately offered to sacrifice for the fish in the lake the tribe's own meager water allotment assigned under the Orr Ditch decree. Realizing that this amount was not nearly enough to stabilize the lake level, they volunteered their water as an initial token. The solicitor for the Department of the Interior declared that allowing their water to flow into the lake for fish life would not be considered a beneficial water use under the law. Since federal water rights were usufructuary, the tribe might well lose legal title to that water; Anglo users elsewhere would quickly claim it. "Water not diverted and used," he declared, "must be allowed to flow downstream for the benefit of other users with subsequent rights in the stream. Water adjudicated for the irrigation of lands of the Indians of the Pyramid Lake Reservation is not available for diversion into Pyramid Lake for the propagation of fish."[17]

After passage of the Washoe Project Act the following year, the Paiutes feared further water loss as soon as the dams began to fill and later to control the floods which constituted the major remaining source of water for Pyramid Lake. Misled by the Interior Secretary's specific assurance of an additional 200,000 acre-feet for the lake as a result of this project, the Council had approved the plan. When tribal figures later showed that 40,000 acre-feet would actually be lost from the small amount the lake received, they withdrew tribal support. Nevertheless, the Washoe Project proceeded. Stampede Dam, built to control upper Truckee floodwaters above Lake Tahoe, was completed. In 1975 another portion of the project, the Marble Bluff Spillway, was finished at Pyramid Lake. As the lake evaporated and its surface level lowered, erosion increased along the river channel near the mouth of the Truckee; the soft sediments there could not resist and were rapidly washed away. To prevent further erosion of agricultural bottomlands, the river was rerouted through the three-mile-long spillway to the nearest outcrop of hard rock, some distance east of its natural course, where a steep chute was carved to bring the river water down to the lake level quickly, so that the water could flow leisurely out into the lake without further erosional damage. A modern and effective fishway which required far less water than the natural river channel was built into the chute.[18]

The third major element of the Washoe Project, the Watasheamu Dam, has been authorized, but construction has not yet begun. A geological study recently done by the Bureau of Reclamation shows that the proposed site would not offer a safe foundation for this massive structure. Nevertheless, as Carson City grows and its domestic water needs increase, pressure mounts for construction of this dam in the near future.[19]

Besides new structures, the Washoe Project required water. To generate sufficient amounts, the federal government instituted for the first time a series of regulations for Newlands Project water-users to control excessive withdrawals. Unlimited irrigation was curbed and allotments were enforced under the Orr Ditch final and Alpine temporary decrees. Despite dire predictions from outraged ranchers and farmers in the Fallon area, no agricultural damage has occurred.[20]

In addition to the Washoe Project, there is yet another threat to Pyramid Lake waters. The Orr Ditch case and later Alpine had adjudicated only the use of waters within the state of Nevada and among users there. The Truckee flows through California before it reaches Tahoe and overflows into Nevada; the Carson is also an interstate stream. Upstream California water-users believed that their interests had not been represented in court. On the other hand, intensified development of the California section of these river drainages threatened Nevada users, as the amount of water reaching the state border declined. Furthermore, Lake Tahoe itself, partly in Nevada and partly in California, became an increasingly valuable property over the years, and the two states contested for control of it. For these reasons, a bistate agreement of some kind was needed, and in 1955 Congress granted consent for the two states to negotiate a final settlement of the interstate stream systems of Lake Tahoe and its tributaries, as well as the Truckee, Carson, and Walker rivers. Such an interstate compact had to be agreed on by the legislatures of both states, as well as by Congress, before it took effect.

The first draft of the compact in 1968 tried to restrict Indian water use severely—only the irrigation use of water as delineated in the Orr Ditch decree was allowed for the reservation:

The maximum amount of water to be recognized as an existing beneficial use of water in Nevada for the Pyramid Lake Indian Reservation *shall be* [30,000 acre-feet] as allocated by Section A of this Article together with any additional water used for domestic or municipal purposes on said reservation; *provided further however,* that the water allocation in Section A of this Article must first be put to beneficial use before any credit will be given for said additional waters to be used for domestic or municipal purposes.[21]

This part of the proposal specifically prohibited Indian water use for purposes other than irrigation, domestic, or municipal applications; it therefore excluded use of water for fish propagation. Further, it froze Indian usage at this designated amount. In addition, the Paiutes themselves were barred from going to court to seek increased allocations; and the United States, acting as their trustee, could sue for changes in beneficial use only if those could be made "without injury to the allocations of either state." Since Orr Ditch had completely allocated all the Nevada flow in average years, any increase in Indian usage meant increasing Nevada's total allocation. Necessarily, such a change would injure California's share and hence be in violation of the above clause. California, on the other hand, was specifically given the right to develop any surplus waters for the use of its growing population in any way it saw fit.

The Department of the Interior strongly recommended that Congress reject this proposal, since it explicitly limited federal powers to exercise its duties as Indian trustee. Again, Indian water rights flow from the *Winters* Doctrine. These are claims for sufficient water to fulfill the intended purposes of an Indian reservation. The decision in the Arizona v. California case declared that these claims are not limited to land actually under production at the time, but are also for potentially irrigable lands.[22] Thus *Winters* rights are an expansible water claim. The proposed bistate compact limited Paiute claims to a fixed quantity. Further, the compact made no allowance for future growth of the Paiute economy. Because of the economic, social, and legal debilities of the past, the Pyramid Lake economy was operating far below its actual potential. If it were limited to its current actual water use, then any opportunity for economic development would be blocked forever.

There were still further legal objections to the proposed compact.[23] The bistate agreement was a subtle yielding of federal jurisdiction, which in effect submitted Indian matters to state control yet did not offer even the protection of state law. Although such a change would undoubtedly have an adverse effect on Paiute water resources, the Indians had not been a party in the negotiations. Furthermore, the compact conceptually separated Lake Tahoe from the Truckee River basin to create two administrative districts. Reclamation planned to stabilize Lake Tahoe, a non-Indian lake, at the cost of total destruction of Pyramid Lake, on an Indian reservation. This plan could be interpreted as discrimination and a violation of civil rights. It would also have regional environmental impact and might constitute a violation of conservation laws.

By 1969, after very brief hearings, the Nevada State Legislature approved the document before Paiutes could marshal resistance. Soon they were joined by the National Congress of American Indians, tribal attorneys, and other interested parties, and together they lobbied the California legislative committees heavily when the bill came up for debate there, asking them to consider the inequities of the matter. Specifically, all other parties except the Pyramid Lake Paiutes could expand their usage against the so-called "surplus" waters, those periodic flood waters which formed the major input for Pyramid Lake. Paiutes alone were to be frozen into the present unsatisfactory situation while others were not. California defeated the proposed compact; part of the reasoning was that Pyramid Lake had vast recreational significance to the whole region. Its maintenance was therefore a legitimate concern of California citizens, and they were unwilling to see it further damaged.

There was an impasse. One state had approved the compact and the other had rejected it. To resolve the deadlock, the Secretary of the Interior met with Governor Reagan of California and Governor Laxalt of Nevada on a private yacht in the middle of Lake Tahoe in the summer of 1969. After only one hour they had a new proposal. Rather than allow Pyramid Lake to decline gradually, it should be drained immediately to a level compatible with its reduced inflow. At that point, with the shoreline firmly established, recreational investment could proceed. This developer's dream was a conservationist's nightmare, for the lake surface would have to be dropped another 152 vertical feet to reach this balance point. The now sparkling lake would become a salt pond in the middle of an ugly barren flat, totally uninhabitable by fish life and thoroughly unattractive to tourists and the recreation-seeking public. This single action would totally destroy for all time any economic potential Pyramid Lake held out to the Paiutes. Both state legislatures joined the Indian outrage, and the suggestion was soon dropped.[24]

Further negotiations produced another proposal in 1971 which met many of the previous bureaucratic objections. Nothing in this draft, it said, impaired any powers of the United States on its own behalf or on behalf of Indian tribes. Nowhere, however, did it acknowledge the right of Pyramid Lake to survive as a viable fish habitat, nor did it recognize the Indians' *Winters* rights. This compact ignored the lake's legal claims to survive, but at the same time allowed it to exist by noblesse oblige. Approved by both Nevada and California, this draft proposal has rested inactively in Congress for a number of years.[25]

In addition to this bistate compact, another threat to Pyramid Lake water rights appeared in the form of a U.S. Supreme Court decision which involved disputed water rights for operation of a national forest.[26] The court ruled that the United States government had implicitly consented to be sued in state courts, and therefore had allowed federal water rights to be decided according to state law. This challenge to federal exemption from state law is potentially extremely threatening to Indians. State legislatures are usually responsive to local interests, which are normally hostile to Indian rights. Therefore, the laws such legislatures generate are not likely to recognize or permit the special considerations from which Indians benefit under federal laws. States can deny the obligations stemming from the historic federal–Indian relationship. In particular, since Nevada did not establish Indian reservations, state law does not provide for *Winters*-type claims to water for reservation purposes. If Pyramid Lake water rights can be driven into state courts as a result of the Eagle County decision, Nevada's hostile attitude toward Indian claims would virtually assure that the Paiutes would lose water and with it practically all potential for economic development.[27]

On the other hand, another recent court decision has offered a more positive hope for future Indian litigation. The act establishing the Bureau of Reclamation in 1902 charged the Secretary of the Interior with effective management of the resources involved in all reclamation projects, including water resources. Between 1903 and 1967, there was absolutely no control over the amount of water withdrawn from the Truckee River for the Newlands Project. Only when the Washoe Project increased the need for water was the Alpine temporary decree entered and new regulations imposed. With assistance from the Native American Rights Fund, the Pyramid Lake tribe filed a suit against Secretary of the Interior Rogers Morton and other officials in 1970, charging him with violations of secretarial trust obligations toward the tribe and maladministration under the Reclamation Act of 1902.

While this case was in court, Morton issued new regulations which said that all Newlands water should be put to efficient use. Unlike the old regulations under the Orr Ditch and Alpine decrees, which allocated fixed amounts to users, the new procedures did not specify quantities. Although the judge was leaning toward an out-of-court settlement, this maneuver led him to set aside the proposed regulations and to call for formal courtroom argument. In another unsuccessful effort to forestall the attack on the Secretary, the Department of Justice made the unprecedented announcement as the hearings opened that it would soon file suit on behalf of the tribe "for the recognition and protection of a water right for the maintenance of Pyramid Lake."[28] Throughout the proceedings, a flurry of new regulations issued from the Secretary's office. The documents called for voluntary water salvage in the Newlands area to placate the Paiutes. Nevertheless, in 1972, the Secretary was found guilty. The judge ruled:

> It was amply demonstrated that water could be conserved for Pyramid Lake without offending existing decrees or contractual rights of the [Truckee-Carson Irrigation] District through better management which would prevent unnecessary waste. ... Under the contract between the Secretary and the District the Secretary has the right to require the District to conduct its affairs in a nonwasteful manner but no such action was taken or is contemplated in the regulation. The opera-

tions of the District are not tightly controlled and water is taken practically on demand without necessary safeguards to prevent improper and wasteful use. This failure to act must be given particular emphasis since the proof showed that the Secretary has not in the past enforced his prior yearly regulations affecting the District and has acquiesced in excessive water deliveries to the farms. ... The Secretary's action is therefore doubly defective and irrational because it fails to demonstrate an adequate recognition of his fiduciary duty to the Tribe. This is also an abuse of discretion and not in accordance with law. ... The burden rested on the Secretary to justify any diversion of water from the Tribe with precision.[29]

This case was a landmark decision in Indian rights. For the first time in history, the United States government was to be held responsible for the proper administration of its trust obligations to Indian tribes.

The Morton case was the first of a series of court decisions in favor of the tribe. Years before, Pyramid Lake and other Northern Paiute groups had instituted a claim with the Indian Claims Commission for land the United States had seized without treaty, seeking damages for the loss of land without a legal transfer. In 1972 the Pyramid Lake tribe successfully removed the question of their water rights lost to Derby Dam and other Truckee drainage developments from the general land-claims case.[30] Three years later the Commission agreed that the tribe had been illegally deprived of a valuable property and awarded them 8 million dollars.[31] While awarding damages, this judgment was not a sale of those water rights; the tribe still retained them under *Winters* Doctrine and aboriginal claim. The decision specifically declared that "both the Pyramid Lake Paiute Tribe and the United States are of the view that no water rights reserved for the Pyramid Lake Indian Reservation have been lost, diminished, or taken by reason of anything that has happened or been done, between 1859 and the present, ... [This award] is strictly for damages sustained by the tribe by reason of its not having received all of the water to which it was entitled under such rights."[32]

More important than the money, however, was the statement contained in the decision that

both the Pyramid Lake Paiute Tribe and the United States are convinced that, as of the date of the establishment of the Pyramid Lake
Indian Reservation in 1859, there was reserved for the benefit of the
Pyramid Lake Paiute Tribe the rights to sufficient water from the
Truckee River for the maintenance of Pyramid Lake, for the maintenance of the lower reaches of the Truckee River as a natural spawning
ground for fish, and for other needs of the reservation, such as irrigation and domestic use."[33]

The court's specific acknowledgement, in the name of the United
States government, of a primary water right for lake and fishery
maintenance, and the subordination of irrigation and domestic water, was an outstanding achievement for the tribe. The Indians' assertion that the primary purpose of the reservation was for fishing had
finally been acknowledged by an official body, and they now had
precedent for a *Winters* claim for maintenance of the lake itself.

The case against Secretary Morton established that the federal
government was responsible for proper management of those Indian
resources which it held in trust. The water-claim settlement acknowledged that the Paiutes of Pyramid Lake had suffered damage as a
result of seizure of their water resources by the United States government. Despite the monetary award, their claim to that water remained unaltered. The next logical step in the legal sequence was to
sue for fulfillment of those rights and for actual return of the water.

The development of such a suit was favored by another recent
event. In 1975, the Department of Justice established a special Indian
Land and Natural Resources Division, a small group of attorneys appointed exclusively to tribal economic cases. Through such specialization, Justice could avoid the previous conflict of interests by which
a government attorney might file a suit one day in the name of a tribe
against the Bureau of Reclamation, only to be assigned a case in favor
of the Park Service against a tribe the next. This reorganization enabled the United States to fulfill its trust obligations to the tribes and
at the same time to protect them against a major offender—the federal government itself.

In December 1973 the Pyramid Lake tribe, supported by the Department of Justice, had filed suit against the Truckee-Carson Irriga-

tion District, civil successor to the Newlands Project, along with 17,000 other water-users in the Truckee River basin. On the basis of *Winters* Doctrine and the acknowledged federal intent to establish the reservation for fishing purposes, the tribe sued for water to maintain the lake and to reestablish its natural fishery. The suit asserted that Paiute water rights had not been fairly adjudicated during the Orr Ditch decision, because their representative, the United States, had restricted its claim on their behalf solely to irrigation water. *Winters* rights, on the other hand, could have been claimed "for irrigating and other useful purposes upon the reservation."[34] Even though no successful *Winters* claim has ever been made for any purpose other than domestic use or irrigation, the tribe contended that among those "other useful purposes" could be the raising of fish. The case was soon assigned to attorneys from the newly formed Land and Natural Resources Division; this began the government's most aggressive defense of Paiute resources in Pyramid Lake history.

Many Truckee River water-users feared that a successful Indian claim would result in drastic reduction of their irrigated acreage. However, studies showed that a great deal of the water needed to stabilize Pyramid Lake could come simply from instituting known, existing, high-efficiency technology and reducing the massive waste which has always characterized TCID irrigation methods. In its present form, Pyramid Lake requires about 385,000 acre-feet annually to be in water balance. It now receives an average of 250,000, leaving it 135,000 acre-feet short. This deficit is the reason Pyramid Lake declines an average of one vertical foot each year. Many studies have tried to discover where the extra 135,000 acre-feet could come from, given present water use in the Truckee drainage.[35]

After the first bistate water compact proposal met defeat in 1969, the governors appointed a task force to study the water issue. It reported that simple changes in management of the Newlands area could provide most of Pyramid Lake's water needs. If water delivery were automated, if sand-bottomed canals were lined with cement, if a few reservoirs made obsolete by pump installations were abandoned, and if the irrigation system changed from open ditches to sprinkler systems, over 85,000 acre-feet of water could easily be salvaged. If some of the more water-wasteful land currently being irrigated were retired, an additional 10,000 acre-feet could be saved. Pyramid Lake then would need only 40,000 acre-feet more to stabilize.

The next effort to itemize salvageable water came in 1972, when the Secretary of the Interior, then embroiled in the suit by Pyramid Lake Paiutes over trust responsibilities, issued a new set of "voluntary" regulations for administration of the Newlands Project. Without any technological improvements, such increasingly efficient water delivery would save 28,000 acre-feet. Predictably, the TCID was outraged at any suggestion for curtailment of its traditional unlimited water-use practices, and there was no compliance with the voluntary regulations.

The Reno Sierra Club was exceedingly concerned with the ecological preservation of Pyramid Lake, Stillwater Wildlife Refuge, and the habitats along the Truckee. Wearying of governmental ineffectiveness, the group formed a citizen task force in 1972. Members with scientific expertise volunteered for a massive study to check bureaucratic statistics and suggest imaginative new solutions. Having no vested interest in any of the water claims, the Sierra Club group was concerned only with the prevention of further environmental degradation, and repeated previous suggestions to modernize Newlands: line canals, cover selected conduits to reduce evaporation losses, institute gauging systems to measure individual diversions, retire marginally productive lands and those without legal water rights, abandon outmoded reservoirs, use sprinkler irrigation in highly porous areas, and install subsurface pumps and drains to lower the water table and reduce salinization.

Secondly, the Sierra Club task force proposed more efficient management of the Lahontan Reservoir. In the summer, Truckee River water could be brought through the canal into the Lahontan Reservoir and be drawn off to irrigate the TCID area through the proposed high-efficiency system. As late summer thunderstorms began and Carson River flow was able to sustain both the reservoir and irrigation needs, the flow through the canal could be halted. Truckee River water, no longer necessary for diversion, could flow down to Pyramid Lake. Winter and spring waters in the Carson exceed the requirements of the irrigation district. With the use of high-compression pumps, the seasonal excess could be moved through the canal back to the Truckee to compensate Pyramid Lake for water lost the previous summer.

The Sierra Club task force believed that the entire 385,000 acre-feet needed to preserve Pyramid Lake could be saved in this way. Its members were further concerned with the Stillwater Wildlife Refuge, that very shallow body of water which supported a rich growth of tules to shield the nesting migratory wildfowl traveling up the Great Western Flyway. Pyramid Lake, being a deep-water lake, had never served this sheltering function, although its sister, now-dry Winnemucca Lake, had. In order to maintain the environmental balance for both fish and wildfowl, the Sierra Club group saw that both Pyramid and Stillwater had to be maintained. Under the proposed plan, Stillwater would survive; in fact, it would benefit. Stillwater had no water right of its own and received only the waste from the bottom of the TCID system. Like all waters at the end of an irrigation system, these were highly saline. Since all water claims on both the Truckee and the Carson would be satisfied by the Sierra Club management plan, Stillwater Wildlife Refuge could be periodically flushed, thus greatly improving its water quality.

There were a few problems with this Sierra Club plan. Because of Lahontan Reservoir's recreational usage, many Anglos opposed any practice which would cause seasonal variation in its water level, and the Sierra Club plan would maintain a slightly lower level than is now customary. Then, in anticipation of the spring floods, that level would be intentionally reduced still farther in winter, when there is little recreational or irrigation need. In addition, the report did not consider the question of economic feasibility. The government has evaded the cost of modernizing TCID water delivery for years, despite numerous efforts of Newlands residents to get improvements installed.

Apparently the water necessary to stabilize Pyramid Lake does exist. It is this water that the Pyramid Lake tribe is now suing to reclaim. Their case is now in the courts. Preliminary questions are still being debated, and it may be many years before the fate of Pyramid Lake is decided (see Epilogue).

That decision on water for Pyramid Lake will also decide the fate of the Paiute people living there. When John Fremont had first come upon this "gem in the desert" in 1844, he described the Indians living there as "very fat, and [they] appear to live an easy and happy life." In the years that followed, that happy life was destroyed by the invasion of an alien people and restriction to a reduced land base. The avaricious conquerors then systematically plundered that remaining scrap of homeland in every conceivable way. Their cattle trespassed freely. Squatters seized lands. Fishermen violated the waters of the lake itself. Although the federal government managed to stop the most flagrant of the fishing violations, it was ineffective in dislodging land grabbers. Federal agencies seized the waters of the Truckee River so necessary to maintain the reservation's most valuable asset, the fish life. Congress removed Wadsworth township, permitted squatters to purchase Indian land at cut-rate prices, and tolerated Anglo exploitation of Indian resources. It stood by while the state of Nevada restricted the Paiutes' right to fish on their own reservation.

Despite this unrelenting attack, Pyramid Lake Paiutes refused to relinquish the lake. They protested and petitioned against every infringement of their rights to fish. They tried to protect their fish from death through spawn-gathering and death through water theft. They went to court. They sought grants to build hatcheries. If the lake continues to decline and eventually becomes uninhabitable to fish life, all their efforts are wasted. The resource on which the tribe had depended before the coming of the whites, the resource which supported them throughout the difficult early reservation years, the resource which is the one valuable possession of the Pyramid Lake Paiutes, will be gone forever.

But they have a plan. They want to establish control of the entire reproduction cycle of the native cutthroat trout and the cuiui completely within the reservation. They want to reestablish the fish populations while the salinity level in the lake is still tolerable. They want to build the lake into a recreation center, not for commercial exploitation but as a haven for Anglo fishermen. The tribe would direct controlled economic growth—motels, restaurants, boat rentals, guide services, and grocery stores. The lake would be the core of a new resort-oriented economy. It would provide a viable economic base for Paiutes for the first time in this century and become a foundation for their children. But all this can happen only if the Paiutes can reclaim enough water to prevent Pyramid Lake from evaporating.

Time is running short. Each year Pyramid Lake's surface level falls another foot; it now stands nearly 100 feet lower than it did when the reservation was established.[36] The Truckee River mouth has moved two full miles into the lake, and the river now dribbles across the great naked sand delta. The surface of the lake has shrunk by 34,000 acres. Salinity has increased over 50 percent.[37] The cutthroat trout is on the threatened species list and the cuiui on the endangered list because neither can spawn in their natural habitats, but must rely completely on artificial propagation.[38]

Every summer the grass around Pyramid Lake dries to a tinder gray. Every summer Pyramid Lake shrivels under a scorching sun. For over a century, Paiute resources have shrunk before the relentless desires of white men. Is the Paiute future to be merely a continuation of the past, until all is gone and even the lake itself is dead? How much longer shall their river run?

Within the broad sweep of American Indian history, events in the Great Basin occupy only a footnote at best. There were no dramatic last stands or prolonged cavalry campaigns against famous chiefs. There was resistance, but it was on a small scale, not flamboyant but persistent and perservering. Today Great Basin tribes do not often make headlines in the national press, occupy government buildings, seize hostages, or defy court orders. They have pursued their lives over the last 130 years gently and without fanfare; they continue to do so today. But this lack of drama does not mean that their experience is of little importance. Many of the issues raised by their quiet past are of great importance to tribes everywhere.

The Northern Paiutes at Pyramid Lake experienced incessant exploitation of their natural resources by the surrounding non-Indian population. They also experienced constant infringement of their civil rights. Such injustices are common to the history of all Indian tribes. As a result, Northern Paiute history, like the history of other Indian peoples, cannot be understood as a separate, isolated stream of events; it can only be comprehended in conjunction with the history of Anglos, their migration, their economic patterns, and their legal system.

The injustices which Anglo-European history has heaped on the Paiutes are not safely relegated to the past. Their history, as with the history of all Indian tribes, did not stop with the shooting. The damage done to Indian peoples did not end with white settlement of the frontier. Instead, it began. As Anglos increased in numbers, so increased the pressures against remnant Indian resources. The open violence of frontier times was transformed into the more subtle, and more invidious, methods of the twentieth century—lobbying, corporate power plays, manipulation of legislative processes, government development projects, and the intricacies of legal title and contracts. Attacks on the Pyramid Lake resource base were made farther and farther from the lake itself, unseen by but not unknown to the residents there.

The Paiutes were vulnerable to this form of attack. Like Indian tribes everywhere, they were themselves politically powerless. A people few in number and despised, they had no direct access to the political system which ruled their lives.

In addition, they suffered the institutionalized disadvantages which Indians alone of all ethnic groups endure. The most obvious of these was administration by the Bureau of Indian Affairs and the federal trust status of reservation land. This was an ambiguous relationship which was both a source of endless frustration and the only bulwark standing between the tribe and Anglo greed. Trusteeship empowered the federal government to decide unilaterally whether to construct an irrigation system at Pyramid Lake, for instance, or to leave the land undeveloped. Since the tribe did not hold clear title to the property, they could not offer it as collateral for bank loans in order to develop the land on their own. The government could decide to allot five acres to each Indian at Pyramid Lake and then sell the remainder of the reserve, or it could arbitrarily relinquish the township of Wadsworth. Before 1934, although the reservation was held in the name of the group as a whole, the tribe could not hire a private attorney to defend that corporate property. Before 1934, the federal government could intervene in all aspects of Indian life, from marriage customs to the schooling of children. It could take these actions without Indian representation or consent.

So too, Indians are alone among ethnic groups for the large body of federal and state laws and regulations which apply to them. For instance, the General Allotment Act, passed without Indian representation in Congress, declared it to be federal policy to break up reservations previously guaranteed to the tribes. The Wheeler-Howard Act countermanded that law and asserted that tribes were viable legal corporations. House Concurrent Resolution no. 108, not even a law, stated in 1954 that it was federal policy to annul any special tribal relations with the federal government as soon as possible. Fifteen years later, a presidential speech again reversed that policy by declaring it "morally and legally unacceptable."[39]

Furthermore, much of the day-to-day administration of reservations is extralegal and exists within the gray zone of federal regulation. Such regulations are changed with each new administration and its new political appointees. Indian agents control life on the reservations. No other ethnic group has such administrators. The personalities and concerns of these agents often have more to do with the development or nondevelopment of a reserve than does national policy. If Reverend Bateman, for instance, had not protested potential railroad claims in the 1870s, virtually all of the rich riverine section of the Pyramid Lake reservation would have been lost. If Alida Bowler had not encouraged and supported the tribal council in their tentative first efforts, they would have taken much longer to become a self-confident, self-governing body.

State laws often discriminate overtly against Indians.[40] Nevada poll taxes prevented Indians from voting in state elections until 1924. Indians could not vote for senators, who thus saw no political reason to defend Indian interests and who in fact led the opposition for decades. Nevada law forbade marriages between Indians and whites until 1919, and did not recognize marriage by Indian custom as legitimate until 1943. State law intentionally damaged the Pyramid Lake fishing industry.

Thus Paiutes, with other Indians, are differentiated from the rest of the people of the United States by an administrative structure and a body of law which apply only to them. In addition, a series of court decisions affects Indians alone. The U.S. Supreme Court made decisions in the 1830s, before Anglos even knew of Pyramid Lake's existence, which profoundly influenced events there. That court, not Congress, declared Indian tribes to be wards of the United States government.[41] These court decisions set the foundation of all Indian policy by making it the exclusive concern of the federal government and denying states all jurisdiction in Indian matters. It was on the basis of these and other precedents that the cases against the squatters Sutcliffe, Depaoli, and Garaventa were appealed to federal rather than state courts. The fact that these cases went through the less hostile federal courts was critical to their success. Again, it was Paiutes' court-defined status as federal wards which placed their tribal properties in trust with the government. It was Paiutes' status as federal wards which enabled them to sue Interior Secretary Morton for mismanagement of those tribal trust properties. Another Supreme Court decision in the *Winters* case established an Indian claim to water under federal law which applied to no other ethnic group.

The Indians' unique position in American legislative, administrative, and judicial structures has left them weak before the threats of large and powerful Anglo interests in the twentieth century. Those threats no longer come from individual white men openly carrying a rifle, but are covert and even more hazardous. In the twentieth century, danger comes from irrigation districts representing thousands of Anglo water-users. Land corporations and interstate power consortia, supported by federal bureaucracies and public belief in the necessity of progress, have taken the conflict out of the local arena and into a distant forum where the battle is waged by surrogates. Nevada has spawned a series of congressmen outstanding for their active defense of Anglo encroachment on Indian properties. Stewart, Newlands, Oddie, Pittman, McCarran—all have records of utter disregard for Indian interests. Their names are infamous in Pyramid Lake history.

Against such powerful congressmen and their Anglo constituency, Paiutes had only the dubious protection of the Bureau of Indian Affairs. "The United States Government acts as a legal trustee for the land and water rights of American Indians," President Nixon declared in 1970. "Every trustee has a legal obligation to advance the interests of the beneficiaries of the trust without reservation and with the highest degree of diligence and skill."[42] Pyramid Lake's history shows clearly that the federal government as a whole and the BIA in particular did not protect Indian property aggressively. They were not responsive to Indian concerns or petitions. They held uniform national policies of agricultural development which showed no understanding of Paiute customs, environment, or culture. They tolerated squatters on Indian lands for generations, and then ceded title to them. The BIA stood by while other government agencies planned to drain Pyramid Lake, the heart of the reservation. The BIA did not press actively for maximal tribal water claims in the Orr Ditch suit. It did not encourage development of the fisheries until Anglo history had made this virtually impossible.

In 1866, an agent said that Paiutes looked "with anxious expectation to that government upon which we have taught him to rely";[43] they have waited in anticipation ever since. During that time, they have discovered that agents' promises of federal protection were empty. Paiute confidence in the BIA crumbled as each new disappointment followed upon the last. They grew distrustful of federal promises and federal projects. Their bitterness stimulated demands to control their own resources, their own development, and their own lives.

While the federal government's role in Indian history has often been one of apathy and ineffectuality, state legislatures have been openly hostile. States are more responsive than the federal government to local interests dominated by non-Indians. These powerful local concerns are nearly always directly opposed to Indian best interests. Nevada early proved itself hostile by asking that Pyramid Lake be abandoned as a reservation and thrown open to Anglo settlement. The state was frequently a powerful and extremely dangerous foe to Pyramid Lake Paiutes in other matters as well.

The increasing role that states are now playing in Indian affairs poses a great threat to Paiutes and to Indians all across the country. For instance, in yet another attempt to get the federal government "out of the Indian business," Public Law 280 enabled states to take over certain functions previously provided by the BIA, such as law enforcement and social services. Paiute interests could be seriously damaged by such a transfer of jurisdiction, particularly in the two areas of game management and water control. For years, Nevada unilaterally attempted to assert control over Indian fishing methods, seasons, and markets. This attempt was unsuccessful when the tribe resisted. Paiutes denied Nevada spawn-gathering privileges and eventually asserted their tribal sovereignty, thus forcing state agents to leave the reserve. The tribe has recently declared that it will control its own fishery and operate it in its own best interest.

Water, the life-blood of economic development in Nevada, is the other critical issue. The Eagle County decision could force federal claims into state courts, which would mean that future decisions would be made based on state rather than federal water law. Such state jurisdiction is dangerous, because those state laws were made by legislatures themselves responsive to local pressures from large Anglo landowners and commercial interests. The premises of such law necessarily favor the vocal political majority. Further, states were excluded historically from dealing with Indian tribes. Nevada law, for instance, was written without any recognition of aboriginal land or water rights. It does not recognize *Winters* Doctrine, which is based on federal trust responsibility for reservation development and federal ownership of the public domain. Therefore, if Paiute water suits were driven into the Nevada court system, they would all be lost.

If water claims are lost and Pyramid Lake shrinks into a saline pond, the Paiutes will become poorer than they are today. And they are poor enough. Throughout the 1960s, between 40 and 50 percent of the Paiute labor force was without jobs.[44] The source of this problem is obvious. There is virtually no industry on the reservation, and the average farm size is seven acres, far too small to support a family in Nevada. Cattle grazed on the tribal pastures provide livelihood for a few. The general store supports one family. Many women sell craft products, but this is not very lucrative because of the distance from urban markets. Until the tribal hatchery was built, the only other source of on-reservation employment was the BIA, directly or through the tribal council. Such jobs depend on the levels of federal funding and fluctuate with each administration in Washington, not with the needs of the local economy.

National statistics show that Indians are the poorest ethnic group in the country.[45] Housing is below regional standards, income is low, and unemployment is high on nearly all reservations. Many private and government analyses try to explain the depressed economy of places like Pyramid Lake by their distance from markets and their rural character. They call them underdeveloped areas and point to their lack of commerce and industry. These reservations have been bypassed by progress, they say.

But the Pyramid Lake Paiutes are not poor because they have been forgotten by history. They are not poor because they were isolated in a backwater of the national economy. Before the coming of the whites to Nevada, Pyramid Lake Indians were not poor. They were among the richest of the native tribes in the Great Basin, because they controlled the mouth of the Truckee River. Other bands came there to gather fish and to share in their bounty. They were an independent people earning their living off their own land, without the need of outside assistance or welfare checks. Throughout the nineteenth century, BIA agents complained of this very independence, that Paiutes would not become farmers because they did not need to. They could always go out to fish or to work in towns or on ranches. But steadily and relentlessly, Anglos siphoned off the resources of the reservation. It was the systematic Anglo theft of valuable agricultural lands, state denial of permission to sell fish, and then destruction of that fishery by government seizure of water from the Truckee River, which made Pyramid Lake Indians poor. Stripped of resources, the reservation could only become the home to poverty.

Pyramid Lake Paiutes became poor not because they were forgotten, but because they were integrated. They were integrated into a national economic system which transferred tribal lands of the West to Anglo ownership. Paiutes did not become poor because they were in an isolated backwater, but because they were drawn into the mainstream of historical events. Within that history, their position was that of the exploited rather than of the exploiter. They were made subject to special state laws and federal policies and to the avarice of the surrounding non-Indian economy. Against these exterior forces they were powerless to defend themselves because of their position under American law. Only when that position changed were the Pyramid Lake Paiutes able to fight again.

The Pyramid Lake tribe has risked much of its future on one single resource which has in the past always provided its sustenance—Pyramid Lake itself. The cutthroat trout and cuiui are part of Paiute cultural heritage. These fish, part of nature which traditional beliefs declare cannot be violated, have been threatened by Anglo action and brought nearly to extinction. The tribe has fought back by investing in hatcheries and engaging in costly lawsuits. If water for Pyramid Lake can be found, if the river continues to flow into the lake, if the lake is not drunk up by the thirsty sun, then Paiutes can hope. They can hope to turn around the trends of the past, to fight successfully against aggressive American values and policies, to strive against systematic legal and social discrimination. They can hope to establish a viable economy, independent of federal assistance and of welfare handouts. If once again the river runs full, it will restore independence to a people. Paiutes will once again draw their sustenance from Pyramid Lake.

Epilogue

Since completion of the manuscript for this book the courts have rejected the suit by the Pyramid Lake tribe and the United States Department of Justice against the Truckee-Carson Irrigation District and other water-users for sufficient water to sustain the lake fishery.

In December 1977, the Federal District Court for Nevada decided against the petition of the tribe. The court held that the issue of water for the fishery had already been decided during development of the Orr Ditch case. First, the court argued, Orr Ditch was a general, friendly case brought to settle all claims to water in the river system. The federal government, as trustee for the tribe, had the responsibility to put forward all defensible claims at that time. The government made a policy decision by not suing for water to sustain fish life or the lake level. By condoning this legal strategy, the court concluded, the Secretary of the Interior implicitly yielded any rights to water for fish life. He had the power to do this because such authority was delegated by the President, who could make or retract executive order reservations and, by implication, property rights in such reservations. Such an abdication of tribal water rights could have been accomplished without tribal knowledge or notification, because property rights in executive order reservations are not compensable interests.

Further, the court argued, the Secretary of the Interior had been given explicit authorization in the Reclamation Act of 1902 to acquire water rights for future reclamation projects through purchase or condemnation, as long as such proceedings were in strict accordance with state law. Since Indian water rights were put into direct conflict with reclamation-project development needs, the problem "was resolved within the executive department of government by top-level executive officers acting within the scope of their Congressionally-delegated duties and authority and were political and policy decisions of those officials charged with that responsibility, which decisions resulted in the extinguishment of the alleged fishery purposes water right."[1] Thus the tribal right had been negated before Orr Ditch even went to court, before the tribal council gained veto power over alienation of tribal resources, without tribal knowledge and with explicit Congressional statement of intent. The District Court ordered that the tribal complaint be dismissed with prejudice in its entirety.

Of course, the tribe rejected this argument and appealed the case. Their defense was based primarily upon claims of conflict of interest and denial of due process of law. In a split decision, the Ninth Circuit Court of Appeals found partially for the tribe on case-specific grounds, denying the argument that the Secretary of the Interior could eliminate tribal control of resources by implicit administrative action, by simply not suing for water under Orr Ditch to maintain the fishery. Executive order reservations, it stated, create a property interest which can only be eliminated by a procedure at least as formal as that which created it. Since there was no subsequent executive order withdrawing water rights, water was not lost through explicit administrative action. Furthermore, Congress never ratified the 1944 judicial decision as law, which would have locked off later suits such as this one. To the contrary, in the Washoe Project Act Congress had specifically accepted the need to restore the Pyramid Lake fishery. Therefore it was not the intent of the legislative branch to remove water resources from the reservation. It remained to be determined if the judicial branch had, with due process of law, taken fishery water from the tribe.

This then was a question of whether tribal interests were adequately represented in the Orr Ditch case, and the Court of Appeals decided that they were not. Since all parties in the suit had been in competition for the same amount of water, each was entitled to legal representation to defend its claim against all other contenders. Both the Newlands Reclamation Project and the Pyramid Lake Reservation were represented by the Justice Department. The Appeals Court held that since Indian resources were not federal property in the same sense that project resources were, but rather were tribal properties held in trust by the federal government, the specific legal standards for proper trust management must apply. Further, it said that government action in the Orr Ditch case failed to meet just standards for protection of property interests by a trustee, because it had not rigorously contended with the project for all possible water for the reservation, specifically water for fish maintenance. The court declared:

> The Tribe and the Project were neither parties nor co-parties, however. They were non-parties who were represented simultaneously by the same government attorneys. ... The very idea of representative litigation is defeated if the representative asserts adverse claims simultaneously. Under most circumstances, such representation is by definition inadequate. ... We assume, but do not decide, that the government's representation of the Tribe in *Orr Ditch* was improper and inadequate.[2]

Thus the federal government failed to overcome its conflict of interests.

This conflict of interests did not invalidate the entire Orr Ditch decision, for the thousands of other parties to that case had acted in good faith and should be able to rely on the decision as final. The government had adequately defended tribal interests against these users in the course of its joint representation. It was only against the reclamation project—and by implication its successor in interest, the Truckee-Carson Irrigation District—that the government had failed to defend tribal property. Therefore, the Court of Appeals found, it was only against TCID which the tribe could now seek further adjudication of claims for fishery and lake waters. This released all parties except TCID from the suit. The Appeals Court sent the case back to the district level to try the water claims between TCID and the tribe.

TCID found this solution unacceptable and appealed to the Supreme Court. Nevada and 19 other Western states, realizing that they too had similar historical cases in their territories and fearing the reopening of massive suits by numerous tribes, joined TCID in the case in *amicus curiae* status, as interested but uncontending parties.

On October 12, 1982, the U.S. Supreme Court accepted this case for rehearing, thus implicitly disagreeing with the legal argument or conclusions of the Court of Appeals.[3] The case was argued on 27 April 1983 and decided by a unanimous court on 24 June 1983. The written decision by Justice Rehnquist merged the Indian fisheries case with two others involving Truckee River waters. The Supreme Court ruled against the tribal petition on strictly historical grounds, but in so doing, enunciated several principles destined to have strong impact on Indian water rights both at Pyramid Lake and elsewhere in years to come.

In rejecting the Pyramid Lake appeal, the Supreme Court concurred with the district court and declared, "It seems quite clear to us that they are asserting the same reserved right for the purposes of 'fishing' and maintenance of 'lands and waters' that was asserted in *Orr Ditch*."[4] The court ruled that the parties were the same in the earlier and in the present suit, despite the fact that both the tribe and TCID had been represented by the federal government in the original hearings. By choosing to perceive both the claim for agricultural waters in the *Orr Ditch* decision and the claim for fishery waters in the present case together under the general category of *Winters* claims, the court ruled that the same parties were suing for the same property under the same legal defense in both suits. Therefore, TCID was being asked to defend itself against the same suit a second time, which constituted double jeopardy. The Supreme Court denied the Pyramid Lake suit.

In so doing, the Court made clear its intention to interpret *Winters* claims narrowly. It declared that "the only conclusion allowed by the record in the *Orr Ditch* case is that the Government was given an opportunity to litigate the Reservation's entire water right to the Truckee, and that the Government intended to take advantage of that opportunity." The resulting action "cannot be construed as anything less than a claim for the full 'implied-reservation-of-water' rights that were due the Pyramid Lake Indian Reservation."[5] That federal action, undertaken at a point in history when the tribe was effectively powerless to intervene and had no knowledge of the long-range implications of such bureaucratic decisions, were defined as forever binding on tribal action.

The Court revealed its motivation for this narrow construction of *Winters* claims. In a footnote lauding the legal doctrines of *res judicata* which it used to decide this case, the Court declared that these principles "perhaps are at their zenith in cases concerning real property, land and water." Quoting an earlier decision, it continued: "Where questions arise which affect title to land, it is of great importance to the public that when they are once decided they should no longer be considered open. Such decisions become rules of property, and many titles may be injuriously affected by their change."[6] With regard specifically to water rights, "a quiet title action for the adjudication of water rights, such as the *Orr Ditch* suit, is distinctively equipped to serve these policies because 'it enables the court of equity to acquire jurisdiction of all the rights involved . . . and thus settle and permanently adjudicate in a single proceeding all the rights, or claims to rights, of all the claimants to the water taken from a common source of supply.'"[7] Thus the argument was for the permanent protection of existing property rights. The question of whose property rights were the focus of this concern became clear in the decision abstract, where the Court made obvious its intent: "These defendants have relied just as much on that decree in participating in the development of western Nevada as have the parties in the *Orr Ditch* case, and any other conclusion would make it impossible finally to quantify a reserved water right."[8] Here again was the nineteenth-century argument of the ultimate value of Progress, coupled with an Anglo-American defense of private property. In western regions of limited water resources, many people fear, as did the Supreme Court here, that privately owned land and water titles are threatened by open-ended Indian water rights reserved for their use by the *Winters* doctrine. As long as *Winters* claims remain unknown in quantity and potentially expansible to meet future tribal needs as they develop in the twentieth century, it is felt that property rights of others face a vague threat. Therefore there is growing political pressure to quantify Indian *Winters* rights through suit, negotiations or agreement, and this decision of the U.S. Supreme Court made clear that once such quantification takes place, it shall be final. Tribes cannot hope for later readjustments despite omission, error, oversight, or inequity, even when the original agreement is arranged *for* them by an arm of the federal government, within the BIA or the Department of Justice.

The second major implication of the Supreme Court decision involved just such federal representation, and again the implications extended far beyond the Pyramid Lake case alone. As we have seen throughout the history of Pyramid Lake, there was question over the performance of federal trust responsibility to properly administer Indian land, water, and other resources. A key argument in the tribal appeal was that an inherent, structural conflict of interest crippled the Department of Justice in its advocacy of Pyramid Lake water rights when that same agency was simultaneously defending opposing Newlands claims. In a broadly phrased ruling, the Supreme Court denied that such a conflict of interest existed:

> It is simply unrealistic to suggest that the Government may not perform its obligation to represent Indian tribes in litigation when Congress has obliged it to represent other interests as well. In this regard, the Government cannot follow the fastidious standards of a private fiduciary, who would breach his duties to his single beneficiary solely by representing potentially conflicting interests without the beneficiary's consent. The Government does not 'compromise' its obligations to one interest that Congress obliges it to represent by the mere fact that it simultaneously performs another task for another interest that Congress has obligated it by statute to do.[9]

By avoiding any discussion of the potentially direct competition for resources and rights and by equating legal representation with routine bureaucratic "tasks," the Court sterilized the issue. Without legal argument and based on appeal only to "realistic" pragmatism, the

Court ignored the realities of political power. Issues involved in Indian legal rights are little known in Washington, resting as they do on a specialized body of law and the representation by a small bureau which lacks political influence and is dwarfed by the powerful Bureau of Reclamation, Forest Service, and Park Service within the very same Department of the Interior. The vulnerability of tribal issues to political decision-making within such a bureaucratic milieu, at a point long before matters reach court hearings or even legal representation, is obvious. The Supreme Court turned its back on this reality.

Further, it established weaker standards for the representation of Indian rights by the federal trustee than are acceptable anywhere else in the legal profession. Pyramid Lake's lengthy dispute over the hiring of a private attorney in the 1950s becomes even more significant. Without such autonomous counsel, tribes will be helpless to defend themselves under such an interpretation of federal responsibility; however, the resulting strain on tribal financial resources will be substantial. Tribes which, through lack of economic means to hire private attorneys, are forced to continue to rely on federal representation, will do so at their own risk.

The ultimate Supreme Court denial of the Northern Paiutes' claim for *Winters* waters for the Pyramid Lake fishery somehow came as no surprise. The 125-year history of Paiute dealings with Anglo-Americans showed a pattern of weak federal protection of tribal resources and toleration of the loss of land to white farmers, pasturage to trespassing cattle, fish from the lake, and massive amounts of water from the Truckee River, taken by an arm of the Government itself. Indian agents were unable to defend against such encroachments, senators aided and encouraged it, and the Bureau of Indian Affairs blocked tribal self-protection by ignoring petitions and manipulating attorney's contracts. The consistency of this historical pattern was not broken by the recent Supreme Court decision. Even its appeal to rugged individualism in competing for federal legal services and staunch defense of private property rights in the name of progress were a fitting part of that history. The form of that history was not to change.

A month after the Supreme Court ruled that Indian claims to Truckee River waters were fixed by the *Orr Ditch* decision, Sierra Pacific Power Company, a defendant in that suit and already a major water user, applied for an increase of its water allocation by 175 second-feet, to be used for municipal and domestic purposes in the Reno area. The following month Washoe County reportedly asked for an impossible 9,000 second-feet, which would consume 512,000 acre-feet annually and require construction of a $10 million facility for its distribution. Waters declared unavailable for the Indian fishing industry were still much coveted by non-Indian urban users.[10]

On October 3, 1983, the Supreme Court rejected the Pyramid Lake Paiutes' intervening appeal in the *Alpine* case, which attempted to ameliorate the impact of the Newlands diversion by modifying Carson River water distributions.[11]

These two Supreme Court decisions dealt a bitter blow to Paiute hopes. But rather than resort to anger or depression, the tribal council met with their attorney to evaluate other basic strategies to gain water for the tribal fish hatcheries. They agreed to continue still-pending suits which asked for more limited and specific water allocations. Their decision was made public in a first page banner headline in the *Native Nevadan*: "The Battle Isn't Over."[12]

The courage and stamina to continue in the face of such repeated defeats has characterized all of the Pyramid Lake Paiute past. It is such fortitude and refusal to give up in the face of overwhelming odds that makes their past more than a short and bitter footnote in history. Paiute expectations for the future are based on the realities of their past and yet, despite all, they have the courage to go on doing what they have always done—defending their home at Pyramid Lake.

Notes

Many of the sources used in preparation of this book are unpublished manuscripts. The vast majority of these public documents are housed in the National Archives in Washington or are duplicates and reproductions of materials from there. Unless otherwise cited, unpublished materials are from federal archival collections of Bureau of Indian Affairs documents. These are housed in Record Group 75, Letters Received by the Office of Indian Affairs. They are filed by Superintendency (Nevada), then by year, alphabetically by author, and sequentially by date of receipt. These files are available on microfilm through the General Services Administration.

In addition, duplicate copies of many letters and memos, often the carbons or office copies, have been deposited in regional archival depositories. Particularly useful were those at Denver, and at San Bruno, California. For convenience, we have also employed various reproduced photocopies of the original manuscripts. Dr. Stewart's extensive personal collection of manuscript copies, built up through fifty years of Great Basin research and testimony in Indian land claims cases, was heavily used. Photoduplicates were also provided to Dr. Stewart for his testimony in the Pyramid Lake water case by the Department of Justice. These were gathered from federal archive repositories and other public sources by the Bureau of Ethnic Research at the University of Arizona (Bureau of Indian Affairs contract H 50C-14209178) under the direction of Thomas Weaver, Theodore Downing, and Dave Ruppert. The Inter-Tribal Council of Nevada also allowed us to scan their photoduplicate collection of agency records.

In addition to unpublished materials from the federal archives, we used manuscript material from the Nevada Historical Society in Reno, particularly their collections of correspondence to and from Nevada Senators and their newspaper clipping files. Finally, Pyramid Lake Tribal Council files are deposited in the Special Collections of the University of Nevada, at Reno, Library. All materials which are housed in either of these two institutions are individually noted.

We should also mention that the University of Nevada, Reno, has an extensive microfilm collection of newspapers published in the state, both short-lived and continuing dailies and weeklies. A great deal of this collection is duplicated at the University of Nevada, Las Vegas, and it constitutes a wealth of information on historical interethnic relations.

All quotations are precisely that, accurate to the words and style of the original authors. Among the delights of historical research are the local slang, creative spelling, expressive punctuation, and conversational sentence structure. We did not want to deny the reader these joyous glimmers from the past, and have preserved the full color of the originals.

KEY TO ABBREVIATIONS

ARCIA   *Annual Report of the Commissioner of Indian Affairs*

BIA   Bureau of Indian Affairs

BIAR   Copy in the files of the Special Projects Office, Bureau of Indian Affairs, Reno

Comm.
Ind. Aff. Commissioner of Indian Affairs

NASB National Archives Regional Center, San Bruno, California

NCAI National Council of American Indians

NHS In the collections of the Nevada Historical Society, Reno

PLTC Pyramid Lake Tribal Council

Sec. Int. Secretary of the Interior

TCID Truckee-Carson Irrigation District

UNR University of Nevada, Reno, Library Special Collections

USGPO United States Government Printing Office

USRS United States Reclamation Service

CHAPTER ONE: THE LAND AND ITS PEOPLE

1. Merle Brown, "Climates of the States—Nevada," *Climatography of the United States* no. 60–26, U.S. Dept. Commerce, Weather Bureau (Washington, D.C.: USGPO, 1960).

2. Beecher Crampton, *Grasses in California,* Calif. Natural History Guides no. 33 (Berkeley and Los Angeles: Univ. California Press, 1974); Edmund C. Jaeger, *Desert Wild Flowers,* rev. ed. (Stanford, Calif.: Stanford Univ. Press, 1941); Julian H. Steward, "Basin–Plateau Aboriginal Sociopolitical Groups," Bureau Amer. Ethnol. *Bulletin* no. 120 (Washington, D.C.: USGPO, 1938; reprint ed., Salt Lake City: Univ. Utah Press, 1970), pp. 21–32; Tracy I. Storer and Robert L. Usinger, *Sierra Nevada Natural History* (Berkeley and Los Angeles: Univ. California Press, 1963).

3. Jesse D. Jennings, "The Desert West," in Jesse D. Jennings and Edward Norbeck, eds., *Prehistoric Man in the New World* (Chicago: Univ. Chicago Press, 1964), pp. 149–174. There is debate over the possible occurrence of a Paleo-Indian Big Game Hunting Tradition in the Great Basin, in association with extinct megafauna which would be similar in economy and age to the Clovis Culture elsewhere. The evidence is uncertain, but most researchers agree that the mixed

hunting and gathering system described here, with focus on lacustrine resources, goes far back in time, regardless of whether another far less well-documented culture preceded it. For our purposes, the existence of such a prior culture, adapted to a different ecological system, is relatively unimportant. See Robert F. Heizer and Martin A. Baumhoff, "Big Game Hunters in the Great Basin: A Critical Review of the Evidence," Univ. Calif. Arch. Research Facility *Contributions* 7 (1970): 1–12; Phillip Wilke, Thomas King, and Robert Bettinger, "Ancient Hunters of the Far West?," Nev. Arch. Survey *Research Papers* 5 (1974): 83–90; Donald R. Tuohy, "A Comparative Study of Late Paleo-Indian Manifestations in the Western Great Basin," ibid., pp. 91–116.

4. John O. Snyder, "The Fishes of the Lahonton System of Nevada and Northeastern California," U.S. Bureau Fisheries *Bulletin* no. 35 (Washington, D.C.: USGPO, 1917), pp. 31–86.

5. Donald R. Tuohy, "Evaluative Report of Archaeological Sites Located near Marble Bluff Dam and Fishway, Pyramid Lake Paiute Reservation, Nevada" (Sept. 1975), typescript in the Nevada State Museum collections and personal communications, 24 Sept. 1975 and 14 June 1976; David T. Clark, "Excavations at One Owl House and Three Moons Eagle" (1976), typescript in the Bureau of Reclamation collections, pp. 198–203.

6. Robert F. Heizer and Alex D. Krieger, "The Archaeology of Humboldt Cave, Churchill County, Nevada," Univ. Calif. *Pubs. in Amer. Arch. and Ethnol.* 47, no. 1 (1956): 6–7.

7. Gordon L. Grosscup, "The Culture History of Lovelock Cave, Nevada," Univ. Calif. Arch. Survey *Reports* no. 52 (1960); Robert F. Heizer and Lewis K. Napton, "Archaeological Investigations in Lovelock Cave, Nevada," Univ. Calif. Arch. Research Facility *Contributions* 10 (1970): 1–86; Llewelyn L. Loud and M. R. Harrington, "Lovelock Cave," Univ. Calif. *Pubs. in Amer. Arch. and Ethnol.* 25, no. 1 (1929): 1–183; Lewis K. Napton, "Lacustrine Subsistence Pattern in the Desert West," Kroeber Anthro. Soc. *Special Pubs.* 2 (1969): 28–89. See also Martin A. Baumhoff, "Excavation of a Cache Cave in Pershing County, Nevada," Univ. Calif. Arch. Survey *Reports* 44, no. 2 (1958): 14–25; Albert B. Elsasser and E. R. Prince, "The

Archaeology of Eastgate Cave," Univ. Calif. *Anthro. Records* 20, no. 4 (1961): 139–149; and Robert F. Heizer and Martin A. Baumhoff, "The Archaeology of Wagon Jack Shelter," ibid., pp. 119–138.

8. W. I. Follett, "Fish Remains from Human Coprolites and Midden Deposits Obtained during 1968 and 1969 at Lovelock Cave, Churchill County, Nevada," Univ. Calif. Arch. Research Facility *Contributions* 10 (1970): 164–174; Lewis K. Napton and Robert F. Heizer, "Analysis of Human Coprolites from Archaeological Contexts, with Primary Reference to Lovelock Cave, Nevada," ibid., pp. 87–129; Heizer and Napton, "Biological and Cultural Evidence from Prehistoric Human Coprolites," *Science* 165 (1969): 563–568.

9. Napton and Heizer, "Analysis of Human Coprolites," pp. 107–108.

10. James F. O'Connell, "The Prehistory of Surprise Valley," Ballena Press *Anthro. Papers* no. 4 (1975); Margaret S. Weide, "Cultural Ecology of Lakeside Adaptation in the Western Great Basin," Ph.D. diss. (1968), Univ. California, Los Angeles. Compare with William Clewlow and Mary Rusco, eds., "The Grass Valley Archaeological Project: Collected Papers," Nevada Arch. Survey *Research Papers* no. 3 (1972); Francis A. Riddell, "The Archaeology of the Karlo Site (Las-7), California," Univ. Calif. Arch. Survey *Reports* no. 53 (1960); David H. Thomas, "An Empirical Test for Steward's Model of Great Basin Settlement Patterns," *Amer. Antiquity* 38 (1973): 155–176.

11. W. I. Follett, "Fish Remains from Site NV-Wa-197, Winnemucca Lake, Nevada," Univ. Calif. Arch. Research Facility *Contributions* 21 (1974): 37–43; Thomas Hester, "Archaeological Materials from Site NV-Wa-197, Western Nevada: Atlatl and Animal Skin Pouches," ibid., pp. 1–36; Phillip C. Orr, "Notes on the Archaeology of the Winnemucca Caves, 1952–1958," Nevada State Museum *Anthro. Papers* 16 (1974): 47–59; Charles Rozaire, "Analysis of Woven Materials from Seven Caves in the Lake Winnemucca Area, Pershing County, Nevada," ibid., pp. 60–97; Donald R. Tuohy and Mercedes Stein, "A Late Lovelock Shaman and His Grave Goods," ibid., 14 (1969): 96–130; Doris L. Randal, "A Barbed Antler Point Found at Pyramid Lake, Nevada," *Amer. Antiquity* 31 (1966): 740–742; Norman Roust, "Archaeological Materials from Winnemucca Lake

Caves," Univ. Calif. Arch. Survey *Reports* 44, no. 2 (1958): 1–13; R. Shutler, Jr., "The Great Basin Archaic," Eastern New Mexico Univ. *Contributions in Anthro.* 1, no. 3 (1968): 24–26; Peter Ting, "A Pyramid Lake Surface Artifact Assemblage Located at or near the 3,800-Foot Elevation," Nevada Arch. Survey *Reporter* 1, no. 8 (1967): 4–11, and "Bone Points from Pyramid Lake," ibid., 2, no. 3 (1968): 4–13; Tuohy, "Evaluative Report of Sites Near Marble Bluff Dam."

12. There is some evidence of stylistic shifts in tool and other artifact types, perhaps reflecting the entry of different ethnic groups into the area, at about 2500 B.C. in Surprise Valley (O'Connell, "Prehistory of Surprise Valley," p. 45) and at 1500 B.C. and A.D. 500 in Warner Valley (Weide, "Cultural Ecology of Lakeside Adaptation," p. 263). Interestingly enough, the period of indisputable lacustrine adaptation of the Lovelock Culture in the Humboldt Valley traces back to just 2500 B.C. (Lewis K. Napton and Gerald K. Kelso, "Preliminary Palynological Analysis of Human Coprolites from Lovelock Cave, Nevada," in Kroeber Anthro. Soc. *Special Pubs.* 2 [1960]: 20–27). Linguists have argued on glottochronological grounds that Numic speakers, including Northern Paiutes, entered the Great Basin within the last 1,000 years (Sydney Lamb, "Linguistic Prehistory in the Great Basin," *Intl. Journal Amer. Linguistics* 24 [1958]: 95–100; Catherine S. Fowler, "Comparative Numic Ethnobiology," Ph.D. diss. [1972] Univ. Pittsburgh). Archaeological evidence to support this estimate is inconclusive at present (Gordon L. Grosscup, "Northern Paiute Archaeology" [1954], typescript; printed in *Paiute IV,* Amer. Indian Ethnohistory Series [NY: Garland, 1974], pp. 1–27). The recent archaeological record, since A.D. 1000, is quite scanty, and the period A.D. 1500–1800 is unrepresented in most areas, making verification or refutation of the migration hypothesis difficult. However, this entire issue is of only tangential importance to the argument presented here, as the critical point is the nature of the economic adjustment, not the linguistic or ethnic identity of the population practicing it. The settlement patterns spanning several ecozones, the migratory annual cycle, the dependence upon multiple resources from both lakeshore and valley, and the resulting dietary patterns and mobility of small human groups, are continuous throughout the prehistoric record in this area. Even proponents of ethnic migration say that

"there is no major change or difference between economic activities of the Lovelock people and the Northern Paiutes. The differences or changes, again, are in forms and techniques of manufacture, while the functions remain the same" (Gordon L. Grosscup, "Lovelock, Northern Paiute, and Culture Change," Nevada State Museum *Anthro. Papers* 9 [1963]: 70).

13. Willard Z. Park, ed., "Tribal Distribution in the Great Basin," *Amer. Anthro.* 40 (1938): 622–638.

14. Omer C. Stewart, "The Northern Paiute Bands," Univ. Calif. *Anthro. Records* 2, no. 3 (1939): 129, 144; Alfred L. Kroeber, "Coefficients of Cultural Similarity of Northern Paiute Bands," Univ. Calif. *Pubs. Amer. Arch. and Ethnol.* 47 (1957): 209–214.

15. Stewart, "Northern Paiute Bands," p. 139.

16. Much of the following description is drawn from the excellent account by Margaret Wheat, *Survival Arts of the Primitive Paiutes* (Reno: Univ. Nevada Press, 1967), pp. 8–16. See also Omer C. Stewart, "Culture Element Distributions: XIV. Northern Paiute," Univ. Calif. *Anthro. Records* 6, no. 4 (1942):231–360.

17. Wheat, *Survival Arts*, p. 10.

18. Robert F. Heizer, "Ethnographic Notes on the Northern Paiute of the Humboldt Sink, West Central Nevada," in Earl H. Swanson, Jr., ed., *Languages and Cultures of Western North America* (Pocatello: Idaho State Univ. Press, 1970), pp. 232–245; Wheat, *Survival Arts*, pp. 12–13.

19. Steward, "Basin–Plateau," p. 27.

20. Sarah Winnemucca Hopkins, *Life Among the Piutes: Their Wrongs and Claims* (NY: Putnam, 1883; reprint ed., Bishop, Calif.: Chalfant Press, 1969), pp. 55–57; Steward, "Basin–Plateau," pp. 34–35.

21. Hopkins, *Life*, pp. 52–53; Nellie Shaw Harner, *The History of the Pyramid Lake Indians, 1843–1959, and Early Tribal History, 1825–1834* (Sparks, Nev.: Dave's Printing and Pub., 1974), p. 22.

22. Julian H. Steward, "The Foundations of Basin–Plateau Shoshonean Society," in Swanson, *Languages and Cultures*, pp. 141–144.

CHAPTER TWO: ARRIVAL OF ANGLOS AND THEIR FRONTIER CULTURE

1. Gloria G. Cline, *Exploring the Great Basin* (Norman: Univ. Oklahoma Press, 1963), p. 123.

2. Sarah Winnemucca Hopkins, *Life Among the Piutes: Their Wrongs and Claims* (NY: Putnam, 1883; reprint ed., Bishop, Calif.: Chalfant Press, 1969), pp. 5–6.

3. W. F. Wagner, ed., *Adventures of Zenas Leonard, Fur Trader and Trapper, 1831–1836* (Cleveland, Ohio: Burrows Bros., 1904), p. 161.

4. Ibid., pp. 162–164.

5. Lalla Scott, *Karnee: A Paiute Narrative*, ed. Robert F. Heizer (Reno: Univ. Nevada Press, 1966; reprint ed., Greenwich, Conn.: Fawcett, 1973), p. 28.

6. Ibid., pp. 29–30.

7. Quoted in Cline, *Exploring*, pp. 176–177.

8. Scott, *Karnee*, p. 22.

9. Hopkins, *Life*, pp. 14–15.

10. Scott, *Karnee*, p. 25.

11. John C. Fremont, *Report of the Exploring Expedition to the Rocky Mountains in the Year 1842 and to Oregon and Northern California in the Years 1843–'44* (Buffalo, N.Y.: Geo. H. Derby, 1851), p. 215.

12. Ibid., pp. 218–219.

13. Hopkins, *Life*, pp. 9, 18–19.

14. Ibid., pp. 19–20.

15. Ibid., p. 12.

16. James Downs, *Two Worlds of the Washo* (NY: Holt, Rinehart, and Winston, 1966), p. 73.

17. Myron Angel, *History of Nevada* (Oakland, Calif.: Thompson and West, 1881; reprint ed., Berkeley: Howell-North, 1958), p. 49.

18. Russell R. Elliott, *History of Nevada* (Lincoln: Univ. Nebraska Press, 1973) pp. 50, 56.

19. Ibid., p. 61.

20. H. Douglas, report of conversation on May 1, 1870, with Piute Indians at Truckee River Indian Reservation, Nevada, 27 May 1870.

21. S. B. Worden, letter to Governor Blasdel of Nevada, 9 June 1866. NHS.

22. "The Walker Lake Reservation: Piute Nomads Holding the Best Land in Nevada," *Daily Nevada State Journal*, 15 Oct. 1884.

23. "The Curse," *Grant County News*, 14 Aug. 1880.

24. "Hoggish Redskins," *Reno Evening Gazette*, 7 Feb. 1883.

25. Frank Campbell, letter to Comm. Ind. Aff., 9 June 1865.

26. "Disposal of Indian Prisoners," *Avalanche* (Owyhee, Idaho Terr.), 25 Jan. 1868.

27. Gov. James W. Nye, letter to Caleb Smith, Sec. Int., 14 Aug. 1861.

28. William Wright [Dan DeQuille], *History of the Big Bonanza* (Hartford, Conn.: American Pub. Co., 1877), p. 196.

29. Statement of Captain Weatherlow, quoted in Sessions S. Wheeler, *The Desert Lake: The Story of Nevada's Pyramid Lake* (Caldwell, Idaho: Caxton Printers, 1967), p. 46.

30. Hopkins, *Life*, pp. 59–65.

31. John Reese, letter to Supt. Ind. Aff. for Utah Terr., 3 Nov. 1861.

32. M. T. Carr, 1st Lt., letter to W. J. Gardiner, Commander, Ft. Crook, Calif., 2 July 1858 (War Dept. Commands, Dept. Pacific, G-71-1858).

33. Howard P. Taylor, "A Thrilling Experience," c. 1900. Typescript, NHS.

34. "Pyramid Lake," *Reno Weekly Evening Gazette*, 19 July 1878.

35. "Degeneracy of the Tribesmen," *Reno Evening Gazette*, 23 March 1910.

36. *Deseret News* (Salt Lake City), 28 March 1860.

37. Angel, *History*, p. 341.

38. Ibid., p. 145; emphasis in the original.

39. *Idaho Statesman,* 6 Oct. 1867, p. 2.

40. Phillip D. Smith, "The Sagebrush Soldiers," *Nevada Historical Soc. Quarterly 5* (1962): 62.

41. William F. Drannan, *Thirty-One Years on the Plains and in the Mountains* (Chicago: Thom. Jackson Pub., 1900), pp. 148–151.

42. Ibid., p. 159.

43. "Doing Up a Band of Piutes," *Denver Field and Farm,* 7 Jan. 1911, p. 8.

44. "The Recent Fight in Paradise Valley," *Humboldt Register,* 5 Aug. 1865.

45. "Soldiers on the Countermarch," ibid., 19 Aug. 1865.

46. J. Holeman, letter to L. Lea, Comm. Ind. Aff., 28 June 1852.

47. H. Dodge, letter to Jacob Forney, Supt. Ind. Aff. for Utah Terr., 4 Jan. 1859.

48. Ibid.

49. J. Reese, letter to Supt. Ind. Aff. for Utah Terr., 3 Nov. 1861.

50. Garland Hurt, letter to Brigham Young, Gov. and *ex officio* Supt. Ind. Aff. for Utah Terr., Sept. 1856. Published as Letter No. 98 in *ARCIA, 1856* (Washington, D.C.: USGPO, 1856), p. 779.

51. Quoted in "Deceptive Indian Agents," *Daily Silver State Journal,* 6 Nov. 1879.

52. Carl Schurz, letter to R. E. Trowbridge, Comm. Ind. Aff., 8 Aug. 1880.

CHAPTER THREE: OPEN CONFLICT

1. Statement of Captain Weatherlow, quoted in Sessions S. Wheeler, *The Desert Lake: The Story of Nevada's Pyramid Lake* (Caldwell, Idaho: Caxton Printers, 1967), p. 52.

2. F. Dodge, letter to Jacob Forney, Supt. Ind. Aff. for Utah Terr., 4 Jan. 1859.

3. Myron Angel, *History of Nevada* (Oakland, Calif.: Thompson

and West, 1881; reprint ed., Berkeley: Howell-North, 1958), pp. 146–147.

4. Ira Eaton, citizen, letter to F. W. Lander, Supt. U.S. Wagon Road Expedition, 31 Oct. 1860.

5. Angel, *History,* pp. 147–148; Weatherlow, statement, p. 48.

6. Angel, *History,* p. 148.

7. Quoted in ibid., p. 149.

8. Quoted in ibid., p. 148; and in Effie Mona Mack, *Nevada: A History of the State from the Earliest Times Through the Civil War* (Glendale, Calif.: Arthur H. Clark Co., 1936), pp. 298–299.

9. Howard Taylor, "A Thrilling Experience," c. 1900. Typescript, NHS.

10. Ibid., p. 2.

11. Ibid., p. 1.

12. Ibid., p. 2.

13. For instance, Ferol Egan, *Sand in a Whirlwind: The Paiute Indian War of 1860* (Garden City, NY: Doubleday, 1972), pp. 78–85.

14. Eaton, letter to Lander, 31 Oct. 1860; emphasis added.

15. Angel, *History,* p. 150.

16. F. W. Lander, letter to A. B. Greenwood, Comm. Ind. Aff., 31 Oct. 1860.

17. F. Dodge, letter to A. B. Greenwood, 9 Aug. 1860; Mack, *Nevada,* p. 302.

18. Sarah Winnemucca Hopkins, *Life Among the Piutes: Their Wrongs and Claims* (NY: Putnam, 1883; reprint ed., Bishop, Calif.: Chalfant Press, 1969), p. 7.

19. F. Dodge, letter to A. B. Greenwood, 23 June 1860; James Mooney, *The Ghost-Dance Religion and Wounded Knee,* Bur. Amer. Ethnol., Smithsonian Inst., 14th *Annual Report,* part 2 (Washington, D.C.: USGPO, 1896; reprint ed., NY: Dover, 1973), p. 771.

20. Taylor, "A Thrilling Experience," p. 2; Effie Mona Mack, "William Morris Stewart, 1827–1909," *Nevada Historical Soc.*

Quarterly 7 (1965): 24; George R. Brown, ed., *Reminiscences of Senator William M. Stewart of Nevada* (NY: Neale Pub. Co., 1908), p. 123; Angel, *History,* p. 152.

21. Angel, *History,* p. 152.

22. Russell R. Elliott, *History of Nevada* (Lincoln: Univ. Nebraska Press, 1973), p. 93; Egan, *Sand,* pp. 107–271; Angel, *History,* pp. 149–164; Mack, *Nevada,* pp. 301–307; Nellie Shaw Harner, *Indians of Coo-yu-ee Pah (Pyramid Lake): The History of the Pyramid Lake Indians* (Sparks, Nev.: Dave's Printing and Pub., 1974), pp. 41–46; Phillip Dodd Smith, "The Sagebrush Soldiers," *Nevada Historical Soc. Quarterly* 5 (1962): 64–65.

23. Angel, *History,* p. 162; Elliott, *History,* p. 93.

24. Dodge, letter to Greenwood, 23 June 1860.

25. Angel, *History,* p. 164.

26. Lander, letter to Greenwood, 31 Oct. 1860.

27. Ibid.

28. Angel, *History,* pp. 164–165.

29. F. W. Lander, letter to A. B. Greenwood, 25 Nov. 1859.

30. Warren Wasson, letter to Gov. James W. Nye, 13 July 1861.

31. Mack, *Nevada,* pp. 307–314.

32. Hopkins, *Life,* pp. 137–202.

33. Ibid., pp. 203–248.

34. Nevada Terr. Legislature, memorial to the U.S. Congress, 19 Dec. 1862; reprinted in *Session Laws of American States and Territories—Statutes of the Nevada Legislature* (Westport, Conn.: Redgrave Info. Resources, 1973; microfiche ed.).

35. Brown, *Reminiscences,* pp. 100, 125.

36. Warren Wasson, letter to Gov. James W. Nye, 20 April 1862.

37. Angel, *History,* p. 169, emphasis in original.

38. Ibid.

39. John C. Burche, letter to Gov. James W. Nye, 1 Aug. 1864.

40. Angel, *History,* p. 169.

41. For instance, William L. Manly, *Death Valley in '49* (San Jose, Calif.: Pacific Tree and Vine Co., 1894; reprint ed., Bishop, Calif.: Chalfant Press, c. 1978); Louis Nusbaumer, *Valley of Salt, Memories of Wine: A Journal of Death Valley, 1849,* ed. George Koenig (Berkeley and Los Angeles: Univ. California Press for Friends of Bancroft Library, 1967); LeRoy Hafen and Ann Hafen, eds., *The Old Spanish Trail: Santa Fe to Los Angeles,* Far West and Rockies Historical Series no. 1 (Glendale, Calif.: Arthur H. Clark Co., 1954).

42. John C. Fremont, *Report of the Exploring Expedition to the Rocky Mountains in the Year 1842 and to Oregon and Northern California in the Years 1843–1844* (Washington, D.C.: Gales and Seaton, 1845), p. 268.

43. Burche, letter to Nye, 1 Aug. 1864.

44. Jacob Lockhart, letter to Gov. James W. Nye, 10 Aug. 1864.

45. Smith, "Sagebrush Soldiers," pp. 33, 64–65.

46. Sarah Winnemucca, letter to the Commanding Officer of Camp McDermitt, 27 Oct. 1868 (War Dept. Commands, Dept. Calif. 695-1-P-1868). The belief that Winnemucca Lake was on the reservation was common in the area at this period, although it later proved false.

47. Hopkins, *Life,* p. 77.

48. Angel, *History,* p. 172.

49. Ibid., p. 174.

50. Smith, "Sagebrush Soldiers," p. 66.

51. F. Dodge, letter to E. S. Parker, Comm. Ind. Aff., 20 Sept. 1870.

52. Jesse Lee, letter to H. Douglas, Indian Agent, 18 Dec. 1869.

53. Hopkins, *Life,* p. 78.

54. Capt. William Kelly, 8th Cavalry, Commanding Camp Harney, Ore., letter to Lt. A. H. Nickerson, Rt. Adjt. 23rd Infantry, AAAG District, 24 June 1868 (War Dept. Commands, Dept. the Columbia, 30-C-1868), encl. no. 3.

55. Ibid.

56. Angel, *History*, pp. 166–177.

57. U.S. Court of Claims, "Opinion of the Court," Snake or Piute Indians of the Former Malheur Reservation in Oregon v. United States, Appeal, docket No. 10, 2 June 1953, p. 23.

58. Hopkins, *Life*, p. 89.

59. Effie Mona Mack, *The Indian Massacre of 1911 at Little High Rock Canyon, Nevada* (Sparks, Nev.: Western Printing and Pub., 1968); Frank V. Perry, "The Last Indian Uprising in the United States," *Nevada Historical Soc. Quarterly* 15: 23–37, 1972.

60. *Nevada State Journal*, as quoted in Mack, *Indian Massacre*, p. 116.

61. "Indians Captured," *Reno Evening Gazette*, 27 Feb. 1911.

62. Quoted in Mack, *Indian Massacre*, pp. 142–143.

63. Frank Campbell, letter to Comm. Ind. Aff., 9 June 1865.

64. Daniel Platt, letter to Sec. Int., 21 June 1865.

65. H. G. Parker, letter to D. N. Cooley, Comm. Ind. Aff., 10 Sept. 1866.

CHAPTER FOUR: RESERVATION LIFE

1. U.S. Const., art. I, sec. 10.

2. Ibid., sec. 8.

3. Cherokee Nation v. Georgia, 5 Pet. 1 (1831); Worcester v. Georgia, 6 Pet. 515 (1832).

4. Felix Cohen, *Handbook of Federal Indian Law* (Washington, D.C.: USGPO, 1942; reprint ed., Albuquerque: Univ. New Mexico Press, 1971), p. 299.

5. Jacob Forney, letter to Frederick Dodge, Nevada Indian Agent, 6 Oct. 1858.

6. F. Dodge, letter to A. B. Greenwood, Comm. Ind. Aff., 25 Nov. 1859.

7. Ulysses S. Grant, executive order, 23 March 1874; reprinted in

Charles J. Kappler, comp., *Indian Affairs: Laws and Treaties* (Washington, D.C.: USGPO, 1904), 1: 869.

8. Cohen, *Handbook*, p. 302.

9. William Vandever, letter to Comm. Ind. Aff., 8 June 1875.

10. "In the Name of Humanity," *Reno Weekly Gazette*, 29 July 1880.

11. Sarah Winnemucca, statement to Carl Schurz, Sec. Int., 15 Dec. 1879.

12. Washington J. Endicott, report of inspection, 3 Sept. 1920, p. 3.

13. Sarah Winnemucca Hopkins, *Life among the Piutes: Their Wrongs and Claims* (NY: Putnam, 1883; reprint ed., Bishop, Calif.: Chalfant Press, 1969), pp. 128–135.

14. C. A. Bateman, letter to F. A. Walker, Comm. Ind. Aff., 30 Sept. 1872; reprinted in *ARCIA, 1872* (Washington, D.C.: USGPO, 1872), pp. 284–285.

15. George R. Pearsons, report of inspection of the Nevada Agency, 24 Feb. 1886, p. 4.

16. W. D. Gibson, letter to Comm. Ind. Aff., n.d.; reprinted in *ARCIA, 1887* (Washington, D.C.: USGPO, 1887), p. 164.

17. W. D. Gibson, letter to J. D. Atkins, Comm. Ind. Aff., 8 March 1888.

18. Lorenzo Creel, Supt. Nevada Agency and Nevada Indian School, letter to Comm. Ind. Aff., 16 Jan. 1909, pp. 2–3.

19. E. C. Watkins, report of inspection to Comm. Ind. Aff., 28 March 1877, p. 6.

20. James E. Jenkins, annual report of the Reno Indian Agency, 1923, pp. 12–13.

21. Endicott, report, pp. 11–12.

22. Ibid.

23. Hubert Hailman, letter to U.S. Prosecuting Atty., 7 Feb. 1914.

24. Jenkins, report, p. 15.

25. Ibid., p. 11.

26. Watkins, report, pp. 30–32.

27. James Nye, Gov. Nevada and *ex officio* Supt. Ind. Aff. for Nevada, letter to Sec. Int., 19 July 1861.

28. C. A. Bateman, letter to H. R. Clum, Comm. Ind. Aff., 30 Sept. 1871; reprinted in *ARCIA, 1871* (Washington, D.C.: USGPO, 1872), p. 560.

29. J. M. Lee, Spec. Agent for Nevada, letter to H. Douglas, Supt. Ind. Aff. for Nevada, 1 Sept. 1870; reprinted in *ARCIA, 1870* (Washington, D.C.: USGPO, 1870), p. 571.

30. George Balcom, Spec. Indian Agent for Nevada, letter to E. S. Parker, Comm. Ind. Aff., 8 April 1871.

31. C. A. Bateman, letter to Edward Smith, Comm. Ind. Aff., 31 Aug. 1874.

32. Lorenzo D. Creel, Special Supervisor, letter to H. G. Wilson, Supervisor in Charge of the Reno Indian Agency, 26 Jan. 1922.

33. C. R. Trowbridge, report to Sec. Int., 13 Sept. 1921.

34. Untitled information page accompanying Map of Areas Irrigated in 1920, Pyramid Lake Project, April 1920, BIA, Irrig. Div.

35. Pyramid Lake irrig. crop report, various years, esp. 1945, 1955, 1963.

36. Irrig. Dist. Two, Pyramid Lake Reservation, Nev., annual report for fiscal year 1929, pp. 141–142.

37. Frank E. Armstrong, report of inspection to Sec. Int., 23 May 1889.

38. Watkins, report, p. 6.

39. Irrig. Dist. Two, annual report, 1929, p. 142.

40. C. A. Bateman, letter to Comm. Ind. Aff., 30 Sept. 1873. Reprinted in *ARCIA, 1873* (Washington, D.C.: USGPO, 1874), pp. 254–255.

41. Irrig. Dist. Two, annual report, 1928, p. 133.

42. Ibid. for 1930, p. 130.

43. Joseph McMaster, letter to Comm. Ind. Aff., 11 Aug. 1883; reprinted in *ARCIA, 1883* (Washington, D.C.: USGPO, 1883), p. 111.

44. James W. Nye, letter to Caleb B. Smith, Sec. Int., 14 Aug. 1861.

45. Jacob T. Lockhart, letter to William P. Dole, Comm. Ind. Aff., 25 June 1863.

46. C. A. Bateman, letter to Edward P. Smith, Comm. Ind. Aff., 8 March 1875.

47. Walter C. Van Emon, letter to C. H. Asbury, Special Ind. Agent for Nevada, 14 Feb. 1913.

48. J. E. Jenkins, letter to H. W. Philipson, 10 Jan. 1923.

49. Elizabeth P. Peabody, *Sarah Winnemucca's Practical Solution of the Indian Problem* (Cambridge, Mass.: John Wilson and Sons, 1886), p. 8.

50. Frederic Snyder, letter to John T. Reid, 30 Jan. 1930. NHS.

51. C. C. Warner, letter to Comm. Ind. Aff., 17 Aug. 1891; reprinted in *ARCIA, 1891* (Washington, D.C.: USGPO, 1891), p. 298.

52. J. D. Oliver, narrative annual report, 29 July 1914, p. 1.

53. Hopkins, *Life,* p. 88; Inter-Tribal Council of Nevada, *Life Stories of Our Native People—Shoshone, Paiute, Washo* (Provo: Univ. Utah Printing Service, 1974), p. 27.

54. "Indian Feels Like Horses Over Rations," *Nevada State Journal,* 9 May 1929.

55. Frederic Snyder, letter to John T. Reid, 16 Sept. 1930. NHS.

56. Hopkins, *Life,* p. 221.

57. Bateman, letter to Edward Smith, 8 March 1875.

58. Hopkins, *Life,* pp. 105–248.

59. Franklin Campbell, letter to H. G. Parker, Supt. Ind. Aff. for Nevada, 1 July 1867.

60. Eugene M. Hattori, "Northern Paiutes on the Comstock: Archaeology and Ethnohistory of an American Indian Population in Virginia City, Nevada," Nevada State Museum *Occasional Papers* no. 2, 1975.

61. Peabody, *Sarah Winnemucca's Solution*, p. 21.

62. Nevada Supt., narrative report to the Comm. Ind. Aff., 1919, sections 2–4.

63. J. E. Jenkins, annual report of the Reno Agency, 1923, narrative section, p. 18.

64. Elmer R. Rusco, "The Status of Indians in Nevada Law," in Ruth M. Houghton, ed., *Native American Politics: Power Relationships in the Western Great Basin Today* (Reno: Bur. Govt. Research, Univ. Nevada, 1973), pp. 59–87.

65. Jesse M. Lee, letter to Henry Douglas, Supt. Ind. Aff. for Nevada, 18 Dec. 1869, pp. 26, 33.

66. J. M. McMaster, letter to Comm. Ind. Aff., 7 Feb. 1882.

67. Henry Douglas, letter to E. S. Parker, Comm. Ind. Aff., 20 Sept. 1870.

68. Joseph G. Jorgensen, *The Sun Dance Religion: Power for the Powerless* (Chicago: Univ. Chicago Press, 1972); David F. Aberle, *The Peyote Religion Among the Navajo*, Viking Fund Pub. in Anthro. no. 42 (NY: Wenner-Gren Foundation, 1966; reprint ed., Chicago: Aldine, 1967); Grace Dangberg, "Wovoka," *Nevada Historical Soc. Quarterly* 11 (1968): 1–53.

69. James Mooney, *The Ghost-Dance Religion and Wounded Knee*, Bureau Amer. Ethnol., Smithsonian Inst., 14th *Annual Report*, part 2, 1892–93 (Washington, D.C.: USGPO, 1896; reprint ed., NY: Dover, 1973), p. 784.

70. C. C. Warner, letter to James Mooney, 12 Oct. 1891, reprinted in Mooney, *Ghost-Dance Religion*, p. 767, n. 1.

71. T. M. McCormick, letter to Sec. Int., 26 May 1894.

72. Mooney, *Ghost-Dance Religion*, p. 1054.

CHAPTER FIVE: LITANY FOR REDUCTION AND ABANDONMENT

1. Frederick Dodge, letter to A. B. Greenwood, Comm. Ind. Aff., 25 Nov. 1859.

2. T. T. Dwight, letter to Comm. Ind. Aff., 9 Jan. 1867.

3. Lander, letter to Greenwood, 31 Oct. 1860.

4. James Nye, letter to Sec. Int., 27 Oct. 1863; reprinted in *ARCIA, 1863* (Washington, D.C.: USGPO, 1863), p. 537.

5. Jacob T. Lockhart, letter to William P. Dole, Comm. Ind. Aff., 25 June 1863.

6. H. G. Parker, letter to D. N. Cooley, Comm. Ind. Aff., 10 Sept. 1866.

7. H. G. Parker, letter to D. N. Cooley, 10 Sept. 1866.

8. *ARCIA, 1866* (Washington, D.C.: USGPO, 1866), p. 30.

9. N. G. Taylor, letter to O. H. Browning, Sec. Int., 30 June 1868.

10. Henry Douglas, letter to E. S. Parker, Comm. Ind. Aff., 20 Sept. 1870.

11. Charles C. Royce, *Indian Land Cessions in the United States,* Bureau Amer. Ethnol., Smithsonian Inst., 18th *Annual Report,* part 2, (Washington, D.C.: USGPO, 1900; reprint ed., NY: Arno Press, 1971), p. 833.

12. T. T. Dwight, letter to Comm. Ind. Aff., 9 Jan. 1867.

13. Henry Douglas, letter to E. S. Parker, 17 Jan. 1870; emphases in original.

14. Henry Douglas, letter to E. S. Parker, 5 April 1870.

15. Ibid.; emphases in original.

16. Douglas, letter to Parker, 17 Jan. 1870; emphases in original.

17. C. A. Bateman, letter to Edward P. Smith, Comm. Ind. Aff., 30 Sept. 1873; reprinted in *ARCIA, 1873* (Washington, D.C.: USGPO, 1873), p. 255.

18. J. W. Powell and G. W. Ingalls, report to Comm. Ind. Aff., 18 June 1873; reprinted in Don D. Fowler and Catherine S. Fowler, eds., *Anthropology of the Numa: John Wesley Powell's Manuscripts on the Numic Peoples of Western North America, 1868–1880,* Smithsonian Contribs. Anthro. no. 14 (Washington, D.C.: USGPO, 1971), p. 115.

19. William Vandever, letter to Comm. Ind. Aff., 8 June 1875.

20. E. C. Watkins, report of inspection to Comm. Ind. Aff., 28 March 1877, p. 13.

21. Franklin Campbell, letter to J. P. Jones, 12 Feb. 1879.

22. Nevada State Senate and Assembly, Joint Memorial and Resolution Relative to Pyramid Lake Reservation in the State of Nevada, 29 Jan. 1877; reprinted in *Session Laws of American States and Territories—Statutes of the Nevada Legislature* (Westport, Conn.: Redgrave Info. Resources, 1973), microfiche ed.

23. 12 Stat. 489, Amend. 13 Stat. 356.

24. C. A. Bateman, letter to Edward P. Smith, 8 Nov. 1873.

25. Ibid.

26. J. D. Bevier, letter to C. Delano, Sec. Int., 18 Nov. 1873.

27. B. B. Redding, Land Agent for Central Pacific Railroad Co., letter to C. A. Bateman, 20 Feb. 1875.

28. A. C. Barstow, Board of Ind. Commissioners, letter to Edward P. Smith, 19 Oct. 1875.

29. William Vandever, letter to Comm. Ind. Aff., 11 June 1875.

30. C. A. Bateman, telegram to Edward P. Smith, 8 Feb. 1875.

31. Ezra A. Hays, letter to Sec. Int., 22 March 1878.

32. C. A. Bateman, letter to Edward Smith, 30 Sept. 1873, p. 255.

CHAPTER SIX: GRAZING TRESPASS

1. Frederick Dodge, public notice, Aug. 1860.

2. 4 Stat. 729.

3. James W. Nye, letter to William P. Dole, Comm. Ind. Aff., 16 Sept. 1862.

4. Ibid.

5. J. M. Edmund, Comm. Genl. Land Office, letter to D. N. Cooley, Comm. Ind. Aff., 12 March 1866.

6. Henry Douglas, letter to E. S. Parker, Comm. Ind. Aff., 31 May 1870.

7. Jesse M. Lee, letter to Henry Douglas, 1 Sept. 1870.

8. C. A. Bateman, letter to Edward P. Smith, Comm. Ind. Aff., 31 May 1873.

9. Ibid., 31 Aug. 1874.

10. William Vandever, letter to Comm. Ind. Aff., 8 June 1875.

11. A. J. Barnes, letter to E. A. Hayt, Comm. Ind. Aff., 15 Jan. 1878.

12. E. A. Hayt, letter to Sec. Int., 22 March 1878.

13. George R. Pearsons, report of inspection to Sec. Int., 9 March 1886, p. 5.

14. H. D. Gibson, Pyramid Lake Agent, letter to H. Price, Acting Comm. Ind. Aff., 20 Dec. 1884.

15. Pearsons, report, 9 March 1886, p. 5.

16. U.S. Cong., Senate, *Survey of Conditions of the Indians in the United States: Part 28: Nevada,* 72nd Cong., 1st sess. (Washington, D.C.: USGPO, 1934), p. 15068.

17. James E. Spencer, letter to E. A. Hayt, 29 Jan. 1880.

18. "Piutes at Home," *Reno Weekly Gazette,* 12 Aug. 1880.

19. Carl Schurz, letter to R. E. Trowbridge, Comm. Ind. Aff., 8 Aug. 1880.

20. Ibid.

21. James W. Nye, letter to Sec. Int., 19 July 1861.

22. Warren Wasson, Carson Indian Agent, letter to James W. Nye, 20 April 1862.

23. Lalla Scott, *Karnee: A Paiute Narrative,* ed. Robert F. Heizer (Reno: Univ. Nevada Press, 1966; reprint ed., Greenwich, Conn.: Fawcett, 1973), pp. 32–33, n. 29, and pp. 133–134.

24. Ira Eaton, letter to F. W. Lander, 31 Oct. 1860.

25. Frederick Dodge, letter to Jacob Forney, Supt. Ind. Aff. for Utah Terr., 4 Jan. 1859.

26. James W. Nye, letter to William P. Dole, 3 Feb. 1862.

27. Frank Campbell, letter to Comm. Ind. Aff., 9 June 1865.

28. Nye, letter to Dole, 3 Feb. 1862.

29. Jesse M. Lee, Special Agent for Nevada, letter to Henry Douglas, 18 Dec. 1869.

30. Henry Douglas, letter to E. S. Parker, Comm. Ind. Aff., 30 Nov. 1870.

31. Felix S. Cohen, *Handbook of Federal Indian Law* (Washington, D.C.: USGPO, 1942; reprint ed., Albuquerque: Univ. New Mexico Press, 1971), pp. 325–332.

32. J. A. Barnes, letter to E. A. Hayt, 28 Jan. 1878.

33. W. M. Garvey, letter to Comm. Ind. Aff., 16 Aug. 1879; reprinted in *ARCIA, 1879* (Washington, D.C.: USGPO, 1879), p. 109.

34. Pearsons, report, 9 March 1886, p. 5.

35. William Armstrong, letter and report to Sec. Int., 23 May 1889, pp. 2–3.

36. U.S. Cong., House, *Agreement entered into between the Indians of Pyramid Lake Reservation and the Commission Appointed under the Provisions of the Act of March 3, 1891*, Ex. Doc. 71, 52nd Cong., 1st sess. (Washington, D.C.: USGPO, 1892), p. 8.

37. D. McCormick, letter to Sec. Int., 26 May 1896.

38. Supt. Nevada Ind. School, annual report to Comm. Ind. Aff., 1913, p. 10.

39. C. H. Asbury, Special Agent at Reno, report of inspection to Comm. Ind. Aff., 23 Feb. 1915, pp. 17 and 20; L. A. Dorrington, report of inspection to Comm. Ind. Aff., 15 March 1916, p. 18; E. B. Linner, report on diversion dams and irrigation, to Com. Ind. Aff., 29 March 1921, p. 9; Senate, *Survey,* p. 15057.

40. This issue has become critical recently in BIA relations with many tribes. Several groups have demanded the right to negotiate their own leases after massive disclosures of submarket royalties in BIA-arranged leases. See "Navajos Demand Larger Share of Energy Wealth: Days of Passive Acceptance Gone," *Denver Post,* 17 Oct.

1977, p. 13; "No More Ripoffs: Crow Tribe Looks to Coal Bonanza," *Denver Post*, 6 Feb. 1978, p. 2.

41. Lorenzo Creel, Special Supervisor, Reno Agency, letter to L. A. Dorrington, Special Ind. Agent in Charge, Reno, 11 March 1919.

42. Washington J. Endicott, report of inspection to Cato Sells, Comm. Ind. Aff., 3 Sept. 1920, p. 40.

43. C. A. Bateman, letter to F. A. Walker, Comm. Ind. Aff., 30 Sept. 1872; reprinted in *ARCIA, 1872* (Washington, D.C.: USGPO, 1872), p. 286.

44. House, *Agreement.*

45. I. J. Wooten, Pyramid Lake Agent, letter to Comm. Ind. Aff., 23 Aug. 1895; and letter to Comm. Ind. Aff., 28 Sept. 1896, reprinted in *ARCIA, 1897* (Washington, D.C.: USGPO, 1897), p. 206.

46. C. H. Asbury, report of inspection to Comm. Ind. Aff., 23 Feb. 1915, p. 14.

47. L. A. Dorrington, report of inspection to Comm. Ind. Aff., 15 March 1916, p. 16.

48. Senate, *Survey,* p. 15055.

49. PLTC, minutes, 15 Jan. 1938. UNR.

50. James W. Johnson, U.S. Atty. at Reno, letter to Arthur B. Heller, settler on Flanagan claim, 2 Dec. 1953.

CHAPTER SEVEN: FISHING TRESPASS

1. 27 F. 2d 16413

2. Asst. Area Dir., memo re problem of water of Pyramid Lake, to the BIA Area Dir., Phoenix Area Office, 17 Dec. 1970.

3. Jesse M. Lee, Special Ind. Agent for Nevada, letter to Henry Douglas, Supt. Ind. Aff. for Nevada, 18 Dec. 1869, pp. 24, 26.

4. Ibid., p. 26.

5. Aaron B. Jerome, 1st. Lt., 8th Cavalry, Fort McDermitt, letter to H. G. Brown, Asst. Adjt. General, Hdqtrs. Dept. of Calif., 5 Aug. 1868; War Dept. Commands, Dept. of Calif.—695-2-P-1868.

6. Jesse Lee, final report, to E. S. Parker, Comm. Ind. Aff., 8 March 1871.

7. Henry Douglas, letter to E. S. Parker, 20 Sept. 1870.

8. Jesse Lee, letter to Henry Douglas, 1 Sept. 1870; reprinted in *ARCIA, 1870* (Washington, D.C.: USGPO, 1870), p. 574.

9. Douglas, letter to E. S. Parker, 20 Sept. 1870.

10. H. G. Parker, Supt. Ind. Aff. for Nevada, letter to D. Cooley, Comm. Ind. Aff., 23 Oct. 1865.

11. A. J. Barnes, letter to Comm. Ind. Aff., 24 Sept. 1877.

12. Ibid.; emphasis in the original.

13. A. J. Barnes, telegram to Comm. Ind. Aff., 19 Dec. 1877.

14. A. J. Barnes, letter to E. A. Hayt, Comm. Ind. Aff., 15 Jan. 1878.

15. Ibid.

16. E. A. Hayt, letter to Sec. Int., 22 March 1878.

17. Poster advertising employment for fishermen on Pyramid Lake, enclosure in A. J. Barnes letter to Comm. Ind. Aff., 2 Nov. 1878.

18. "Expelling the Fishermen," *Nevada State Journal*, 21 Jan. 1879.

19. Jesse M. Lee, final report to E. S. Parker, 8 March 1871, p. 10.

20. "War on the Fishermen," *Nevada State Journal*, 19 Jan. 1879.

21. "The Pyramid Lake Reservation," *Territorial Enterprise*, 30 Jan. 1879.

22. "The Pyramid Trouble," *Reno Weekly Gazette*, 30 Jan. 1879.

23. "The Pyramid Fishermen," *Nevada State Journal*, 20 Feb. 1879.

24. "The Pyramid Trouble."

25. "The Pyramid Fishermen."

26. "The Fishery Trouble," *Nevada State Journal*, 23 Jan. 1879.

27. "War on the Fishermen."

28. James N. Ely, letter to E. A. Hayt, 9 June 1879.

29. James E. Spencer, letter to E. A. Hayt, 21 Nov. 1879.

30. James E. Spencer, letter to R. E. Trowbridge, Comm. Ind. Aff., 6 Oct. 1880, pp. 4–5; emphasis in the original.

31. "The Reservation Fishermen," *Reno Weekly Gazette,* 10 July 1879.

32. Spencer, letter to Trowbridge, 6 Oct. 1880, p. 2.

33. Ibid.

34. Ibid., pp. 7–8.

35. J. M. McMaster, Supervisor of the Nevada Indian Agency, letter to Comm. Ind. Aff., 31 Aug. 1881; reprinted in *ARCIA, 1881* (Washington, D.C.: USGPO, 1881).

36. Sec. of War, letter to Sec. Int., 10 Sept. 1884.

37. William Vandever, report of inspection to Comm. Ind. Aff., 8 June 1875, p. 2.

38. C. A. Bateman, letter to Edward P. Smith, Comm. Ind. Aff., 14 Jan. 1875, p. 3.

39. Sen. William Stewart, letter to A. B. Upshaw, Acting Comm. Ind. Aff., 21 July 1888.

40. W. D. C. Gibson, letter to D. G. Atkins, Comm. Ind. Aff., 8 March 1888, pp. 10–11.

41. T. M. McCormick, report of inspection to Sec. Int., 26 May 1894, p. 5.

42. H. D. Huntington, 1st Lt., 2nd Calvary, letter to Post Adjt., Fort Bidwell, Calif., 20 Aug. 1884.

43. Statement of the Piute Indian tribe residing in the Pyramid Lake Indian Reservation, 1 Feb. 1913, BIA letters received, 27088–1913–Nevada–056.

44. "Indians in War Paint at Pyramid Lake," *Carson City News,* 15 June 1915.

45. J. D. Oliver, letter to J. M. Gale, private citizen of Reno, 26 Dec. 1917.

46. Washington J. Endicott, report of inspection to Cato Sells, Comm. Ind. Aff., 3 Sept. 1920, pp. 27–29.

47. James E. Jenkins, letter to H. W. Philipson, Farmer in Charge, 16 May 1924.

48. U.S. Cong., House, Comm. on Ind. Aff., *Hearings to Investigate the BIA: Part 3: Hearings in the Field*, 78th Cong., 2nd sess. (Washington, D.C.: USGPO, 1945), p. 1167; see also U.S. Cong., Senate, Subcomm. Ind. Aff., *Survey of Conditions of the Indians in the United States: Part 28: Nevada*, 72nd Cong., 1st sess. (Washington, D.C.: USGPO, 1934), p. 15069.

CHAPTER EIGHT: LAND TRESPASS

1. F. Dodge, Ind. Agent for the Carson Valley, Utah Terr., letter to Jacob Forney, Supt. Ind. Aff. for Utah Terr., 4 Jan. 1859.

2. F. Dodge, letter to A. B. Greenwood, Comm. Ind. Aff., 23 June 1860.

3. F. Dodge, letter to A. B. Greenwood, 9 Aug. 1860.

4. H. Douglas, Supt. Ind. Aff. for Nevada, letter to E. S. Parker, Comm. Ind. Aff., 31 May 1870; J. D. Bevier, inspector, letter to C. S. Delano, Sec. Int., 18 Nov. 1873.

5. Lt. J. M. Lee, Special Agent, letter to Henry Douglas, 20 Dec. 1869.

6. E. L. Hiekman, citizen, letter to Gov. H. G. Blasdel, October 1867. NHS.

7. Ibid.

8. F. Campbell, Ind. Agent at Walker River, letter to Comm. Ind. Aff., 30 Aug. 1868; reprinted in *ARCIA, 1868* (Washington, D.C.: USGPO, 1868), p. 145.

9. Hiekman, letter to Blasdel, October 1867.

10. Lee, letter to Douglas, 20 Dec. 1869.

11. PLTC, minutes, 23 May 1937. UNR.

12. U.S. Cong., House, *An Agreement Entered Into Between the Indians of the Pyramid Lake Reservation and the Commission Appointed under the Provisions of the Act of March 3, 1891*, Ex. Doc. 71, 52nd Cong., 1st sess. (Washington, D.C.: USGPO, 1892), p. 5.

13. 4 Stat. 729, sect. 10.

14. D. N. Cooley, Comm. Ind. Aff., *ARCIA, 1866* (Washington, D.C.: USGPO, 1866), p. 30.

15. J. M. Lee, letter to Henry Douglas, 18 Dec. 1869.

16. J. M. Lee, letter to Henry Douglas, 14 March 1870.

17. Henry Douglas, letter to E. S. Parker, 16 Feb. 1870.

18. C. A. Bateman, Ind. Agent for Pyramid Lake, letter to E. P. Smith, Comm. Ind. Aff., 31 May 1873.

19. S. F. O'Fallon, inspector, report to Sec. Int., 19 Jan. 1910, p. 17.

20. C. A. Bateman, telegram to E. P. Smith, 8 Feb. 1875.

21. C. A. Bateman, letter to E. P. Smith, 8 March 1875.

22. E. A. Hayt, Comm. Ind. Aff., letters to Sec. Int., 22 and 26 March 1878.

23. James E. Spencer, Ind. Agent at Pyramid Lake, letter to E. A. Hayt, 21 Nov. 1879; emphasis in the original.

24. J. W. Whitehead, squatter at Pyramid Lake, letter to Comm. Ind. Aff., 11 Feb. 1880.

25. "Trouble at Pyramid Lake," *Reno Weekly Gazette,* 5 Feb. 1880.

26. James E. Spencer, letter to R. E. Trowbridge, Comm. Ind. Aff., 14 June 1880.

27. Ibid.

28. Joseph McMasters, Ind. Agent, letter to Comm. Ind. Aff., 15 Aug. 1884; reprinted in *ARCIA, 1884* (Washington, D.C.: USGPO, 1884), pp. 126–127.

29. S. S. Sears, Ind. Agent, letter to Comm. Ind. Aff., 27 Aug. 1890; reprinted in *ARCIA, 1890* (Washington, D.C.: USGPO, 1890), p. 147.

30. 26 Stat. 1009.

31. House, *Agreement,* p. 21.

32. Ibid., p. 11.

33. Ibid., p. 7.

34. Ibid., p. 14.

35. Ibid., p. 6.

36. Ibid., p. 11.

37. Ibid., p. 16.

38. Sen. William M. Stewart, letter to William Webster, atty. in Reno, 16 Feb. 1892. NHS.

39. S. 3, 54th Cong., 1st sess., 1895.

40. I. J. Wooten, Ind. Agent at Pyramid Lake, letter to Comm. Ind. Aff., 11 Feb. 1896; emphasis in the original.

41. Albert K. Smiley, "Report of June 27, 1895," in *Twenty-Seventh Annual Report of the Board of Indian Commissioners, 1895* (Washington, D.C.: USGPO, 1895), p. 15.

42. Ibid., p. 16.

43. Dave Numana, Pyramid Lake Paiute, letter to Comm. Ind. Aff., 19 June 1905.

44. Indian Appropriation Act of 24 June 1904, sect. 26.

45. Fred B. Spriggs, Supt. Nevada Ind. Agency, letter to Comm. Ind. Aff., 18 Sept. 1905; reprinted in *ARCIA, 1905* (Washington, D.C.: USGPO, 1905), p. 257.

46. S. F. O'Fallon, inspector, report to Sec. Int., 19 Jan. 1910, pp. 27–28.

47. W. H. Code, Chief Engineer, Ind. Irrigation Service, letter to Sec. Int., 12 Oct. 1910.

48. Statement of the Piute Indian Tribe of Indians Residing in Pyramid Lake Reservation (unsigned), 1 Feb. 1913; in the "Letters Received" correspondence of Comm. Ind. Aff.

49. Frank Pierce, Acting Sec. Int., letter to Atty. Gen., 28 Aug. 1909.

50. C. H. Ashbury, Special Agent at Reno, report of inspection to Comm. Ind. Aff., 23 Feb. 1915, p. 37.

51. William Woodburn, U.S. Dist. Atty. at Reno, letter to L. A. Dorrington, Special Ind. Agent at Reno, 31 May 1917.

52. Dorrington, letter to Cato Sells, Comm. Ind. Aff., 31 May 1917.

53. U.S. Cong., Senate, *Report on S. 225, Bill for the Relief of Settlers and Townsite Occupants of Certain Lands in the Pyramid Lake Indian Reservation,* Report no. 301, 67th Cong., 1st sess. (Washington, D.C.: USGPO, 1921), p. 4.

54. Ibid., p. 3.

55. Ibid.

56. Reno Agency, narrative report for 1922, p. 20.

57. Washington J. Endicott, report of inspection to Cato Sells, Comm. Ind. Aff., 3 Sept. 1920, pp. 41–42.

CHAPTER NINE: SQUATTERS AND THEIR FRIENDS IN THE SENATE

1. William C. Darrah, *Powell of the Colorado* (Princeton, N.J.: Princeton Univ. Press, 1951), p. 336.

2. Sen. William M. Stewart, letter to J. W. Ross, Board of Trade, 6 July 1887. NHS.

3. William Stewart, letter to H. M. Yerington, citizen, 7 April 1892. NHS.

4. Ibid.

5. "To secure the relinquishment of the Indian title to a portion of the Pyramid Lake Indian Reservation in said state and for other purposes." This began as Senate bill 1749, 52nd Cong., 2nd sess., and reappeared as S. 3, 54th Cong., 1st sess.; HR. 7579, 54th Cong., 1st sess.; and S. 2873, 55th Cong., 2nd sess.

6. William Stewart, letter to Allen C. Bragg, newspaper editor, 16 Dec. 1891. NHS.

7. "Pyramid Trout," *Wadsworth Dispatch,* 12 Oct. 1892.

8. W. A. Jones, Comm. Ind. Aff., letter to Sec. Int., 6 Jan. 1898.

9. Albert K. Smiley, Board of Indian Commissioners, letter to E. Whittlesey, Sec. Board of Indian Commissioners, to be forwarded to Sec. Int., 1 May 1895.

10. I. J. Wooton, Nevada Agency, letter to Comm. Ind. Aff., 11 Feb. 1896.

11. Jones, letter to Sec. Int., 6 Jan. 1898.

12. T. M. McCormick, Inspector, report to Comm. Ind. Aff., 26 May 1894.

13. 30 Stat. 571, 594.

14. J. H. Frimple, Asst. Comm. Gen. Land Office, letter to Comm. Ind. Aff., 27 April 1903.

15. U.S. Cong., Senate, *Report on S. 225, a Bill for the Relief of Settlers and Townsite Occupants of Certain Lands in the Pyramid Lake Indian Reservation, Nevada,* Report no. 301, 67th Cong., 1st sess. (Washington, D.C.: USGPO, 1921), p. 5; L. A. Dorrington, Special Agent, report of inspection of the Nevada Agency and School, to Comm. Ind. Aff., 15 March 1916, p. 13.

16. S. F. O'Fallon, Inspector, report of inspection of the Nevada Agency re trespassers at Pyramid Lake, to Comm. Ind. Aff., 19 Jan. 1910.

17. Washington J. Endicott, Inspector, report of inspection to Cato Sells, Comm. Ind. Aff., 3 Sept. 1920, p. 43.

18. Ibid., pp. 19–20.

19. Senate, *Report on S. 225,* p. 2.

20. Endicott, report, pp. 41, 42.

21. L. A. Dorrington, letter to Cato Sells, 31 May 1917.

22. L. A. Dorrington, letters to Comm. Ind. Aff., 2 July and 8 Nov. 1917.

23. Senate, *Report on S. 225.*

24. C. R. Trowbridge, Inspector, report on settlers on Pyramid Lake Indian Reservation, Nevada, to Albert B. Fall, Sec. Int., 6 Sept. 1921, p. 18.

25. Ibid., p. 36.

26. Ibid., p. 67.

27. Ibid., p. 15.

28. Senate, *Report on S. 225,* pp. 3 –4.

29. Trowbridge, report, pp. 40 –41.

30. Lorenzo D. Creel, Special Indian Agent, letter to James E. Jenkins, Supt. Nevada Agency, 22 May 1922.

31. U.S. Cong., Senate, *Report on S. 1309, a Bill for the Relief of Settlers and Townsite Occupants of Certain Lands in the Pyramid Lake Indian Reservation, Nevada,* Report no. 341, 68th Cong., 1st sess. (Washington, D.C.: USGPO, 1924).

32. Douglas Clark, Asst. Land Field Agent, report on Wadsworth townsite, to Fred Baker, Land Field Agent, BIA, 3 March 1938.

33. U.S. General Land Office, Dept. Interior, unsigned office memorandum, file code "K" MMJ, 1930. Copy in General Land Office files, National Archives, Washington, D.C.

34. Comm. Ind. Aff., memorandum to Sec. Int., 19 Dec. 1929, pp. 39, 40.

35. U.S. General Land Office, memorandum.

CHAPTER TEN: NEW CHALLENGES, NEW STRENGTHS

1. Charles H. Burke, Comm. Ind. Aff., letter to William M. Kearney, atty., 13 May 1929.

2. Nevada Indian School, annual report to Comm. Ind. Aff., 1913, p. 16.

3. James E. Jenkins, Supt. Nevada Agency, letter to Henry W. Philipson, Farmer-in-Charge, Pyramid Lake Agency, 23 Jan. 1923.

4. Washington J. Endicott, report of inspection to Cato Sells, Comm. Ind. Aff., 3 Sept. 1920, p. 13.

5. Lorenzo D. Creel, Special Supt., letter to James E. Jenkins, 11 July 1922.

6. Dave Gibson, Paiute, letter to Comm. Ind. Aff., enclosed in John T. Reid, citizen, letter to Sen. Tasker L. Oddie, 8 Feb. 1932. NHS.

7. U.S. Cong., Senate, Committee on Indian Affairs, *Survey of Conditions of the Indians in the United States, Hearings: Part 28:*

Nevada, 72nd Cong., 1st sess. (Washington, D.C.: USGPO, 1934), p. 15084.

8. 48 Stat. 984; 25 U.S.C. 461.

9. Felix S. Cohen, *Handbook of Federal Indian Law* (Washington, D.C.: USGPO, 1942; reprint ed., Albuquerque: Univ. New Mexico Press, 1971), p. 129.

10. Faun Mortara, "Political Resources Available through the Wheeler-Howard Act: A Case Study," in Ruth Houghton, ed., *Native American Politics: Power Relationships in the Western Great Basin Today* (Reno: Bureau of Govt. Research, Univ. Nevada, 1973), p. 57.

11. PLTC, minutes, 8 March 1939, 22 Jan. 1940, and 28 Nov. 1947. UNR.

12. Alida Bowler, Supt., letter to Comm. Ind. Aff., 23 April 1935.

13. PLTC, minutes, 18 Feb. 1936. UNR.

14. For example, PLTC, minutes, 4 Oct. 1946. UNR.

15. 48 Stat. 985, sect. 16.

16. 60 Stat. 1049.

17. James E. Curry, Atty., letter to Albert Aleck, Chairman, PLTC, 3 Oct. 1950. UNR.

18. Dillon S. Myer, Comm. Ind. Aff., statement on proposed attorney contract regulations, February 1951, pp. 3, 8; emphasis in the original. BIAR.

19. James Curry, memorandum to PLTC, 14 March 1951. UNR.

20. James Curry, letter to Dillon Myer, 27 Feb. 1951.

21. John Collier, news release, 28 Feb. 1951.

22. "Attorney Answers Attack Levelled by Indian Bureau," *Reno Evening Gazette,* 25 Oct. 1950.

23. PLTC, memorandum, 23 Oct. 1951. UNR.

24. Myer, statement, p. 9.

25. U.S. Cong., Senate, Committee on Interior and Insular Affairs, *Attorney Contracts with Indian Tribes,* Report no. 8, 83rd Cong., 1st sess. (Washington, D.C.: USGPO, 1953).

26. E. Reeseman Fryer, Supt., letter to Avery Winnemucca, Chairman, PLTC, 5 Oct. 1950.

27. 48 Stat. 984.

28. Douglas Clark, Asst. Land Field Agent, report on Wadsworth townsite to Fred Baker, Land Field Agent, Field Service, BIA, 3 March 1938. BIAR.

29. PLTC, minutes, 10 March 1948. UNR.

30. Alida Bowler, letter to John Collier, 15 April 1938.

31. PLTC, minutes, 24 March 1948. UNR.

32. PLTC, minutes, 2 May 1958. UNR.

33. PLTC, letter to John Collier, 26 July 1934. Carbon copy in UNR.

34. PLTC, minutes, 29 Nov. 1936. UNR.

35. Nevada State Legislature, resolution to the Congress of the U.S. favoring passage of S. 840, 1937. In the National Archives, Records of the U.S. Senate, Committee on Interior and Insular Affairs, 83rd Cong., relating to Nevada, "Pyramid Lake" folder.

36. PLTC, minutes, 17 Dec. 1936. UNR.

37. PLTC, minutes, 26 Jan. 1937. UNR.

38. PLTC, minutes, 15 Jan. 1938. UNR.

39. 48 Stat. 985.

40. Alida Bowler, letter to John Collier, Comm. Ind. Aff., 15 April 1939; emphasis in the original.

41. PLTC, letter to Franklin D. Roosevelt, President of the United States, 21 March 1938. Copy in UNR.

42. Lawrence Williams, Chairman, PLTC, letter to William Boyle, U.S. Atty. at Reno, enclosing tribal council resolution, 3 Dec. 1938.

43. U.S. Cong., Senate, Committee on Indian Affairs, *Authorizing Patents Issued to Settlers, Pyramid Lake Indian Reservation, Nevada, Hearings,* 75th Cong., 1st sess. (Washington, D.C.: USGPO, 1937), p. 50.

44. PLTC, minutes, 5 Dec. 1939. UNR.

45. U.S. v. Garaventa Land and Livestock Company et al., 38 F. Supp. 191; 129 Fed. 2d 416.

46. U.S. v. Depaoli et ux., 139 Fed. 2d 225.

47. John Collier, letter to PLTC, 14 April 1944.

48. Oscar L. Chapman, Asst. Sec. Int., letter to the Atty. Genl., 3 Jan. 1944.

49. PLTC, minutes, 21 April 1944, 20 Sept. 1946, and 28 Nov. 1947. UNR.

50. E. Reeseman Fryer, letter to M. P. Depaoli, 31 Dec. 1948.

51. PLTC, minutes, 23 Jan. 1948. UNR.

52. Ralph M. Gelvin, Supt. Carson Indian Agency, letter to Comm. Ind. Aff., 20 Oct. 1947.

53. Ted Haas, BIA Chief Counsel, letter to Ralph Gelvin, 24 Oct. 1947.

54. E. Reeseman Fryer, letter to Avery Winnemucca, Chairman, PLTC, 19 April 1949; PLTC, notes from meeting with Supt., 9 June 1949. UNR.

55. Avery Winnemucca, letter to E. P. Carville, tribal atty., 14 June 1949. Copy in UNR.

56. Ralph M. Gelvin, Genl. Supt., Colorado River Agency, letter to Albert Aleck, Sec., PLTC, 5 July 1949.

57. PLTC, minutes, 10 May 1950. UNR.

58. James E. Curry, letter to E. Reeseman Fryer, 3 Aug. 1949.

59. Mastin G. White, Solicitor Genl., Dept. Justice, letter to U.S. Atty. Genl., 10 May 1950.

60. James Curry, letter to Louis R. Bruce, 3 Oct. 1950. UNR.

61. Harold L. Ickes, "McCarran and the Paiute Indians," *Washington Post,* 13 Oct. 1950.

62. Patrick McCarran, letter to Peter C. Petersen, 22 July 1950, quoted in Mortara, "Political Resources," p. 56.

63. Quoted in John Collier, news release, 28 Feb. 1951.

64. PLTC, resolution, c. 31 March 1952. UNR.

65. Senate, *Authorizing*, p. 1.

66. Ibid., p. 6.

67. Cohen, *Handbook*, pp. 299–300. This was verified in the textbook case from McCarran's own district, U.S. v. Walker River Irrigation District [104 F. 2d 334; 11 F. Supp. 158; 14 F. Supp. 10 (1939)], and reconfirmed in the Alpine decision (see Chapter 11).

68. Senate, *Authorizing*, p. 10.

69. Quoted in A. J. Liebling, "The Lake of the Cui-ui Eaters: II," *New Yorker*, 8 Jan. 1955, p. 49.

70. Quoted in ibid.

71. Quoted in ibid.

72. Senate, *Authorizing*, p. 10.

73. Quoted in Liebling, "Lake: II," p. 46.

74. Senate, *Authorizing*, p. 12.

75. U.S. Cong., House, Committee on Indian Affairs, *Pyramid Lake Indian Reservation, Hearings on S. 24*, 78th Cong., 1st sess. (Washington, D.C.: USGPO, 1943), pp. 55–72.

76. Quoted in Liebling, "Lake: III," *New Yorker*, 15 Jan. 1955, p. 46.

77. Senate, *Authorizing*, pp. 68–74.

78. U.S. Cong., Senate, *Authorizing Patents Issued to Settlers, Pyramid Lake Indian Reservation, Nevada*, Report no. 5, Calendar no. 3, 76th Cong., 1st sess. (Washington, D.C.: USGPO, 1939).

79. PLTC, letter to Pres. Franklin D. Roosevelt, 21 March 1938. UNR.

80. Quoted in ibid.

81. PLTC files. UNR.

82. "Pyramid Paiutes Use Modern Weapons," *Nevada State Journal*, 24 March 1938.

83. Nevada Legislature, resolution, 1937.

84. House, *Pyramid Lake*, p. 24.

85. PLTC, minutes, 11 March and 29 April 1943. UNR.

86. Alida Bowler, letter to Avery Winnemucca, 2 Aug. 1949.

87. Curry, letter to Bruce, 3 Oct. 1950.

88. James Curry, letter to Alida Bowler, 23 Aug. 1949.

89. PLTC, minutes, 18 June 1948 and 4 Jan. 1963. UNR.

CHAPTER ELEVEN: THE RIVER AND THE LAKE

1. William H. Veeder, "Federal Encroachment on Indian Water Rights and the Impairment of Reservation Development," in U.S. Cong., Joint Econ. Committee, Subcommittee on Economy in Govt., *Toward Economic Development for Native American Communities,* 91st Cong., 1st sess. (Washington, D.C.: USGPO, 1969), pp. 479–482.

2. Quoted in Mary Ellen Glass, "Water for Nevada: The Reclamation Controversy, 1885–1902," Nevada *Studies in History and Pol. Sci.,* no. 7 (1964): 32.

3. John M. Townley, "Soil Saturation Problems in the Truckee–Carson Project, Nevada," *Agricultural History* 52 (1978): 280–291.

4. Merle Brown, "Climates of the States—Nevada," U.S. Dept. Commerce, Weather Bur., *Climatography of the United States* no. 60–26 (Washington, D.C.: USGPO, 1960); George Hardman and Cruz Venstrom, "A 100-Year Record of Truckee River Runoff Estimated from Changes in Levels and Volumes of Pyramid and Winnemucca Lakes," *Trans. Amer. Geophysical Union* 20 (1941): 71–90; S. T. Harding, "Recent Variation in the Water Supply of the Western Great Basin," Univ. Calif. Water Research Center Archives *Report* 16 (1965).

5. Quoted in "Report of the Proceedings of the Nevada State Irrigation Convention, Opera House, Carson City, Nevada, 9 October 1891" (Carson City: Nevada State Printing Office, 1891), p. 11.

6. Herbert I. Bennett, "The Truckee–Carson Irrigation Project," *Sci. Amer.* 46: 9 (September 1905): 216.

7. "Pyramid Lake Indian Reservation to be Opened," *Nevada State Journal,* 19 June 1907.

8. Lorenzo D. Creel, Special Supervisor, Reno Indian Agency, letter to H. G. Wilson, Supervisor-in-Charge, 28 Jan. 1922.

9. Lorenzo Creel, letter to Comm. Ind. Aff., 18 Jan. 1922. See also John M. Townley, "Truckee Basin Fishery, 1844–1944," Univ. Nevada Water Resources Center *Pub.* no. 43008 (1980): 66.

10. Creel, letter to Comm. Ind. Aff., 18 Jan. 1922.

11. Nevada State Fish Commission, *Biennial Report of the State Fish Commission, 1909–1910* (Carson City: State Printing Office, 1911), pp. 12–13.

12. C. A. Engle, Supervising Engineer, Ind. Irrig. Service, letter to Comm. Ind. Aff., 6 May 1924, p. 2.

13. Ibid., p. 3.

14. Ibid., p. 4.

15. Sen. Tasker L. Oddie, letter to the President, 23 July 1929.

16. William Zimmerman, Comm. Ind. Aff., letter to Sen. Patrick McCarran, 22 Sept. 1927.

17. E. B. Meritt, Comm. Ind. Aff., letter to A. P. Davis, Dir., USRS, 6 May 1922.

18. John F. Richardson, Mgr., Newlands Project, memo to Dir., USRS, 23 May 1923.

19. C. A. Engle, Report on conditions affecting fish life in Pyramid Lake and Truckee River, 31 Jan. 1924, p. 4.

20. Engle, Report, p. 7.

21. Lorenzo D. Creel, letter to Comm. Ind. Aff., 27 May 1909.

22. L. A. Ballinger, Sec. Int., letter to Sec. Commerce and Labor, 25 Oct. 1919; Carson Indian Agency, narrative report, 1929; Chief, Admin. Div., letter to Dir. Irrig. Div., BIA, 13 March 1930.

23. M. J. Madsen, U.S. Bur. Fisheries, Preliminary Survey of Pyramid Lake, Nevada, 1935, p. 4.

24. F. J. Sumner, Investigation of the present status of the Pyramid Lake Fishery, Nevada, 30 June 1938, p. 40.

25. Alida C. Bowler, letter to Comm. Ind. Aff., 24 June 1936.

26. Project Engineer, Newlands Project, letter to Dir., USRS, 28 July 1908.

27. James E. Jenkins, Supt., Reno Indian Agency, narrative report, 1923, p. 21.

28. D. W. Cole, Project Mgr., Newlands Project, Report on water supply for Pyramid Lake Indians, 31 Oct. 1910, pp. 2–3. In the collections of Bur. Reclamation files, U.S. Nat. Archives, Denver.

29. C. R. Trowbridge, Report on settlers on Pyramid Lake Indian Reservation, Nevada, to Albert B. Fall, Sec. Int., 6 Sept. 1921: appended affidavit from John F. Richardson, 6 Aug. 1921.

30. C. Coggesall, Supt. Reno Agency, letter to Comm. Ind. Aff., 31 Aug. 1921.

31. H. W. Philipson, Farmer-in-Charge, letter to Lorenzo Creel, 30 Aug. 1923.

32. Engle, Report, p. 19.

33. Charles Burke, Comm. Ind. Aff., letter to Elwood Mead, Comm. Reclamation, 1 Oct. 1925.

34. Charles Burke, letter to Frederic Snyder, Supt. Reno Agency, 1 Oct. 1925.

35. Supt. Carson Ind. School, letter to Comm. Ind. Aff., 15 Feb. 1926.

36. Jose A. Zuni, Supt., Nevada Ind. Agency, letter to John T. Artichoker, Phoenix Area Dir., BIA, 15 June 1972.

37. Dir., USRS, letter to Chief of Construction, 20 Aug. 1919. In Bur. Reclamation files, U.S. Nat. Archives, Denver.

38. Supt. Irrigation, annual report to W. M. Reed, Chief Engineer of the U.S. Ind. Irrig. Service, 1919, p. 12.

39. John F. Truesdell, Special Asst. to Atty. Genl., letter to Comm. Ind. Aff., 26 May 1919; emphasis added.

40. Ibid.

41. Lorenzo Creel, letter to Charles Burke, 18 Jan. 1922.

42. 207 U.S. 564 (1908). Therefore Indian water claims are not based on explicit legislation, but on judicial interpretation. For a more

thorough discussion, see Felix Cohen, *Handbook of Federal Indian Law* (Washington, D.C.: USGPO, 1942: reprint ed., Albuquerque: Univ. New Mexico Press, 1971), pp. 316–319; Monroe Price, *Law and the American Indian* (Indianapolis: Bobbs-Merrill, 1973), pp. 310–329; David H. Getches, Daniel M. Rosenfelt, and Charles F. Wilkinson, *Federal Indian Law* (St. Paul: West Pub. Co., 1979), pp. 586–616; Veeder, "Encroachment"; Michael Nelson, "The *Winters* Doctrine," Univ. Arizona Arid Lands Studies *Information Paper* no. 9 (1977).

43. U.S. v. Winans, 198 U.S. 371 (1905).

44. There is still legal debate on this point, since there is also good precedent to argue that executive orders create the same compensible title in reservation land as do treaties, and that all reservations, regardless of origin, have the same stature before the law. See the debate as outlined in the references cited in Price, *Law,* p. 802, and Nelson, "*Winters,*" pp. 114–142.

45. Conrad Investment Co. v. U.S., 161 Fed. 829 (1908).

46. Arizona v. California, 373 U.S. 546 (1963).

47. U.S. v. Orr Water Ditch Company et al., temp. restraining order, U.S. District Court for Nevada, 13 Feb. 1924.

48. James E. Jenkins, Supt. Reno Agency, letter to Comm. Ind. Aff., 20 Jan. 1925.

49. Elwood Mead, memo for Sec. Int., 22 Aug. 1934.

50. John F. Richardson, telegram to Dir., USRS, 30 Aug. 1923.

51. C. R. Trowbridge, Report, p. 18.

52. James M. Dixon, Sec. Int., letter to Sen. Tasker L. Oddie, 21 Aug. 1929.

53. Oscar L. Chapman, Asst. Sec. Int., letter to Comm. Ind. Aff., 19 May 1934.

54. U.S. v. Orr Water Ditch Co. et al., temp. restraining order, U.S. District Court for Nevada, 13 Feb. 1924, p. 87.

55. Reno Ind. Agency, minutes of a meeting with a delegation from Pyramid Lake, 20 Jan. 1925.

56. D. S. Stuver, Supt. Newlands Project, letter to Frederic Snyder, 26 Aug. 1926.

57. Frederic Snyder, letter to Comm. Ind. Aff., 18 May 1927.

58. John F. Richardson, memo to Comm., USRS, 9 Feb. 1925.

59. Harry C. Dukes, Water Master, letter to Thomas B. Snoddy, Supt., Reno Ind. Agency, 5 Dec. 1931.

60. William Zimmerman, letter to Oscar Chapman, 4 June 1934.

61. BIA, Irrig. Div., memo on water supply at Pyramid Lake, 10 Oct. 1934.

62. A. L. Haight, Atty. for TCID, letter with encl. to Elwood Mead, 18 April 1935. In Bur. Reclamation files, U.S. Natl. Archives, Denver.

63. U.S. v. Orr Water Ditch Co. et al., U.S. District Court for Nevada, Equity no. A-3 (1935).

64. George P. Miller, Exec. Sec., Calif. Div. Fish and Game, 16 April 1942; S. O. Harper, Chief Engineer, Newlands Project, memo to District Engineer, USRS, 19 May 1942; Walker Young, Acting Chief Engineer, memo to the Comm., USRS, 30 June 1942; Haight, letter to Mead, 18 April 1935.

65. Ethelbert Ward, Special Asst. to Atty. Genl., memo re proposed Truckee River Agreement, 9 May 1934.

66. Roy W. Stoddard, TCID Atty., memo re proposed Truckee River Agreement to Asst. Atty. Genl. Blair, 21 May 1934.

67. Walter Wilson, "Water and Indian Culture at Pyramid Lake," paper read to Great Basin Anthro. Conf., Reno, 5 Sept. 1964.

68. *Session Laws of American States and Territories—Statutes of the Nevada Legislature* (Westport, Conn.: Redgrave Info. Resources, 1973), microfiche ed., 1st legis., p. 32. See also Martha C. Knack, "The Effects of Nevada State Fish Laws on the Northern Paiutes of Pyramid Lake," *Nevada Historical Soc. Quarterly* 25 (1982): 251–265.

69. *Session Laws,* 4th legis., pp. 109–110.

70. Ibid., 8th legis., pp. 179–180, sect. 9.

71. Nevada State Legislature, Joint Memorial and Resolution Relative to the Pyramid Lake Reservation to U.S. Cong., 6 Feb. 1885, in ibid., 12th legis., pp. 143–145.

acre-feet per acre. The court agreed with the TCID claim, reaching a higher total amount of water necessary to irrigate these lands. Any such water must necessarily be diverted from the Truckee, water which would otherwise flow into Pyramid Lake. Because of this, potential damage to tribal property was finally recognized and the Pyramid Lake Tribe was allowed to join the appeal of the case as *amicus curiae* (friend of the court, not as a party) and—a privilege rarely granted—permitted to intervene actively and present argument before the Circuit Court of Appeals. The implication of this decision for Washoe Project development and Pyramid Lake is still very much in doubt, because of the reversal by the Court of Appeals in US v. TCID (see Epilogue).

21. Quoted in Robert Leland, "The California–Nevada Compact: Another View," *Govt. Research Newsletter* (Bur. Govt. Research, Univ. Nevada, Reno) 7, no. 6 (March 1969): 2.

22. 373 U.S. 546 (1963).

23. William Veeder, "An Analysis of the Bistate Compact and Task Force Report," January 1972; reprinted in part in *Govt. Research Newsletter* (Bur. Govt. Research, Univ. Nevada, Reno) 10, no. 7 (April 1972): 8–12.

24. Alvin M. Josephy, Jr., "Here in Nevada a Terrible Crime . . .," *Amer. Heritage* 21, no. 4 (June 1970): 93–100.

25. Terry J. Reynolds, "Western Nevada's Water Problems—Part Two," *Nevada Public Affairs Report* (Bureau Govt. Research, Univ. Nevada, Reno) 14, no. 3 (Dec. 1975): 5; John Fordham, personal communication to senior author, 8 July 1980.

26. U.S. v. District Court (Eagle County [Colorado]), 401 U.S. 520 (1971).

27. Monroe E. Price, *Law and the American Indian* (Indianapolis: Bobbs-Merrill, Co., 1973), pp. 189 and 322; U.S. Cong., Senate, Committee on Interior and Insular Affairs, Subcommittee on Indian Affairs, *Indian Water Rights, Hearing, 25–26 March 1974*, 93rd Cong., 2nd sess. (Washington, D.C.: USGPO, 1974), esp. testimony by Frank Tenorio, pp. 9–18; David H. Getches, Daniel M. Rosenfelt, and Charles F. Wilkinson, *Federal Indian Law: Cases and Materials* (St. Paul, Minn.: West Pub. Co., 1979), pp. 586–616.

28. Quoted in "The War of Ghosts, 1902–1972," *Native American Rights Fund Announcements* 1, no. 6 (November–December 1972): 11.

29. Pyramid Lake Paiute Tribe of Indians v. Rogers B. Morton et al., civil action 2506-70, U.S. District Court for District of Columbia (1972); this case is currently under appeal.

30. 28 Ind. Cl. Comm. 256.

31. "Pyramid Lake Votes to Accept U.S.A. $8 million," *Native Nevadan* 10, no. 9 (May 1975): 2.

32. 36 Ind. Cl. Comm. 256, 261.

33. Ibid., 259.

34. Conrad Investment Company v. United States, 161 F. 829, 9th Circuit Court (1908).

35. Dinn Cosart and Allen R. Wilcox, "Water and Pyramid Lake: The Problem and A Solution," *Govt. Research Newsletter* (Bur. Govt. Research, Univ. Nevada, Reno) 11, no. 7 (April–May 1973): 1–7.

36. See Figure 5, Chapter 11.

37. From 3,300 parts per million to 5,200 ppm by 1971. Pyramid Lake Task Force, "Final Report" (Washington, D.C.: USGPO, December 1971), p. 2.

38. U.S. Dept. Commerce, Bur. Fisheries, *Newsletter,* May 1980.

39. President Richard M. Nixon, "Message to Congress on Indian Affairs," 8 July 1970; reprinted in Alvin M. Josephy, Jr., *Red Power: The American Indians' Fight for Freedom* (NY: McGraw-Hill, 1971), p. 216.

40. E. Rusco, "The Status of Indians in Nevada Law," in Ruth M. Houghton, ed., *Native American Politics: Power Relationships in the Western Great Basin Today* (Reno: Bur. Govt. Research, Univ. Nevada, 1973), pp. 59–87.

41. Cherokee Nation v. Georgia, 5 Pet. 1 (1831); Worcester v. Georgia, 6 Pet. 515 (1832).

42. Nixon, "Message," pp. 225–226.

43. Franklin Campbell, letter to H. G. Parker, Comm. Ind. Aff., 22 Aug. 1866.

Designer :   Janet Wood
Compositor :   Innovative Media Inc.
Text :   10/12 Sabon
Display :   Sabon Roman and Italic